HENRY V

Also by Dan Jones

NONFICTION

Powers and Thrones: A New History of the Middle Ages

Crusaders: The Epic History of the Wars for the Holy Lands

The Templars: The Rise and Spectacular Fall of God's Holy Warriors

Magna Carta: The Birth of Liberty

The Wars of the Roses: The Fall of the Plantagenets and the Rise of the Tudors

The Plantagenets: The Warrior Kings and Queens Who Made England

Summer of Blood: England's First Revolution

FICTION

Wolves of Winter (Essex Dogs Trilogy 2)

Essex Dogs (Essex Dogs Trilogy 1)

HENRY V

THE ASTONISHING TRIUMPH OF ENGLAND'S GREATEST WARRIOR KING

DAN JONES

VIKING

VIKING
An imprint of Penguin Random House LLC
penguinrandomhouse.com

First published in hardcover in Great Britain by Apollo, an imprint of
Head of Zeus, part of Bloomsbury Publishing Plc, London, in 2024
First United States edition published by Viking, 2024

Illustration credits may be found on page 387.

LIBRARY OF CONGRESS CATALOGING-IN-PUBLICATION DATA
Names: Jones, Dan, 1981– author.
Title: Henry V : the astonishing triumph of England's
greatest warrior king / Dan Jones.
Description: New York : Viking, [2024] |
Includes bibliographical references and index.
Identifiers: LCCN 2024012345 (print) | LCCN 2024012346 (ebook) |
ISBN 9780593652732 (hardcover) | ISBN 9780593652749 (ebook)
Subjects: LCSH: Henry V, King of England, 1387–1422. | Great
Britain—History—Henry V, 1413–1422. | Great Britain—Politics and
government—1399–1485. | Great Britain—Kings and rulers—Biography.
Classification: LCC DA256 .J66 2024 (print) | LCC DA256 (ebook) |
DDC 942.04/2092 [B]—dc23/eng/20240404
LC record available at https://lccn.loc.gov/2024012345
LC ebook record available at https://lccn.loc.gov/2024012346

Printed in the United States of America
2nd Printing

DESIGNED BY MEIGHAN CAVANAUGH

For D.

Many times he read his books, surrendered to hard work
The king was brave, an archer, all idleness he shirked.

THE *Versus Rhythmici* OF HENRY V

Fellas, let's go!

HENRY V, OCTOBER 25, 1415

CONTENTS

PART 2

KING

1413–1422

IRELAND
Drogheda
Dublin
Kilkenny
Wexford
Waterford
Irish Sea
ANGLESEY
Conwy
Chester
Glyndyfrdwy
Sycharth
Harlech
Shrewsbury
Aberystwyth
Leominster
Hereford
Gloucest
Grosmont
Monmouth
St Davids
WALES
NORTH
Lancaster
Seve
Bristol
Exeter
CORNWALL
E
N
Eng

ENGLAND, WALES, AND IRELAND IN THE EARLY FIFTEENTH CENTURY

London
ENGLAND
Southampton
English Channel
Harfleur
Touques
Caen
NORMA
Falaise
ALENÇON
Alençon
BRITTANY
MAINE
Battle of
Baugé
ANJOU
Loir
Nantes
Bay of Biscay
Poitiers
POITOU
La Rochelle
N
0
50
100
Miles
GUYENNE
Bordeaux

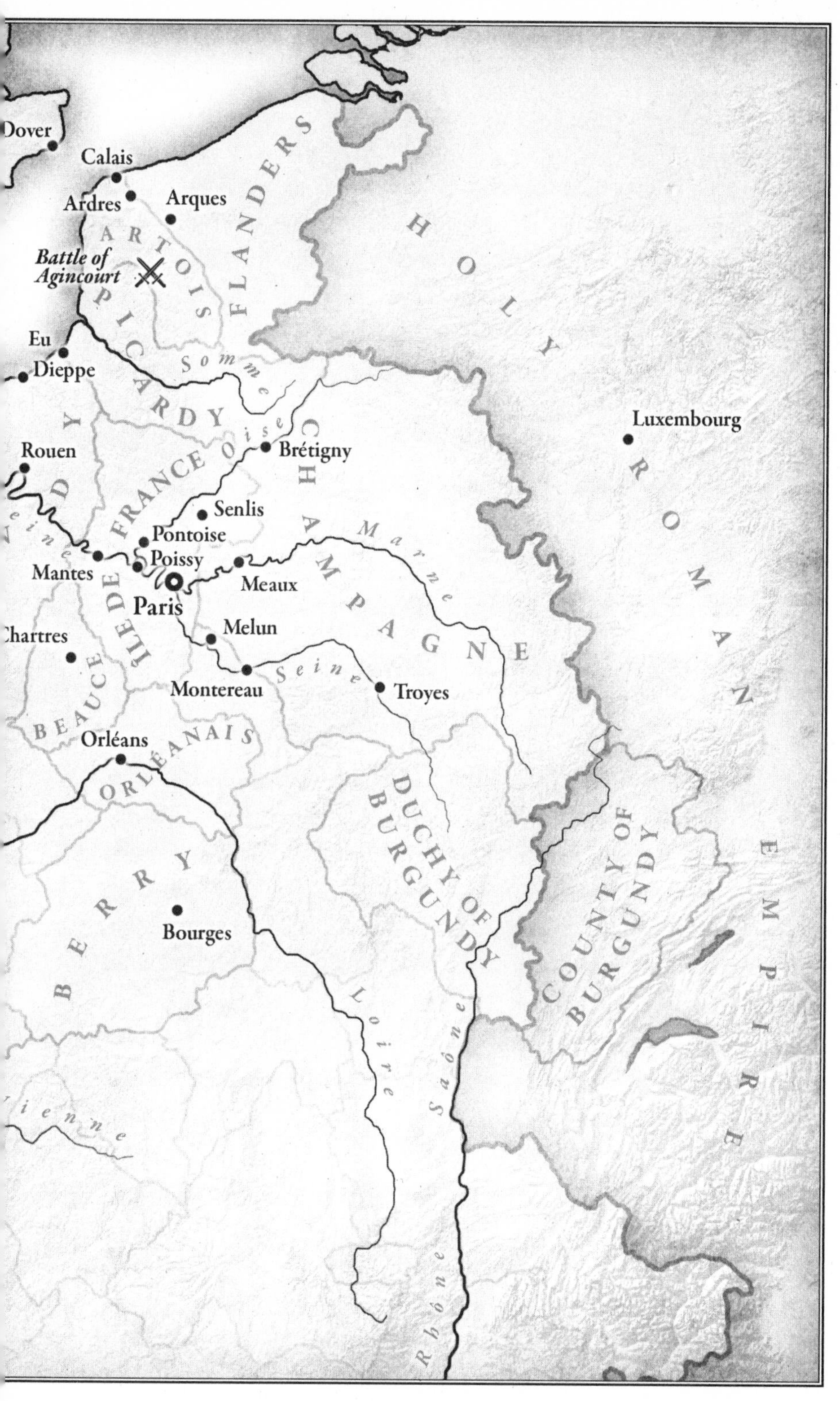

FRANCE IN THE EARLY FIFTEENTH CENTURY

INTRODUCTION

The doctor is nervous. John Bradmore is the best surgeon in England. He has a famous practice in London. He attends on rich and powerful clients, including the king. He has the supreme self-confidence—bordering on arrogance—common to elite surgeons since the days of the ancient Greeks.

But this case is different.

In the course of his career, Bradmore has proved time and again that he can heal patients other surgeons have written off as incurable—often by daring and inventive means. He has cured a woman of scrofula—an infection of the lymph nodes so awful it is commonly thought to respond only to the touch of monarchs. He has developed a technique to cure drooping eyelid bags. He has saved a London carpenter who accidentally slashed an artery in his arm with a chisel, by cauterizing the wound with a powder of his own invention.

Bradmore once spent nearly a month restoring to health a royal servant—the master of pavilions—who had succumbed to "diabolical temptation" and attempted suicide, sticking a dagger to his guts and running into his office wall. But none of those cases had been so delicate, nor so high-profile, as the one he is about to take on.

It is July 1403, and Bradmore has been summoned one hundred miles from his home in London to Kenilworth Castle: the palace-fortress in the English Midlands that is the historic home of the mighty dukes of Lancaster. It is a long journey, on uneven roads, toward a part of the country that is riven with disorder.

But traveling is not the problem, even at this time of great turbulence, during which England teeters on the brink of all-out civil war. Nor is dealing with the demands of wealthy clients.

What makes this job different is what is at stake.

The patient who lies at Kenilworth, having defeated every other doctor who has seen him, awaiting Bradmore's attention as a matter of last resort, is one of the most important members of the Lancastrian dynasty.

He is a teenage boy, born in Monmouth sixteen years ago, who has survived the lurching, bloody times through which he and England have recently lived. He is a promising warrior, a prodigious lover of music and literature, an avid sportsman and hunter.

He is the eldest son and heir to a man who four years ago became the first Lancastrian king of England, Henry IV.

He is Henry, Prince of Wales.

Henry is almost certainly going to die.

A few days ago, on July 21, at a battle fought just north of Shrewsbury, in the borderlands between England and Wales, he was hit in the face with an arrow shot from a longbow.

How exactly this happened is not altogether clear. Henry ought to have been wearing a helmet with a visor protecting his face. Perhaps he lifted the visor, or removed the helmet entirely, to take a drink or get a better view of the chaotic, blood-soaked battlefield. But *how* it happened does not matter now. The fact is that several days ago the iron head of an arrow tore into Henry's face just to the right of his nose. It sheared through his cheek, tearing cartilage and flesh before lodging itself, six inches deep, in the back wall of his skull.

At some point someone—probably Henry himself—tugged at the arrow shaft, and it came away from the arrowhead. That must have seemed, in the panic of the moment, to have dealt with the worst of it.

Far from it. Once Henry left the battlefield, having performed, by all accounts, very bravely, it was obvious that he remained in mortal danger. It was only thanks to the miracle of a few millimeters that the arrowhead did not instantly blind him, damage his brain, or kill him outright. All the same, he still has a one-ounce chunk of metal embedded inside his head.

So having been saved by one miracle, Henry now needs another. Bradmore needs to provide it. Unless this arrowhead is removed, it is only a matter of time before it either shifts and damages the nerves and blood vessels inside his head—or blood poisoning sets in.

Bradmore has an idea how he might remove the arrowhead, then seal and heal the wound. His bag holds all he needs: blocks, called tents, for opening wounds; honey- and wine-based antiseptics; clean dressings; and a tool he has designed himself, a little like a speculum, with which he hopes to grip the arrowhead and tease it out without causing further damage to the flesh. He knows how to make pastes to stem bleeding, creams to control the rate of healing, and oils to flush out entry wounds. He has a lifetime of experience and a steady hand.

Yet like any good surgeon, Bradmore knows there are things he cannot control. Dirty metal in human flesh, close to the brain stem: experience tells him there is a high risk of the patient going into seizure. ("The fear of the spasm . . . was my greatest fear," Bradmore writes later.) A fit could be brought on simply by the catastrophic damage already wrought on the delicate tissues of the patient's head. It could be caused by secondary infection: the painful toxic spasms that today we attribute to tetanus. If it occurs it will probably prove fatal.

What's more, even if seizure is avoided, this is still going to be a long operation, involving many hours of painstaking surgery without reliable anesthetic, followed by weeks of diligent aftercare. Bradmore will have to be at his best for all of it. His patient will have to be abnormally tolerant of pain. And God will have to be on their side.

So Bradmore has good reason to be nervous. This will be among the most difficult operations anyone in England has ever performed. The odds are stacked against him, even if he does everything well. And if he makes the slightest mistake there is a good chance he will be remembered as the man who killed the eldest of the king's four sons and redirected the line of succession to the English crown.

The consequences of failure are clear. But what Bradmore cannot comprehend are the consequences of success.

For what he does not know—what no one can possibly know, including the patient himself—is that if this sixteen-year-old lying stricken at Kenilworth lives, he will grow up to be someone very special.

He will be the king regarded by most generations after him as the greatest medieval ruler England ever had.

This teenage boy will one day be Henry V.

Henry will be the general who wins the battle of Agincourt; the conqueror who achieves the long-standing Plantagenet dream of seizing the crown of France.

He will be the politician who understands better than any other of his time how to assert himself as a statesman on the foreign stage while still maintaining harmony in domestic politics.

He will be the monarch who does the most to promote the English language as the preferred tongue of poets and patriots.

He will be the king who is lionized by the generation who knew him, idolized by those who followed, and eventually mythologized by William Shakespeare.

Although Henry V will reign for only nine years and four months, dying at the age of just thirty-five, he will loom over the historical landscape of the later Middle Ages and beyond, remembered as the acme of kingship: the man who did the job exactly as it was supposed to be done.

He will be considered the closest thing his age ever produced to one of the Nine Worthies. A titan. An English Alexander.

A young Henry VIII will regard his predecessor and relative Henry V as an idol to be mimicked to the point of obsession. Shakespeare will deploy Henry V as a character study in youthful folly redirected to grave and sober statesmanship. In the darkest days of the Second World War, the example of Henry's victories in France will be offered by British filmmakers as encouragement to a people existentially threatened by Nazism. Even Winston Churchill, who has mixed feelings about Henry, will call him "a gleam of splendor" in the "dark, troubled story of medieval England."[1]

Well into the late twentieth century Henry's name will retain the power to enchant and entrance. True, around once in every generation a historian will do their best to bring Henry down a peg, usually by casting him as a cold, violent, overambitious warmonger whose campaigns in France caused great human suffering and were eventually proven, because they did not endure forever, to be a colossal waste of money and time. But these are generally voices crying in the wilderness.

More often than not, those who appreciate what a medieval king was supposed to be and do will echo the judgment made in 1972, by one of the finest, most levelheaded, and most influential medievalists of the modern age, who told an audience that he considered Henry "the greatest man who ever ruled England."

Does Henry deserve that name? I believe he does. But why he deserves it is not a question that can be answered with regard to a single battle—his triumph at Agincourt in 1415—nor by appeal to a simple preference for our kings manly and warlike.

To understand why—and how—Henry V was so spectacularly successful in his day, why he was so widely admired after his death, and why his reputation has impressed so many historians over so many centuries, it is necessary to take stock of his life in the round.

Henry lived a short life, and was king for only a quarter of it. What made him such an extraordinary and effective figure (putting aside luck, which like all great historical figures he exploited when it came along) lies as much in the twenty-six years that preceded his coronation as in the subsequent nine. Many historians have praised Henry for what he managed to do as king—noting that he dragged England out of the doldrums into which it had sunk during the baleful reign of his cousin Richard II (1377–1399) and the turbulent one of his father, Henry IV (1399–1413), balancing astonishing military achievements with stable and consensual domestic government.

Yet what is habitually underappreciated is the degree to which Henry was prepared to do that job by the time he ascended the throne in 1413. To understand the king, one must understand the prince. That is the premise around which I have conceived and structured this book.

This is a new biography of Henry V. I have been waiting to write it for some time.

More than a decade ago I published *The Plantagenets*, a narrative history that covered that dynasty's history from the accession of Henry II in 1154 to the deposition of Richard II in the Lancastrian revolution of 1399. Two years later I produced a companion volume known as *The Wars of the Roses*. That book began in 1420 and concluded in 1525.

Between those two I left a *Henry V*–shaped gap.

It was not the case that the subject did not interest me. Quite the opposite. It was that the subject fascinated me so much I wanted to wait until I was a little more experienced in my writing to take him on.

For Henry V is nothing if not a challenge. He is one of the most intriguing characters in all of medieval history, yet at the same time one of the hardest to pin down.

Henry had a reputation for being austere to the point of desiccation, yet he was also theatrical and astonishingly adept at the art of public spectacle.

He was a hardened warrior, a dyed-in-the-wool soldier who exercised the power of life and death over his enemies from his early teens, and (notoriously) gave the order for a mass slaughter of prisoners of war at Agincourt. Yet he was also creative, artistic, and literary, with a bookish temperament and a talent for composing music and playing a number of instruments, including the harp.

He was a leader who made his share of mistakes, misjudged his friends and family members, and took gambles that brought him and others to the edge of ruin. Yet he always seemed to triumph when it mattered.

He was a king who did more than any other to bring England back from the brink of economic torpor, poisonous political faction, and scorn on the European stage, and his reign is a case study in the art of leadership in a time of crisis, which feels especially apposite as I write these words today. Yet through his singular triumph—the effective conquest of the French crown and the northern half of the French kingdom—he sowed the seeds for three generations of calamity at home, in the form of the Wars of the Roses.

He was his father's son, who honored and rescued the fortunes of the Lancastrian dynasty that had snatched the crown in 1399. But he often seemed to owe more in his manner of kingship—and his sympathies—to his father's hapless, histrionic predecessor, Richard II: the king whom the 1399 revolution displaced.

These competing elements in Henry's character make him a difficult but an attractive subject for a biography. So too does the generally distorted shape of Henry's popular historical reputation, which tends to focus far too narrowly on the miraculous victory at Agincourt, and not enough on his life before he was a king, and after he was a conqueror.

All in all, it has long seemed to me that given the extraordinary nature of Henry's achievements, the dramatic intensity of his relatively short life, and his singular cultural importance to English history, Henry deserves a volume all his own.

That is why for the last decade I have planned to write a biography that would comprise a standalone portrait of king and man, while also serving as a final volume to be read alongside *The Plantagenets* and *The Wars of the Roses*: not quite the third part of a trilogy, but the final panel in a triptych.

This is that book.

I have already said a lot about the story you are about to read, but two more things seem to me to be worth noting before we begin.

The first concerns structure. As I have already suggested, books about Henry V are often lopsided. That is to say: they concern themselves very heavily with the years during which he was king (1413–1422) and very little with the years of his life beforehand (1386–1413).

This strikes me as a mistake. Henry V enjoyed a long, eventful, and invaluable apprenticeship to the office of monarchy. He was not born to be king, but from around the age of ten he was in close proximity to royalty, and from the age of thirteen he was a politically and militarily active heir to the throne.

Yet only Shakespeare—working in the realm of theater and choosing to hang his narrative on an almost wholly fictitious characterization of the young Henry as a tearaway, womanizing drunk—seriously grasps that to understand Henry, we must understand "Hal," the young man and prince, in equal measure. This book tries in its structure to address that imbalance. Almost every other serious biographer of Henry has treated the twenty-six years of his apprenticeship as a short prelude to the real business of his life's story. Here, you will find that Henry does not become king until exactly halfway through the story.

The second thing I must say relates to style. It is traditional to write history books in the past tense. I have always done so myself. History is by definition the study of things that happened. (Or, if you like, things that *have* happened.) It usually makes sense to describe them in such a way.

Usually. But not always.

It is possible that trying to write a biography of a medieval person may be a contradiction in terms. In the modern sense, the word "biography" implies a degree of psychological insight and inspection of a subject's interior world that is generally impossible given the nature of medieval sources.

Henry V was not a Queen Victoria. He did not—so far as we know—keep a diary. What personal remarks and reflections we can collect from him must be scraped from sources that were never created with the purpose of cracking open his mind for the benefit of future scholars. For the most part, what we have are his orders and his actions. Nothing else.

How, then, do we animate Henry V? How can we bring ourselves as close as possible to the man while remaining responsible historians? How can we get to know him, without straying into the realm of Hollywood fantasy?

My response to those questions, which I present here humbly but unapologetically, is through narrative style, by writing the story of his life in present tense.

Henry rides. He fights. He prays. He plans. He rules.

He is next to us as he does it all. We are living, as he does, on the edge of the next decision, and on the cusp of the next crisis. We are jolted out of our comfortable place in the distant future, and must wrestle with the medieval world in real time, with him.

I hope the effect of this slightly untraditional approach is that Henry will become, in the pages that follow, a man whom we will live alongside. I hope you will find, as I have, that there is a man of surprising depths and tastes, who carries with him a range of contradictory influences built up across the course of his life, which swirl around him as he grows up.

I hope you will enjoy, as I have, seeing how Henry tries increasingly to live his life behind a mask that betrays as little of this as possible. And I hope you will experience the same thrill that I have in peering behind that mask.

Henry is going to do as he will. We will do it with him, and I hope that in the end, we will feel that we know him better than we thought we possibly could.

This is Henry V.

Enjoy the ride.

Dan Jones
Staines-upon-Thames
Spring 2024

PART 1

PRINCE

1386–1413

My God! A wonderful land is this, and fickle, which hath exiled, slain, destroyed or ruined so many kings, rulers and great men, and is ever tainted and toileth with strife and variance and envy . . .

King Richard II

1

THE BOY IN THE BLACK STRAW HAT

The young woman labors in a chamber above the gatehouse of Monmouth Castle, a squat stronghold at the confluence of two rivers in the lush, green borderlands between England and Wales.

Her name is Mary de Bohun. She is little more than a child herself: a blond slip of a girl, just sixteen or seventeen summers old, with high brows and eyes wide-set in a round face that tapers to a little bobble chin, her hair a tumbling mass of golden curls.[1]

Mary is a pretty girl, or at least will later be drawn that way to flatter her. But laboring a firstborn is not pretty. It is a burden and a duty. The burden was given by God at the Fall to all the descendants of Eve: a "great pain and great dis-ease," which can drive a woman to despair, "weening that she might not live."[2] The duty is the one given by noble society to all young women like Mary, who have been wedded to powerful men to serve as vessels for their dynasties. She must bear children as often as she is able.

This is the first time Mary is doing her duty: the first baby she is bringing into the world.[3] Most likely she is frightened. If she is not, she should be. One day bearing children will kill her.

Mary has been married since she was about twelve. There was a time she thought she might be a nun, like the quiet sisters of the order of St. Clare who taught her lessons. But that time ended abruptly on February 5, 1381, in a manor house two hundred miles from here, when she wed her husband, a teenage nobleman called Henry Bolingbroke, who was himself not quite fourteen.

Much is given to young couples like Bolingbroke and Mary, and their wedding was a lavish show. It was paid for by Mary's father-in-law, John of Gaunt, duke of Lancaster, uncle to the king, and the greatest lord in the land. At the party, Gaunt gave Mary the gift of a ruby. Her new sisters-in-law gave her trinkets of cups and drinking jugs.

And in time, her new husband, young Bolingbroke, gave her a baby. Here, today, above the gates of Monmouth Castle, that child comes roaring into the world.

The date of his birth will not be well remembered, for at the time it is not thought really to matter. But much later will it be fixed, in an astrological tract that links the child's future prodigy to the perambulations of the heavenly bodies.

With improbable certainty, the future stargazer marks it:

September 16, 1386.

Eleven twenty-two a.m.[4]

A boy is born.

He is given the same name as his father.

The young lord Henry breathes.[5]

The England to which Henry is born is a realm of 2.23 million people, who are ruled by a king and governed by a few thousand members of a small, closed aristocratic and clerical caste.[6] To be born into this caste confers huge privilege: wealth unimaginable to almost everyone else, a longer life expectancy, a better diet, more legal freedoms, and the dignity of having one's deeds and affairs recorded for posterity. It is a ticket to power.

True, the realm has institutions that organize and check this power:

Crown, Church, and Parliament, as well as courts of law, universities, and merchant guilds. These have their particular rules and norms, developed over centuries. Yet while power is expressed through office, it is *controlled* by the members of a few dozen landowning families such as the one into which Henry has been born: a high-born cabal whose pasts and futures are enmeshed by intermarriage. These are the people who own land, dispense justice, lead armies, and elide their personal goals with those of the realm at large.

Things have been this way since time out of mind, strongly resistant to all but the most gradual change. Five years before Henry's birth, in the chaotic summer of 1381, ordinary folk across England rose up in rebellion, murdering their betters and demanding that lordship itself be abolished. Their demands were ignored and their rioting savagely punished. The rebels asked, "when Adam delved and Eve span, who then was the gentleman?"[7] But learned opinion cares nothing for utopian couplets. "If it is natural for man to live in the society of many, it is necessary that there exist among men some means by which the group shall be governed," it answers.[8]

That *means* is through blood-bound aristocracy. So it is a stroke of luck for young Henry to be born into this world as the firstborn son of the firstborn son of the noble house of Lancaster.

The patriarch of the house of Lancaster is Henry's forty-six-year-old grandfather John of Gaunt. Gaunt is by a long measure the richest and most powerful nobleman in England. He is a soldier, a diplomat, a patron of writers including Geoffrey Chaucer, and the protector of radical theologians such as John Wyclif. He has a large family, including children by two wives—Bolingbroke's late mother, Blanche, and the current duchess, Constanza of Castile—as well as one mistress, Constanza's lady-in-waiting Katherine Swynford, who will in time become duchess herself.

As well as being duke of Lancaster, Gaunt holds four more earldoms, and his landed estate—which sprawls from Lancashire and the Midlands out to Wales and East Anglia—is larger than anyone's but the Crown's.

He is the eldest of three surviving sons of the late king Edward III; his younger brothers are forty-five-year-old Edmund Langley, duke of York, a guileless homebody with little interest in, and no instinct for, politics or soldiering, and thirty-two-year-old Thomas of Woodstock, duke of Gloucester, erudite, widely admired, but aggressive and unwilling to suffer fools, among whom he numbers his, Gaunt's, and Langley's nephew, the nineteen-year-old king Richard II.

Gaunt has a tricky relationship with Richard, too: there are times when the king has toyed with the idea of murdering him. But he has a better instinct for handling his nephew than many others. What is more, Gaunt has pretensions to a crown of his own. At the time of young Henry's birth, he is abroad with an army of five thousand men trying to lay claim to the crown of the Spanish kingdom of Castile and León, to which he has a say in right of his wife, Constanza.

This, then, is what leadership of the house of Lancaster looks like. This, in good time, is what the baby Henry can expect to inherit. He could become a Spanish king. At the very least, he will one day be one of England's premier noblemen—so long as Gaunt and Henry's nineteen-year-old father, Bolingbroke, manage to steward the Lancastrian inheritance and hand it down to him intact, without himself falling foul of their capricious relative, the king.

When Henry is born, Richard II has been king for nearly a decade, since 1377, when he was ten years old. His parents were first cousins: Edward III's eldest son, Edward (a peerless warrior known much later as the "Black Prince"), and the king's niece Joan, the "Fair Maid of Kent." When Richard was crowned, the whole country celebrated and London erupted in a frenzy of wild thanksgiving. Old king Edward had ruled for half a century and although in his pomp he had been one of the greatest monarchs in English history, his reign had lapsed into corruption, faction, and decay.

So Richard was heralded as a savior. But as he has grown up, he has not turned out that way. He has a highly developed sense of the ritual and visual spectacle of kingship, and an awesome conception of royal majesty as ministerial and even priestly. But his instincts in government have tended toward peace abroad and tyrannical severity at home—more or less the reverse of what is expected of a Plantagenet king.

Bolingbroke is almost exactly the same age as Richard, and as different in temperament as it is possible to be. For a time the boys were raised side by side.* They were knighted together, aged ten, on St. George's Day, April 23, 1377, by their frail and senile grandfather Edward III. Just a few months later, when Edward died and Richard was crowned his successor, Bolingbroke was given a role at the heart of the coronation pageantry: standing guard over Richard holding the ceremonial sword Curtana.†

In the first years of Richard's reign, Bolingbroke regularly attended the boy-king's court, dressing in exquisite fabrics and furs, exchanging gifts, gambling at tables, hunting, falconing, and even jousting.[9] The lads experienced alike the terrors of the 1381 rebellion, as violent crowds ransacked London, lynching high royal officials including the archbishop of Canterbury, burning Gaunt's Savoy Palace to the ground, and breaking into the Tower of London. Bolingbroke escaped capture or worse only because a loyal soldier called John Ferror hid him in a wardrobe until the danger had passed.

But in recent years the cousins have grown apart: Richard has surrounded himself with a clique of favorites from which Bolingbroke is pointedly excluded. They include the king's former tutor, Simon Burley, and the despised twenty-four-year-old Robert de Vere, duke of Ireland, whose easy command of the king's attention will inspire later rumors that the duke has bewitched or seduced him.[10]

Yet the toadies are a symptom of the problem, and not the cause. The king is grand, theatrical, and physically imposing. Yet he is also flittish, quarrelsome, and petulant. He loves the trappings of monarchy but does

---

* Richard was born on January 6, 1367. Bolingbroke was probably born on April 15 of the same year.

† Thought variously to have been wielded by England's sainted Saxon king Edward the Confessor and by the legendary knight Tristan.

not truly understand the grave office he holds. Instead of admitting this and seeking the support of able men, he promotes sycophants and convinces himself he is threatened by enemies who are trying to hold him back. Richard is easy with lavish gifts but even easier with cruel words. Sometimes he is violent: a few months before young Henry's birth he punched the earl of Arundel with sufficient force and little enough warning to knock the earl to the ground.

As we shall see, political trouble is bubbling, and it will not be long before it boils over.*

Still, Richard is the king, and it is at his pleasure Bolingbroke remains in line to inherit the many titles and vast estates of his father, Gaunt. It is with the king's blessing that he bears his family's junior title of earl of Derby. It was with the king's say-so that he married young Mary de Bohun in 1381, bringing into the Lancastrian orbit Mary's share of the huge Bohun inheritance: the earldoms of Hereford, Essex, and Northampton.† It will be with Richard's approval that, in time, young Henry, still in the first weeks of his life, will grow up to assume his own place in the Lancastrian family's hierarchy and the public life of England.

First, though, young Henry must survive.

He is considered a scrawny baby, in an age that does not favor the feeble.[11] Even in ordinary times, at least one in five children born in Europe never see their second birthday; nearly one-third will die without reaching full adulthood.[12] When Henry is born the dangers are greater than ever. For decades, Europe has been tormented by recurring waves of a pandemic known as the Black Death. This pestilence has already slashed England's population in half. Still it returns for more victims, and now,

---

* See chapter 3.

† The Bohuns have also garnered significant personal prestige over the generations: as lusty participants in the Scottish wars of Edward I, the French wars of Edward III, and, latterly, a crusade to smite the Mamluk rulers of Egypt, on which Mary's late father Humphrey helped pillage Alexandria.

overwhelmingly, it comes for the young. When the plague first arrived, it struck at children and adults alike. But when it surged three years before Henry's birth, nine in ten of its victims were children.[13]

There are many theories on how best to avoid infection: vomiting daily on an empty stomach, sweating out toxins by going to bed and drinking warm ale infused with ginger, or bloodletting.[14] Obviously these are not suitable for tiny babies. So at Henry's baptism—a rite that typically involves a child being marinated in salt, oil, and saliva before being dunked three times in the font—prayers are said asking for the protection of a recently deceased Augustinian canon: John Thwing of Bridlington.

Thwing was well-liked in life. He swore an oath of chastity at age twelve, attended diligently to his studies at Oxford University, and went on to pursue a blameless monastic career. A verse biography recalls his pleasant countenance, and explains that "when others slept, full oft he woke, praying to God full busily, both in his youth and his old age." He was said to be "right wise . . . and merciful . . . discreet in his manner and not vengeful, full of pity and reason."[15] Miracles reported at Thwing's tomb since his death in 1379 suggest that his spirit has healed the sick, raised the dead, and banished demons.[16]

Both of Henry's parents are fond of Thwing: a commentary on his life and holy deeds has been composed for Mary's late father, Humphrey. Bolingbroke will go to Thwing's tomb for guidance and protection in moments of crisis throughout his life. He may hope this chaste and holy man of Bridlington provides in some way a moral model for their firstborn son.

For now, though, whether through Thwing's intercession or the simple chance of fate, the plague leaves Henry alone.

And so he grows up.

Youth has its phases. For Henry's first seven years he will be a child, living in what scholars call a state of *infantia*. Between seven and fourteen comes boyhood (*puerita*); thereafter adolescence, which some consider to last until the age of twenty-one but others think is only truly over when a man reaches thirty or even thirty-five—roughly the average life expectancy at birth* for a male child born into a well-off family.[17]

At first Henry the child lives in petticoats and satin gowns of scarlet and white, surrounded by women.[18] A wet nurse called Joan Waryn suckles him, and he remembers her all his life.[19] Later a governess, or "mistress," is appointed: her name is Mary Hervy.[20] In charge of all is Mary de Bohun, his mother, so recently emerged from her own adolescence.

Mary is elegant and pious and the household shines with her pleasures. She loves fine clothes and beautifully bound prayer books. She keeps dogs and parrots as pets, and plays chess on a silver board. To mark her eighteenth birthday she washes the feet of poor women and gives them sixpences. Bolingbroke visits as often as he can, and even when he is away—as he is a great deal—he sends his wife gifts of fruit, nuts, and fresh seafood.[21] Above all, there is music. Mary plays the harp. She plays the guitar and sings. She composes music on staves she draws herself with a ruler. Minstrels and musicians entertain the household and their guests. Young Henry grows up with the sound of horns and drums and voices in his ears. It is a love he will never lose.

Under Mary's care this bright, lively household and its nursery move around England. Henry learns to walk, run, and play in the great castles and palaces of the duchy of Lancaster. His mother takes him to Leicester and Peterborough. They stay with John of Gaunt's second wife, the duchess Constanza, at Tutbury in Staffordshire. They go to Kenilworth, a red sandstone fortress-palace in the Midlands, which rises from the cool, flat waters of a man-made lake called the Mere, and over which John of Gaunt's workmen swarm as they remodel the Lancastrian headquarters into a palace fit for a would-be king. Between these places, Henry learns to enjoy the traditional outdoor hobbies of rich boys: hunting, fishing, riding, and running.[22]

As the family travels, they grow in number. Mary is regularly pregnant. Henry is barely a toddler when, in late 1387, he has a baby brother,

* Life expectancy at birth in the Middle Ages is dragged down by the heavy incidence of child mortality. Life expectancy at twenty-five years old is fifty-eight.

given the stirring Lancastrian name of Thomas.* In June 1389 comes another brother, John, and then, in October 1390, Humphrey, named for Mary's late father. Two sisters, Blanche and Philippa, appear in 1392 and 1394. By the arrival of the last, Henry has left the royal nursery. He is no longer in his petticoats, but wears linen shirts and green-and-white gowns lined with squirrel fur, with a scarlet cap in the winter and a black straw hat to shade his face in the summer. He washes himself with soap ordered from London, and stays up after dark by the flicker of a night-light in his bedroom.[23] He has survived childhood and is ready to be taught.

He learns his lessons in the schoolroom and the saddle. For boys a noble life is physical, and Henry must learn to ride, hunt, and fight—then practice relentlessly. ("For he that arms shall haunt, in youth he must begin / Of all arts under heaven, use is a master," writes one poet of the age.)[24] His parents buy him the kit he needs: saddles, swords, birds, greyhounds, armor. When he is sick, they send for the best doctors to hasten up from the capital and attend him. They appoint trusted friends and servants to oversee his education, among them Peter Melbourne, a childhood companion of Bolingbroke's, born to a family who has been in Lancastrian service for decades, whom John of Gaunt regards almost as a surrogate son.

Meanwhile, Henry takes to his books as naturally as he takes to the physical pursuits. There is much to admire in his mother's prayer books: gorgeous, precious, vibrant things; she also owns a handsome copy of the tales of Lancelot and the knights of Arthurian Britain, graphically illustrated with images of these legendary worthies feasting in their hall.[25] But Henry has books of his own, too. Aged eight he is presented with a collection of seven volumes to teach him Latin grammar.[26]

If these books are as conventional as the rest of his noble education seems to be, they contain texts abounding with pagan and Christian wisdom. Henry studies Greek fables by Aesop, Roman proverbs by Cato, and

* Thomas, earl of Lancaster, was the belligerent cousin of Edward II who led the baronial opposition against Edward until his defeat at the battle of Boroughbridge in 1322, after which he was beheaded as a traitor.

stories said to have been recorded by the severe, brilliant Cistercian monk St. Bernard of Clairvaux.[27] He learns Latin, the universal language of the Church, and French, the common tongue of the European aristocracy. He opens his mind to insights distilled from two thousand years of civilization. He absorbs what he reads. He is intelligent and thoughtful. He will never be a scholar, but from a young age he is literate in Latin, French, and English—the last of which is reemerging from its status as a peasant tongue to become for the first time in centuries a language of high literature and even government letters. From his earliest years Henry is well-read and interested in the world of words and ideas: an admirer of men who wield the pen as well as the sword.

His mother dies in 1394, at Peterborough, killed by the trauma of delivering the sixth of her children, Henry's youngest sister, Philippa. She is no more than twenty-five.

Mary's death comes as the family are already mourning another of their number: John of Gaunt's wife, Constanza. The two women's funerals take place on consecutive days in July, at the Church of the Annunciation of Our Lady of Newark, in Leicester.* This fine place is designed to be a Lancastrian ducal mausoleum, sanctified by the presence of a relic: a single needle from Christ's Crown of Thorns, plucked from its place by the king of France and given to the dynasty's late patriarch, Henry Grosmont.

And so the youngest Henry of the Lancastrian family lays his mother to rest before he is even eight years old. He is just old enough to remember her—or at least to form a clear idea of what her memory is and to cherish it. Mary has taught him and his brothers to love music, to love learning, to love books, to love God. He memorializes her by loving all these himself.

Henry worries that Mary has not been given quite the honor in death her life merited.[28] For now, though, he can only mourn her and go on. He

---

* Long since destroyed: a few ruins can be viewed in the heritage center of De Montfort University.

travels with his siblings for a time to live with Mary's mother, Joan FitzAlan, countess of Hereford, at Bytham Castle in Lincolnshire. His education continues as he passes his eighth birthday, then his ninth. But as his tenth birthday comes around, it becomes clear that Henry cannot live much longer as a child. He is his father's eldest son. And his father is Henry Bolingbroke. Whether he likes it or not, English politics will soon drag him away from the schoolroom and out into the adult world.

Henry is barely out of boyhood when the England beyond his safe round of Lancastrian castles bursts in. He will learn through hard experience that it is a world of peril. A world of rebellion. A world of exile. A world of death.

Above all, it is a world shaped by the peculiar character of King Richard II.

2

THE PRICE OF PEACE

Henry leaves England for the first time in late October 1396, aboard one of a fleet of ships heading from Dover to Calais, where he is to be a guest at King Richard's wedding. The world of diplomacy and international relations awaits—specifically, an introduction to the politics of a conflict in which he will come to be a defining figure: the Hundred Years War.*

He has fine new things for the occasion, including four saddles decorated with silver gilt fittings.[1] He needs to look his best, because a party for the ages is planned. King Richard is marrying the eldest daughter of the king of France, Charles VI. Their union will slot home the last piece in a delicate diplomatic jigsaw puzzle that has been many years in the solving. England and France have been at war for nearly sixty years: a conflict that has ruined thousands of lives and put huge strain on both realms' finances and polities. This marriage will halt hostilities for a long time,

---

* It is proper here to point out that "the Hundred Years War" is a historians' term coined in the nineteenth century, which was not in use in the fourteenth.

sealing a truce projected to last for twenty-eight years. Richard and Charles intend to celebrate.

To that end, teams of engineers, builders, and caterers from England and France have been hard at work for two months near Ardres: neutral ground between the English town of Calais and the French town of Guînes.* They have been erecting a temporary city of more than two hundred shimmering pavilions, protected by a large wooden palisade.

Among the pavilions will be kitchens and dressing rooms, kennels and stables, chapels and washrooms. The stylish English king will have a wardrobe department capable of supplying dozens of outfit changes. His treasurers need secure storerooms to accommodate the wagonloads of presents Richard is bringing for the bride's family: "immense gifts of gold, gems, and silk, and of precious vessels."[2]

For a week this tent city will whirl with barons and ladies, knights and bishops, soldiers, servants, and priests, clerks, cooks, and hangers-on. The guest list will run to the thousands. There will be games, plays, and music. There will be feasts and dances. Regulations have been issued forbidding "clamors, brawls, disputes or insulting words."[3] The stakes—and the costs—are high. But the place is ready. Everything is set up, says one author, "in splendid fashion."[4]

Henry travels with his father in John of Gaunt's Lancastrian party. He is ten years old, out of childhood: old enough to grasp why he is there. This is the first diplomatic summit Richard has ever held with another great monarch, and the king is pulling out all the stops. That means showing off his entourage: turning up flanked by as many of his nobles, friends, and family as he can muster.

The presence of youngsters like Henry is essential to the dignity of the king's traveling court. Boys like Henry represent the future. They are also bargaining chips. Indeed, talk of arranging a wedding for Henry abounds while they are in France. The names of various princesses of noble blood

---

* In 1520 Ardres will also be the site of the Field of Cloth of Gold: Henry VIII's peace conference with Francis I.

have been bandied back and forth as possible wives for him, most notably that of Marie, the five-year-old daughter of the duke of Brittany.

As it happens, nothing comes of this, but the mere mention of it should remind Henry of what he is.

A boy, yes. Flesh and blood and soul.

But he is more than that, too. Part of something much greater: a body politic, whose needs he must serve.

What has brought the English to Calais? Henry must by now know at least the broad sweep of the history.

England and France have been at war for fifty-nine years. Ever since the Norman Conquest of 1066, English rulers have held territories in France, and have therefore been drawn into armed contests to expand or defend them. But the particular origins of *this* war lie in the year 1337, when Henry's great-grandfather, Edward III, intervened in a succession crisis in France, claiming the French crown was his by legal and moral right, and committed himself to proving that fact by military conquest.

Since then, the war has defined relations between England and France, and has dragged in neighboring realms including the Spanish kingdoms, Scotland, and the counties of the Low Countries. It has consisted of periods of intense, bloody fighting, interspersed with lulls during which both sides plot their next move.

In 1360 peace seemed finally to have been made. After the English captured the French king Jean II at the battle of Poitiers, Edward forced from his defeated enemy the Treaty of Brétigny, by which he, Edward, gave up his claim to the French crown in exchange for a vast sum of money and a huge swath of French territory, most of it in southwest France around the duchy of Guyenne. But in 1369, the peace of Brétigny collapsed. It has never been resurrected, so for nearly three decades, full-blown war has never been more than an ill-tempered word or diplomatic impasse away.

For some, this is welcome. There are hawks on both sides of the Channel, who question the desirability, wisdom, and possibility of a peace on any terms but the most favorable to their own kingdom. There have been long periods when this war has given the English in particular an outlet for the militarism of their male ruling classes and a ready source of plunder, booty, and ransoms. The loudest and most consistent pro-war voice on the English side belongs to the king's youngest uncle, the duke of Gloucester, whose tongue is almost as sharp as his sword. Gloucester dismisses the French as being "full of hot air . . . vanity and presumption" and scorns his nephew the king as "unwarlike . . . indifferent to arms" and a disgrace to the memory of his father and grandfather.[5]

Gloucester's words consistently find a willing audience. As one knight of Richard's court puts it, even amid a general disillusionment with the expense and bloodshed of the conflict, the public reveres veterans* "who have been great warriors and fighters and [who have] destroyed and won many lands."[6]

Set against attitudes like these, however, is the unpleasant truth that the war is placing heavy strain on the public finances and political unity of both kingdoms. English parliaments complain bitterly and often about the enormous cost. Pragmatists point out that it is not entirely clear what victory for either side would really look like, nor how it might be achieved. Anti-war polemicists argue that Christian-on-Christian violence in the west is an obstacle to a more righteous enterprise: crusading. Muslims, writes a French cleric in 1395, must be delighted that the traditional crusading realms of France and England are at war, for it fosters "the increase and progress of their most wicked religion and the weakening of our own true law and faith."[7]

Both Charles VI and Richard II incline toward these arguments. Neither has the stomach nor the resources for the vast military surge that would force a settlement on their own terms. The French king has officially condemned a conflict in which "so many evils have occurred, so

---

* A common sentiment in times of unpopular conflicts. During the Vietnam War of the 1950s to 1970s and the Gulf Wars of the 1990s and 2000s, this was known as being "against the war, but for the troops."

many Christian souls perished, so many churches have been destroyed and women raped."[8] The English king agrees.

Hence the truce. Under its terms, England and France will refrain from fighting each other for as long as many of its architects live. They hope their example will stir princes throughout Europe into settling their own squabbles and rallying against their mutual, infidel enemy: the Ottoman Turks, whose sultan has recently sent armies rampaging through the Christian Balkans. (A large crusading army has in fact already departed on a doomed mission to stall Ottoman designs on Hungary, Bulgaria, and, ultimately, Constantinople.) And they hope an accord between England and France will help heal a long-running papal schism, in which two popes claim legitimacy: an English-backed pontiff in Rome and a French-backed one in Avignon.

It is not quite a full peace. But it is the next best thing.

Why, though, a wedding? The reason is, on the face of it, simple. A little more than two years ago, on June 7, 1394, King Richard's first wife, Anne of Bohemia, died of plague. She was twenty-eight years old, and had been married to Richard since they were both fourteen. Richard has never been an entirely stable or predictable king, and Anne's death inspired in him extreme, performative fits of anguish.

He had the palace where Anne died—a beautiful Thames-side retreat at Sheen—torn down. He vowed never to set foot again in any building they had visited together. At Anne's funeral the earl of Arundel arrived late, and Richard attacked him, beating him with a stick before having him thrown in the Tower of London.

Yet in tragedy lies opportunity: as a bachelor, Richard can marry again. Royal weddings are the highest-value currency of international relations. For one thing, they are typically lucrative for the groom: Isabelle's dowry is said to run to nearly a million francs. For another, they can seal truces and peaces. And of course, they are also vital for dynasty building, an issue that in Richard's case seems pressing. The king is nearly thirty, but has no full siblings and—as yet—no children. (It is possible that his long marriage to Anne of Bohemia was deliberately chaste: Richard admires St. Edward the Confessor, who ruled in pious celibacy. He also adores his male friends.) If Richard dies tomorrow a number of relatives will vie to replace him. His first cousin once removed, Roger Mortimer, earl of March, will head the queue for the crown. The Lancastrians—Gaunt, Bolingbroke, Henry himself—may not be far behind. But this is not a cheering prospect. England is always a far happier realm when a king's heir is a child of the body rather than a member of his extended family.

So even a boy of Henry's age can understand how Richard's soon-to-be-solemnized second marriage, to Charles VI's daughter Isabelle, richly meets the needs of statecraft. All the same, he may well wonder how a princess like Isabelle is going to help Richard with his second great marital need: that of producing some princes of his own.

It is not that there is anything amiss with the girl, whose portrait has been sent ahead for Richard's approval. Nor is there any suggestion that she will be unable to bear children in her time.

The problem is that her time lies some way in the future. Isabelle of Valois, daughter of Charles VI of France, was born in the Louvre in Paris on November 9, 1389.

She is not quite seven years old.

On the morning of Thursday, October 26, 1386, Henry is in Richard's vast entourage as the king rides out of Calais to the fluttering, glittering pavilion field at Ardres.

As Calais recedes, he has the chance to appreciate the sheer scale of the city, England's nearest enclave on the French side of the strait. Its seaward aspect was visible when his ship landed: the harbor guarded by a fort and gun battery mounted on a sandbank known as the Risbank. But viewed from here, on land, Calais is even more impressive. Around the city runs a soaring circuit of defensive walls, which merge into the defenses of a sturdy castle. These walls are protected by two deep moats fed from the salt water of the harbor. Beyond sprawls sucking marshland, passable only by man-made causeways. Here and there, on islands in the marsh, stand other fortresses: little defensive nodes securing this prized port from any attempt to take it back into French hands.

As the English pass out of Calais through the marshes, Henry may learn from Lancastrian veterans around him just how much blood and sweat their ancestors spilled to win Calais exactly fifty years ago.

During the hard winter of 1346–47 King Edward III, along with Richard's father (the Black Prince) and Henry's great-grandfather William de Bohun, earl of Northampton, led a brutal eleven-month siege to starve the city into submission. It was an expensive, difficult operation. Only when Calais's garrison had expelled every useless mouth and were reduced to eating rats and contemplating cannibalism did the defenders open the gates.

So this is what war is, Henry can reflect. This is what a warrior king must do.

The first meeting between King Richard and Charles VI takes place the next day, Friday, October 27, in the middle of the afternoon. The scene is minutely choreographed.

To emphasize the harmony between the two camps, King Richard parades flanked by the French dukes of Berry and Orléans. He wears a long gown of scarlet, notes one observer, with a hat dangling pearls.[9] King Charles wears a knee-length cloak of red velvet hooped in black and white and a black hat studded with jewels.[10] He is accompanied by John of Gaunt and the duke of Gloucester. On both sides, hundreds of disarmed and dismounted knights file behind.

The monarchs draw together at a pillar hammered into the ground in the middle of the pavilion field, and their attendants fall to their knees as they greet one another, exchanging spiced wine, gold rings, and other goodwill tokens: Charles presents Richard with a wine jug; Richard gives Charles a beer glass. They make a joint vow to found a church on the spot where they have just met.

Then the two kings and their closest advisers disappear into one of the pavilions and do not emerge until after nightfall.

As they go, Henry may reflect on the strangeness of these two men, neither of whom is quite the archetype of kingship. Richard is at least familiar. The king is tall and well-built, standing at six feet, several inches above average height. He has a long face softened by round, boyish cheeks and a short, fluffy beard; his eyes boggle within heavy lids, framed by high, curved brows. He typically wears a haughty resting expression intended to convey majesty, yet in truth he looks more like he has caught a faint bad smell. He stammers a little. He spends huge sums with mercers and tailors and always dresses magnificently—today he wears scarlet; on another it will be white and green; on a third he may appear clad all in gold. All of this leaves a deep impression on Henry, as his later life will show.

Yet Richard's grand manner and pomp serve to emphasize the ways in which he is *un*kingly. He does not fight. He does not sire children. He inspires caution, even terror, but not respect. Henry may compare him unfavorably with the vision of kingship and knighthood contained in his mother's books of Arthurian lore. Or he may contrast Richard with his own father, Bolingbroke: a proven, worldly warrior who jousts and loves women.

But then there is Charles VI. The French king is no less strange than Richard. Charles is almost two years younger than the lanky popinjay who will soon be his son-in-law. Like Richard, he has an instinct for the grandeur of kingship, and is no weakling. Charles's problem is his health, which is poor, and has been for the last four years.

In 1392 Charles suffered the first of a series of psychotic episodes in which he lost command of his senses. When madness overcomes him, he has been known to attack his own relatives and servants—sometimes fatally. Sometimes he cannot recognize even his own queen, Isabeau of Bavaria. Last year during a relapse, it is whispered, Charles became convinced he was the reincarnation of St. George.

Charles's unpredictable mental health and the severity of the episodes of illness he suffers has placed great strain on French government. Factions vie for control of the realm when he is incapacitated. Poison is slowly seeping through French politics. Henry cannot possibly know just how rotten things are becoming in the palaces of Paris, or just what heavy concerns weigh on the minds of the French king's advisers amid the bright pavilions at Ardres. But he will, in time.

The next day of the royal conference is a washout, with rainstorms so violent it seems "as if the cataracts of heaven [are] opening for the first time."[11] The kings continue to discourse in private, but outside the tempest sweeps across the countryside and lashes the tents, battering some so hard that they collapse. The following day is not much more exciting: it is a Sunday, and reserved for prayer. However, on the fifth and final day—Monday, October 30—the rain clears, the prayers abate, and it is time for the final moment of the pageant. What unfolds is both symbolic and all too real. Henry, presumably, sees it all.

With the politicking done, Richard and Charles meet for the final time at the central point of the peace field. They and their advisers have discussed many important things: the exchange of military garrisons in Normandy, the dowry to be paid as part of the marriage alliance, strategies for trying to force an end to the papal schism, a possible joint military expedition against the duke of Milan and—most controversially—Richard's wish that Charles might send him aid against his own subjects, should he ever need it. Now the talking is over. So this time Charles brings with him his daughter Isabelle, carried by the dukes of Berry and Burgundy and trailed by "a brilliant procession of noble ladies, adorned with crowns of gold and precious stones."

Isabelle is dressed as France itself: she wears a golden diadem on her head and a blue dress sewn with gold fleurs-de-lis. She is crying. As she is presented to Richard, he thanks her father for giving him such a fine gift, but these kindly words—which will come to characterize a blandly avuncular relationship between the man and his child bride—can scarcely comfort her. She is so young that her dolls have been packed with her jewels and clothes.

Isabelle is taken off by English ladies to be comforted and prepared for her new life as a queen, which will begin with her marriage in Calais and proceed to a time living in her own household, to await puberty, womanhood, and (perhaps) the king's full attention.

Meanwhile the crowds, in which Henry is still present, stay and wait for the last pieces of diplomatic business to be transacted. Proclamations of joint policy on the papal schism must be made. Treasure to the value of some 300,000 gold francs (£50,000) must change hands, weighed out in coin, crowns, jewels, plate, jugs, and other trinkets.

This is the stuff of diplomacy, and it is why they are all there. Perhaps by now, Henry is restless to return home. He may well have a lot of questions. He may wonder to himself what it feels like to be a man, a king. To marry strategically and on that foundation to build political settlements. He may consider whether peacemaking is the highest goal of kingship, or if the natural state of Englishmen and Frenchmen is war. He may even fantasize about what he would do, were he ever given the supreme responsibility of a crown on his head and a realm at his back.

He does not know that in time he will find out. More than that, indeed. Under very different circumstances, in an entirely different world, Henry will find his own way to force a peace between England and France. It will not look at all like Richard's way, though the two of them will have one thing in common.

Henry, too, will one day take a daughter from the poor, afflicted, mad king Charles of France.

3

"BEHOLD, I WILL OPEN YOUR GRAVES"

On the evening of Henry's eleventh birthday, Sunday, September 16, 1397, Henry's father hires a plush house on London's Fleet Street and throws a party. Henry and his brother Thomas, as Bolingbroke's two eldest children, are allowed to attend. It is almost a year since Henry went to Calais, and appearing in public at his father's elbow is now becoming a regular feature of his life. It is as much a part of his education as his studies of his Latin books and his training in the saddle and with the sword.

The house Bolingbroke rents belongs to a wealthy skinner and city politician called John Rote. It is a grand place to entertain, for Fleet Street is a smart address. The riverside avenue runs from the walled City of London down to the sprawling royal palace complex at Westminster. Along its length, set back behind walls and hedges, lie grand friaries, the lawyers' offices of the New Temple, and a run of fine private homes. The buildings on the south side of the road boast long gardens with their own wharves onto the Thames.*

---

* The Lancastrian family once owned the biggest and most famous house on this street, the Savoy Palace. But Henry cannot remember it. Five years before he was born, during the great rebellion of 1381, rioters targeted property belonging to his grandfather John of Gaunt.

Given the fine surroundings and the importance of this occasion, Henry and Thomas are dressed stylishly, wearing new gowns made for them by the family's tailor, Adam Garston.[1] As the boys mingle, adjusting to the feel of their unfamiliar robes, there is much for them both to take in. They listen to their father's minstrels play. They watch the revelries laid on for the guests, who are brought to the house on barges steered by boatmen wearing Lancastrian livery. They admire a display of brightly painted birds: doves, curlews, and parrots painted by the king's official artist under their father's commission.

It is a fine scene, because it needs to be. The guest of honor at the party is King Richard, who will, the next day, be presiding over the first day of a parliament. Over the years, Richard's parliaments have tended to be the stage for high, even bloody, drama. In September 1397 there is a feeling that this parliament is likely to be explosive.

Henry and Thomas must realize their father is on edge. The whole of London is on edge. The city is packed with soldiers. The Lancastrians have five hundred men-at-arms and a thousand archers billeted in and around London. The king is said to have a bodyguard of two thousand archers from the county of Cheshire: his private lordship, which he has turned into a recruiting ground for what amounts to a private militia.

What is more, although most of the great and good of the English nobility are in the capital—and many of them in attendance at Bolingbroke's party—there are some extremely significant absentees. The king's uncle, the hawkish, outspoken duke of Gloucester, was arrested in the summer. He has been imprisoned in Calais for eleven weeks, and no word has been heard from him.

Two other senior noblemen—the earls of Arundel and Warwick—are also under arrest, and have been held respectively in the Tower of London and Carisbrooke Castle on the Isle of Wight. Legal cases are being prepared against all three of these peers, based on offenses they gave the king more than ten years earlier, and are rumored to be high on tomorrow's

---

Thanks to them the Savoy is a ruined shell, plundered, burned out with gunpowder, and never rebuilt.

parliamentary agenda. The fate of Gloucester, Arundel, and Warwick must be on the minds—and lips—of all the adults at Bolingbroke's party. Young Henry and Thomas may worry about who else might be dragged into the parliamentary proceedings, and at what cost.

Amid the glamour and the music of the party, it is impossible to ignore the fact that English politics is curdling. Plots are being hatched and re-hatched. Alliances are shifting and twisting. Ancient grievances that have been festering for years are being re-aired, and old enemies sniff the air, trying to sense their moment to strike.

Dangerously close to the heart of these matters is the host of the party, Henry's father. He had his own part to play in the events of a decade ago that have now led to Gloucester's, Arundel's, and Warwick's imprisonment. His fate, as much as theirs, may be determined by how his cousin Richard decides to proceed when tomorrow's parliament opens. Bolingbroke knows, and his sons may well know, too, that he is caught up in events beyond his control.

Bolingbroke turned thirty this year. He is a famous man, who in the eleven years of young Henry's life has seen and done as much as any other man in England. He has traveled the world, proven himself a vigorous Christian warrior, and raised a young family. Yet he has also become snared in the political brambles of Richard's reign, and now faces his moment of maximum jeopardy.

The crux of it is this. In 1386, the year Henry was born, Bolingbroke joined a faction of noblemen who took the teenaged King Richard to task for the inadequacies of his kingship. There were many problems, but two stood out. The first was Richard's failure to take control of the war with France—which was at that point going so badly that it seemed likely that the French were about to launch a full invasion of England's south coast. The second was Richard's enchantment with a small group of favorites, most notably Robert de Vere, the duke of Ireland.

The three leaders of the noble faction were the men whom Richard now has in custody: Arundel, Warwick, and Gloucester. At a parliament in the autumn of 1386 (later nicknamed the Wonderful Parliament) they led demands for Richard to sack his struggling and unpopular chancellor, Michael de la Pole, earl of Suffolk. When Richard resisted, Gloucester threatened him with deposition.

In the short term, this threat worked: Suffolk was removed and condemned for corruption, and the three lords established a council to take over government for a year, with a mandate to carry out reform. They effectively stripped the king of all his power and returned him to a state of minority. But in the medium term their actions had dire consequences.

As is perhaps unsurprising for a man crowned king just after his tenth birthday, Richard has long had a sense of righteous psychological attachment to the dignity of kingship. He does not take kindly to being thwarted.

In 1386 he was obliged to do as his more senior lords said. But he began almost immediately to wriggle out of their control. The next year, Richard secured a judgment from the highest judges in England, declaring that the lords were traitors and ought to be punished as such. In response, Gloucester, Arundel, and Warwick issued a proclamation known as the Appeal of Treason, in which they argued that the real traitors were in fact Richard's henchmen, most notably de Vere, de la Pole, a senior judge called Sir Robert Tresilian, and a powerful London merchant named Nicholas Brembre. Both sides began raising troops and preparing for civil war.

This was the point at which Henry's father, Bolingbroke, was drawn into the affair. He and Thomas Mowbray, earl of Nottingham, threw in their lot with the older lords, forming a coalition known collectively as the Appellants.*

To defend himself and the king, de Vere raised an army of several thousand troops from the northwest of England and marched them toward London. On a gloomy, foggy late December day in the Cotswolds the Appellants intercepted de Vere with an armed force of their own. In a small battle at Radcot Bridge, in Oxfordshire, Bolingbroke trapped de Vere's men against the banks of the Thames, "attacked them as public

---

* The name derives from the Appeal of Treason the older lords had issued.

enemies and caught almost every one."[2] De Vere got away: he "gambled on life or death, and spurring his horse, cast off his gauntlets and his sword . . . and plunged into the Thames, and thus escaped with wonderful daring."[3] But he could no longer stay in England. De Vere fled to France, where, to Richard's immense sorrow, he died in 1392, from injuries sustained while hunting wild boar.

De Vere's exile was a personal tragedy for King Richard, and political humiliation followed quickly on its heels. Bolingbroke and the other Appellants spent Christmas 1387 debating what to do with the king. They considered the idea of deposing him, but ultimately decided only to remove the most objectionable of his remaining favorites. In January 1388 the Appellants purged the king's household and the judiciary. The following month at a new parliament (known as the Merciless Parliament) de Vere, de la Pole, Brembre, and Tresilian were condemned to death. Tresilian and Brembre were hanged and had their throats slashed. Three of Richard's closest friends from his household were also executed, including his childhood tutor, a decorated knight called Simon Burley.

Richard was almost as attached to Burley as he was to de Vere. The older knight had been a close friend of both his parents; at Richard's coronation he had carried the ten-year-old king on his shoulders. Richard pleaded for Burley's life, and Bolingbroke and Mowbray were inclined to spare him. But Arundel, Warwick, and Gloucester were adamant that he should die. At the start of May, Burley was beheaded on Tower Hill.

By the spring of 1388 the Appellants had achieved their goal of separating the king from those whom they believed were the most malign influences around him. But Richard never forgot the pain of de Vere's exile and the violent deaths of Burley and his other friends, and became "filled with an ardent desire to exact revenge for the bitter rebuke which he had endured."[4] The Appellants believed they had been acting in the best interests of the kingdom. Unwittingly, they had lit in Richard a smoldering desire to have his revenge.

In 1397 he is ready to wreak that revenge in stunning, pitiless, theatrical fashion. Henry is going to be present in Westminster and London to witness it.

The day after Bolingbroke's party at John Rote's house, Parliament opens in Westminster. Henry and Thomas are allowed to watch at least some of the proceedings; they have new robes for this occasion, too. What unfolds is an extraordinary exercise in political performance: governance transformed into a sort of danse macabre. This is the first time Henry has seen a parliament. Strange and chilling though this one is, some of its lessons will remain with him all his life.

The opening of Parliament is always a significant occasion. Parliamentary assemblies are the largest possible meetings of lords and commons, the latter group mostly comprising urban burgesses and knights of the shire. They are summoned at the king's pleasure to the venue of his choosing, and usually shadowed by a simultaneous assembly of the clergy, known as convocation. They can take place once a year, twice a year—or with gaps of several years between them. Generally, though, they are called when the king needs to raise money through taxation, which can only be collected with Parliament's approval. Since the earliest parliaments of the thirteenth century, a convention has developed that, in exchange for grants of taxation, the lords and commons are allowed to complain about the management of the realm, make formal requests for reform, and raise weighty matters that cannot be dealt with in the course of ordinary political life.

That calculus—of taxation in exchange for reform—can work well under a king who is prepared to engage constructively with his critics, and who is able to discern between legitimate complaints and loudmouths blowing off steam. Richard II, however, is not that king. Over the course of his reign he has become addicted to the theatrical opportunities offered by great gatherings of the political nation, but at the same time is painfully touchy about even the tiniest perceived slights to his royal dignity.

When Henry and Thomas join the crowds who come to witness the opening of Parliament in September 1397, the tone is immediately set. Parliament's normal gathering place would be in the great hall of Westminster Palace, but Richard is having the hall's roof rebuilt, under the direction of the famous mason Henry Yevele.* So the lords and commons gather in a large marquee in the palace yard. Richard presides, as one chronicler puts it, "in greater splendor and solemnity than any king of [the] realm ever had before."[5]

Positioned around the marquee are thousands of Richard's Cheshire archers. These guards strike some observers as little more than criminal thugs: "by nature bestial . . . ready to commit any sort of crime . . . people who in their own localities [are] scarcely regarded as worthy to pull off their masters' boots."[6] And indeed, this is the point of them. During the most recent parliament before this one, in January 1397, various aspects of official policy had been heavily criticized. Scorn was heaped on Richard's plans to join his father-in-law Charles VI on an invasion of Milan, the poor state of defenses on the Scottish border, the pernicious raising of private armies by English lords, and the excessive costs of the royal household. The king was enraged then, and wishes no repeat now. His archers' presence delivers an unsubtle warning. Step out of line, and there will be trouble.

That same message is delivered by the king's chancellor, the bishop of Exeter. Giving the traditional opening speech of the parliament, he takes as his theme a text from the book of Ezekiel.[7] "I will make them one nation in the land," he proclaims, "and one king shall be king over them all; and they shall be no longer two nations, and no longer divided into two kingdoms."†

The bishop explains what this means. "For the good governance of every king three things [are] required," he says. "First, that the king have the power to govern. Second, that the laws by which he ought to govern should be kept and justly executed. Third, that the subjects of the kingdom should be duly obedient to the king and his laws."[8]

---

* Yevele's hammer-beam roof of Westminster Hall survives today; it is one of the biggest medieval timber-beam roofs in Europe and a sight well worth taking a tour of the Houses of Parliament to see.

† Ezekiel 37:22.

Put together, the biblical verse and authoritarian commentary seem clear: Richard wants peace and harmony in his kingdom, but this can only be achieved by absolute adherence to his royal will.

Yet there is something darker to it, too. If Henry and Thomas have paid attention to their scriptural studies, they will recall the preceding verses in this chapter of Ezekiel. God takes the prophet to the desert and shows him the dry bones of men who are long dead. He orders Ezekiel to preach to the bones and Ezekiel obeys. Then "there was a noise, and behold, a rattling; and the bones came together, bone to its bone. And as I looked, there were sinews on them, and flesh had come upon them, and skin had covered them."* As this undead army arises God asks Ezekiel to give them one last rousing message on his behalf. He has him say: "Behold, I will open your graves, and raise you from your graves, O my people; and I will bring you home."†

To anyone who knows this passage, the chancellor's speech is chilling. The chancellor seems to be saying that for King Richard, peace means reconciliation, and reconciliation demands that old scores be settled. The king intends to bring his country together. But first he will have satisfaction in the name of old friends.

Whether Henry and Thomas are allowed to stay in Westminster for the rest of the parliamentary session or they are sent back to John Rote's Fleet Street mansion is not known. But they, along with the whole capital and the land beyond, must follow with growing horror the events that unfold in the following days.

First, the speaker of the commons—an experienced parliamentarian and Lincolnshire landowner named Sir John Bussy—comes to the king and the lords and formally accuses the three older Appellants of 1386–88 of treason.[9] (These accusations had previously been made to the royal council several weeks earlier by a group of Richard's loyal lords, styling

* Ezekiel 37:7–8.

† Ezekiel 37:10–12.

themselves "counter-Appellants.") Then, on Friday, September 21, the first of the old Appellants, Richard FitzAlan, earl of Arundel, is brought before the parliament to stand trial for his actions ten years ago.

Arundel claims the benefit of a general pardon issued at the time, and argues that on that basis he has no case to answer. But the steward of England, presiding over the trial, tells him he has no claim, and that he is a traitor who deserves to die.

The steward of England is young Henry's grandfather, John of Gaunt.

Arundel, who has come to the parliament dressed for martyrdom, with a red cloak on his hood, rounds furiously on Gaunt, and on Speaker Bussy. He accuses Gaunt of treachery and tells Bussy: "I know all about you and your crew, and how you have got here: not to act faithfully, but to shed my blood."[10]

Then Bolingbroke speaks up, and speaks to divisions among the Appellants ten years ago—divisions that presumably explain why he is lined up among the free men in Parliament, and Arundel is a prisoner.

Bolingbroke claims that in 1386 Arundel plotted to make the king a prisoner, casting him as the ringleader and zealot of the movement. Arundel shouts, "You lie in your teeth!"[11] But this is the wrong audience. The king now steps in, to point out that Arundel once refused to have mercy on his beloved tutor Simon Burley. The implication is that he now deserves none himself. Arundel is hot with rage, but there is no more damning witness against him than Bolingbroke, and no hope of pity from the king.

So the end is a formality. As Arundel splutters, Richard calls for judgment. It is for Gaunt to pass the sentence, and he hands down the only one he can. Arundel is told that he has forfeited all his lands and titles. Then he is marched out of Westminster to London. Like Burley, he is to be killed as a traitor on Tower Hill.

If young Henry is not in the crowd of gawpers who follow the fifty-one-year-old earl's steps to the scaffold, then he must surely see and hear the masses as they pass John Rote's house: "a great crowd of citizens who mourn [Arundel] as much as they dare."[12] He may see the earl himself, walking as coolly as if "he had been asked out to dinner."[13]

At the Tower, the headsman is waiting for Arundel. The full sentence for treachery is the torture of drawing, hanging, and quartering, with the agonies of disembowelment and castration. In respect of his noble birth, Arundel is spared this. The executioner will simply remove the earl's head with an ax. Arundel tests the ax blade with his thumb, then kneels down to die. After the blow is struck, his body allegedly rises, headless, and stands with dignity for the length of time it takes to say a paternoster.[14] This is a sure sign that he has heen admitted, as one writer puts it, "to the fellowship of the saints."[15]

His has been a shocking end. But Arundel will not be the only one.

Why, young Henry and Thomas may whisper to each other, as Arundel marched to his death, is their father safe, when his old allies are not?

It is a very good question. After Arundel is dead, his brother, Thomas, is brought before Parliament. Thomas was an Appellant ally, but since then he has served a long stint as Richard's chancellor, and last year was appointed his archbishop of Canterbury. He seemed safe. Yet his involvement with the Appellants has never been forgotten, and now revenge is served cold. As a churchman he avoids his brother's fate, but he is deprived of his see and sent in exile to Italy.

Next, the king's uncle, the duke of Gloucester, is summoned. But he does not come, for reasons that shock the whole parliament. Gloucester has been in prison in Calais, where his jailer is none other than Thomas Mowbray, earl of Nottingham, the former junior Appellant. When Mowbray is asked to produce his prisoner to the parliament, he reports that Gloucester has died. He does *not* reveal the true circumstances: several weeks ago, Gloucester was smothered with a pillow in the back room of a Calais pub called Princes' Inn, on the king's direct orders. These facts will emerge in time and can probably be guessed at straightaway. But for the moment, everyone must simply accept the new reality emerging before them: this is a noble bloodbath.

Finally, there comes the earl of Warwick. He is hauled before the parliament in a pathetic state, "sobbing and whining and begging the king's mercy in all things and bemoaning the fact that he had ever associated with the Appellants."[16] It is not very edifying, but this pitiful display saves his life at least. Warwick, like Arundel, is stripped of his lands and titles, but rather than facing the headsman, he is exiled forever to the Isle of Man.

And so in short order, all three of the senior Appellants are dealt with, ten full years after their betrayal of the king. One executed, one murdered, one banished in tears. Yet Bolingbroke and Mowbray live, and needed to do no bleating or crying at all.

The reason is clear, and young Henry and Thomas must see it, whether they can admit it or not. Their father acquiesced in Richard's revenge. He and Mowbray are free because they have helped, in their different ways, to ensure the shameful deaths of men who were once their allies. Given the choice between sticking to their principles and saving their own skins, they have chosen their skins.

On the last day of the parliament they reap the rewards, along with the other lords who have backed Richard over his former critics.

Bolingbroke is made duke of Hereford. Mowbray is made duke of Norfolk. Other high titles are handed out like sweets, so many of them to such unworthy recipients that people snigger and call the new nobles "duketti," or "little dukes."[17] But all sniggering must be done with care now, for Richard's tyranny has arrived and it is real. The parliamentary session is suspended on September 30, with the king demanding oaths from all those present to uphold the things it has done.

Then the king hosts a banquet to mark an interval in proceedings, and everyone goes home. They are to reconvene in January, at Shrewsbury. What awaits them there is anyone's guess.

4

ROUGH JUSTICE

Henry's father, the newly minted duke of Hereford, spends the months that follow the Revenge Parliament in the king's orbit, traveling between Westminster, Windsor, and the king's Oxfordshire palace of Woodstock.

He lodges his younger children in a fortified Herefordshire manor house called Eaton Tregoz: the home of John of Gaunt's attorney Sir Hugh Waterton, who oversaw Bolingbroke's own education when he was a boy.[1] Eleven-year-old Henry, however, does not stay with his siblings. He is with his father, to witness the turmoil at the royal court firsthand. It is an extraordinary thing to see. A dangerous new political climate has settled over England since the Revenge Parliament.

Following the purge of the Appellants, Richard's approach to kingship, which has always tended toward the theatrical and capricious, now goes entirely unchecked. The king exults in his own majesty. Indeed, he adopts "majesty" as his preferred form of address—a style that will be adopted by most English monarchs after him. He sits aloof in court, dressed in blazing gold cloth and silks, attended by sycophants, playing a game that demonstrates his absolute power. He casts his gaze around a room; whomever it lights upon must fall to their knees and grovel.

Richard also recruits more and more men to his private army, membership of which is connoted by a little badge bearing his royal symbol, the white hart. He sends out "blank charters" to those great men he distrusts—essentially, all of them—demanding they affix their seals to clean sheets of parchment, which he may later use against them, filled in with fake confessions or recognitions of debt.[2]

Meanwhile the Cheshire archers, his bodyguards and private militia, run wild. As the court travels, they terrorize the people of England. They "beat and wound with impunity the king's faithful subjects."[3] They rob ordinary folk of their goods and possessions. They rape and kill. And they speak to the king in honeyed tones, calling him by the pet name "Diccon" and telling him he can always sleep securely while they are around.

An artwork commissioned by the king around this time shows Richard as he presumes to see himself: kneeling in the company of his favorite saints—Edmund the Martyr, Edward the Confessor, and John the Baptist. He greets the Virgin Mary and the Christ child, who are surrounded by angels wearing white harts, seemingly about to bless him and offer him their protection.[4]

Is this madness or melodrama? Narcissism or simple tyranny?[5] Writers who choose to fawn rather than hold Richard to account lap it up. They rejoice that Richard's royal majesty is no longer "obscured by a hostile source—but now, soaring in arms over the mountains, and bounding over the hills with his might, [the king] has dispersed the clouds with his sun, whose light shines ever more brightly."[6] Others are not so sure. Among the common people of England a rumor abounds that the earl of Arundel's body has miraculously recoupled with his severed head. This is taken as a sign that the king's triumph may be hollow and even short-lived.

Henry is in a better position than most to judge. And it is possible that he falls in with the fawners. Decades after this fact, the first writer commissioned to make an account of Henry's life will claim that Richard frequently shines his kingly light on the young man in a way that is either very flattering or terrifyingly passive-aggressive. According to this writer, Richard is wont to say "right often in open audience of the court . . . 'Of the greatest of my house shall be born a child, whose name shall be Henry, which for his knightly acts and resplendishing virtues shall be renowned throughout the world.'" That Henry, Richard tells his courtiers, is Bolingbroke's son.[7]

We do not know how Henry responds. But it is perfectly possible that Richard's show of imperious majesty is attractive to a child's mind—which is probably why Richard, himself an overgrown teenager, enjoys it so much. Certainly, in later life, Henry will show both a deep and abiding respect for Richard's memory and an instinctive grasp of high political theater. He surely learns at least some of this from watching Richard at first hand.

In the new year, Henry's role in the drama of Richard's reign moves from that of observer to participant. Once more, it is his father who drags him in.

At the Revenge Parliament in the autumn, Bolingbroke abetted the destruction of his former Appellant allies. The fifth Appellant, Thomas Mowbray, had an even closer and bloodier hand in things, overseeing the murder of the earl of Gloucester in Calais.

Both men were handsomely rewarded for their complicity. Yet neither is safe, and when they meet on the road to London in early December 1397, Mowbray unloads his fears. He tells Bolingbroke that they are both "about to be undone." He alleges that the king and his cronies are plotting to have Bolingbroke and John of Gaunt murdered, partly out of personal spite, partly to remove Gaunt and Bolingbroke from the line of royal succession, and partly so they can confiscate and plunder the vast duchy of Lancaster estates.[8]

The way Bolingbroke later tells the story, he reacts to these allegations with horror and disbelief. He exclaims, "God forbid!" and tells Mowbray that the king has "sworn by St. Edward to be a good lord to him and to all others." He asks Mowbray how anyone could ever trust such a feckless king.

That's just it, replies Mowbray. No one *can* trust him. For even if the king and his allies don't get to them this time, "they will still be intent on destroying us in our homes ten years hence."[9]

He leaves Bolingbroke with that thought, and Bolingbroke does the only sensible thing he can. He tells his father, John of Gaunt, what he has heard, and asks for his advice. Gaunt takes the matter to the king, and when Parliament reopens at the end of the month in Shrewsbury, the last two Appellants come before it wrapped up in a full-blown intrigue. A special parliamentary committee is set up to investigate Bolingbroke's claims against Mowbray, which Mowbray understandably denies. When the committee finally makes its report, it advises that since this is all a matter of hearsay and that Mowbray disputes Bolingbroke's entire story, the two lords should fight a duel to decide whose word is true.

Duels between peers of the realm are rare. The Church has frowned on the use of forms of ordeal to determine judicial cases ever since the Fourth Lateran Council of 1215. In the same year, the Magna Carta stated clearly that in England the judgment of a man's peers was to be the preferred means of dispute resolution. True, a celebrated duel was fought just over a decade earlier in France, pitching a Norman knight called Jean de Carrouges against a squire called Jacques Le Gris to settle an accusation of rape.* But this case did not involve noblemen, nor did it pertain to high politics; moreover, it caused a stir precisely because it was so unusual.

Nevertheless, in 1398 the idea of a staged battle between two of his greatest subjects appeals to the king. So Richard agrees. He sets a time and a place for combat to take place: Monday, September 16, at a tournament field in Coventry. There, Bolingbroke and Mowbray must defend their honor in a fight to the death. God will ensure that the innocent man

---

* This case was the basis for the 2021 film *The Last Duel*, which made the 1386 battle between Carrouges and Le Gris a vehicle for a ponderous meditation on the politics and ethics of twenty-first-century sexual abuse.

wins. Bolingbroke and Mowbray will have five months to prepare for his judgment.

The summer of 1398 must be, for Henry, a time of nerves, excitement, wonder, and terror. His education, both literary and physical, has told him that these sorts of things happen: scripture teaches that God intervenes in the world to see that justice is served, while the classical histories and Arthurian romances portray combat as the ultimate measure of a man. But now this is real. On the day of his twelfth birthday, it will be happening to his father. To his family. To him.

Henry can comfort himself at least with the knowledge that his father is good at fighting. Indeed, Bolingbroke spent many of Henry's youngest years absent, honing his martial skills. In the aftermath of the Appellant affair, Bolingbroke took himself away from the seething English court and threw himself into a self-guided program of chivalric adventure, designed to burnish his reputation and sharpen his command of lance and sword.

In 1390 he traveled to Saint-Inglevert, in northern France, to take part in a tournament organized by the most famous knight in western Europe, Jean "Boucicaut" Le Maingre;* Bolingbroke rode ten jousts against the great man and was praised by poets afterward for his talent.[10] Next, he traveled to the Baltic coast of northern Europe to take part in a crusade against the pagans of Lithuania.† He fought two seasons with the Teutonic Knights: the German military order that oversees Baltic crusading from their headquarters in Marienburg. Then, in the autumn of 1392, he disappeared again, on a spectacular tour of the Mediterranean, which took him to Venice, Corfu, Rhodes, Cyprus, and, finally, Jerusalem. He returned from this adventure in the summer of 1393 with exotic souve-

---

* Boucicaut is an almost cartoonish paradigm of knighthood, famed for having fought in his first battle when he was twelve years old, and for being so athletic that he could perform backflips in full armor.

† Boucicaut had also crusaded against the Lithuanian pagans in 1384.

nirs, including a parrot for young Henry's mother and a leopard given to him by the king of Cyprus.[11]

So, Henry can reassure himself, his father knows what he is doing. What's more, the king has allowed him to remain at liberty during the months before the duel, whereas Mowbray is locked up, first in Windsor Castle and later in the Tower of London. Henry, Thomas, and their siblings must follow with grim fascination their father's preparations: he travels almost ceaselessly around his estates, staying in the eyes and hearts of his tenants. They will be aware that he is exchanging letters, gifts, and envoys with Europe's leading combat experts. He contacts his old sparring partner Boucicaut, who is now marshal of France and a crusading hero. The duke of Milan, Gian Galeazzo Visconti, takes on the task of supplying Bolingbroke's armor, and sends to England four expert armorers to adjust its fit.[12]

A betting man would incline toward Bolingbroke in the contest. But only slightly. And the stakes are as high as they could be. The loser of the duel will likely be killed. His reputation will be shredded. The king may decide to disinherit and impoverish his family. Henry will know his father must win. He will know that nothing but victory will do.

On the last day of August 1398 official invitations to the duel are sent out. In the first weeks of September dignitaries from all over England and western Europe begin arriving at Coventry to the tournament ground.

When the day arrives, Monday, September 16, everything is as the king wants it: picture perfect, almost dreamlike. The duel will begin in the saddle and will likely be finished on foot, so Henry's father has his horses, his armor, his lance, and a pavilion stitched with red roses. He carries a shield painted with a bright red cross. Mowbray is in finery of his own.

The king presides over all, radiant and solemn. His Cheshire archers, thousands of them, surround the lists, forbidding any man to touch the barriers, under pain of losing a hand. Richard hears the combatants' oaths, with Bolingbroke declaring that he will prove by force of arms that

Mowbray is "a traitor, false and recreant to God, the King, his realm and me."[13] He orders the tournament ground to be emptied of anyone but the two men who must prove their right. The crowd falls silent, the barriers are opened, and Bolingbroke and Mowbray advance to the ground where they will fight, and perhaps die.

But after Bolingbroke has taken "seven or eight paces toward his adversary to do his duty," the king rises from his seat and cries out, "Ho! Ho!"[14] He orders the two men to surrender their weapons and return to their pavilions. Then he disappears into his private quarters to prepare his next dramatic flourish. Two hours later he reemerges, and has his decision proclaimed to the confused crowds of spectators.

"Henry of Lancaster, Duke of Hereford, appellant, and Thomas Mowbray, Duke of Norfolk, defendant, have both appeared here valiantly, and . . . ready to do his duty like a brave knight; but because the matters are so weighty between the two lords, it is decreed by the King and council, that Henry of Lancaster shall quit the realm for the term of ten years, and, if he return to the country before the ten years are passed, he shall be hanged and beheaded."[15]

The crowd erupts. When they are quietened, Mowbray's sentence can also be heard: "Thomas of Mowbray, Duke of Norfolk, shall quit the realm for the rest of his life, and shall choose whether he would dwell in Prussia, in Bohemia, or in Hungary, or would go right beyond sea to the land of the Saracens and unbelievers; that he shall never return to set foot again on Christian land; and that all his lands shall remain in the King's hands."[16]

The men are given five weeks to pack their things and go.

What is a twelve-year-old boy to make of this? So much is happening all at once. There is the splendor of the tournament and the high, romantic drama of its interruption. There is the astonishing caprice of a king who calls for God's judgment and then substitutes for it his own. Then there is the realization that Henry will lose his father for a decade. That this may be the first step toward the ruin of his whole family.

Speculation is swirling about the deep purpose of the king's decision—if indeed there is one, beyond simple self-aggrandizement. Does it represent a genuine concern on Richard's part for finding a fair solution to a dispute between two of his most senior peers? Is it a blatant, if absurdly convoluted, scheme to be revenged on the last two of the Appellants?

Or is it something else again? Since the king seems more inclined to Bolingbroke than Mowbray, some muse that Richard intends to reduce Bolingbroke's lighter sentence still further, so that he may serve six years, or even fewer.[17]

Cynical observers disagree. One conspiracy theory holds that "the king had been told by a fortune-teller that the duke of Norfolk would win the contest, which pleased him greatly, since he longed for the downfall of the duke of Hereford; once they had joined battle, however, it seemed to him that the duke of Hereford was going to win, so the king ordered the duel to be halted."[18] According to this line of thinking, it will be Mowbray, not Bolingbroke, who will be back early. Whatever the case, Henry can bank on not seeing his father for a long time.

In the short time Bolingbroke has before his banishment begins, he makes what provisions he can for all six of the children. The younger three—Humphrey, Blanche, and Philippa—will remain with Sir Hugh Waterton at Eaton Tregoz, with a small group of servants to take care of them, including maidservants to make sure the little girls' hair is always tied up neatly, and a chaplain who says mass with the children every day for the soul of their dead mother, Mary.

Henry's nine-year-old brother, John, is lodged in London with the capital's sixty-year-old grand dame, Margaret Brotherton, duchess of Norfolk. A granddaughter of King Edward I of England and a great-granddaughter of Philip III of France, Margaret keeps an opulent household between the city and Framlingham Castle in Norfolk. John will grow up surrounded by great luxury and learning to speak perfect French.[19]

Thomas and Henry have stayed with Margaret before, but they will not remain with her this time. Bolingbroke has decided he will take Thomas, just turned eleven, into exile with him, as part of a household that will include hundreds of servants and wagonloads of treasure and living commodities. There are no restrictions on where they may travel, so they will be going first to Paris, and then perhaps on to Italy or the Spanish peninsula, where one of Bolingbroke's sisters is queen of Portugal and another queen of Castile.

Thomas ought to be excited by this grand adventure, even if its circumstances have been trying. Henry may well envy him, and wonder if this suggests his father has a favorite son. Yet his father does not have a choice, nor does he. He is one of the senior males of the house of Lancaster, and if anything happens to Bolingbroke during his exile, he will be its scion.

That matters. The family's patriarch, John of Gaunt, is approaching his sixtieth birthday. It is by no means certain he will be alive by the time Bolingbroke's term of banishment is up. Bolingbroke is allowed to appoint attorneys in England to handle any legal matters pertaining to inheritance while he is gone. But he is banned under pain of treason from asking to come home early. If Gaunt dies and Bolingbroke is still in exile, Henry will be the one who must fight for the Lancastrian estates. So he is going to reside in the only plausible place for an adolescent on whose shoulders hangs such a weighty inheritance.

He will stay in England, with his grandfather Gaunt, in the orbit of King Richard.

5

"FAIR COUSIN"

Winter approaches and Henry lives in limbo.

By the end of October 1398 his father and Thomas have settled in Paris, and through messengers they send news occasionally back to England, keeping Henry and his siblings up to date on their situation.

It is not all bad. They have been welcomed graciously by Charles VI, who is enjoying a period of lucidity between relapses into madness. Bolingbroke is feted everywhere he goes, and lives in style at the Hôtel de Clisson, the palatial residence of the storied Breton soldier Olivier de Clisson. He collects a decent income from England, since Richard has allowed him to continue to draw the revenue from the lands of his late wife, Mary de Bohun. He is considering spending some of it on joining a French crusade to be led by Marshal Boucicaut against the Ottoman sultan Bayezid, the better "to make the time of his banishment pass the sooner away. He may even marry again: a match with the duke of Berry's daughter has been loosely floated. Nevertheless, he is somewhat prone to melancholy 'on being thus separated from his family.'"[1]

Henry may feel the same way. For here he remains in England, where the king is not mad, but certainly bad and dangerous to know.

Like his younger brothers John and Humphrey, scattered across England in their own surrogate households, Henry continues his education, developing his artistic and knightly interests. He plays the harp. He studies chess.[2] He takes care of his sword, the scabbard of which he keeps wrapped in a sheet of fine black silk.[3] He visits his maternal grandmother, Joan, countess of Hertford, whom he loves dearly.[4] But he spends most of his time living with his grandfather John of Gaunt in his duchy of Lancaster headquarters at Leicester, still watched over by the steady eye of Gaunt's retainer Peter Melbourne.[5]

The loyal Lancastrian servant Melbourne may try to cheer Henry with stories of the times he once spent overseas with Bolingbroke: when he joined him on crusade in Prussia; when they went on pilgrimage to Jerusalem. Perhaps Henry imagines himself doing all this one day. Perhaps when he is older he will go and visit his father. Certainly, he will be a man before Bolingbroke comes home.

Or so it seems until the winter settles in.

As the nights shorten and the grounds freeze, it becomes clear that Gaunt is not well. His eldest son's banishment has stolen something vital from him, and now the duke of Lancaster falls into what a chronicler will call a "sudden languor, both from old age and heaviness that his son was so sorely treated."[6] He takes to his bed, a magnificent piece of furniture, draped in gray-blue sheets stitched with gold roses and white ostrich feathers.[7] He will not or cannot rise.

In Leicester Castle, physicians bustle along the corridors, offering grave opinions to the household, which is overseen by Gaunt's third wife, Katheryn Swynford. The prognosis is serious enough that a messenger is sent to Paris to inform Bolingbroke that his father labors "under so dangerous a disease it must soon cause his death."[8] King Richard comes to visit, speaking to Gaunt "right courteously . . . with pleasant words of comfort." He brings Gaunt some secret state documents to read, perhaps to keep his mind busy.[9] A later, scurrilous rumor, put about by an inveterate enemy of the Lancastrian family, will state that Gaunt shows the king his penis, which has supposedly putrefied as a result of his "frequenting of women."[10] This is not a vice Richard seems troubled by, so it seems improbable that the rumor is true.

On February 3, 1399, Gaunt dies, aged fifty-eight.[11] The duke has lived an eventful life, and despite intense provocation has managed to remain on cordial terms with his nephew the king until the end. He has not always been popular with the ordinary folk, particularly in London, where his support for the late radical academic John Wyclif has earned him the scorn of the citizens. Certain chroniclers call him a "great adulterer."[12] Whether or not this is so, Henry's grandfather has been the true statesman of Richard's reign, and he is mourned with great, if unorthodox, solemnity.

Gaunt's will includes an unusual request that his body be laid out, unburied and unembalmed, for forty days after his death.* The executors of his will—who include Henry's loyal guardian, Peter Melbourne—see that his wishes are respected, so it is not until March 16 that he is buried near the altar at St. Paul's Cathedral in London, next to his first wife, Blanche: the grandmother whom young Henry never met.

Henry and his siblings are all bought mourning robes of black to wear at the funeral; even the little girls, Blanche, six, and Philippa, four, wear head-to-toe black with matching shoes.[13] On the day their grandfather is buried, the children see the crowds of paupers gathered to receive extravagant gifts of alms; hermits, lepers, and friars have also received generous handouts. They see St. Paul's flicker by the light of the many candles that surround Gaunt's putrefying corpse. (These are arranged in groups: ten for the commandments he has broken, seven for the deadly sins commit-

* Gaunt's reasons for this are obscure, and debatable. It may have been a precaution against being murdered—so that if he had met a violent end, it would become public knowledge. Equally, it could have been a dramatic display of piety, so that the decay of the mortal flesh might serve as a lesson to all who saw it. (If the latter, it would make more sense of the story about Gaunt showing Richard II his rotten genitals.)

ted, five for the human senses he has offended.)[14] It is undoubtedly a memorable, if somber day.

In Paris, meanwhile, Bolingbroke holds a requiem mass, attended by Charles VI and a whole bevy of royal dukes. There is much sympathy for him among the French court, who have found this exiled and now orphaned son of Lancaster "an amiable knight, courteous and pleasant to everyone."[15] And there is dismay on his behalf when messengers arrive just days after Gaunt's English funeral to tell Bolingbroke what is now common knowledge in England.

King Richard has decided not to allow Bolingbroke to claim his inheritance as duke of Lancaster. He is taking the lands into temporary royal management. He has forbidden Bolingbroke from taking over the hereditary Lancastrian post of steward of England, granting it instead to their one surviving uncle, Edmund Langley, duke of York. And he has extended Bolingbroke's term of banishment from ten years to life.

Under the terms of this harsh new royal decree, Henry's father will never have Gaunt's titles or estates.

He will never return to England.

In the turbulent aftermath of Gaunt's death and his father's dispossession, Henry has to move out of Leicester Castle. He and Peter Melbourne have been summoned by King Richard to attend upon him in person.

Richard, seldom bolder than when he has just thrown his weight around, has concluded that having snatched the duchy of Lancaster he is in a mighty enough position to attend to even greater business. He has been vexed throughout his reign by a desire to impress his majesty upon a traditionally unruly corner of his dominion: Ireland.

Henry and Melbourne have been told they must follow him, in part so that the king can burnish himself with an entourage of impeccable nobility and in part so that Richard can keep an eye on Henry. If Richard truly believes Henry is the child prophesied to take over the crown one day, then this is a sensible decision—better to have the young man where he can see him. Equally, Henry may simply be an insurance policy. The king cannot seriously expect Bolingbroke to accept his disinheritance with meek civility. Henry is in this context a guest who might easily be turned into a hostage, should Bolingbroke get any rash ideas.

Henry, for his part, has no choice but to obey. The Lancastrian inheritance has been snatched by the king. Gaunt's household has ceased to exist with the old statesman's death. His father cannot help him. Peter Melbourne cannot do anything—Richard has stripped him of several of his duchy of Lancaster offices, and completely overridden his capacity to execute Gaunt's will.[16] So Henry has no means to support himself, unless and until the king decides to grant him an estate, a title, and a living of his own. Richard instructs the royal exchequer to allow Henry to draw up to £500 per year to support himself. This is a generous stipend, but it is not a fortune. What's more, its granting exposes Henry's reliance on Richard's variable favor. His best hope of any meaningful inheritance is now to obey the king, hope his favor continues, and maybe one day even become one of his pet noble duketti.[17] Whatever he thinks of Richard, that is the reality of his situation.

In the three weeks that follow Gaunt's funeral, Henry and Melbourne are moved into the royal court and ordered to prepare for a military expedition. They buy arms, armor, and military sundries. They spend nearly £50 with a London skinner called John Freningham. They have heard enough about Ireland to know what they need to acquire for the journey. Ireland is going to be cold, and wet.

Henry and Melbourne have to make their preparations quickly. The king wants to set off for Ireland before the spring is out.[18] But from now on, events will move rapidly, and not favorably for Richard. For in Paris, political opinion entertains no doubt about what has happened. "The king of England was very ill-advised not to recall [Bolingbroke]," writes one chronicler. "To say the truth, if the king had wisely considered the consequences, he would have done it: affairs would not have turned out so miserably as they did."[19]

Ireland is a strange place for the king to go—indeed, for any English king to go. Not one has been there since Richard's ancestor King John, nearly two hundred years before. Although the Plantagenets claim nominal lordship over the island, and once drew a significant income from it, the reality of their influence by Richard's day amounts to a network of semiloyal Anglo-Irish noble families who doff their caps to the Crown when they must, and an increasingly helpless colonial government dug in at Dublin, which is financed at a steep annual loss from Westminster.[20]

Richard has long been determined to reverse the decline of English control over Ireland. To that end, he has already visited, during the winter of 1394–95, when he took several thousand troops on a tour from Waterford to Drogheda, via Dublin. He satisfied himself on the basis of one brief visit that he now understood all Ireland's problems.*

In a letter to his council on that occasion Richard explained that there were three types of Irishmen: "Irish savages, Irish rebels, and the obedient English."[21] Solving the Irish question, he had concluded, was simply a matter of reconciling all three to his own command, hearing their promises of fidelity, then sending over the most willing of his English friends to deputize for him in his absence. For some reason this policy has failed; Richard's return in 1399 is his attempt to reboot it.

Henry and Melbourne sail from Milford Haven to Waterford on the first day of June, in the company of the king and a vast host amounting to virtually the entire English court. Richard's favored nobles of the duketti appointed in 1397 are with him, along with boatloads of Cheshire archers. English attitudes toward the "Irish savages" are not kind: even the stevedores working in Waterford harbor are described by one observer as "wretched and filthy people, some in rags, others girt with a rope, had the one a hole, the other a hut for their dwelling."[22]

The royal army rides from Waterford to Kilkenny, then waits there a

* This remains a common English delusion.

while, as they try to locate a particular chieftain named Art MacMurrough, who has aroused Richard's wrath. MacMurrough is no fool, and at the approach of the English he has vanished into the forest. Richard is left to distract himself by having his men burn the homes of ordinary villagers. Misery is duly spread around and, buoyed by this small triumph, Richard sends for a group of young men from among the army and tells them they are to be made knights. Henry is foremost among the group he picks. If he has wondered whether he is in favor with the king, now he knows.

Making noble boys into knights at the outset of a military campaign is traditional: Richard's father, the Black Prince, was dubbed at age sixteen on a beach in France before the famous Crécy campaign of 1346. This is Henry's turn. The king orders a space to be cleared in the middle of his troops, with pennons and banners hoisted. As the king performs the ritual, he calls Henry "fair cousin" and tells him, somewhat cryptically, to be worthy and valiant, "for you have some valiant blood to conquer."[23]

A writer who observes this scene is adamant that there is no dark ulterior motive at work here: Richard performs the ceremony out of "true and entire affection."[24] In any case, Henry cannot resent being made a knight: this is a natural and expected step on his life's path. Yet he must be nervous, too. Henry knows his father well enough to suspect that he is unlikely to consider his son's knighthood and admission to the royal favor a fair exchange for the duchy of Lancaster.

While Henry and Melbourne are here with Richard chasing shadows through the forests, Bolingbroke and Thomas must be boiling with rage in Paris. Will his father act? What will he do? And how long will the king's favor toward him, Sir Henry, last if Bolingbroke decides to test the terms of his exile?

Buoyed by a fresh band of young knights, Richard's army slogs through forests in pursuit of disobedient Irishmen. When provisions run low, the group grows hungry and miserable. When they are resupplied with victuals including fine Spanish wine, they all drink too much and the ordinary troops quarrel and fight.

Meanwhile, the elusive Art MacMurrough is sighted but not subdued, and when invited to a parlay with one of Richard's noble advisers, he tells him he is the rightful king of Ireland, then rides away. So the party presses on, and by July 1 they have arrived at Dublin.

The weather is shocking when they arrive, the wind blowing so sharply that no ships can enter or leave the city's port for a few days. But when the "outrageous tempest" blows itself out, a vessel arrives with a message that is "the occasion of much sorrow."[25]

Henry's father is no longer in Paris.

Knowing Charles VI would never approve of him breaking the terms of his exile, he has made a pact with the French king's brother, Louis, duke of Orléans, a reckless and controversial character who schemes for power at his brother's court and tends to make trouble wherever he goes.*

Orléans bought him the time and political cover he needed to escape the capital and board a small ship at Boulogne. From there, Bolingbroke sailed for England, and has made land at Ravenspur in Yorkshire. He has no army with him—just a few dozen loyal servants. But he has brought along two more exiles: Thomas Arundel, the former archbishop of Canterbury who was banished by the 1397 parliament that executed his brother the earl of Arundel, and the earl's seventeen-year-old son and heir, Thomas FitzAlan.

Bolingbroke is said to be heading into his late father's lands, announcing to Lancastrian loyalists that he is back.

He is assuring everyone who will listen that he has only come to claim his rightful inheritance as duke of Lancaster. The king's uncle, the duke of York, has responded by mustering an army to see him off. But towns are already opening their gates to him, and his father's former followers are flocking to his side.

If Richard cares about his realm at all, now is the time to stop chasing

---

* Vividly and notoriously at the masquerade known as the Bal des Ardents in 1393, Louis accidentally set fire to four revelers' costumes. All four died, and Louis's brother, King Charles, narrowly escaped with his own life.

after roughnecks like Art MacMurrough and hurry back across the Irish Sea.

Those who are near the king when he receives this news see that it shocks him to the core. He turns pale with horror and rage.[26] He calls a council of his advisers and they agree to do the only sensible thing, which is to head back to England and face down the would-be duke of Lancaster. Then he summons Henry to his presence. For at least the second time in a month, Henry stands face-to-face with the king.

"Henry," says Richard. "What your father has done to me is truly a waste . . . I am very sorry for you, because thanks to his misdeeds, he may well have cost you your own patrimony."

It is a delicate moment for the young man. He must decide in an instant to whom he shows his loyalty.

Henry summons his most adult voice, and answers: "I'm sad to hear this rumor. But I believe I am innocent of what my father has done."[27]

He is only stating the obvious. He can have no idea how events will unfold from here, and he probably realizes he is not going to be allowed to witness them at first hand. Mercifully, the unvarnished truth satisfies Richard. He does not punish Henry, but simply confirms that there is no chance he will be going home to England anytime soon.

Instead, Henry is packed off thirty miles north of Dublin to Trim Castle: a stronghold on high ground beside the river Boyne with a cross-shaped keep, thick stone walls, and huge gatehouses. He has company there: his eighteen-year-old cousin Humphrey, son of the murdered earl of Gloucester, and Eleanor de Bohun, Henry's mother's sister.

Richard has instructed that the young men are not to be poorly treated—for the time being. But they are to be kept ignorant and at arm's length from whatever is to take place in England between Henry's father and the king.

Nearly two months will pass before Henry finds out how this feud between the two cousins has unfolded. As he will learn later, it is a time of the highest political and constitutional drama, whose effects will shape English history for many decades.

At the end of the summer a ship puts into port in Dublin. It belongs to a man from Chester called Henry Dryhurst, and it has come to fetch Henry and Humphrey and bring them home, along with a large consignment of red wine and "the furniture of a chapel and its ornaments," which King Richard left in Ireland when he departed to deal with Bolingbroke's disobedience.

As well as a berth back to England for the two boys, however, Dryhurst's sailors bring with them extraordinary news of what has happened in the past few weeks.

Henry's father has not simply returned to claim his duchy of Lancaster, his estates, and his honorary titles.

He has led a full-blown rebellion, gathering a large popular force behind him, seizing and executing the most egregious of Richard's supporters, and capturing Richard himself and imprisoning him.

One cousin has the other in his possession. There can surely be only one outcome. Richard is going to be deposed, either by cajolement or by force. A new king will be appointed in his place.

Henry Bolingbroke is to be crowned King Henry IV.

Henry will be his heir.

6

"A MAN IS RULING"

When Henry arrives back in England and travels to Chester in the middle of August 1399, death is in the air.

The city is the capital of King Richard's loyal county: the recruitment hub for his notorious bodyguard of archers. Cheshire has been a Ricardian heartland. Now a stake stands hammered into the ground outside the city's east gate. On it is set the recently severed head of one of Richard's most ardent supporters.

Perkin Leigh was a forest warden in the sprawling woodland known as Delamere. In the eyes of the new party sweeping to power in England, he was also a perverted "great malefactor" who liked to dress up as a monk and inflict "countless oppressions and extortions on the inhabitants of the region."[1] Leigh has been decapitated in his phony monk's garb. Now his dead eyes gaze blindly out from a city that has abandoned its former master.

Leigh is not the only dead man. Henry learns that his father, at large in England with an army at his back, has already captured and slaughtered several of Richard's closest advisers: William Le Scrope, earl of Wiltshire; Sir John Bussy, the speaker of the commons who had presided over the

Revenge Parliament of 1397; and a ubiquitous councilor called Sir Henry Green.

A glance at the countryside around Chester tells Henry that there are countless more unnamed who have also lost either their lives or their livelihoods. When his father's men swept through Cheshire, they were allowed to do their worst.

"For two years [the Cheshiremen] had ceaselessly inflicted murders, adulteries, robberies, assaults, and other insufferable wrongs upon the kingdom," writes one chronicler.[2] Their collective punishment is the ruination of their county: Bolingbroke's army has "devastated the land everywhere, wasting the meadows and the crops." Churches have been ransacked: "doors and chests broken open and everything carried off."[3] Henry must come to terms with all of this—and what it suggests about the character of his father's return from exile.

He must also process a death that Bolingbroke and his partisans have nothing to do with. On the journey by land and sea from Trim to Chester,* Henry's eighteen-year-old cousin Humphrey fell sick. He deteriorated so rapidly that it will later be said he was poisoned.[4] By the time Henry and the party returning from Ireland reached Chester, Humphrey had breathed his last. So the boy with whom Henry has passed his summer's imprisonment in Trim Castle is now a corpse, while Henry is alive.

What effect Humphrey's death has on Henry we do not know for sure. But the two young cousins spent a summer together at Trim, and during that time they may well have found common ground for conversation beyond the basic facts of their imprisonment. Like Henry, Humphrey grew up in a literate household overseen by a bright mother from the Bohun family: the library at Humphrey's family seat in Pleshey was full of French romances, Arthurian stories, histories of the crusades, and beautifully bound and illustrated religious texts, some of them bought specifically for

---

* The chronicler Adam Usk says Humphrey died on Anglesey while returning to England. Other accounts say variously that he was drowned at sea, or made it to Chester and died there. Humphrey's mother, Eleanor de Bohun, was said to be so distraught at his death that she too died, of grief.

Humphrey.[5] If the boys bonded during their weeks of limbo, it could have been over their mutual knowledge—and certainly in Henry's case, love for—literature.

Now they will never talk again. As Henry returns to Chester and takes stock of what is happening in England, he may ask himself what sense there is in death claiming Humphrey and sparing him. It will not be the last time he has cause to wonder why God seems so intent on keeping him alive.

When Henry arrives in Chester, his father is ahead of him. In fact, he is already on his way south to London, and as he goes, he takes with him a precious cargo: King Richard.

The sequence of events by which the king has fallen into Bolingbroke's hands will later become the stuff of legend, and Henry will have many opportunities, official and unofficial, to hear the story told.

In outline, it is this: Henry's father landed in Yorkshire in late June 1399 and marched through Lancastrian territory, gathering troops. Richard returned from Ireland to try to arrest his progress only in late July. By this time it was already too late. Bolingbroke had thousands of troops, a groundswell of public support, and tacit agreements with key nobles either to support his cause or not to obstruct it. One of these noblemen was his uncle Edmund Langley, duke of York, whom Richard had left in nominal charge of the realm. Another—even more important than Langley—was Henry Percy, earl of Northumberland, the most powerful magnate in northern England. Northumberland, fifty-seven years old, is a veteran border dynast who is in equal parts pragmatic and pugnacious. He has lived through enough changes in royal government to have long ago set aside attachment to any one faction for its own sake, and trims his alliances to suit whatever outcome he thinks will be most helpful to his own interests in the borderlands between England and Scotland. Northumberland has calculated that his cause will be best served by backing Henry Bolingbroke against Richard. So in July 1399 he did not just acquiesce, but actively helped Bolingbroke chase down the king.

Richard, meanwhile, came back from Dublin with only a fraction of his army at his back and no meaningful plan to take back his grip on his realm. This meant he was able to do nothing to resist Bolingbroke, save scampering around the coast of Wales, trying to drum up more troops. In this he had no success. Eventually he took refuge behind the massive walls of Conwy Castle with a handful of supporters. On August 14 the earl of Northumberland went to Conwy to coax him out, which he did by telling Richard that Bolingbroke had sworn he was back in England only to claim his inheritance, and not to threaten the crown. Reluctantly, Richard agreed to leave the castle, but as soon as he did Northumberland arrested him.

The next day Northumberland took the king to meet Bolingbroke at the nearby castle of Flint. According to one onlooker, Bolingbroke appeared in full armor to meet his cousin at the castle gate, and immediately began scolding him. "It is commonly said among your people that you have, for the last twenty or twenty-two years, governed them very badly and far too harshly," he said. He offered to help Richard mend his ways.

Mending ways was not quite what Bolingbroke had in mind for England and its incorrigible king. But whether or not Richard read the offer of help as euphemistically as it was intended did not matter. He was trapped, and he seemed defeated.

"If it pleases you, fair cousin, it pleases us well," he said.[6] From that point on he has been in Bolingbroke's keeping and at Bolingbroke's mercy.

Precisely where Henry goes and what he sees during the tumultuous weeks that follow his own return from Ireland do not leave a clear mark on the record. Most likely he follows in his father's wake, as Bolingbroke rides from Chester, via the Midlands, to London. By the end of September at the latest, Henry is in London, too. Once there, he discovers there is plenty for a young man to marvel at.

The king is locked in the Tower of London. Henry's father is in charge in all but name. Henry initially finds him staying at the bishop of London's palace near St. Paul's Cathedral, after which Bolingbroke moves into the spacious Clerkenwell priory belonging to the crusading order known as the Knights Hospitaller. Lolloping around him in these temporary homes is Henry's father's new companion: a large greyhound who once belonged to Richard but has now, like much of the rest of the country, defected.

The new pet is only light relief, however. Henry's father is manically, all-consuming busy. He visits John of Gaunt's tomb in St. Paul's for the first time, and he weeps bitterly and publicly at the sight of his father's grave.[7] He holds round upon round of meetings with lawyers and historians, bishops and noblemen. He commissions propaganda sheets to be distributed around England, accusing Richard of having collaborated with foreign powers to extort his magnates and of plotting to keep the English peasant-folk "in greater subjection and harder bondage than any Christian King had ever held his subjects."[8]

Bolingbroke is consumed by work because he is faced with a task of the utmost complexity. He can scarcely be blamed for coming back to England to claim his inheritance. But his pursuit of his rights has led the country into deep, dangerous waters. Bolingbroke claims publicly—just as he told Northumberland—that he has come only to seek justice and help Richard improve his own standard of government. But no one believes him to be serious. Richard's track record of taking dire revenge on those who threaten his majesty means Bolingbroke has gone too far to settle for his duchy. He has not come to correct Richard. He has come to replace him.

The big questions are: with whom, and how.

The first of these is easier to answer than the second. Richard has produced no heir of his body: the only child in his immediate family is his nine-year-old wife. Nor has he applied his mind seriously to a credible succession plan. His preference as his heir presumptive is a boy called Edmund Mortimer, whose claim rests on his descent in the female line from Edward III's second son, Lionel, duke of Clarence.* But Edmund is only

* Edmund inherited the status of Richard's preferred heir when his father, Roger Mortimer, died in 1398.

seven years old. In time, his claim to the English throne will come to matter—and it will cause particular torment to Henry. But in the present circumstances, Edmund is not a serious alternative to Richard II.

There is only one realistic candidate to be the new king: Bolingbroke himself. Through John of Gaunt he is a grandchild of Edward III. He is an adult, a proven warrior, and a man of the world. He also happens to have possession of Richard II. None of these things on its own amounts to an incontestable claim to the crown. But given the circumstances, the combination is just about enough.

Yet this raises the second question: how is such a transfer of power to be justified and carried out? Since the Norman Conquest only one English king has been forced to abdicate the throne: Edward II. But Edward was replaced by his eldest son and heir, Edward III. Traumatic as that event was, it could be framed as simply the early transfer of power from father to son.

This is not *that*. So Bolingbroke's assumption of the crown must consist of a makeshift blend of procedural sleight of hand, spin, political lobbying, and sheer force of will.

Henry must watch and learn. The day will come when he, too, will have to dethrone a king.

On Saturday, October 11, Henry is knighted for the second time. This is unusual. Then again, everything in England is unusual at the moment.

The parliament assembled to do away with King Richard has done its job. On Michaelmas, September 29, Richard was visited in the Tower of London by a delegation of lords, bishops, knights, and learned doctors, and asked to vacate the throne. An official account, known as "The Record and Process," stated that he agreed cheerfully to do so.[9] A less partial witness recorded that Richard was in fact "greatly incensed."[10] He had previously harangued visitors to his rooms with complaints that England was "a strange and fickle land" given to destroying its greatest men.[11] Now he demanded "to have it explained to him how it was that he could resign the crown and to whom."[12] Bolingbroke visited later to do just that, and his answer was blunt: it was happening, there could be no negotiation, and Richard needed to get on with it.

The following day, Parliament met in Westminster Hall. The assembled estates of the realm were told that the king had renounced his title and handed over the signet ring that symbolized his majesty to Bolingbroke. Would they accept his decision? "Yes, yes, yes," they yelled. Speaking in English, rather than courtly French or clerical Latin, Bolingbroke proposed himself to be the new king, on three grounds: "that I am descended by right line of the blood" from the thirteenth-century king Henry III; "that God of his grace has sent me, with the help of my kin and my friends to recover it"; and that had he not stepped up, England would "be undone for default of governance and undoing of the good laws."[13]

The throne stood empty in the hall, draped in cloth of gold. Bolingbroke's fellow former exile Thomas Arundel, acting as archbishop of Canterbury, led him to it. Bolingbroke sat, to more cheers, and Arundel preached a sermon. England would now be ruled by grown-ups, he said. "When a boy reigns . . . willfulness reigns and reason is exiled . . . constancy is put to flight and then great danger threatens. From this danger we are now liberated, for a man is ruling."[14]

Henry's second knighting takes place eleven days after all this, on the weekend preceding his father's coronation on Monday, the thirteenth. He is one of forty-six new knights made that day, three of whom are his brothers: Thomas, John, and Humphrey. It must be exciting for the siblings to be back together. Yet they must also realize that their father is striving to make a clear, serious break from the vapid foppery of his cousin's reign, and that they are expected to play their part in this tone change.

The ceremony, which takes place at the Tower of London, is elaborate and serious. The boys bathe, take instruction on the duties of knighthood from older men, keep vigil in one of the Tower's chapels, make confession, and hear mass before they can be dubbed with a sword. They are thus inducted into a new military fraternity, which will one day become known as the Order of the Bath.*

Of the forty-odd other young men knighted alongside Henry and his brothers, many are of their generation, and several are the scions of families who have suffered under Richard. They include the eldest sons of the Appellants of 1386: Thomas FitzAlan, seventeen, heir of the murdered earl of Arundel, and Richard Beauchamp, also seventeen, whose father is the exiled earl of Warwick. Had Henry's cousin Humphrey, his companion in Trim Castle, survived their trip home from Ireland, he too would likely have been a part of this grand occasion, for it represents the honoring of a youthful aristocratic generation who will in their own turn carry the collective burden of ruling England.

On the afternoon of Sunday, October 12, Bolingbroke's coronation procession begins. Despite lashing rain, Henry and his brothers set out with their father from the Tower of London, where Richard still languishes, to ride through London and out along Fleet Street to Westminster. Henry is at his father's side as they and thousands of others proceed slowly along streets hung with colorful, expensive cloth and lined with fountains that bubble with free wine. Henry, his brothers, and their fellow Knights of the Bath wear green, priestly cloaks. Their father wears gold. His head is bare. Around his neck hangs a pendant advertising his grandfather Edward III's claim that he and his successors are also kings of France.

Right now, for Bolingbroke, just being king of England will do. The party arrives at Westminster and the king and his sons lodge in the abbey for the night. The next day, Monday, October 13, the coronation proper takes place. Bolingbroke is taken once again to a throne draped in gold cloth. He is stripped to the waist and anointed on his torso and head with holy oil supposedly given by the Virgin Mary to the martyred archbishop

* The Order of the Bath was only formally constituted as a military order in the eighteenth century, during the reign of George I.

Thomas Becket more than two hundred years previously.* He is invested with all the treasures of a king: spurs, scepter, staff, slippers, bracelets, and a crown made for his cousin Richard.[15]

Henry is at or near his side for all of this, carrying Curtana, the same ceremonial sword Bolingbroke bore at Richard's coronation. Then he and his brothers ride at the head of the procession accompanying their father, now King Henry IV, from the abbey church to Westminster Hall for a feast of incredible variety. Here Henry stands behind his father once again as the banqueting party devours chickens, herons, egrets and even eagles, boar's heads, venison, and rabbit. He continues to hold Curtana throughout, while beside him stands Henry Percy, earl of Northumberland, bearing the sword Bolingbroke held when he landed in Yorkshire on his return from exile.

It is surely an exhausting, perhaps bewildering, time for Henry and his brothers. Henry is still only thirteen. Thomas is twelve, John ten, and Humphrey has just turned nine. It has been only one year since their father was exiled, their lives upended, and their futures thrown into uncertainty. Now their father is the king, and they are knights and princes: the nucleus of a new Lancastrian royal family. Nothing like this has happened in England since the Norman Conquest of 1066.

The case Henry IV made to the parliament and the realm to justify what he has done is that by right of blood, conquest, and suitability, he and the house of Lancaster deserve their newfound royalty. Some of his partisans argue that in fact this dynastic revolution was inevitable, foretold eons ago by the Arthurian wizard Merlin.[16] But what has been justified by rhetoric must now be clung to by action. Archbishop Arundel has preached that the realm will be governed by men. If the new princes want to take some part in this, they will have to grow up fast.

This applies particularly to Henry. Parliament reopens immediately

* The Virgin had let it be known that the first English king to be anointed with this oil would accomplish great deeds, including the conquest of France and liberation of Jerusalem from the heathen; Richard II had discovered it in the Tower of London and asked to be anointed with it midway through his reign; this being deemed improper, the magic oil was used for the first time on Henry IV.

after his father's coronation, and one of its first pieces of business is to lavish titles upon him. He becomes Prince of Wales, duke of Cornwall, and earl of Chester. A few days later he is awarded the duchies of Lancaster and Aquitaine (also known as Guyenne). His right to eventually succeed his father as king is approved, confirming that Henry IV's kingship is a full dynastic revolution and not the beginning of a form of electoral monarchy in England. Henry even has a mini coronation of his own: in recognition of his new position he has a little gold circlet placed on his head and his father gives him a ring, rod, and kiss of peace.

So there is no escaping it. At thirteen years of age, Henry has progressed from boyhood with his mother, playing his harp and wearing a black straw hat, through a short and topsy-turvy adolescence full of loss and peril, to have adulthood thrust upon him. He is heir to the crown, and the ennoblements heaped upon him are real. He is not to be a Ricardian duketto, but a working prince: apprenticed and thrown into the fray immediately, fighting to help his father keep hold of a crown that is about to be contested on many sides, all at once.

7

PRINCE OF WALES

Trouble begins right away.

For all the chants of "yes, yes, yes" that echoed around Westminster Hall when Henry Bolingbroke proposed to become Henry IV, not all his subjects are truly pleased to see him replace the old king.

Richard's former favorites have mostly been treated leniently by the new regime: besides the executions of Bussy, Le Scrope, and Green during Bolingbroke's invasion, the only notable revenge killing has been the hanging, drawing, and quartering of one of the men who murdered the earl of Gloucester at Calais in 1397; the offender's right hand is currently impaled on a spike on London Bridge.[1]

By and large, Henry has watched his father operating with measured restraint. The duketti have been stripped of the titles awarded them in 1397, but otherwise left at large. Henry IV has also resisted calls to put Richard on trial.

Yet the usurper's task—of rewarding his supporters while reconciling with survivors of the old regime—is difficult. The house of Lancaster is a large bloc. As well as Henry IV and his six children, there is another branch to the family: the Beaufort offspring of John of Gaunt's third wife, Katherine Swynford, which includes the brothers John, Henry, and Thomas Beaufort and their sister, Joan. The new king also has obligations to families like the Percys of Northumberland who have helped put him on the throne. Out in the shires of England there are thousands of men who picked the winning side in 1399 and expect to be rewarded with grants of land, office, and cash.

And since there are winners, there must be losers. Despite Henry IV's preference for reconciliation with Richard's closest advisers and allies, a small cabal realize their days of dominance are over, and will likely never return, unless they act drastically and fast. They determine to try to put their old master back in charge.

Conditions appear to suit them, not least because Henry's father is distracted on many fronts. The king must review every government appointee in the realm, from the great offices of state to the sheriffs in the shires. He must consider how England's erstwhile enemies in France and Scotland will react to the upheaval of regime change. To make things worse, he must try not to scratch his head. The holy oil passed down from the Virgin Mary to Thomas Becket, which was slathered all over the king's chest, back, and scalp when he was crowned, has left him with a chronic case of lice, which has caused his hair to fall out.

The downgraded duketti see all this. And so Richard's half brothers the earls of Huntingdon and Kent, along with the earls of Salisbury and Rutland, begin plotting. They know breaking Richard out of jail is not an option, for by October Richard has been taken out of the Tower of London by boat. "Weeping and wailing that he wished he had never been born," the deposed king has been transported to Leeds Castle, in Kent, and thereafter to the secure and remote northern stronghold of Pontefract.[2] So rather than trying to lay hands on him, the plotters decide to mark the occasion of his thirty-third birthday—January 6, 1400—by murdering his replacement: during the new year's Epiphany celebrations, at a jousting tournament to be held at Windsor Castle, they plan to snatch Henry IV and his sons and do with them as they will.

Fortunately for Henry and his family, the plot is betrayed. The earl of Rutland is a cousin to both the old king and the new. At a critical moment, just days before the kidnap attempt, Rutland gets cold feet. He confesses the plot to his father, Edmund Langley, duke of York, who promptly informs the king.

The first that young Henry knows of all this is on January 4, when his father summons him and his brothers, informs them that they are in mortal danger, and orders them to ride with him as fast as they can into London. Henry is not feeling at all well—a sickness has swept around the court that will later be attributed to an attempt to poison the royal family.[3] Nevertheless, he and his brothers hurtle from Windsor to the capital, where Henry's father puts them in the care of the mayor and declares a state of emergency. The ports are closed. A call for troops go out. The first test of the new Lancastrian regime has begun.

Over the following days the country trembles, and the noble blood Henry IV tried to avoid spilling finally runs. Having missed their chance to seize the royal family, the rebel earls try to march along the Thames valley with their small band of followers, hoping sympathizers will rally to their side. They are met by general hostility. Their supporters melt away and the earls scatter to try to escape the kingdom. Salisbury, Kent, and Huntingdon are caught and killed, along with several dozen of their supporters. Some are lynched by angry mobs; others face official, if summary, justice. One observer is shocked to see "bodies, chopped up like the carcasses of beasts killed in the chase, being carried to London, partly in sacks and partly on poles slung across pairs of men's shoulders."[4] It is a grim end. And it is a stark lesson for Henry IV.

Rebels cannot be allowed a figurehead. There cannot be two kings in the kingdom.

By the end of the next month, the Epiphany rebels' hero, Richard, has been starved to death in Pontefract Castle. Opinions vary as to whether he wastes away of his own accord, having "realized his hopes had been dashed and there was now no chance of escaping," or whether he is denied sustenance by his jailors and thereby slowly murdered.[5] Or perhaps he is not really dead at all. One French observer fantasizes that the king's murder is a hoax, and that he has been taken to an even more obscure hiding place.[6] To try to scotch such conspiracy theories, the king has Richard's corpse brought south from Pontefract to be displayed in an open coffin at St. Paul's before its burial at Kings Langley in Hertfordshire.

When Richard's cortege moves through London, Prince Henry walks behind it with his father and the rest of the royal family. It is a moment that makes a deep impression on him, and as he grows up he will dwell on it, feeling that some terrible wrong has been done. Before Richard's fateful trip to Ireland, he had made detailed arrangements for his funeral. He wished to be buried in a tomb he had commissioned at Westminster Abbey, alongside his late wife, Anne of Bohemia. He wanted his body to be clothed in velvet, and each of his fingers to be adorned with a ring set with a precious gem.[7]

It was all typically overblown and vainglorious, but Richard nonetheless took time and care over the details, believing that his immortal soul and historical memory depended on the arrangements. His last wishes have been ignored entirely. Prince Henry may reflect that when Richard had the chance and good cause to treat *him* badly—in Ireland in 1399—he exercised restraint. (A monk who writes a verse history of Henry's life will spell this out explicitly: "King Richard raised you and loved you . . . he nurtured you with a covenant of honor.")[8] He can do nothing about it now, but he will come to believe that, whatever wrongs Richard did the Lancastrian family, and however much his death was unavoidable and even deserved, it is always better to preserve the dignity of high office than to disparage it. As he will discover, the political unity of the realm depends on it.

Having survived the Epiphany Rising, Henry prepares to take on his first duties in service of his father's crown. Already he has been touted around on the marriage market: in November 1399 Henry and his siblings are offered to the king of France as possible spouses for the French royal family, in an attempt to make up to Charles VI for having deposed his son-in-law.*

But Henry's father wants more from him than marriage. The titles lavished upon him as Prince of Wales, duke of Aquitaine, and duke of Lancaster demand that he take an active role in the defense of the realm.

At his first parliament in 1399 the king announced that he would go to campaign against the Scots, who have been raiding in northern England and sending impertinent letters to the English court addressing Henry IV as duke of Lancaster rather than king.† In early June 1400 he calls for men to come with him "in armor, with horses and in other manner of war."[9]

He amasses thirteen thousand troops, and sends a demand to the aged king Robert III (along with his twenty-year-old son, David, duke of Rothesay, who is the power behind his throne) to appear in Edinburgh to pay homage to him. Henry IV claims—with a degree of historical license—that Scottish rulers have been obliged to defer to their English counterparts ever since the time of the legendary king Brutus. Robert thinks otherwise, so Henry IV invades his kingdom.

Prince Henry and his brother Thomas are taken north for the expedition, each of the boys with a small company of men under his banner. (Henry has nominal command of seventeen men-at-arms and ninety-nine archers.) They join a campaign that lasts only two weeks, during which fortnight the English cross the border, march around a bit, decline a Scottish offer to settle the dispute with a pitched tournament, and then retreat as supplies run low.[10] During this time the Scots amuse themselves by hiding in woodland and snatching English soldiers who wander off from the main army, torturing and mutilating them. All this is made

---

* For understandable reasons, Richard's ten-year-old widow, Queen Isabelle, burns with a particularly righteous hatred of Henry IV. She is to be returned unharmed to the French, but the insult to her and her family is considerable.

† The English, for their part, have failed for many years to address the kings of Scots by their royal title. So this is tit for tat. But more than one war in human history has begun over a raspberry.

worse by appalling weather: rain lashes down almost ceaselessly this year from May until November, ruining crops and causing widespread famine and disease. It is not an awesome display of fire and fury. But it does allow Henry his second chance to study a military campaign.

He can see, if he takes an interest, how the royal army is raised: by calling up all those in England who receive a personal income (known as an annuity) from the king to come and fulfill their obligations. He can marvel at the huge quantities of supplies required for even a few days in the field: tons upon tons of flour, salt, wine, beans, fish, cheese, and bacon, all loaded onto ships with pious names like *Trinity of the Tower* and *Holy Ghost*. He can peek into the crates of weapons that are dragged into the English camp and see thousands of arrows, crossbow bolts, axes, lances, guns, and spare pieces of armor. And he may notice his father scratching his lice-ravaged head at the challenge of financing his campaign, as royal officers are sent out to beg, wheedle, and bully loans from merchants in England's cities, and even staff in the royal chancery are asked to contribute to the war chest out of their own pockets.

In other words, although in Scotland Henry is not exposed to the full horror and pity of war, he does get a chance to learn more about the other side of combat: the dull, detail-heavy, expensive, complex business of logistics and supply husbandry, without which no war in history has ever been fought, let alone won.

It is all part of an education. Yet Henry's main training ground in the arts of princely diplomacy and warfare over the course of his teenage years does not lie in Scotland. In fact, he will learn his craft in Wales, in a war more long-lasting and dangerous than anything he saw with King Richard in Ireland or his father in Scotland.

The figure who draws him into Welsh affairs is a high-born, well-educated, combat-hardened man in his midforties. He is described by a poet as an "eagle, delightful beyond measure, fine-helmed . . . generous with a gift, golden son."[11] His legend is destined to live forever in the annals of Welsh nationalism.

His name is Owain Glyndŵr.

Wales has a long, proud history of independence under the lordship of high native princes—or did have until, in the 1280s, Henry's ancestor Edward I smashed the political power of the Welsh and garrisoned Snowdonia with a chain of vast stone fortresses advertising and enforcing the might of the English crown. The castles at Caernarfon, Beaumaris, Conwy, Harlech, and elsewhere are permanent reminders of the colonization that English kings have effected in Wales, mutilating the countryside and killing off the native kings. During the early years of Henry IV's reign, Owain Glyndŵr leads a rebellion that seeks to overturn the dismal century of Welsh subjugation and kick the English out of the principality forever.

The Glyndŵr bloodline runs back to the heyday of the princes, but Owain has not seemed much of a separatist before now. Indeed, he has cultivated good relations with his English neighbors to the east.[12] He trained as a lawyer in Westminster. During the reign of King Richard he fought against Scots and French in the military retinue of the late earl of Arundel. He is married to an English girl called Margaret Hanmer, whose father is a royal judge, and he and Margaret keep a fine house at Sycharth, in Powys (part of his estate of Glyndyfrdwy), which is replete with all the modern fittings of a substantial lord: chapel and bakehouse, orchards and fishponds, deer parks and a mill.

In September 1400, however, something in Owain's respectable career goes suddenly awry. The immediate cause is likely a petty squabble with an English lord, Reginald Grey of Ruthin, whose lands in north Wales abut Glyndŵr's own. But the broader context is an excited sense among the Welsh that Bolingbroke's revolution provides their best opportunity in 120 years to push back against arrogant English overlordship.

In mid-September 1400 Owain folds his personal desire to needle Grey into the mood bubbling up among his compatriots. He gathers together several hundred friends to join him in burning and robbing the town of Ruthin. To dignify his warlording, Owain precedes it by proclaiming himself to be the real Prince of Wales, out to retrieve his true inheritance. He does so, perhaps not randomly, on September 16: Henry, Prince of Wales's fourteenth birthday.[13]

This is audacious, but it meets with an enthusiastic reception—which gives Owain the confidence to keep going once Ruthin has been torched. For a week or so he and his followers ride around firing and plundering other border towns. He sends a couple of his cousins, named Rhys and Gwilym ap Tudur, to wreak havoc on Anglesey.

This invites a predictable response. An English force hastily raised from the men of three nearby counties rides out under a local dignitary named Hugh Burnell, and without much ado they scatter Owain's troublemakers. It looks as though a brief flash of disorder has been stamped out.

But Owain is only getting started.

Owain Glyndŵr's claim to be Prince of Wales puts him squarely at odds with young Henry, who holds that title by his father's grant, solemnly confirmed by Parliament. And now that Henry is fourteen, his father decides he should learn to defend what is his. So in October 1400 Prince Henry is sent to Chester, the border town he last saw when he was returning from his imprisonment in Ireland and his father was taking his first steps toward removing Richard from the throne. His mission is to suppress Owain's revolt by any means necessary.

This is a daunting task, so Henry is given trusted men to support him. His household is managed by his stalwart servant and companion Peter Melbourne, who takes the office of chamberlain. In addition he has two governors: first a knight called Sir Hugh Despenser; then, after that gentleman's death in October 1401, Thomas Percy, earl of Worcester, brother of Henry Percy, earl of Northumberland, who remains the Lancastrians' most important supporter in the north of England. A full council is also sent to advise Henry on policy. The dominant voice on the council belongs to yet another member of the Percy clan: Northumberland's vastly experienced thirty-six-year-old son, also named Henry Percy, but better known as "Hotspur."

Few men in England have a heartier appetite or aptitude for fighting than Hotspur. Impatient, headstrong, and fierce, he is, as one writer of the age notes, "always the first in the skirmish at the barriers."[14] Another calls him "the flower and glory of Christian knighthood."[15] Hotspur has sharpened his tusks doing battle in Ireland and, like the king, he has been a crusader, fighting the infidel in Prussia and Turkey. (His nickname has been given him by the Scots, who have seen his aggressive demeanor at first hand.) As a young man Hotspur served Richard II loyally in France, spending some time as steward of Richard's household, and since the age of twenty-four has been a member of the elite chivalric club known as the Order of the Garter. Yet, like his father, Hotspur was in the vanguard of the Lancastrian revolution of 1399, helping to keep order in the county of Cheshire as Richard was overthrown.

Over the winter of 1400–1401 there is not much for Prince Henry, Hotspur, and the council to do. The king has sent orders that any rebels who come to Chester to submit to young Henry will receive a royal pardon. But there are not many takers. So it is a dull winter. In London the king spends Christmas entertaining the Byzantine emperor Manuel II Palaiologos, who is touring Europe begging Christian rulers to donate to his defense of Constantinople against the Turks; Eltham Palace is full of impecunious, white-robed Greeks with long hair and unkempt beards, who are entertained by a tournament, mumming, games, and sports.[16] In Chester, meanwhile, Prince Henry waits in vain for the Welsh to come and apologize for vandalizing border towns.

They do not come. All the same, there is a creeping feeling that when spring comes the mountains will spit out the rebels and a new cycle of violence will begin. Prince Henry is in London in February 1401 to attend Parliament, where he hears ominous news from the university towns of Oxford and Cambridge that Welsh scholars have been abandoning their books, taking off their gowns, and returning home to join a nativist movement. Welsh laborers are also reported to have been heading for the land of their fathers, laying down their tools and taking up "arms, bows, arrows and swords and other weapons of war, such as they had not done at any time since the conquest of Wales; on account of which it seems probable that they intend to start another, new rebellion."[17]

This would seem to demand serious preparations to deal with an attack. Unfortunately, at this moment the Crown is hard-pressed for money. King Richard's bloated, luxurious court and expedition to Ireland has left little ready cash for the new government to spend. Henry IV has a large payroll of his own supporters who helped him to power, and he has hardly improved the royal finances with his Scottish foray. Parliament is not at all minded to make large grants of taxation for heading off trouble that has not yet broken out. Instead, the commons try to legislate rebellion away, passing a swath of laws restricting the property rights of Welshmen and making it easier to prosecute felons across the border. This is simple populism, designed by an English parliament to please itself, without any thought for whether the Welsh are really likely to be mollified by being reduced to second-class citizens. When Parliament closes, it is clear that if Henry is going to defend his principality, he will have to do so out of his own pocket.

As winter ends, the rebellion blazes back into life on Good Friday 1401 at the gatehouse of Conwy Castle.[18]

The massive, round-turreted fortress built by Edward I broods over the river estuary it guards. It is the strongest and most imposing of all the fortresses Longshanks stamped on the Welsh landscape, and it is by design impossible to take by storm. On April 1, however, all but five of its garrison are attending mass at a chapel in the town when a carpenter who has worked there before presents himself to the gatekeepers and asks to be let in to finish an overdue job.

The carpenter is a traitor. As the gates swing open to allow him into the castle compound, a band of forty Welsh rebels appear behind him. They are led by Glyndŵr's relative Gwilym ap Tudur and include men with roughneck names like Dafydd ap Gruffydd Fantach ("Dai No-Teeth"). They rush in, kill the guards, and seize control of the castle.

This lightning military coup is not masterminded by Owain Glyndŵr. Rather, it is a glorious victory for the Tudur brothers—Gwilym on the inside and Rhys lurking in the mountains nearby—who have decided to use the castle as a means of negotiating royal pardons for their roles in the previous year's violence.

Their gambit works. Hotspur rushes to Conwy, blockades the castle, and opens talks with the rebels. After a month Prince Henry is sent to join him, but it still takes until May or June to reach a breakthrough, when Gwilym ap Tudur agrees to hand over nine of his fellow rebels as prisoners in exchange for freedom and pardons for all the others.

While this solution is painstakingly bargained out, there is constant correspondence between the king, who bridles at any solution that seems soft on the rebels, and Hotspur, who is on the ground and sees how difficult anything but a negotiated settlement will be to enforce. Hotspur's approach of pragmatic dealmaking eventually wins out, but when the nine prisoners are handed over and pardons are issued to the remaining three dozen, the English are smarting. It is clear that the captives at least, must be treated roughly if any sort of message is to be sent to other would-be rebels in Wales.

Since Henry is the most senior lord on the spot at Conwy, he must take responsibility for their punishment. In view of the embarrassment and inconvenience they have caused, there is only one choice. All the same, it is a grave command for a young man to give.

Henry orders that Gwilym ap Tudur and his fellow rebels must stand and watch as the comrades they have betrayed are "drawn and then disemboweled, hanged, beheaded and quartered."[19]

Henry is still some months short of his fifteenth birthday, but he has begun to exercise the power of life and death—and there is no hint in the chronicles that describe this time that he has any qualms about it. What is more, his decision to make sure that the Tudurs understand the human cost of their pardons suggests he has already developed an instinct for the delicate psychology of justice. His father, monitoring events from afar, clearly regards this difficult and bloody experience as a useful lesson for Henry. His letters to his "most beloved" heir are full of lessons to be adduced from the work at hand: "remember, dear son, that it is cheaper and easier to defend a castle than to reconquer it once it is lost," he writes in June.[20]

All in all, however, events of the summer of 1401 are unsatisfactory for everyone. Far from dousing the flames of Welsh rebellion, the debacle at Conwy Castle and its gory conclusion suggests that the English have soft bellies and only a small appetite for sustained warfare. Owain Glyndŵr has a challenge to meet in matching his kinsmen's daring, and perhaps sees a chance to secure a royal pardon for himself in similar fashion. All over Wales, events at Conwy have inspired a bold new spirit of insurrection against English lordship.

More concerning than any of that, though, is the attitude of one leading lord on the English side. Hotspur has been brought to Wales to help young Henry to whip the principality into shape. But he is not at all happy with the resources he has been given to do the job. During the early summer of 1401, as events at Conwy are unfolding, Hotspur writes to the royal council in London. He complains of the "pillaging and mischief" that is becoming widespread in Wales and recommends that "good and hasty measures ought to be immediately adopted by sea as well as by land." Hotspur notes that his oversight of Wales is costing him, personally, a small fortune. And he asserts, in prickly fashion, that "all the country is without doubt in great peril of being destroyed by the rebels if I should leave."[21]

This may be true. Hotspur is probably within his rights to speak plainly. But contained in this grouching letter is a warning for the future. The war to put down the Welsh rebellion is destined to be long and draining. It will test the character of all those involved. Already Hotspur is showing signs of a self-important and querulous nature, which will shortly come to pose an existential threat to the house of Lancaster and Henry, Prince of Wales.

8

"GREAT PAIN AND DILIGENCE"

At the height of Gwilym ap Tudur's audacious hijack of Conwy Castle, Henry's father writes to him with a tough message. Although in April 1401 Henry is still only fourteen, and his father reassures him that he remains his "most dear and most beloved son," the king also tells him baldly that it is his personal responsibility to sort out the disorder that is rocking his principality.

Conwy is a case in point. "As the said castle was taken through the negligence of your constable," the king writes, "[you must] cause to ordain that by a strong hand the said castle may be restored." The king couches his words in polite French, but there is no mistaking the lesson he wishes Henry to draw: he has been given high authority, but with it comes accountability. "This charge ought not to appertain to anyone but you," explains Henry's father, and to an intelligent young man like Henry, these words must sting.

The king is not totally without sympathy. He tells Henry that he knows the job is not easy, and accepts that it is becoming difficult to find the funds in Wales to meet the costs of firefighting a growing rebellion. Yet he refuses to let Henry have this as an excuse for failure. Whatever it costs to pacify Wales, his father says, will be reimbursed from the treasury in London. This may raise a young eyebrow: Henry must know as well as everyone else in England that his father is hardly awash with funds for military campaigns. All the same, the message is clear: Henry has been given a task, and it is up to him alone to see it through. For Henry's "great pain and diligence" so far, his father "very specially render[s] you good thanks."[1] But the subtext of the message is plain. Holding the title of Prince of Wales is a privilege and a challenge, the two things being indivisible. Henry has been granted a right that must be defended. His father wants to see him rise to the occasion.

Needless to say, this is easier said than done, and the most obvious problem is finance. Money is short everywhere, and the means of raising it in the provinces are sometimes alarmingly hand-to-mouth. Henry's brother Thomas has been sent to Ireland to cut his teeth there as royal lieutenant, and is enduring a miserable time, so short of money to police that lordship that his counselors are reduced to selling his jewels and plate to pay soldiers' wages.[2] For Henry in Wales, things are not much better. In theory, he is expected to fund Welsh peacekeeping from Welsh revenues. But these are dwindling away to nothing, for with a rebellion in full swing, tenants refuse to pay their rents and any notion of raising taxation is little more than fantasy. Henry receives money from his duchy of Cornwall and earldom of Chester, but even if he pumps every penny of this into Welsh operations, it will not be enough for the task in hand—and will leave him unable to meet the ordinary expenses of his household.

In the autumn of 1401 Henry's father accepts that whatever lesson he would like Henry to learn in Wales, his son needs military support as well as paternal encouragement to do his job. In October, therefore, the king brings several thousand troops into Wales to help Henry pursue Owain Glyndŵr. Owain has been stirring up trouble across the northwest, marching from Caernarfon to Aberystwyth, flying a faux-Arthurian flag emblazoned with "a golden dragon on a white field," and holding festivals of verse and song* at which bards compete to flatter him as a hero predicted by the prophecies of Merlin.[3] The insult to Lancastrian authority is palpable—and intolerable. Yet despite the surge of troops, neither the king nor Prince Henry—nor indeed anyone else—can lay a finger on him. The insurrection in Wales is a guerrilla operation of the slipperiest sort and Owain is a master of gliding away from trouble once he has set it in motion. At one point Owain makes contact with the king, via intermediaries, offering to submit to the English crown in return for the sort of generous pardon that was granted to his Tudur kinsmen at Conwy. Whether or not Henry is inclined to take him up on this is irrelevant. The king angrily refuses.

In 1402 the crisis widens and deepens. First, it becomes clear that Owain has ambitions for a rising that go beyond freedom for the Welsh. English agents intercept letters addressed from him to the king of Scots and lords of Ireland, imploring them to join forces with him to make war on "our and your mortal enemies, the Saxons."[4] At the same time, a rumor begins to spread around England that King Richard II is still alive: this story is spread through networks of friars, who are also said to be raising money from ordinary people to funnel into Wales to support the rebels there. Buoyed by cross-border support and funding, Owain grows ever bolder, and early in the year he captures his old enemy Lord Grey of Ruthin, with whom he quarreled at the outset of the revolt, and releases him only on the promise of a ransom payment of 10,000 marks.

Encouraged by the success of this banditry, on June 22, 1402, Owain next ambushes an English force led by Sir Edmund Mortimer, a twenty-five-year-old nobleman and cousin of the king who is one of the most powerful landowners in the borderlands known as the Welsh Marches. At a fierce battle at Bryn Glas, not far from Offa's Dyke, as many as one thousand English troops are slain. Horrific reports circulate of Welsh women rushing onto the battlefield after the fighting to mutilate the English dead: cutting off their genitals and stuffing them in the corpses'

* It is not totally anachronistic to call these the early fifteenth-century equivalent of "poetry slams."

mouths "with testicles hanging out of the teeth above the chin," or cutting off noses and pressing them down the slain men's throats.[5] The carved-up dead are left where they lie rotting, stinking, and denied a Christian burial.

Bryn Glas is little short of a disaster. For besides the slaughter, the humiliation, and the blow to morale, Sir Edmund Mortimer is snatched on the battlefield: "taken captive . . . and denied of all his goods."[6] And now Henry and his father are in a quandary. If they ransom Sir Edmund, they will be putting money directly into rebel pockets, and encouraging even more hostage taking in the future. Deciding that they must play a long game, the king forbids Sir Edmund to ransom himself. There is logic to this, which Henry can probably appreciate. But there is also logic to what happens next. In November 1402 Sir Edmund decides that he will do better to throw his lot in with Owain, "in order to mitigate the rigors of his captivity." He turns rebel, and marries Owain's daughter Catherine to seal the alliance.[7]

Thus a military crisis rolls into a dynastic one. For one thing, Sir Edmund Mortimer is the uncle of another Edmund Mortimer: the ten-year-old earl of March who has a strong claim to the English throne and was once Richard II's preferred heir. His alliance with Owain now offers the Welsh rebels the tantalizing prospect of having a credible alternative to Henry IV and the Lancastrians to parade around and use as they will.

Just as serious, Sir Edmund is also the brother-in-law of Hotspur, scion of the Percy family, and one of the key figures installed to support Henry as Prince of Wales. His defection to the rebel side throws into relief tensions that have been growing between the Crown and the Percys. In Wales, Hotspur has been growing disillusioned with the king's policies for some time. He enjoys the prestige that comes with the sense that king and prince need him to prop up their regime in the west. Yet he finds the actual business of deputizing for Prince Henry not only unrewarding but personally expensive. He strongly favored allowing Sir Edmund Mortimer to buy his freedom from Owain Glyndŵr when that gentleman was captured, and is beginning to find the king's unwillingness to negotiate with the rebels extremely vexing.

This is not the only point of friction between the houses of Lancaster and Percy, but it is a serious one all the same. Sir Edmund Mortimer's defection to the Glyndŵr cause in 1402 forces Hotspur to ask himself some fundamental questions. He—and his powerful Percy relatives—begin to question whether in supporting the Lancastrian family's revolution of 1399, they have backed the wrong cause.

In February 1403, with the rebellion in Wales showing little sign of abating, Prince Henry, now sixteen, gains a stepmother. Joan of Navarre, dowager duchess of Brittany, arrives in England by ship, putting in at Falmouth after a choppy crossing of the Channel. She is greeted as though an angel has descended from heaven. Henry IV goes to meet her in Winchester, bringing with him a retinue of well-bred nobles and relatives, as well as luxurious gifts, including a huge roll of gold cloth and a jewel-studded collar that cost hundreds of pounds. Henry's brothers John and Humphrey—now thirteen and twelve respectively—present Joan with a pair of gold tablets.

On February 7 the king's half brother Henry Beaufort, bishop of Lincoln, marries the king to his new queen at St. Swithun's Minster in Winchester. And just under three weeks later Joan is crowned in Westminster Abbey. There is great feasting to mark the occasion, and performers from the City of London entertain the royal couple with "outrageous appareilling." Then comes a jousting exhibition, in which the twenty-one-year-old nobleman Richard Beauchamp, earl of Warwick, plays the role of queen's champion. (Beauchamp has recently become earl of Warwick, succeeding his Appellant father, who returned from exile on the Isle of Man but died in 1401.) At the coronation jousts, the new earl comports himself most "notably and knightly."[8]

Joan's arrival is a welcome moment of relief for the king and his family after three and a half extremely difficult years. But the joys of matrimony do not mark the end of their travails. In fact, 1403 will thrust the Lancastrian dynasty into a state of existential crisis, and Prince Henry will be in the midst of it.

On April 1, 1403, just weeks after the royal wedding, and exactly two years after the Conwy Castle raid, the king appoints Prince Henry as royal lieutenant of Wales, giving him full command of his own principality. He is given a force of three thousand troops, along with orders to make "a frontier of garrison forts of men-at-arms and archers" who can make forays into the Welsh countryside to make it safe and bring to justice "such rebels as can be found."[9] He has men around him he knows and trusts—his household chamberlain and old mentor Peter Melbourne is on hand to give advice, accompanied by a personal company of nine archers. Having had more than two years to acclimatize to the demands of the role, Henry follows his orders vigorously, wholeheartedly buying into the idea that the best form of defense against Owain Glyndŵr is all-out attack.

In early May, little more than a month after his formal appointment, Henry rides out of his base in the town of Shrewsbury to punish Owain for his ongoing impertinence. On his return he dictates a letter to his "dearest and entirely well beloved" father to describe what has happened. It brims with youthful bravado—the details of the raid almost tumbling over one another on the page.

Owain, reports Henry, has been gathering men for the purpose of "raiding and also fighting if English men wished to resist him." Worse than this, he has been boasting of his prowess—a challenge to Prince Henry's dignity as well as his military capability. Because of this, Henry writes, "we took our men and went to . . . [Owain's] principal house named Sycharth, where we supposed to find him if he wished to fight in the manner he said." On arrival, however, "we found no man, and so we set fire to the whole place and several other houses of his tenants around."

Henry reports with pride that he has also done serious damage to Owain's properties at his estate of Glyndyfrdwy, where "we fired a fine lodge in its park and all the country around it." He has captured one of the rebel's key allies, who offered a ransom of £500 for his freedom: "This was not accepted, but he was put to death." Henry goes on to mention briskly some other notable escapades on this foray into rebel country: in Merioneth "we set fire to a fine and well populated country." He signs off respectfully, asking that God has his father "always in his holy keeping."[10] This is a calm end to a letter that is otherwise skittish with pride and excitement at an adventure that has felt like giving Owain an overdue taste of his own medicine. It is not so long ago that the king challenged a fourteen-year-old Henry to step up and show he deserved the name of prince. At sixteen he is eager to show that he has listened.

Unfortunately, Prince Henry's promotion to head up Welsh affairs and his enthusiastic embrace of the job rankles with the Percys. The lieutenancy of Wales had been Hotspur's at the start of Henry IV's reign, along with a swath of other Welsh offices, including the constableships of several important castles. Hotspur's uncle, Thomas Percy, earl of Worcester, has also been heavily involved in Welsh affairs, acting as the king's deputy in south Wales and as Prince Henry's personal governor. Hotspur in particular has complained about the burdens of the office. Nonetheless, neither he nor his relatives relish losing their preeminence to the teenager.

So in the spring of 1403, when Prince Henry takes over the formal lieutenancy of Wales and sets about showing how he means to exercise his power, it triggers in the Percy family an outburst of grievance. They roll together in their minds their perceived demotion in Welsh affairs with other frustrations they have been nursing against the Lancastrian crown: Henry IV's refusal to allow them a free hand to ransom hostages their men have taken during fighting in the Scottish borders, along with a more general feeling that they are not paid promptly or well enough for their service to the realm.[11] Sometime in the spring of 1403 they take a fateful decision. On Monday, July 9, they show their hand.

On that day, Hotspur appears in Chester, the capital of Prince Henry's earldom of Cheshire, and announces to the townsfolk a piece of astonishing news. He tells them that King Richard II, once so beloved in this part of the country, did not die in Pontefract Castle in 1400. He is alive, well, and ready to make a glorious return.

Indeed, says Hotspur, in eight days' time King Richard will appear in public, at the head of an army commanded by Hotspur's father, the earl of Northumberland. Together, they are going to behead the Lancastrian snake. Their chief aim is to depose the usurper who calls himself Henry

IV. But first they intend to go to Shrewsbury, the English town from where Welsh operations are now being directed, and snatch the king's heir, Prince Henry.

Evidently, Hotspur is lying.

He does not have King Richard anywhere to hand, for despite persistent rumors to the contrary, King Richard is long dead. Nor, for that matter, is Hotspur's father, the earl of Northumberland, about to come anywhere near the Welsh Marches. He is in the north, preparing to make a sortie against Cocklaw Castle, a stronghold near the town of Hawick, in the Scottish borders.* Whether he knows about, or approves of, his son's actions is a matter that will be fiercely debated later on.

However, despite (or because of) the outrageous nature of Hotspur's claims, crowds flock to his side as he sweeps through Cheshire on his way to Shrewsbury.[12] One chronicler describes these folk as a "multitude of imbeciles of both sexes, defrauded by desire"; they are particularly stirred up by the presence at Hotspur's side of a charismatic hermit who has a good track record of predicting major political events.[13] But if the crowds are gullible, they are also dangerous. Over the coming days the ranks of Hotspur's army swell, and many who arrive to join the anti-Lancastrian movement are wearing King Richard's livery badge of the white hart. They include significant numbers of the Cheshire longbowmen who were so feared during the darkest days of the old king's reign.

It is a little over forty miles from Chester to Shrewsbury, where in July 1403 Prince Henry is preparing another raid into Wales in pursuit of Owain Glyndŵr, who is currently stirring up his countrymen in Pembrokeshire. So the news of Hotspur's rising does not take long to reach him. And there cannot be the merest scrap of doubt in his mind about the

---

* Cocklaw Castle, near Hawick, had been besieged unsuccessfully by Hotspur in April 1403. A deal was struck with the garrison captain that if the Scots did not relieve the siege by midsummer, it would be handed over. This sparked preparations in England and Scotland alike for a staged battle to decide the castle's fate. The earl of Northumberland was focused on this when Hotspur headed toward Shrewsbury in rebellion.

seriousness of the movement, for no sooner does the news arrive than it is confirmed by the disappearance from his household of Thomas Percy. The earl, who still holds the formal post of Henry's guardian, absconds and rides off to Chester, taking with him a cache of coin and more than two hundred troops.

This is far from the first crisis Henry has faced in his young life. But it is certainly the most serious. It is a little over three months since he was awarded full responsibility for his principality. Now he must rally its forces—such as they are—to defend him against other Englishmen. The stakes, suddenly, could not be higher. Everyone knows what happens to fallen monarchs: Prince Henry has walked behind the open coffin of the one his family starved to death in Pontefract Castle. If Hotspur is not defeated, the same fate will assuredly befall his father. It will likely be his, too.

Mercifully for Prince Henry, his father is closely informed about Hotspur's treachery. What's more, he is nearby. The king has been traveling north from London with a force of troops to take to Scotland, to join the pitched battle the earl of Northumberland has planned at Cocklaw Castle. He is in Nottingham on Thursday, July 12, when he hears of the Percy rebellion. He turns immediately west, heading toward his eldest son in Shrewsbury. As he forces a march through the English Midlands, the king sends out a flurry of royal commands: ordering every county sheriff within one hundred miles to send him musters of their able-bodied fighting men and to lock up anyone giving off even the faintest scent of treachery.

What news reaches the prince in Shrewsbury during the next few days speaks only to rapidly escalating danger. The king is on his way, but Hotspur leads him by a day or two. By Tuesday, July 17, the Percys are at Lichfield, just forty-five miles from Shrewsbury. Hotspur has abandoned his pretense of resurrecting Richard, but the Percys have issued a series of accusations against the king, claiming he lied in 1399 about his intention to seize the throne, that he murdered Richard II, that he has overtaxed the realm, packed Parliament with lickspittles and denied the ten-year-old Edmund Mortimer, earl of March, his right to the throne.[14]

There is enough truth in these denunciations, and enough momentum behind Hotspur's army, to keep them rolling forward; Hotspur also threatens to lynch or decapitate anyone who fancies they might desert his cause.

If Henry clambers onto Shrewsbury's walls at the end of the week, he can see Hotspur's army gathering in the green countryside, watered by the river Severn. There are perhaps fourteen thousand of them, including longbowmen from Cheshire and the neighboring counties.[15]

Hotspur and Worcester have made their base around three miles upriver at a hamlet called Berwick. Some of them have been yelling up to Shrewsbury's gatekeepers to give them food. Not surprisingly, the demands have been ignored.

A siege will be difficult to defend. And there are rumors from the west that Glyndŵr is on his way to join up with the Percys. These things ought to be enough to strike dread into Henry's heart. Yet to the south of Shrewsbury is a far more welcome sight. His father, the king, has marched with the speed and purpose that characterized his invasion of Richard's realm in 1399. The royal army, cobbled together as it is from the force Henry IV was taking to Scotland and the county musters he has summoned on his diversion, is arriving en masse. By Friday the twentieth, the king and his son are reunited. Together they take a decision. It is a decision that reflects Prince Henry's instinct to attack troublemakers head-on.

They will not wait for the Percys to make another move in their direction. That evening they and their combined forces will move out of Shrewsbury and go on the offense. They will ford the river Severn and make camp at the nearby Augustinian abbey of Haughmond.

Then, in the morning, they will ride against the Percys.

The country outside Shrewsbury is abundant with summer crops on the morning of Saturday, July 21, as Prince Henry and his father break camp at Haughmond Abbey and carefully lead their troops toward where Hotspur and his uncle Worcester are drawing their own men up, in a field "sown with many peas."* [16]

Both sides realize that any window for settling their dispute peacefully is almost closed. During the last week Henry's father has—despite his general distaste for negotiating with rebels—tried repeatedly to parlay with the Percys. Through messengers sent to Thomas Percy, "the king proposed to depart without slaughter and to [take the matter] to parliament," remembers one writer later.[17] But Prince Henry's erstwhile governor has refused all compromise. Writers will later condemn Thomas Percy for his "false counsel and wicked stirring."[18] In reality, Henry and all the others in the royal army must appreciate that Thomas knows he and Hotspur have gone too far with their rebellion to back out now. Trampling pea shoots underfoot, the royal army therefore lines up on a ridge across the field from their enemies: in sight, but out of range of longbow shot.

Henry has seen many extraordinary things in his short life. But neither he nor anyone else has seen anything like this. It is more than eighty years since Englishmen have fought Englishmen in battle. It is true that for two generations men-at-arms and archers from all corners of the British Isles have done battle in France, Scotland, the Spanish kingdoms, and beyond in the Hundred Years War. But never have armies containing such huge numbers of the longbowmen who have been so deadly in the continental wars faced each other on English soil.[19]

Henry's father has divided the royal army into three divisions, giving command of one to himself, one to the twenty-five-year-old earl of Stafford, and the third—the rearguard—to Prince Henry himself. He has also dressed up two of his knights in armor identical to his own, to conceal his real location on the field.

What does the sixteen-year-old prince hear, see, smell, and feel? We cannot read his intimate thoughts. But it would be strange if he did not feel a tangle of powerful sensations and emotions all at once: the weight

* The claim in one account that Hotspur ordered his men to tie the pea stalks together "in such a way that they would be an obstacle to those who approached" seems to betray the chronicler's unfamiliarity with the realities of both agriculture and combat.

and heat of the plate armor that he has practiced wearing since he was a boy; the heft of the sword in his hand; the smell of the sweat and the fear that rises from the men around him, be they ordinary archers with slender, curved shafts of yew in their hands, or men-at-arms clanking in their protective gear.

Henry has read and learned about war since his schooldays. He has seen combat and sieges. He has been on raids deep into the Welsh hills he can see beyond the pea field in which he now stands. He has burned houses and spilled men's blood. None of it has prepared him for what is about to come.

When the final overtures for peace have been made and refused, a little after midday, the trumpets and drums sound. The cry "Advance banner!" goes up. Then, to a chorus of yells, the quiet hiss of arrow-shot begins on both sides.

Soon the sky is hailing sharp death.

Battles are not neat or orderly. They lurch and sway with a movement of their own. Terror ripples through the field, unpredictably. With both sides using longbows, the casualties are heavy from the beginning. Within minutes of the first call to advance, thousands of royal troops have panicked and are trying to flee the very first shower of the Cheshiremen's arrows.[20]

Not long after, the land is strewn with hurt and dying men and animals on both sides. "Kin slew kin and neighbor slew neighbor," writes one appalled chronicler.[21] When the lines push up against one another, the blood runs all the faster.

One of the knights dressed up as the king is cut down. The earl of Stafford is killed. On Hotspur's side, the earl of Douglas, a Scottish prisoner of war whose fate has been a matter of contention between the king and the Percys, is hit, agonizingly, between the legs with an arrow; he will lose one of his testicles.

All around, thousands of other men, high-born and ordinary, are falling. There seems to be no end to it. The hardest press of the fighting moves here and there around the field, and occasionally a triumphant cry will go up from one side or the other: cheers of support for Henry's father, or cries of "Henry Percy, King!" The two sides are evenly matched in numbers, commitment, and weaponry. They fight through the afternoon, the summer sun moving slowly through the sky above them, shining down impassively on one of the worst bloodbaths in English history.

Henry fights amid it all, but it is exhausting, thirsty, terrible work. At some point he lifts his visor—perhaps to take a drink, perhaps to get a clear sight of the changing melee all around him. Something hits him in the face, below his right eye.

He pulls at it. A shaft of wood comes away.[22]

Adrenaline is a powerful thing. Hands grab him and try to drag Henry off the field, but he will have none of it. And the battle is reaching a crucial turn. On the right of the royal lines, Stafford has fallen and Hotspur is urging his men forward into a disintegrating body of royal troops.

The whole front is beginning to rotate.

Henry sees his moment. He rallies the men around him on the left to push forward and round into the Percys' wheeling flank.

It is a pivotal moment in the battle. As Henry's men advance, they begin to encircle the rebel army. The fighting becomes closer and more intense.

The sun is dipping now, and a moon is rising. As the light fades, the battle turns decisively toward the royal army. Henry's sally breaks the enemy lines. The rebels begin to lose their order and their self-belief. The end is in sight.

By nightfall the battle is over. And when it is, Henry's side has won. The king survives. Thomas Percy is taken prisoner. Hotspur is hacked down and killed, along with hundreds of the Cheshire archers who followed him, wearing the badge of the dead king Richard.

During the night the sky falls black as the moon is eclipsed. The next day the king comes onto the battlefield. He weeps over Hotspur's body, but later has it sent to Shrewsbury to be sat in the street, where passersby can see for themselves that the traitor is dead. The corpse is later quartered and sent to the four corners of the kingdom. Thomas Percy is executed and his head, once it has been struck off, is dispatched to be impaled on London Bridge. The rest of the dead are tipped into pits hastily dug as near as possible to the battle site.

Prince Henry, however, sees none of this. The arrow that hit him in the face has left its metal tip inside him, "buried in the furthestmost part of the bone of the skull to the depth of six inches." Once his battle-craze has left him, and the killing on the pea field is done, it is clear he is in a parlous state.

Henry is taken first to Shrewsbury and then to Kenilworth and the surgeon John Bradmore is sent for from London to try to save his life.

As Bradmore hastens to the Midlands, and the axman's blade falls on the rebels' and traitors' necks, and the nameless fallen are piled into trenches, and the king begins the long process of setting his reign on course, beginning with the foundation of a church on the doleful battle site at Shrewsbury, Prince Henry lies in his family's greatest castle, not knowing if he has been chosen to live or to die.

The Lancastrian dynasty has survived its first great test. But whether Prince Henry will survive to one day lead it lies entirely in God's hands.

9

"HIS MIRACULOUS POWER"

The hot weeks of high summer 1403 pass and Henry remains in Kenilworth Castle, hovering between life and death. Each day the surgeon John Bradmore comes to do something painful to his face.

At first Bradmore is opening the wound that the arrow from an unknown archer ripped: teasing wider the ragged cut made by the arrowhead, and pressing in linen plugs drenched with rose-scented honey to clean the angry, swollen flesh.

Then, one day, the surgeon pushes metal tools deep inside Henry's head, gripping and wiggling and teasing out the arrowhead lodged somewhere at the back of his skull, as a roomful of anxious servants watch on.

Then comes the longest, dullest part: three weeks of daily washing and sealing of the wound. The bright, sharp sting of a liquid that smells like wine and burns when it touches broken skin. A daily ritual of dressing and re-dressing the gash in his face, with warm poultices applied to the back of his neck. Finally a slathering-on of some dark, waxy, fatty paste that smells of herbs, which Bradmore hopes will help the skin heal without leaving too monstrous a scar.[1]

Even with the standard numbing agents of the day—alcohol and a cure-all potion known as theriac,* whose active ingredients include snake venom—the pain can only be intense.[2] But pain is a natural part of life. And Henry endures it.

What may be more difficult to manage for this energetic and active young man are the long hours of boredom. Many slow days of recuperation pass, each full of time to ponder. Do Henry's thoughts turn to memories of the sky raining arrows at Shrewsbury? Or to Hotspur, his mentor turned enemy, who is now rotting in quarters above town gates in the four corners of England? Does he consider the peculiar afterlife of Richard II, the king who predicted great things for him, and who men across the realm seem determined to will back from the dead?

We can surmise one thing with confidence. As Henry suffers and recovers at Bradmore's nimble hands, he contemplates the mysteries of a merciful God who has once more spared him from death, and decides that once he is well enough, he will do something serious to show his thanks.

By September, his wound has closed, and the surgeon has departed back to his practice in London. Henry is fit to travel, but his father—though he could dearly use his son's help in the struggle against Owain Glyndŵr—accepts that he needs time to recuperate.

Henry uses this opportunity in a telling way. Rather than heading west, once more into the bear pit of his Welsh principality, he strikes out in the opposite direction. He goes east, to Kent and Norfolk, to make a pilgrimage to the famous shrines at Canterbury and Walsingham.[3]

Canterbury and Walsingham are famous throughout England. They are renowned, indeed, across Europe. Both have been adored for centuries by ordinary pilgrims and great lords alike. It has been the particular habit of English kings and princes to visit these holy places at

* Henry's great-grandfather Henry Grosmont, first duke of Lancaster, had written about the healing properties of theriac in his famous devotional text *The Book of Holy Medicines*.

moments of crisis—either to seek deliverance from their troubles or to give thanks for their salvation.

Canterbury's history as a destination for royal pilgrims is part glorious and part notorious. The city's splendid Gothic cathedral, with its community of canons, was founded in 597 CE by St. Augustine, sent to England by Pope Gregory the Great to convert the heathens. During the twelfth century, the cathedral was where Archbishop Thomas Becket was cut down at Christmas by thugs in the service of King Henry II. Since then his tomb has become a phenomenally popular shrine, as famous for its glorious golden feretory, set between a marble base and painted wooden cover, as for the hundreds of miracles reported by those who have prayed there.[4] Becket's shrine is the destination of the poet Geoffrey Chaucer's fictitious pilgrims in *The Canterbury Tales* (a book written under the patronage of Prince Henry's grandfather John of Gaunt): the gaggle of storytellers are going "the holy blissful martyr for to seek, that them hath helpen when they were sick."[5]

Henry has certainly been sick. But he also has a direct family tie with Becket, through his father: it was with the miraculous vial of oil presented to Becket by the Virgin Mary, and rooted out of storage at the Tower of London by Richard II, that Henry IV was anointed at his coronation. When Henry arrives in Canterbury, he finds the citizens have cleaned the streets for his arrival and strewn the ground with sand.[6] And when he kneels before the martyr's tomb in Canterbury, he has every cause to thank Becket for protecting his father in the heat of battle earlier that summer.

Walsingham, in Norfolk, has a rather more curious history. Like Canterbury, it is a celebrated pilgrimage destination in its own right. There has been a place of worship there since the time of the Romans. The present shrine dates to 1061, when a noblewoman called Richeldis enjoyed a series of religious ecstasies during which she was transported back to the simple wooden "Holy House" where Mary and Joseph lived in Nazareth: the venue for the angel Gabriel's Annunciation. When Richeldis returned from her reverie, she was inspired to build an exact replica of the Holy House. A generation later her son, Geoffrey, founded a priory to guard it. The site came soon to be referred to as England's "new Nazareth."

So when Henry visits Walsingham, traveling the long route north, via Newmarket, known as the "Palmers' Way," he is in one sense merely following in the footsteps of countless thousands of other Christians who have traveled there over the ages on the understanding that to step inside the Holy House is to make a proxy visit to Nazareth itself.* Like all those other pilgrims, when he arrives at the richly appointed priory and visits the shrine he can enjoy the sensory pleasures of a sanctum that has been lavished with private devotion—and rich gifts of jewels, precious cloths, and altar furnishings—since the time of the Saxons. At the heart of the shrine is a carved wooden figure of the Virgin. She sits enthroned with Christ on her lap. In the light of the candle that burns perpetually before her glitters a golden crown that was given her by the devout thirteenth-century king Henry III.[7]

All this is magnificent and awesome. But, just as at Canterbury, there is personal resonance for Henry at Walsingham. As the prince prays before the statue of Mary, it would also be natural for him to think once more of his parents. Of course, his father visited the original Nazareth when he traveled to the Holy Land in the 1390s. But Walsingham may bring more vividly to mind Henry's mother, gone now for half his life. She too was a Mary. She too was holy: so pious she could have become a nun. She too loved jewels and fine things. Walsingham would have suited her.

Then there is his wider family: the Plantagenets, who have ruled England since 1154. For generations, they have adored this place. And Walsingham has been a special magnet for teenage heirs to the throne who, like Henry, have narrowly escaped danger. When Edward I was a young man he felt he had cheated death while playing chess; having completed a game, he got up from the board, whereupon a large rock fell out of the ceiling, landing exactly where he had just been sitting. He came to Walsingham to give thanks for his stroke of fortune. Later, Edward III first came to the shrine at age sixteen, following his involvement in his father's

* A similar idea can be seen at work today in the round Temple Church in London, first built by the Knights Templar in the twelfth century in deliberate imitation of the Church of the Holy Sepulchre in Jerusalem.

deposition and murder. And after surviving the great peasant rebellion of 1381, a sixteen-year-old Richard II also came, on a tour that took in other East Anglian shrines.

So as Henry travels about the southeast of England on his pilgrimage after Shrewsbury, he is placing himself—either deliberately or just instinctively—in a long royal tradition. It is as though he is doing more than just giving thanks for God's grace in saving his life. He is looking ahead to the next phase of his life, in which his personal piety will become an increasingly central part of his public character, even as he continues to perform his assigned role as a warrior prince.

Henry is eased back into a role in government during the first half of the year 1404, but he does not immediately go back to the front line in Wales. Instead, his first major public duty is to attend a parliament, which opens in January 1404 and lasts until mid-March. There, he can see the immense strain that weighs upon his father simply to keep his reign afloat. Henry IV is undoubtedly a more levelheaded and responsible king than Richard II ever was. Yet after nearly five years of his reign it is clear that he is bedeviled by a set of problems unique to his own circumstances. Richard was the rightful king, but a fool. Henry's father is a capable man, but a usurper. Sometimes it is hard to know which of these positions is worse.

What is easy to see is that the Lancastrian regime faces huge problems. In the north of England royal agents are struggling to bring to heel rebels from the Percy affinity who have been holding castles including Alnwick, Bamburgh, and Warkworth against the king. Henry IV would like to bring sweeping change to the north, and will appoint Henry's younger brother John as his official lieutenant there when he reaches fourteen. But for now the king has little choice but to reconcile with the dissidents, for the Percys hold such a dominant position across the north that without them he cannot hold the borderlands against the Scots. Moreover, Henry Percy, earl of Northumberland, commands a worrying degree of support among his fellow lords and the parliamentary commons. At the parliament of January 1404, therefore, Henry's father is forced to come to a rapprochement with Northumberland: accepting that whatever role he had in his son's rebellion, it did not amount to treason, and issuing him a suspended fine rather than any more severe penalty.

This is bad. But it is not all. In Wales, Owain Glyndŵr sees the English at war with themselves and grows bolder than ever, so that the entire principality is more or less in constant revolt, with English castles under siege, English lords chased away from their Welsh lands, and Owain beginning to plan parliaments of his own, as he seeks to turn the rhetoric of independence into political reality. In the Channel, pirates have long been running wild, raiding and plundering English ports with impunity. At the French court, a war faction is now gaining influence around Charles VI, led by Louis, duke of Orléans, the nobleman who turned a blind eye to Bolingbroke's departure from his exile in Paris but has now repositioned himself as an anti-English firebrand. Ireland is no more submissive to English rule than it has been for a decade, and Prince Henry's brother Thomas has been recalled from his post there with no obvious success to boast about. Meanwhile, in England, rumors still abound that Richard II remains alive, squirreled away across the Scottish border but about to stage a return. Despite the king's regular prosecutions and gruesome executions of gossip spreaders, the legend of a once-and-future Richard seems impossible to stamp out.

The solution to most of these problems comes down to one thing: money. In Parliament Henry hears his father plead at length that he has far too little. But the parliamentary commons are stubborn and grudging about granting the king the taxation he says he needs. Only through long and fractious negotiation is Henry IV able to wheedle out of them funds to keep his government solvent until the end of the year, and even then he must accept humiliating conditions, such as slashing costs in his royal household and dismissing trusted servants. This is more than just an insult to the royal dignity of the sort that would have sent Richard II into a fit of conniptions. It points to a much more serious problem, which is that Henry IV seems unable to convince his subjects that he can be trusted with their money. Their underlying assumption seems to be that his legitimacy as king is dubious and his future far from assured, and there is a sense that they are hedging their bets and withholding their tax grants in case the next challenge to his rule should prove successful and a new king—be it a miraculously reanimated Richard or the twelve-year-old Mortimer scion, Edmund, earl of March—should come and ask for the same thing all over again.

Midway through the parliament Henry IV attempts to tackle the legitimacy problem head-on. He summons all the members of the lords and commons to gather together and swear an oath of obedience, not just to him, but also to Prince Henry: "my most honored lord the prince . . . and to the heirs of his body," or, failing that, to Henry's brothers, Thomas, John, and Humphrey.[8] Since fine words cost nothing, the parliament falls into line. But they grant only a meager tax, which when it is collected is gobbled up in a matter of weeks.

So the parliament, which represents the seventeen-year-old Prince Henry's return to political life, is hardly a resounding success. Yet in its failures, there are lessons for Henry. One is that no war can proceed without taxation, and no taxation can be collected without a happy parliament. Another is that a king can rule successfully only when his legitimacy is beyond doubt. This, perhaps, is the most positive lesson the parliament has to offer. Although his father's demand for an oath of obedience to Prince Henry and his brothers speaks to desperation in the moment, it holds promise for the future.

As the more astute members of the parliament may understand, when Prince Henry or one of his brothers lawfully succeeds his father, the question of legitimacy will disappear. The stain of usurpation will be removed. The talk of a revived Richard or a king Edmund Mortimer will recede. The longer the Lancastrians keep scrapping for their future, the greater their chances of survival will become.

By the summer of 1404, Henry is ready to go back to Wales. Since the battle of Shrewsbury permanently removed Hotspur and Thomas Percy from the principality and rendered Henry temporarily unfit for high command, military activities are being led in the south by thirty-year-old Edward, duke of York (the former earl of Rutland whose cold feet had betrayed the Epiphany Rising of 1400), and in the north by twenty-two-year-old Thomas FitzAlan, earl of Arundel. Henry is given a gentle reintroduction to Welsh affairs: he stations himself roughly between these two older noblemen, in the towns of Hereford and Leominster, at the head of a compact force of fifty men-at-arms and one hundred archers.[9]

His task, for the time being, is to hold the line. The situation is, frankly, dire. English authority within Wales has collapsed almost entirely, consisting of little more than isolated garrisons holding out against sieges. Major fortresses have fallen, including, most shockingly, the massive coastal castle at Harlech. Welsh raiders are pressing into English counties. Owain Glyndŵr's pretense to Henry's title of Prince of Wales is looking more plausible with every month that passes: the rebel leader will hold his first Welsh parliament this year, in Machynlleth, and he is in the process of finalizing a military alliance with France that will see the French provide naval support to his cause. And the English have run out of money. Needless to say, Henry's officials cannot collect tax in his principality, so he must continue to draw on his income from his duchy of Cornwall and earldom of Cheshire, supplemented by borrowing from anyone who will lend to him. He pawns his jewels and plate and wheedles with the royal treasury for whatever it can send him. When he is obliged in the late autumn to ride into Wales with his brother Thomas to relieve a siege of the castle of Coity in Glamorgan, he must beg the lords in the parliament held at Coventry (the second called that year) to contribute loans. He asks his father respectfully by letter to "remember my poor estate and that it is not in my power to continue here unless something different be ordered for my stay, and that these expenses are intolerable for me to bear."[10] It is hardly very dignified, and the words must be painful for him to write.

Throughout the second half of 1404 and 1405 Henry and his fellow lords on the Welsh borders are stretched to the limits of their resources and at times their patience. In the summer of 1404, Henry's cousin the duke of York is forced to plead with the garrisons of English-held castles inside south Wales to fight on unpaid until their wages can be rustled up.[11] When Henry petitions the November 1404 parliament for a few hundred marks to make "hasty and adequate assignment for stationing 129 men at arms and 256 archers in the said parts [i.e., the English border counties] for the safeguard of the same," the polite words of his official request can only barely conceal his desperate frustration.[12]

Yet by early 1405 Henry's mood has changed. The second parliament of 1404 has agreed to a much larger tax grant than the first did, on the condition that the king appoint independent treasurers to see that the proceeds are spent only on the war. Henry forges a good relationship with these treasurers, and they in turn ensure that he is better funded than he has been at any time previously. Crucially, he has the good sense, experience, and fortune not to waste this newfound solvency. Slowly but surely he reprovisions castles, organizes raids into Welsh territory, and establishes a reliable network of informants to forewarn him of rebel activity.

In March 1405 he is informed that several thousand Welsh have gathered in Monmouthshire and attacked the prosperous English town of Grosmont—a serious loss and a symbolic insult to the Crown, since it was the birthplace of the famous first duke of Lancaster, Henry Grosmont, the prince's great-grandfather. Henry sends in a small but well-drilled force of his household knights, led by a Shropshire knight called Gilbert Talbot, the patriarch of a family of soldiers who is destined to be a trusted military captain of Henry's in years to come.

Under Talbot's direction the English troops intercept the Welsh, scattering them and slaughtering all they can. For the first time in a long while, Henry can summon the spirit of his early days in Wales. He writes joyfully to his father to tell him that his men "held the field and conquered all the said rebels, and killed of them according to loyal account . . . some say eight hundred, some say a thousand."[13]

In the aftermath of this rare, cheering victory, Henry is eased back toward the position of overarching authority he held in 1403: he is created lieutenant of north Wales for a year, and moves back to Chester with three thousand men under him. He is growing into command; he is trusted by his father, whose letters spreading the news of his victory fairly burst with pride at the achievements of "our most dear son the prince."[14] He is gathering a reputation as a capable, brave young man in whose hands the difficult counterinsurgency campaign against the Welsh may not be doomed after all.

Who deserves the most credit for this upturn in fortunes? There is no doubt in Henry's mind. The improved royal finances at the turn of 1404–5 have certainly been critical. Having a less prickly and self-serving group of counselors around him than the Percys has not hurt, either. But Henry knows that these are only incidental things in the grand scheme of his life and his military career. He reserves his greatest thanks for God. His own letters abound with pious praises. When things are at their most difficult, he tells his father: "I will raise all that is possible for me in resistance of the rebels and salvation of the English territories to the very best of my small power according as God shall give me grace." When he is reporting to the king his men's triumph on the battlefield, he writes: "I verily pray that God may show for you his miraculous power in all parts. Praised be he in all his works . . . I pray to God that he may preserve you always in joy and honor, and grant to me that I may [be able to] solace you speedily with other good news."[15]

These are conventional turns of phrase, but the prince's letters are alive with them. He has been marked by his survival of Shrewsbury in more ways than one. He is learning the art of military command in a long and sapping war. He is coming to appreciate how vital logistics and finance are before an army can take to the field. But more than anything else he is developing a sense that nothing in the field of war is possible without unwavering faith in the will of the Almighty.

10

CRIMES AND PUNISHMENTS

Prince Henry goes to Chester in March 1405 to take up his new position as lieutenant of north Wales, still aglow with his men's success in crushing the Welsh at Grosmont. There is plenty still to do to run Owain Glyndŵr to ground and reestablish English mastery in the principality. Yet he has barely any time to come seriously to terms with the situation before events in England drag his focus elsewhere.

The pull on his attention comes from his father. In 1405 King Henry faces two different challenges to his rule, and both will come to require the support of his eldest son.

The king's first difficulty is a seemingly endless train of plotters against Lancastrian rule. The second is his health, which, from the summer of 1405, starts to collapse. Henry IV's trials of legitimacy and well-being will frame the realm's politics in 1405 and 1406. They will compromise and circumscribe Prince Henry's attempts to carry out his duties in his principality. Yet at the same time they will propel the prince ever closer to the center of royal power. Before long he will be both ready and impatient to take a leading role in England's government.

Any hope that the Lancastrian victory at Shrewsbury would have put an end to schemes to topple the king has vanished within a few months of the battle. In the summer of 1404, as Henry is returning to active duty in the Welsh borders, his father is dealing with a tangled conspiracy to place a fake Richard II on the throne. It is masterminded by Maud, countess of Oxford, the mother of Richard's one-time favorite Robert de Vere, and William Serle, a Ricardian favorite exiled in Scotland.

This plot is foiled and the plotters punished according to their station, which is to say that Maud is pardoned, while Serle is dragged around behind a horse in half a dozen English cities on a hurdle, hanged half to death in each of them, and finally ritually disemboweled and beheaded at the Tower of London. This momentarily squashes rumors of Richard's survival, but in the old king's place anti-Lancastrian dissidents now attach their hopes to young Edmund Mortimer, the boy who was Richard's preferred candidate as successor, and whose uncle of the same name is now married to Owain Glyndŵr's daughter.

Since 1399 Edmund, thirteen, and his younger brother, Roger, eleven, have been living under royal supervision in Windsor Castle and the royal residence at Berkhamsted, where they have been raised and educated with Henry's younger siblings. But in early 1405 the boys are broken out of their genteel confinement at the behest of another noblewoman, Lady Constance Despenser, whose brother is Prince Henry's cousin and co-commander in Wales, Edward, duke of York. Lady Constance bribes a locksmith who knows his way around Windsor Castle. The locksmith provides copies of the necessary keys. On February 13 the boys are snatched and hustled away through the countryside to the west, roughly in the direction of Wales.

The plot is rapidly thwarted. Edmund and Roger are recaptured quickly near Gloucester and once again the conspirators are punished in a manner deemed fitting to their social status: the duke of York and Lady Constance are imprisoned for a few months each, while the locksmith is decapitated. But the fact that it reached such an advanced stage is hardly encouraging.

Nor is this all. There are rumors of another plan, foiled in its early stages, involving kidnapping the king from Eltham Palace at Christmas 1404. It is said that the royal circle is a hotbed of treachery, with men looking both ways, uncertain even after five and a half years that Henry IV is secure on his usurped throne. Gossips question the loyalty of even staunch allies such as Archbishop Arundel of Canterbury.

These are troubling times for the royal family and it is cold comfort that no plot has yet succeeded. Prince Henry, of all people, must appreciate just how perilous things are, and how disastrous it would have been for Welsh affairs had young Edmund and Roger been delivered to the hands of their uncle, Sir Edmund Mortimer, at Owain Glyndŵr's court. Owain's policy of reaching out to other traditional English enemies who might make common cause with him is paying off. French troops and military supplies are starting to be delivered to Wales, a surge that is guaranteed to make Henry's task there more difficult. How much tougher might it be if Owain obtains a credible alternative king of England to parade around?

There is not much time to think about this, for yet another crisis now unfolds. In May 1405, three months after the plot to free the Mortimers has failed, the king is in Hereford, preparing to lead troops into Wales to support Henry's struggle against Owain. The arrival of extra bodies for the fight is, as always, welcome. Yet in the middle of the month, the king is forced to abandon his campaign and withdraw his men before they have even set foot across the border. Even more serious trouble has erupted elsewhere, which tears him away from the Welsh theater and sets in motion one of the most turbulent and transformative periods of his reign. The focus of the rebellion this time is the north, where a number of loosely connected uprisings have broken out at once. Leading the most serious is the second-most senior churchman in England: Richard Scrope, archbishop of York.

The king inherited Archbishop Scrope from Richard II. Worldly (or at least widely traveled) and straightlaced, Scrope has not, to date, seemed a likely figurehead for a rebellion. In fact, in March 1404 Scrope conducted a solemn ceremony to translate the body of Henry IV's favorite holy man,

St. John Thwing of Bridlington,* from an ordinary grave into a shrine at Bridlington Abbey. However, on May 17, 1405, Scrope gives a firebrand sermon in York inveighing against the king's onerous tax policies and corruption he alleges to be rife in the royal household. A libelous manifesto, almost certainly written by Scrope, is copied out and pinned up around the city. It alleges that the king is a murderer, perjurer, and usurper whose time on the throne has run its term.

So persuasive is Scrope's message—and so fragile is the peace in the north of the kingdom—that by the end of May eight thousand men and women have responded to the call to arms and are camped on moorland north of the city. They are halted by the arrival of an army under the command of Ralph Neville, earl of Westmoreland, and Prince Henry's younger brother John—now sixteen years old and apprenticed to the role of warden of the northeast. John and the earl tell Scrope that the king will be happy to negotiate. But they then promptly arrest the archbishop and imprison him in Pontefract Castle.

When the king arrives in the area a few days later, it is evident that negotiation is the last thing he has in mind. Scrope's citizen army has disbanded and its members are rapidly realizing the error of their ways. They pour out from the city to meet Henry dressed in their undershirts like a pack of ragged beggars and throw themselves miserably to the ground, crying out for mercy. The king commands them to gather outside the city on Monday, June 8, and see what sort of mercy he has on offer. They are horrified to see Archbishop Scrope and his closest noble ally, Thomas Mowbray (the nineteen-year-old son of the duke of Norfolk with whom the king quarreled and nearly dueled back in 1398), led out on the back of ponies as prisoners. The two men are condemned to death and promptly beheaded in front of a windmill.[1]

---

* Thwing was elevated to sainthood a mere twenty-two years after his death, in a bull issued by Pope Boniface IX on September 24, 1401. The miracles attributed to John Thwing in his lifetime include lifting a very heavy ladder to help a widow escape a house fire, turning water into wine, and surviving a blow from a heavy stone because he was praying so intensely. Many healing miracles have been reported at his tomb after his death.

Not since Thomas Becket—at whose tomb Prince Henry recently prayed—has an archbishop been so brutally treated by an English king. Never has a monarch in this realm so flagrantly ignored the convention protecting churchmen from capital punishment at the hands of royal law. But the king's patience with rebels has been exhausted. By killing Scrope he attempts to show his realm how close to the end of his tether he is.

Yet the insult to Church dignity is enormous, and the provocation to God himself nearly as great.

Scrope's death, shocking as it is, does not immediately bring peace to the north, for at the same time as the citizenry of York is rising under the doomed archbishop, elsewhere the old troublemaker Henry Percy, earl of Northumberland, is also reviving the spirit of insurrection that led his son and brother to their doom at Shrewsbury. At least half a dozen Percy castles are garrisoned against the Crown, and it is at this point that Prince Henry is drawn directly into the fray, as he is summoned from Chester to support his father in the next stage of operations. By late June Henry has left Chester and arrived at Newcastle. In early July he moves with the king to Berwick, where the vast fortress is held against the Lancastrians by Percy loyalists.

At Berwick Henry sees—and hears—one of the most effective modern weapons in his father's armory. Berwick Castle's walls snake around a steep rise overlooking the river Tweed and have been built huge and strong to withstand the endemic warfare in this border region. The king has neither the manpower nor the time to waste on a conventional siege. So for the first time on English soil he brings up cannons: squat, fat-nosed, stinking iron pots that give off much heat and smoke as they fire lumps of rock against their target.

Cannons have been used by English armies on the continent for only about sixty years.* They are not yet powerful enough to blow holes in the

---

* The first use of cannons on the battlefield in western Europe was when a few guns were deployed by Edward III's men at the battle of Crécy in 1346.

thick stone walls of a well-built castle; in that sense their bark is more threatening than their bite. But at Berwick, barking is enough. After a long bombardment in which stones pelt the fortress but are "shattered by the hardness of the walls," one shot hits a tower window next to a staircase and kills a defender standing beside it.[2] The garrison, frightened by the novelty of the bombardment, lose their nerve and surrender; the king executes half a dozen of them. This prompts the nearby Percy ancestral fortress at Alnwick to give up as well. The earl is not at home, having fled into Scotland, but he is declared a traitor in his absence. Although he remains at large, his days of stringing along the king are over. With them, the northern revolt is coming under control.

Prince Henry's diversion to the north provides him with valuable long-term experience—a decade later in a very different war he will show he has learned how to use cannons to good effect to reduce obstinate cities and fortifications. Yet in the moment of July 1405 things are complicated. It is clear even by the time Henry joins up with his father's army that something is not right with the king.

Henry IV is not yet forty years old, and has always been handsome, winsome, and charming in person. Suddenly, as if overnight, he has physically changed. He is weak and tired, and the skin of his face and hands is covered in a mass of ugly, painful welts and lumps.

These disfiguring marks, it seems, appeared days—or even hours—after he ordered Archbishop Scrope's death. They are so alarming that they strike most observers as being a symptom of "leprosy"—a catch-all medical diagnosis that in the fifteenth century can refer to a whole spectrum of debilitating conditions, not least the ailment that will one day become known as Hansen's disease, a bacterial infection that slowly eats away at the fingers, toes, nose, and eyes of sufferers. The most confident writer of the day calls the king's affliction "leprosy of the most horrible and worst sort."[3]

Yet that description seems at odds with the sudden onset of the condition.[4] In the fullest telling, soon after Archbishop Scrope was beheaded, the king stayed overnight at a village seven miles from York. He awoke in the middle of the night in a terror, screaming that traitors were "throwing fire" over him. His servants calmed him down with a stiff drink and soothing words, but by now the king was covered in pustules that stood out on his skin like nipples and had to take a full week's rest to regain his strength.[5]

When Henry arrives in the north to help with the siege of Berwick Castle, he finds his father somewhat recovered, and even protesting to be "in good health, thanks to the mercy of the Creator." But he is plainly not well.[6] Henry may remember a few isolated times from days gone by when the king was ill: a bad back in 1397, a passing sickness treated by John Bradmore in 1403, and another bout in 1404.[7] But this is different—or will prove to be.

Both men now bear the marks of war on their faces: Henry in the scar (presumably)* left by Bradmore's surgery in 1403, and his father with a rash of angry boils visited on him, many think, as divine punishment for killing an archbishop. Severe illness will play a decisive role in both of their lives in years to come.

For Henry this fate lies a long way off. For his father, it is imminent.

In March 1406 Henry travels to Westminster to attend another parliament, which his father has called to address the realm's ongoing problems. He has a keen interest in the parliament's business, for he is now once more in charge of the Welsh war, having been promoted to lieutenant for the entire principality with five thousand men under his command. But he is also aware that the realm is beginning to look to him as a leading light in government and that, given his father's faltering health, he must be ready to take full command at any moment.

The very fact that the parliament is near London speaks to the parlous

* Curiously, no contemporary mentions a scar on Henry V's face, which, unless Bradmore's unguents were as effective as modern plastic surgery, would surely have resulted from his surgery after Shrewsbury. Henry's best-known portrait likenesses (Royal Collection RCIN403443 and NPG 545) show him in profile, with the right side of his face hidden, though this could be because they are sixteenth-century artworks, possibly copied from a medal.

state of political affairs. Initially, writs went out summoning lords and commons to Coventry, in the Midlands. The venue was then changed to Gloucester, so that the meeting could be as close as possible to Prince Henry's base of operations in the Marches. The Welsh leader has taken the mighty coastal castle of Harlech, and has been marching troops as far east as the royal command center in Worcester. Worse, Owain is now in alliance with the renegade earl of Northumberland, who has entered Wales from Scotland. Between them they have drawn up a document known as the Tripartite Indenture, a plan to split England and Wales three ways, dividing rule between themselves and Sir Edmund Mortimer. However, an even more urgent crisis—reports of a French fleet gathering in the Thames estuary to invade London—has meant that Parliament has been relocated once again, to the capital, where it assembles in the Painted Chamber of Westminster Palace: a long room gloriously decorated with wall murals showing biblical scenes and allegories of the Virtues and Vices.

Given the ongoing challenges facing Crown and realm, the parliament is expected to be a noisy, rigorous assembly. The king has packed the commons with knights and burgesses personally connected to the duchy of Lancaster. The commons speaker elected, Sir John Tiptoft, is one of the most loyal knights of the king's personal chamber. Yet the king's intention in apparently rigging the parliament is not to create a pliant forum of patsies who will defer to majesty without question or quibble—as Richard II tried to do at his most tyrannical. Rather, Henry IV wants tough questions from people he trusts.[8] They, in turn, want to see the prince at his father's side.

When Parliament opens on March 1, the king's debility is obvious. Very little business is transacted over the course of the month, and by April 3, rumors are circulating about "the royal person of our lord the king," to which the king takes grave offense.[9] Speaker Tiptoft is forced to apologize on behalf of the gossipers as Parliament adjourns for Easter—there is a limit to the amount of plain speaking that the king is prepared to tolerate. But once the Easter break is over, it is clear that the whispers were correct.

On April 28 Henry IV is suffering a "maladie in the leg" and a "grand abcesse," and is too ill to ride. He promises to come as soon as he is able—a matter of a few days. In fact he does not come at all, but instead stays downriver from Westminster in London, staying at the house of Thomas Langley, the chancellor and bishop-elect* of Durham and conducting business by letter. Parliament has to recommence without him.

Details of what is wrong with the king are tightly guarded, and the commons have been warned about speculating. It is possible—perhaps likely—that he is recovering from a stroke. Whatever the case, throughout May and June Henry IV is nowhere to be seen in public. On May 22 he sends word that he cannot "fully to devote his attentions to [government] as much as he would like" and names a council led by Thomas Arundel, archbishop of Canterbury, to take over all functions of administration except for selecting officials and issuing pardons. This is a very serious and barely precedented renunciation of royal duty. Everyone knows what it means, and—without saying as much—the Lancastrian parliament starts making provision for the king's long-term incapacity or sudden death.[10]

These preparations take several forms. In light of the foreign situation—French troops are aiding Owain Glyndŵr and French ships are now preying on English vessels in the Channel—they make demands for non-British subjects to be deported. One of the king's Beaufort half brothers, John, earl of Somerset, is sent to secure Calais, England's most important military base on the continent. But, most important, the ground is laid for the transfer of royal power to Prince Henry. In an extraordinary statement made by Tiptoft on June 7, presented along with a restatement of the order of succession to the throne, Henry is praised for the "humility and obedience which he has shown towards our sovereign lord the king his father."

---

* A Henry IV loyalist, Langley was a churchman and bureaucrat whom the king tried to appoint successively as bishop of London and archbishop of York (to replace the executed Scrope) but whose elevation was blocked by Rome as punishment for Langley's help in the deposition of Richard II. He served as chancellor from 1405 to 1407 and was enthroned as bishop of Durham in September 1406.

Tiptoft notes that God has "endowed [Henry] with a good heart and as much courage as any worldly prince could need." And he notes that while Henry is capable of making decisions, he is also "genuinely and graciously willing to be contradicted, and to conform to the wishes of his said council and their ordinance, in accordance with whatever seems best to them, setting aside entirely his own will."[11]

This is far from idle praise. The king, who languishes close to death, was handed his royal status in October 1399 by a parliament that recognized not only his military victory over Richard II but also his personal fitness for the job at hand. Then, the same archbishop Arundel who is now heading the emergency council to govern in Henry IV's name stood in the nearby Westminster Hall and argued that the new king deserved his status because he was "a wise and prudent man . . . who, with God's help, wishes to be ruled and advised by the wise men and elders of his realm."[12] It is no coincidence that in June 1406 the same virtues are officially identified in the younger Henry. In constitutional terms, Parliament is restating its novel claim to judge the personal suitability of a man to be the monarch. In a practical sense it is laying down the path for Prince Henry to succeed to the throne.

What Henry—still only nineteen years old—makes of this is known only to him. It is no doubt pleasing to hear such fine words rained upon him. It must also be daunting to realize that the awesome responsibilities of government may soon lay upon his shoulders. But there must be a large part of him that is impatient to have the praise wrapped up so that he can get back to the task he is supposed to be carrying out: fighting Owain Glyndŵr and old Henry Percy, the rogue earl of Northumberland.

That being so, we can perhaps sense Henry's own hand behind one of the final statements made in Parliament on June 7, when Tiptoft asks that "our lord the prince should be instructed to go to Wales with all possible haste; considering the news which [is] arriving daily concerning the rebellion of the earl of Northumberland and the other rebels thereabouts."[13]

In time, this plea by the speaker, enrolled on the parliamentary records, will read like an admonition to the prince for neglecting his duties in his own principality. Nothing could be further from the truth. The

1406 parliament grants Henry generous funding to lead the Welsh war. It thanks him for his service and urges him to continue it. And it makes unequivocal provision for him to succeed his father as king at the point when Henry IV's failing health gives out and he dies.

The reality for Henry is that for the foreseeable future he is going to have to combine his role in Wales with at the very least a visiting presence at the parliament and royal council that is taking command of his stricken father's government. That will ask a lot of him. But as he reaches adulthood Henry is beginning to prove that whatever is asked of him, more often than not, he will deliver.

11

"VIRTUOUS PRINCE"

Henry's father is ill, but he is not ready to die. This is a problem for the king himself. It is an even more serious problem for everyone else. A semifunctioning king is far worse for the realm than a dead one.

Throughout the summer of 1406 the king receives the close attentions of his doctors. John Bradmore attends him and is granted funds to buy new robes so that he may look the part as he does his job. It may be around now that Henry IV is treated for a prolapsed rectum, via an unpleasant procedure pioneered by a fourteenth-century physician, which involves applying hot ointment to the protruding section of intestine in an attempt to chase it back to its rightful home.[1]

In July the king is fit enough to set off on a ten-week religious progress around the east of England. The going is slow, in part because he is drained by sickness and in part because the weather is shocking. Rains have been lashing the whole of western Europe for months and England has not escaped: the riverbanks have burst and roads are clogged with mud.

Nevertheless, the king finds his way to a number of shrines well known as healing sites. As Henry did in 1403, he goes to Walsingham to visit the

Virgin Mary in her Holy House. He adores the relics of St. Edmund the Martyr in Bury, Thomas Becket's hair comb at Thetford, and a piece of the True Cross at Wymondham. In Lincolnshire he stops at Bardney Abbey, where the abbot allows him to kiss relics associated with the seventh-century king of Northumbria, St. Oswald.[2] This is a rare treat: most ordinary pilgrims never even lay eyes on the relics they come to venerate. Evidently Henry IV and the abbot both consider that the king needs all the miraculous intervention he can get.

Prince Henry joins his father in the early part of this tour, at Lynn, on the coast of Norfolk. However, his purpose is not to repeat his own pilgrimage of three summers earlier. Rather, he comes to bid farewell to his youngest sister, twelve-year-old Philippa, who is leaving England to marry King Eric of Sweden, Denmark, and Norway.

Henry finds young Philippa surrounded by queenly splendor that will befit her new rank. Lynn is magnificently arrayed. The fleet of fourteen ships that lies at anchor in the harbor, ready to take Philippa across the North Sea, is led by the king's own ship *The Ghost of the Tower*, which is decked out in cloth of crimson and gold.[3] Philippa is radiant, her wardrobe now crammed with regal costume: her gowns gold-embroidered with noble birds and beasts and sewn tightly with pearls, her boots cobbled of soft leather in the latest styles, her hats made of silk and beaver fur to guard her against the Scandinavian cold.[4] She packs books: a staggeringly beautiful illustrated book of hours that was once their mother's, and a medical handbook compiled for her by her father's surgeon.[5] She is attended by 150 personal servants.

Henry is not the only of Philippa's siblings who comes to see her off. He is joined in Lynn by his younger brothers Thomas, eighteen, and Humphrey, fifteen. Of the three of them, Humphrey may feel the strongest wrench at watching Philippa prepare to depart: he spent most of his childhood with his sisters, lodged at Eaton Tregoz when their father was in exile and at the royal castles of the Thames valley after he became king. The elder of the girls, Blanche, has already left England: she departed in 1402 to marry a German nobleman named Louis, elector palatine of the Rhine. Now Philippa is going, too.

However it affects Humphrey, this is no small moment for Henry, either. He may be feeling sentimental about his youth—for around this time he makes a generous grant to Peter Melbourne of two pipes of wine a year for the rest of his life.[6] For all of them, the years of childhood are now over. They are grown up, and finding their roles in service of the Crown. Thomas is preparing to govern Ireland. John is learning to be lieutenant of the north. His baby sister is now about to become a queen. If his father's pilgrimage to the holy shrines of England does not build on the difficult work that Bradmore and the other royal doctors have done, it will not be long before he, Henry, is a king.

In the autumn of 1406, the parliament that originally assembled that March, and which lavished such high praise on Prince Henry before it went into recess, reopens for a final session in Westminster. By the time it closes it will have lasted for nine months—earning it the nickname the Long Parliament. For Henry, though, the great length is less consequential than the provisions it makes in its final weeks for his formal role in government under his ailing father.

Since the Long Parliament opened in the first months of the year, the political issues facing England have developed. There are some reasons to be cheerful. A major blow has been struck against the Scots with the capture at sea of their eleven-year-old heir to the throne, Prince James, whose father has now died, meaning that James I of Scotland is an English prisoner in the Tower of London, where he will remain for the next eighteen years.

Set against these are continuing challenges. Ireland remains part-governable at best, and Henry's brother Prince Thomas is not considered ready to go back and take full command in his own right. The French have abandoned plans to invade the English mainland, but have been sending raids deep into the English-held territory of Guyenne, penetrating as far as its capital, Bordeaux. They are also said to be planning an assault on Calais, which must be defended at any cost.

And of course, there is Wales. The spirit of rebellion is flagging in certain critical regions: the island of Anglesey is on the verge of making peace with the sheriff of Chester, who has blockaded the Menai Strait, cutting off Anglesey from the mainland. In the south, exhausted insurgents in Glamorgan and the Gower have laid down their arms.[7] Owain Glyndŵr's aura is fading: in recent fighting his brother has been killed and his son has been captured; the French have declined to send him fresh troops; it seems that popular disillusionment with his leadership and general war-weariness are setting in. All the same, Owain remains at large. Important castles such as Aberystwyth and Harlech are still held against the Crown. And the earl of Northumberland is loose—perhaps in the principality, perhaps back in Scotland—dodging the traitor's death he has been condemned to suffer if and when he is caught.

To deal with all this—indeed, any of this—the English political classes in Parliament must set up a system of government that can accommodate Henry's father's rocky health. The summer's long shrine tour has not restored the king to full vigor; he remains so fragile that he is not judged fit to work more than two days a week. If the realm is to be ruled in an orderly fashion until such time as he recovers—or dies—a formal royal council must be established.

This is a special kind of problem. Ordinarily, formal councils are set up only when the king is a child or has been behaving so badly that he cannot be trusted. They are almost always open to abuse, and can be deadly dangerous for the councilors who sit on them, who might at some later date find themselves persecuted for having infringed on the royal prerogative. Richard II's reign made this absolutely clear.

Yet in 1406 there is an equally cautionary example of the dangers of *not* setting up a robust system of proxy government for a malfunctioning king. It is to be found in France. There, the court of the periodically insane Charles VI has for fourteen years been poisoned by the tussling of his brothers and cousins for control. Factions dominated by the king's charismatic brother, Louis, duke of Orléans, and his devious, aggressive cousin John the Fearless, duke of Burgundy, are sailing the French realm close to the winds of civil war. Just how desperate affairs in Paris will become has not yet been revealed, but even in late 1406, it is obvious that the French example is to be avoided at all costs.

With this in mind, during the last months of the year, the Long Parliament contrives to avoid this sort of disaster. A council with a tight and fixed membership of sixteen is established to carry out the routine business of running England while the king remains sick. The official documents establishing this arrangement emphasize that this is a last resort: that the members of this council "would not in any way take this responsibility upon themselves unless the king of his own will and account wanted to instruct them especially to do this."[8]

This council and other royal officers of high rank are ordered to carry out their duties in accordance with a set of rules known as the Thirty-One Articles, which prohibit council members from misusing royal funds or trying to use their influence on the king to pursue private quarrels. The council is to check in with the king every Wednesday and Friday to be sure that he agrees with their policy decisions.

It is not perfect. But it makes the best of a bad situation.

Naturally, Prince Henry is given a seat around the council table. He does not lead it; that position will fall to Thomas Arundel, archbishop of Canterbury, who will also become lord chancellor—the highest-ranking official in the royal bureaucracy. All the same, his involvement is essential. For one thing, Henry is a key figure in the struggle to restore order in Wales, which is bound to occupy much conciliar attention and financial scrutiny. More important, as Henry is his father's eldest son and heir, his presence lends weight to the council's decisions. It ought, in theory, to minimize the chance of its members being later accused of lèse-majesté.

So in December Henry takes the same oath as the other councilors, promising before Parliament to "carry out, perform and cause to be enforced to the best of his loyal power the common law of the land and the statutes and ordinances made and ordained in the past, both for the king's household as well as for the good governance of the kingdom of England."[9]

These are no platitudes. The king's illness is effectively an open-ended constitutional crisis. And in constitutional crises, the first principles of government must be spoken aloud.

It is all far from ideal. Yet at the same time, this is the best training a monarch-in-waiting could possibly have. Over the next two years, Henry's role on the council and his relationship with Archbishop Arundel will drill into him the first principles of the English constitution. It will deepen his understanding of the business of rule, teach him the value of political partnerships and, effectively, complete his education in the technical aspects of government.

It will also make him impatient for the day when he can wear the crown in his own right—which will in turn create significant tension between him and his father.

All that, however, lies in the future. Henry's first task as 1407 dawns is to turn his attention back to Wales, and the thorny issue of putting Owain Glyndŵr out of business.

A vital skill of the warrior prince, which Henry learns in depth during the years 1407–8, is the ability to look in two directions at once: seeing at the same time the enemy in the field and the allies at home on whose goodwill and trust success ultimately depends. In his young career so far, Henry has experienced war at its most decisive and dramatic. Now he will come to understand the role of patience, persistence, and political spin in winning battles before a bowstring has been drawn in anger.

In the first half of 1407 Henry begins planning an attack on the castle at Aberystwyth, which has been held by rebels for four years. Aberystwyth, which sits on the coastline of central Wales, is an ambitious target, but a critical one. Heavily fortified in the thirteenth century under the supervision of the English crown's greatest ever castle engineer, Master James of St. George, it was given a significant refurbishment by Richard II's father, the Black Prince. With robust defenses including ditches, a seawall, and large towers, taking Aberystwyth back from the rebels will be expensive and difficult.

To that end, Henry must reassure the council—bound by the Thirty-

One Articles to ensure they do not waste a penny of war taxation—that he knows what he is doing. The attack on Aberystwyth is set for the summer. Throughout the spring Henry attends around two-thirds of the royal council's meetings, and, little by little, funding and matériel begin to be delivered to his cause.

In May he contracts with the council to take a personal force of six hundred men-at-arms and eighteen hundred archers into Wales for a term of six months.[10] (The ratio of three bowmen to every man-at-arms will become a striking feature of his military planning for years to come.) In June, cannons of the sort that scared the wits out of the rebel garrison at Berwick are moved out of the royal armory at the Tower of London and transported to Bristol, whence they will be taken by ship to west Wales. An elite leadership team is appointed to support him, including his cousin the duke of York—now back in royal favor after his sister's plot to release the Mortimer boys in 1405—and Richard Beauchamp, the twenty-five-year-old earl of Warwick, who is a veteran of the battle of Shrewsbury and becoming a good friend and ally. These experienced generals will bring with them a crack squad of hardened veterans of the Welsh wars.

Despite these carefully laid plans, the assault on Aberystwyth does not go well. One of the prized English cannons, a gun named "Messenger," explodes on firing—a spectacular and noisy embarrassment. Those guns that do not self-destruct make no serious mark on the castle's defenses.[11] After a few weeks of bombardment the garrison tire of the noise and negotiate a deal to surrender and save their skins, unless Owain should appear to relieve them before November 1. This deal is struck in hope rather than expectation. Yet, somewhat surprisingly, Owain turns up with enough reinforcing troops that he can break Henry's siege lines and enter the castle to take personal command of its defense. As autumn approaches and a parliament is called to meet in Gloucester to review the council's work and negotiate another round of war funding, Henry is forced to abandon Aberystwyth.

On the surface, this looks like a painful defeat. "This last mishap was worse than the first," sniffs one chronicler.[12] The commons assembled at the Gloucester parliament moan theatrically that the Welsh "have grown even more rebellious than before, to the great damage and injury of the whole realm of England."[13] Yet if Henry has failed to take Aberystwyth, he has taken significant steps forward in understanding how to manage his own side. And as the Gloucester parliament is closing, Henry performs some theatrics of his own.

On the final day of the parliament, the commons' speaker, Thomas Chaucer,* invites him to come before the whole parliament and receive a commendation for his continuing "great labor and diligence" in the Welsh cause. This might easily be the cause for some cynical grumbling against privileged youth, in light of the failure to take Aberystwyth. But Henry reads the room perfectly.

Kneeling humbly before peers and commons in the refectory of Gloucester Abbey, Henry does not try to explain or even address his own role in Wales. Rather, he says he has heard whispers that his cousin the duke of York has proven an incompetent leader of men at the siege of Aberystwyth. In fact, Henry says, "had it not been for [York's] good advice and counsel," he and his company of men "would have suffered very great peril and loss." His cousin has served, he says, "in such a way as to support and embolden all the other members of the aforesaid company . . . he is a loyal and valiant knight in all that he does."[14]

It is a perfectly weighted piece of political stagecraft, deflecting attention from the course of the war and his own role in it, while asking the parliament to appreciate what great sacrifices are made by those who are out in the wilds of Wales at the sharp end of the fighting. And it has the desired effect. Speaker Chaucer rallies behind Henry's speech. Everyone who has served in Wales so far, Chaucer thunders, "should be commended and given credit . . . [and those who have] fled or departed from my lord the prince's company without having obtained permission or license to do this should be punished and chastised as an example for the future."

---

* Geoffrey Chaucer married Philippa Roet, the sister of John of Gaunt's third wife, Katherine Swynford. Their son Thomas Chaucer, born around 1367, was therefore a cousin of Gaunt and Katherine's "Beaufort" children, and closely associated with the Lancastrian cause.

The same day the parliament grants a tax intended to support the war effort for another two years. This grant does not rely on Henry's canny performance. But his words ensure that the show goes on.

Within three months of Henry's appearance before the Gloucester parliament, the rebellion in Wales is in full retreat. During a winter so cold that birds fall out of the sky and lie frozen on the ground, Henry is perpetually in motion.[15] He continues to attend as many council meetings as he can, and his commitment to the process of government pays off. In February 1408 the council agrees to divert to Wales some money earmarked for the defense of Guyenne. Later in the spring Henry is granted expenses to take five hundred men-at-arms and fifteen hundred archers back into west Wales for another campaigning season.

Before going back into the principality Henry makes a pilgrimage to Yorkshire, where he visits the remains of St. John Thwing of Bridlington in the new shrine consecrated by the now-dead archbishop Scrope. This is a considerable detour, but it is worth the inconvenience to give thanks to the saint for his continued good favor. For in February 1408 God has granted the Lancastrians a victory that eliminates one of their long-standing tormentors. On February 19 the sheriff of Yorkshire has engaged Henry Percy, the renegade earl of Northumberland, heading a small armed force with which the earl has decided, in desperation, to invade England.

At a short skirmish fought on Bramham Moor, the sheriff has defeated the earl's troops and killed their wanted leader. His body has been "immediately despoiled and the head cut off," reports one chronicler, adding that "the common people mourned greatly for the earl's misfortune, remembering the splendor of the man and his glory and honor."[16] Not so Henry, who leaves 5 marks as an offering at the shrine in Bridlington, and may well consider that for the protection John Thwing continues to offer his family, this is a very reasonable price.

After his sojourn in the north, Henry turns back to Wales once more. The first duty there is to finish the task begun at Aberystwyth. There he sticks to his guns, continuing to direct cannon fire against the fortress, while also making plans to besiege Harlech Castle, inside which Sir Edmund Mortimer is holed up.

Although results do not come immediately, there is a sense that the tide in Wales is turning. Soon Henry decides he can afford to leave day-to-day siege operations to his captains and base himself eighty miles away at Hereford, or even one hundred miles away in Worcester: border towns from which he can remain connected to the course of the war but also in touch with the council. His cautious confidence seems to be well placed. As Henry's men blast at Aberystwyth's walls during the summer of 1408, the revolt turns from a full-blown insurrection back to its original form: a fractured guerrilla campaign pursued by die-hard rebels who hide in the mountains and forests and show their faces only occasionally before melting away.

By the end of the summer, it is all but over. Even if the terse words of a Welsh chronicle belie the enormous effort expended by besieged and besiegers, they tell the story of the summer of 1408 well enough: "A second siege came to [Aberystwyth] castle, and it was won before leaving it. And from there the host came to Harlech. And there died many of the nobles of Wales, and in the end [they were] forced to give the castle to the English."[17] Aberystwyth falls before the end of the year. By February 1409 the English troops remaining at Harlech are in a mopping-up phase.

A biography of Henry written a generation later frames the victories of this year as a great personal triumph for the prince and an example of his willingness to endure enormous hardship in the name of victory. Of the action at Aberystwyth, the author records that "the siege was not without pain and disease on the part of the prince and his company, but it was much more terrible for those who were lodged within the castle . . . the most virtuous prince, not wearied with pain, after he had long besieged this castle to the king's great cost and expense, and not without the effusion of much blood, obtained the castle, and subdued the residue of Wales under the king's obedience, except one person, whose name was Owain."[18]

Even if Owain remains at large, having escaped Aberystwyth once more before its fall, several more Lancastrian nemeses are dead by the end of the year. Northumberland's head is set up on a spike above London Bridge soon after his death at Bramham Moor. At Harlech, Mortimer finds that his luck has run out, too. He is killed in the fighting, and his wife, Owain's daughter, is sent off to prison in London, along with her children. In later years the events of Sir Edmund's unusual life will inspire songs that are sung at feasts where the memory of the doomed struggle for Welsh independence is kept alive. But this is of no importance to Henry or his father. What matters to them is that this Mortimer can no longer torment the Lancastrian crown from afar.[19] Little by little, piece by piece, the crises that have dominated the first decade of Henry IV's reign are melting away.

Yet as one set of problems recedes, another rises up to take its place. Since his father first fell ill, Henry has proven a highly competent servant of the Crown. Without encroaching on his father's majesty, he has absorbed important lessons about military strategy, tactics, logistics, and finance. He has proven he can work harmoniously in the council chamber and share field command, and he has shown a flair for the dramatic, performative aspects of public office when managing Parliament. In Wales he has forged relationships with fighting men who share with him outlook, attitude, and now experience; men such as Richard Beauchamp, earl of Warwick, and John Oldcastle will be mixed up in his affairs for many years to come.

No doubt, he has made mistakes—cutting a deal with Aberystwyth in 1408 when a harder-nosed commander might have pushed on for victory. But he has found a way to put these right without losing face or the trust of his allies. And as he grows up, he will shed any inclination to treat his enemies leniently. Toughness and a near-total lack of sentimentality will become hallmarks of his political character.

When Harlech Castle falls in February 1409, Henry is twenty-two years old and a grown man. He has received a more intense apprenticeship, without the burden of kingship itself, than any English heir to the throne since Edward I, a century and a half before him. However, although this will be the key to the extraordinary future that lies ahead of him, in the short term it is destined to drive a wedge between Henry and his ailing father.

Not for the first time in Henry IV's reign, there are effectively two kings in the kingdom. But there is only one crown. Prince Henry is beginning to think—not unreasonably—that he is ready to take on some if not all of the responsibilities of kingship. But his father—as well as other important members of his family—have other ideas. Henry's ambition, born in large part from the success of his apprenticeship, will in time become the most serious challenge facing the Lancastrian regime.

12

COUPS AND COUNCILS

On the evening of November 23, 1407, Louis, duke of Orléans, the charming, charismatic, womanizing thirty-five-year-old younger brother of the insane king Charles VI, steps out of the Hôtel Barbette in Paris, where he has been visiting the queen, Isabeau of Bavaria.

The queen is Louis's closest political ally and—so it is whispered—his lover. She has recently borne a child that may or may not be his. That evening the two of them have dined together, but around eight o'clock a servant has arrived from the king's palace, the Hôtel Saint-Pol, asking that Louis take his leave of Isabeau and come to deal with some important government business.

This is not an unusual request. Together, Isabeau and Louis of Orléans lead the dominant faction on the royal council, which has been governing France for fifteen years, ever since King Charles's first attack of madness in 1392. During the king's "absences"—those times when he runs wild through his chambers insensible, slathered in his own feces, screaming that he is on fire—the council taxes and spends, makes war and peace, dispenses justice and hands out the juicy spoils of royal patronage. Control of the council confers immense power and responsibility. But it is also a good way to make enemies.

Having been summoned by the king, Louis leaves the queen and sets out into the dark street. He rides on a mule, surrounded by a handful of servants carrying torches. Louis is singing cheerfully as he rides. But as his group passes a house on the corner of the Rue des Blancs-Manteaux, a dozen thugs holding axes and clubs burst into the pool of flickering torchlight.

It is a fast, brutal attack. The hoodlums set about Louis's servants, smashing two of them to the ground and killing one of them. They wrestle the duke from the saddle, hurl him to the muddy street, and lay into him, battering his head and torso so badly that his skull is crushed and his brains spill out. They break his right arm. They mangle his left: one of the men heaves an ax and chops off the duke's left hand.

Before long the commotion raises the residents of the street: a neighbor opens their window and starts screaming. But by then the job is done. The gang's ringleader, a man in a red cape who is probably a career grifter from Normandy called Raoul d'Anquetonville, appears from the doorway of the house where the men were lying in wait. He calmly calls a halt to the attack and gives the order to flee. The gang sets fire to the house where they were hiding, then leap onto horses and gallop off through Paris's gloomy streets. They leave behind them a pool of blood, a cloud of smoke, and the wails of Louis of Orléans's surviving servants, who stand howling into the night sky that their master is dead.[1]

It is a vicious and bloody murder, but it is no random attack. Within weeks investigators have concluded that Louis's murder was masterminded by his first cousin and chief rival on the royal council, John the Fearless, duke of Burgundy.

John, thirty-six, is a squat, stubborn, ruthless, hardheaded, and violent crusading veteran. Three years ago he inherited his duchy and his factional preeminence from his late father, Philip the Bold, and he has spent almost all of the time since quarreling with Louis of Orléans. The two men had been formally reconciled by their elderly uncle, the duke of Berry, just days before Louis was murdered. It now appears that for John the Fearless this rapprochement was a charade.

In the immediate aftermath of Louis's slaying, John the Fearless pretends to know nothing. But once it becomes clear that he is the prime suspect, he switches tack, admitting that he ordered the hit to save the realm from Louis, who, he claims, was plotting to seize the throne.

Shock, mixed with fear of the duke and his populist appeal, grips the French council. Rather than facing down the brazen duke of Burgundy, they try to appease him. They summon John to meetings and allow him to explain away his actions. But ultimately, they allow him to get away scot-free. In the spring of 1408, when the king enjoys a brief moment of partial respite from his lunacy, John secures a royal pardon and is attempting to take control of the council.

Yet even if he is officially forgiven, John the Fearless's murder of the king's brother, the most celebrated peer of the realm, cannot be forgotten. During 1408 a powerful anti-Burgundian faction begins to form around the murdered duke's thirteen-year-old son, Charles of Orléans. Its members include the duke of Berry; the vigorous eighteen-year-old John, duke of Brittany; and young Charles's father-in-law, Bernard, count of Armagnac, from whom the new faction takes its nickname.

Rivalry between the Burgundians and the Armagnacs will shape the course of French politics for nearly three decades. It will bring about the grisly deaths of many more great princes of the land and drag France into all-out civil war. And it will eventually prove the making of Prince Henry, whose intervention in the Burgundian-Armagnac dispute will provide the opportunity for his most famous deeds.

Yet in 1407–8 the murder of Louis, duke of Orléans, does not offer the English a glimmer of hope so much as a dreadful warning of what might become of them, too, if they do not deal sensitively with their own periodically incapacitated king.

During Christmastime 1408 Henry IV lies close to death at his favorite palace, Eltham. The illness that first gripped him in 1405 has proven resistant to all remedies. The chancellor, Archbishop Arundel, offers spiritual comfort to the ailing king. Although a succession of the finest doctors are brought in, led by an Italian named David Nigarellis, from Lucca, they can do little more than scratch their heads.

In preparation for death, the king is moved to Greenwich in the new year, and there he makes his will. Declaring himself a "sinful wretch" who has "misspended" his life, he asks to be buried in Archbishop Arundel's cathedral at Canterbury, and provides for a chantry chapel of priests to sing masses for his soul and thereby ease it through purgatory. He asks that his servants have any wages owing to them paid—naming the grooms of his chamber, who have dealt most intimately with him during his sickness. Separately, he orders another chapel to be built on the battlefield at Shrewsbury where, five and a half years earlier, the thousands of dead were slung into a common pit.[2]

The witnesses to the king's will include several other members of the council, including Arundel and Sir John Tiptoft, the speaker of the Long Parliament who has been serving as royal treasurer. Henry does not witness the document, which is perhaps not surprising. At this moment he is focused on reducing Harlech Castle and seeing that Owain Glyndŵr's rebellion does not flare back into life. Yet if he cannot leave this task to attend his father on his deathbed, the king still has Henry in his mind. He appoints his eldest as the executor of his will, asking him to "fulfil truly all things" in his testament. This, he says, "I charge my foresaid son upon my blessing."[3]

However, in 1409, Henry does not have to respond to the charge, for instead of dying, Henry IV rallies. By March he is well enough to leave Greenwich for Eltham once more. The following month he writes to Archbishop Arundel to thank him, and God, for "the good health I am in."[4] By the early summer he is convalescing at Windsor and in July he and Henry sit in public in London and watch a four-day theatrical performance of the whole history of the Bible, from Adam's arrival in the Garden of Eden to the Apocalypse. Somehow or other he has made an astonishing recovery. Yet this is perhaps not entirely good news. As a result of Henry IV's incapacity, and Prince Henry's excellent discharge of his duties in Wales during the last two years, the center of power in English government has shifted. However the king's health waxes and wanes, it is clear to all that it cannot be relied upon. Someone must take firm and definite control.

That someone is Henry.

Piece by piece, over the course of 1409 Henry will move to insert himself and his closest allies to key roles in government. Senior noblemen such as the earl of Westmoreland—Henry's brother John's mentor in the north—begin to address their letters to "My lord the prince and the lords of the council, acknowledging his apparently unstoppable"[5] rise to power. And as Henry's star waxes, his own style of rule, his personal preoccupations, and his beliefs about who should (and should not) hold office start to emerge.

As Henry begins to assert himself at the heart of royal government in 1409, he can for the first time in a long time think about matters beyond Wales. This is in large part the result of work he has done there since 1407. Aberystwyth and Harlech Castles have been recovered. Henry's Welsh revenues are beginning to recover, so that his officers can collect taxes in places where they would just a few years earlier have been lynched. Edmund and Roger Mortimer, the boys whom Owain would have liked to put on the English throne, are moved into Henry's custody.

Owain's name can still excite the bards, who compose poems in praise of the hills and forests in which he and his diminishing band of rebels hide: "grove of tall trees full of outlaws, broader than meadow, moon or seas."[6] But the truth, barely disguised by the poets, is that Owain is now little more than an isolated and desperate guerrilla captain. He will remain at large for another six years, but his heyday has passed, and his claim to be the "real" Prince of Wales has faded from a fiscal-military reality to a romantic dream.

This means that as 1409 goes on, Henry can turn his attentions elsewhere—specifically, to France. Notwithstanding the turmoil in Charles VI's mind and court, the threat of a French invasion of English territory has been real for a decade. Between 1403 and 1407 the most aggressive anti-English voice at the French court was that of Louis, duke of Orléans.

His silence has now been assured by John the Fearless's ax-wielding thugs. The truce Henry saw brokered when he was a little boy, sealed in the shimmering pavilions of Ardres between Richard II and Charles VI, still, theoretically, holds. Yet there is much work to be done to see that it does not collapse. French troops have been raiding deep into English lands in Guyenne. A bloody series of coastal raids has seen tit-for-tat amphibious attacks between towns of the English south coast—Portsmouth, Southampton, Falmouth—and the settlements opposite them in Normandy and Brittany.

The biggest physical prize for the French, without question, is Calais: the English military compound and mercantile powerhouse visible from the chalk cliffs of Kent. As Henry's mind turns from Welsh affairs to French in 1409, he is clear that Calais must be defended vigorously and at any cost.

In part, this is a military project. Calais needs a generous and constant supply of men, weapons, and money to keep its garrison and network of forts on high alert against any assault. To this end, Henry presses the cautious chancellor Archbishop Arundel regularly to keep payments flowing. In late February 1409 he also secures his own appointment as constable of Dover and warden of the Cinque Ports, effectively assuming personal responsibility for protecting the important trading towns of Kent and Sussex from French raiding and piracy.

Yet as a military strategist of a later age will observe, war is politics pursued by other means. So while Henry presses for defensive reinforcements for Calais, he also involves himself in diplomatic courtesies between the English council and the French court. A short series of home-and-away jousting matches are arranged between English and Burgundian knights in London and Lille, at which combat on tournament grounds decorated with cloth of gold and arras gives way to feasting on fried minnows, roast porpoise, and venison.[7]

In the meantime, Henry's household chamberlain is sent to Paris to explore the possibility of a marriage between the prince and Charles VI's youngest daughter, a slight seven-year-old named Catherine. This has the uncanny ring of history repeating. The sad example of Princess Isabelle, who came to England to be queen at roughly the same age and was packed off home again in high dudgeon after the Lancastrian revolution of 1399, surely cannot escape the minds of Henry or anyone else involved in the discussions. But dynastic politics seldom allows too much for sentimentality. Henry's and Catherine's fates will remained tangled for many years to come.

One of Henry's most delicate tasks as he starts to grip the levers of power in the spring of 1409 is what to do with his twenty-one-year-old brother Thomas.

When it was thought at the start of the year that their father was dying, Thomas returned from his latest short posting in Dublin, where he has been serving sporadically as lieutenant of Ireland. Thomas was in all likelihood relieved to get away. As Henry may recall from his own youth, and the weeks he spent accompanying Richard II chasing Art MacMurrough around Wicklow, Ireland is a fearsomely difficult and rather unappealing place for an English prince of any age to go. Thomas was first officially made their father's deputy in Ireland in 1401. Since then he has been there only twice: once between November 1401 and November 1403, and again from August 1408 to his return at the time of the king's illness in the new year of 1409. During that time, not surprisingly, he has failed to control chronic infighting among the most powerful Anglo-Irish families, nor has he really found a way to stamp out rebellion by the native people. The area of English control shrinks with every passing year and the roads are unsafe to Englishmen. Thomas has experienced this firsthand, having been wounded in a skirmish near Kilmainham.

Once the crisis of their father's health has passed, therefore, Thomas does not seem in any hurry to go back to his post. However, he is very much insistent on drawing the lieutenancy's pay packet, a budget amounting to nearly £8,000 a year. This rankles with Henry, who has spent the last six years and more in Wales learning how to make inadequate funding go a long way. And so emerges the first hint of a rift between the king's eldest two sons.

The first round of their tussle is won by Thomas. Henry's inclination, which he makes no real effort to hide, is to sack his brother and appoint a more experienced man to the job: Sir John Stanley, who serves as steward of Henry's household. Stanley, a gruff, pragmatic northerner, is a veteran of Shrewsbury who speaks in a deathly growl as the consequence of having taken an arrow in the throat during that battle.* But Thomas clings to his post, successfully convincing the council to allow him his pay while making no plans to actually go back to work.

In response, Henry tries to reduce the burden his younger brother places on the royal finances by having his retainers removed from the payroll of their father's court. Yet here again Thomas bests him, by going over the council's head to the king. Henry IV has great affection for his second son. A special bond may well have formed between them when the older man took Thomas with him during his exile in Paris. Or it may be that the king is feeling sentimental about his children in general: in the summer of 1409, the king hears that Blanche, his eldest daughter, has suddenly died in Germany at the age of sixteen. Whatever the case, when Thomas comes to him for money, the king indulges him, writing wheedling letters to the council asking them "from his heart" to grant Thomas as much cash as they can.[8]

None of this reflects well on any of the parties concerned. It is stiff-necked and overbearing of Henry to take on his brother in the fashion that he does. It is sneaky of Thomas to run to their father. And it is weak of the king to allow himself to be so manipulated. Yet it is easy to see how family resentments played out in administration and government can go wrong very quickly. English affairs are not yet in the same murderous straits as French. But unless Henry can establish himself as the single source of alternative power during his father's drift in and out of sickness, they might easily go that way.

---

* Henry will eventually get his way and send Stanley to Ireland after his accession as king, where Stanley carves out a reputation as a brutal bogeyman.

His unsuccessful tussle with Thomas notwithstanding, as autumn 1409 approaches Henry has fully emerged as a dominant voice on the royal council; from September he is party to the majority of its official decisions, and in December he advances still further. When the new year dawns, he is not only an active and engaged councilor but the undisputed council leader, exercising powers that amount almost to a formal regency. It is an audacious power grab.

As usual, Henry IV's health is the prompt for this new thrust toward preeminence. In October 1409, the king is so poorly that an official of the royal kitchen is paid to walk from England to Jerusalem "for the convalescence and health of the king's person."[9] New doctors join the royal medical team, including a Jewish physician from Bologna, whose summoning to England ignores a law that has been in place for more than a century barring Jewish people from the realm. But no spiritual or medical cure avails, and in the weeks leading up to a new parliament in January 1410 the king is once more too unwell to do his job.

That job is to secure from the country the first grant of taxation in three years, to address a growing problem of lawlessness, and to assure the nervous population that the realm is not about to be invaded by the French. Official summonses to the parliament are sent out in October 1409, calling on representatives to assemble in Bristol, though the venue is later changed to Westminster, in January 1410. As the date of the parliament approaches, Prince Henry begins to plot changes in government that he believes will inspire Parliament to throw its support—and its money—behind the council.

What transpires is part cabinet reshuffle and part coup, in which Henry's targets include the two most cautious and senior bureaucrats on the council: the chancellor, Archbishop Arundel of Canterbury, and the treasurer, Sir John Tiptoft.

These are bold choices to attack, and the fact that Henry goes after these hitherto reliable public servants suggests he is developing a ruthless quality that was missing as recently as 1407, during the first phase of the siege of Aberystwyth. Arundel and Tiptoft have shouldered difficult, unglamorous work in bringing royal spending under control for the past three years. But Arundel in particular is growing old and rigid in his ways. Increasingly, his budget-paring instincts do not sit well with Henry. The chancellor's and treasurer's attempts to restrict the spending of the royal household create constant friction with courtiers and servants whose wages regularly go unpaid. Their proposal in November 1409 to halve the budget of Calais's garrison at a moment when it seems likely that John the Fearless, duke of Burgundy, is planning a direct assault suggests they are men whose long devotion to difficult work has blinded them to the bigger political situation.

Henry does not have the authority to purge the royal council on a whim. But he does have an eye for opportunity. In early December, Henry convinces his father that both men should be fired. On the eleventh, Arundel is asked for his resignation. Ten days later, Tiptoft goes, too.

What follows is the reshaping of the royal council according to Henry's wishes. Over Christmas the king holds on to the great seal—the chancellor's chief instrument of office. By the time Parliament opens, he has agreed to accept Henry's choices for Arundel's and Tiptoft's replacements.

The new chancellor is to be Thomas Beaufort, the youngest of the king's three half brothers by John of Gaunt and Katherine Swynford. The new treasurer is Henry, Lord Scrope, nephew of the rebel archbishop of York executed in 1405.

Both of these men have links with Henry IV. But generationally and temperamentally they are closer to his eldest son. Thomas Beaufort, who becomes one of the few nonchurchmen of his age to occupy the office of chancellor, is at thirty-three years old already a veteran soldier. He fought at Shrewsbury, held Welsh castles against Owain Glyndŵr during the darkest days of the rebellion, and has subsequently forged a successful career in the navy, commanding fleets in the English Channel and preventing the blockade of Calais. Scrope also fought at Shrewsbury, and has enjoyed a successful diplomatic career since then, accompanying Henry's

1. Henry's mother, Mary de Bohun, was a pious, literate woman who loved luxury goods, beautiful books, and music. She married young and died when Henry was still a child. When he became king, he honored her memory with a fine tomb effigy in the Lancastrian mausoleum at Leicester.

2. Henry's father, Henry Bolingbroke, lays claim to the vacant throne of his cousin Richard II. The clerics and lords of England look on somber-faced. The consequences of this usurpation haunted Henry IV for the rest of his life.

3. Henry was born above the gatehouse of Monmouth Castle on September 16, 1386. Wales would play an important part in his youth, as he learned the arts of war suppressing the rebellion sparked by Owain Glyndŵr.

4. John Thwing of Bridlington was a favorite saint of Henry IV, in whose reign he was canonized. Henry followed his father's example, paying his respects at Thwing's shrine after some of his hardest campaigns in France.

5. Conwy Castle was seized by Welsh rebels of the Tudor family in April 1401. Henry, then a teenage Prince of Wales, was tasked with winning it back. His father wrote to him during the siege to explain that since Conwy was lost on his watch, it was his responsibility to recover it. This was a hard early lesson in the realities of warfare.

6. Henry Percy the younger, better known as Hotspur, was one of the most admired and decorated knights of his day. His relationship with Henry IV soured when he was asked to help Prince Henry defend Wales. Hotspur was killed at the battle of Shrewsbury in 1403; this modern statue at Alnwick Castle commemorates him.

7. Henry was taken to Ireland by Richard II at age thirteen in 1399 and knighted beside a forest during Richard's pursuit of a native chieftain called Art MacMurrough. Richard was kind to Henry, allegedly predicting that he would become king. Henry honored his memory by having him reburied in Westminster Abbey.

8. The Great Seal of Owain Glyndŵr of which this is a replica, shows him enthroned as a rival Prince of Wales to Henry. The experience of fighting for the right to a royal title in Wales foreshadowed Henry's struggles as king to enforce his claim to be king of France.

9. John of Gaunt was Henry's grandfather and the most senior nobleman in England until his death in Leicester Castle in February 1399. Legend has it that on his deathbed he showed Richard II his rotting penis as a warning against fornicating with women. Both Richard and Henry V seem to have taken that advice to heart.

10. Thomas Hoccleve addressed his *Regiment of Princes* to Henry, giving him lengthy instruction on the qualities to be found in a great ruler. This page includes an image of Geoffrey Chaucer, whose family was allies and friends of the Lancastrian dynasty.

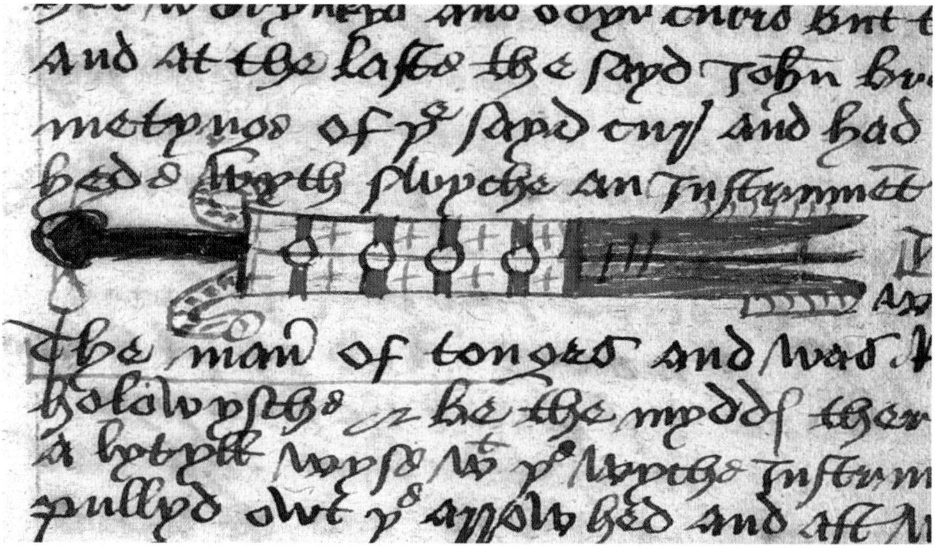

11. The royal surgeon John Bradmore saved Henry's life in 1403, using a bespoke medical tool to remove an arrowhead from deep within Henry's skull. Bradmore's notes and sketches are a fascinating insight into the procedure.

12. This portrait of Henry V was painted between 1504 and 1516. It may be in profile because it was copied from a medal; it may be from an image posed to hide a scar Henry carried from his injury at the battle of Shrewsbury and the subsequent surgery.

13. The German emperor Sigismund of Luxembourg was a pivotal figure in ending Europe's long-running papal schism. He was an honored guest in England in 1416, during which time he donated several relics of St. George to Henry and signed an anti-French peace deal.

14. Henry's brother Thomas, duke of Clarence, was a rash, brave soldier. Perhaps their father's favorite son, Thomas eclipsed Henry for a time, but thereafter became a loyal general. His death at the battle of Baugé in 1421 was a personal blow and a huge setback for Henry's war in France.

sister Philippa when she traveled to marry in Scandinavia, then visiting Paris as part of an English embassy.

These are no-nonsense figures whom Henry likes and trusts. And as he recasts the royal council to his own liking, they are joined by others cut from the same cloth. One is the grand and worldly Henry Beaufort, who has been elevated from bishop of Lincoln to occupy the rich see of Winchester. This Beaufort—the middle of Prince Henry's three uncles—was made a bishop in his twenties despite a distinctly secular mien, served as chancellor earlier in the reign, and has sat continuously on the king's council since February 1403.[10] Beaufort has been close to Henry since he was a child, having briefly been his tutor.* He shares Henry's concern for the security of Calais and he is keen to see the day that Henry succeeds his father; in 1406 while in France he is said to have spread the rumor that Henry IV would soon abdicate in favor of his eldest son.[11]

Two more councilors are Thomas FitzAlan, earl of Arundel, and Richard Beauchamp, earl of Warwick—noble and soldierly men, both allies of Henry's age in their late twenties.† They sit around the table with a small clutch of others, exclusively noblemen and churchmen, whose fortunes are hitched to the Prince of Wales.

It is, in one sense, a clique. Yet its members have been selected not solely because they are partisans of the prince, but also to project the sense that this is a moment of urgency in which men of action are needed.

The new council's first task is to persuade Parliament that they are serious about their responsibilities. On January 27, 1410, the assembly opens in the Painted Chamber at Westminster. The commons elect a

---

* Although not at Oxford University. The story that Henry V spent a year at Queen's College, Oxford, while Beaufort was chancellor of the university is almost certainly a myth.

† The other councilors in 1410 are Nicholas Bubwith, bishop of Bath and Wells; Henry Chichele, bishop of St. Davids; and Hugh, Lord Burnell, a veteran of the Welsh wars. Initially appointed, but then excused from duty on the grounds that they are fiercely busy in the north, are Thomas Langley, bishop of Durham (another ex-chancellor), and Ralph Neville, earl of Westmoreland (mentor in the north to Henry's brother John).

staunchly Lancastrian speaker, Thomas Chaucer—son of the great poet Geoffrey and nephew of the Beaufort brothers—who performed the same role at the last parliament.

Bishop Henry Beaufort gives the opening address. He takes as his theme a phrase from the Gospel of Matthew: *Decet nos implere omnem justiciam* ("It is fitting for us to fulfill all justice").*

This is a pointed choice of passage. The phrase comes from Matthew's description of Jesus being baptized by John the Baptist: a moment in which power and promise are transferred from the prophet to the savior. And surely every person assembled in the Painted Chamber knows what else is written—and said—in this passage. John the Baptist announces that "after me comes one who is more powerful than I, whose sandals I am not worthy to carry," while at the moment of baptism, a voice from heaven cries, "this is my Son, whom I love; with him I am well pleased."

These are hardly subtle sentiments. But Henry and his new allies are not inclined at this moment to subtlety. They know there is work to do, and a pressing need to do it. With this in mind, they feel they have no choice but to frame this moment as a symbolic passing of the mantle of rule, from the languishing king to the vigorous son.

Yet this is not all they are doing. As well as serving to stir up excitement about the arrival of a new leader, Bishop Beaufort explains how the text on which he addresses the parliament applies to the political and military situation facing England. There are, he explains, two pillars to the concept of "justice" (or, as *justiciam* could be translated, "righteousness").

In the first place, justice should be taken to mean restoring and maintaining public order in England: it is the government's duty to see that "laws had been and were kept and obeyed." In the second, justice means maintaining the realm "without its borders": specifically with regard to keeping the peace on the Scottish border and, even more urgently, defending Calais from the designs of the French, and particularly John the Fearless, duke of Burgundy. These are more than just important political goals. They are righteous duties.

---

* Matthew 3:15.

Peacekeeping and defense of the realm have always been the two essential duties of any king: this is why the double-sided royal seal typically shows the king in two guises: with scales of justice and a sword. They are, in a sense, the essential compact of kingship: the king offers peace at home and safety from invasion, and the realm supports him. As Beaufort's address hints, and subsequent events will show, Henry understands this concept of kingship instinctively. A just, righteous ruler will give his people discipline and his enemies nightmares. The bishop is promising that Henry and his newly minted council intend to do just that.

Once it is in session, the parliament of January 1410 does what parliaments usually do, which is to say it complains a good deal about the state of the realm, grumbles about every royal demand for finance as though it ought to be possible to govern the country for free, and then hands over a grant of taxation.

This can be a rough ride, as it is supposed to be. But ultimately it is a safe one. The commons have been sufficiently well packed with men associated with Henry and the duchy of Lancaster to eventually take the new regime at its word. So although the parliament is not short—it sits for four months, in two sessions—by May it has agreed to back the newly constituted council and voted through a reasonably generous grant of taxation.

In that sense, it is a success. As it breaks up, Henry can believe that he has secured the backing of the English polity for his new role as de facto regent for his father. But he is also in no doubt about just what a huge task that is going to be.

13

HOLY FIRE

Parliament is still in session on the afternoon of Wednesday, March 5, 1410, when Henry goes to Smithfield, just outside the walls of England's capital, to see a man burned alive.

The occasion has excited the whole of London. The condemned is a tailor from Evesham called John Badby, and his crime is believing the wrong thing. More than a year ago Badby was arrested and hauled up before his local bishop for denying that the bread broken by priests celebrating mass (known as the "host") is the real body of Christ. In Badby's view, this is simple common sense. A priest, he says, has no more power to magically transform a sliver of unleavened loaf into a morsel of Jesus than does the filthiest street-sweeper.[1]

Unfortunately, what passes in Badby's corner of the Midlands for free thought frankly expressed is an outrage against the teachings of the Church, and a breach of a law known as *de heretic comburendo* ("On the Burning of Heretics"), passed in 1401 to try to stamp out preaching by Lollards.

"Lollard" is an insulting term applied to people inspired by the teachings of John Wyclif—the radical Oxford theologian who was active in the

1370s and 1380s under the protection of Henry's grandfather John of Gaunt. Lollards believe in church reform. They despise the idea of churchmen holding wealth and property. They dismiss as superstitious nonsense concepts such as transubstantiation (the bread and wine of the Eucharist literally becoming Christ's body and blood). They reject many other commonplaces of Christian practice—including baptism, confession, priestly ordination, and the adoration of images.

Taken all together in their most extreme forms, this set of beliefs is a century before its time: well out of step with both high Church doctrine and the ordinary religious observation of the English people. Opponents of Lollardy describe Wyclif as an "idol of abomination" and his followers as "shits."[2] Parliament imposed harsh penalties on those preaching Lollard ideas "as a lesson to others of this evil sect, thus readily to end their evil preachings and make them adhere to the Christian faith."[3]

Yet every now and then certain Lollard ideas gain traction, either among politicians who wish to tap Church wealth, or with open-minded laymen who reach the limits of their surrender to the mysteries of the faith and decide to say something bold. Just such a person is John Badby, and on March 5 he must choose to recant, or be cast into the fire.

By the time Henry sees Badby brought to Smithfield, the tailor has been in prison for over a year—the standard term allowed to convicted heretics to think about the errors of their ways. He is, understandably, "of rough appearance."[4] In the past week he has been reexamined twice.

On Saturday, March 1, he was interrogated at Blackfriars by a panel of judges led by Archbishop Arundel, so recently ousted as chancellor, and including Henry's council members, Bishops Beaufort, Chichele, and Bubwith. There Badby repeated his erroneous views, saying that if Christ himself were present he would tell the Lord the same things: that if every piece of bread consecrated on every altar in England turned into a bit of him, there would twenty thousand Christs roaming around the realm all at once. Arundel told him he would have one more chance to revise his opinions on the matter, then Badby was locked in a cell for a few more days' contemplation.

He was brought back for another interview on the morning of March

5, and there he gave the authorities little choice as to his fate. He argued that the host was an inanimate object, valuable only as a symbol. As he spoke he became increasingly belligerent. At one point a spider crawled across his face, and he showed it to his judges, saying that every living object, be it a spider—or for that matter, a toad—was worth more than an inanimate piece of bread.

This was more than Arundel and his fellow bishops could stomach. They formally condemned Badby as a heretic and—as the law demanded—handed him over to the royal authorities to face his bodily punishment: burning at the stake.

All of which is how Badby came to be tied to a post in Smithfield, with bundles of dry wood piled around his feet and a wooden barrel placed around his body to hasten his immolation. Given the high-profile nature of the case, this is also why Prince Henry, freshly appointed leader of the royal council and the face of his sickly father's royal government, came to be present among the crowd, preparing to watch him die.

Henry's position as regards Badby is conflicted. Of course he has seen men executed before. He passed his first death sentence on Gwilym ap Tudur's rebels outside Conwy Castle back in 1401, when he was just fourteen years old. He has hacked the heads off Owain Glyndŵr's henchmen and boasted about it. Henry knows full well that inventive, agonizing judicial punishments, such as the repeated partial hanging and public gutting of a traitor like William Serle, are simply part of the world, and have often been inflicted on men he knows intimately, from the starvation of Richard II to the beheading and quartering of Thomas Percy, earl of Worcester. No prince can afford to flinch at the sight of blood or the smell of roasting human flesh.

Yet Badby is more than just a criminal heretic. He represents a fork in the road—a choice that will define Henry as a man and, in time, a ruler.

Lollardy is not a mainstream sect. It is not even an organized movement. But it has adherents in important places: among scholars at the University of Oxford, among knights and lords in Parliament, and even among Henry's own friends. Sir John Oldcastle, one of Henry's most reliable captains during his years in Wales, a man who helped reduce Aberystwyth Castle in 1407 and has recently been elevated to the nobility as Lord Cobham, openly associates with religious radicals and is developing contacts in Bohemia, homeland of the notorious Lollard-style heretic Jan Hus.

This matters. What matters more is timing. Lollards are not routinely killed in England. In fact, despite laws prescribing remedy for its adherents, only one Lollard has been tried and burned in the last ten years—a chaplain called William Sawtre, who went to the stake just as the anti-Lollard legislation was being passed in 1401. In general both Church and Crown have preferred gentler methods of combatting the heresy: confiscating books, inspecting schools, and arresting preachers. But March 1410 is not a normal time.

The reason that Badby has been brought forward at this precise moment is that members of the 1410 parliament, which is still in session, have submitted for debate an extraordinary bill heavily influenced by Lollard ideas. This bill seeks to solve the Crown's perpetual financial woes by enacting sweeping confiscations of Church land and property. The authors of the bill claim that if the Crown were to seize back all the lands wasted by clerics, England could be transformed. They calculate that the king could afford to create fifteen new earls, fifteen hundred knights, and more than six thousand esquires; he could found fifteen universities and a hundred poorhouses and sustain thousands of new, godly clerics living in honorable penury.[5] Even after all this he would have an income of £20,000 a year for ordinary business before he needed to ask Parliament for taxes.

The bill is controversial, to say the least. It is of obvious concern to men like Arundel, whose job it is to protect the Church, its teachings, and its wealth. But Henry, at the head of his reshuffled council, with a mandate to bring new ideas and new approaches to government, is theoretically in a position to take it seriously. He could choose to solve all England's financial woes at a stroke, enriching the Crown beyond the wildest dreams of any king since the Norman Conquest. But the price will be to throw his lot in with Lollards and Lollard sympathizers: not simply protecting them, as John of Gaunt did Wyclif, but swinging entirely behind their movement.

The measure of whether he is prepared to do this or not—a test of what sort of ruler he aspires to be—stands inside the barrel, on top of the woodpile, tied to a stake at Smithfield. His name is John Badby.

The stories of what Henry does at Smithfield that afternoon will excite the pens of chroniclers in London and beyond. For, as the torches smoke and the crowd murmurs, Henry displays the same gift for political theatrics and public display that he did when he fell to his knees at the Gloucester parliament of 1407. Indeed, his actions echo Richard II's during a long-ago moment of extreme political tension: when Richard dramatically halted the duel between Henry's father and Thomas Mowbray, just as the combat was about to begin.[6]

As Badby stands waiting to die, he resists Archbishop Arundel's final plea for him to abandon his heresies. So Henry decides that he should have a go. He approaches Badby at the stake and asks him gently to "hold [to] the very right belief of [the] Holy Church," promising him that he will be well looked after if only he abandons his errors.[7] Badby refuses. To test the point, the chancellor of Oxford University steps forward with a piece of the host and asks Badby what he makes of it. "Holy bread," says Badby, "and not God's holy body."[8]

Since there is apparently nothing more to be done for the man, the executioner comes forward with a torch and lights the woodpile around him. The flames lick up; the wooden barrel around Badby's body catches light, and the tortures of burning alive begin. The wretched man starts screaming in fright and pain, bellowing "pitiably in this moment of extreme peril."[9]

This awful stage of the execution ought not to last very long, for Badby will soon pass out from pain or smoke inhalation. Yet Henry steps forward again and calls for the burning barrel to be lifted and the crackling wood around Badby to be kicked away. As one chronicler later tells the tale, Badby is by now half-dead—and perhaps as horrified at being denied his end as he was at meeting it. But he revives just enough to hear Henry tell him that if he recants "he should keep his life and obtain pardon and receive three pence daily from the royal treasury for the rest of his life."[10]

It is to no avail. Badby has come this far with his principled death and croaks he wants to see his fate through. "He would naught but continue forth in his heresy," writes another contemporary. So Henry has the barrel placed back over him once more and the fire stoked. "And so it happened that this meddler burned to ashes there at Smithfield, miserably dying in his sin."

Henry has tried to rescue Badby, and in one sense he has failed. He merely prolonged the obstinate tailor's last tortures, without saving him from the future torments of damnation. Yet the theatrics have also been a self-serving triumph. Given that Badby was to be burned to death anyway, Henry has cleverly played two roles at once. He has acted the reasonable, merciful prince, concerned for the soul of every sinner in England. Yet he has shown himself strong enough of heart to see that justice is done when it must be.

In political terms, he has trodden an even cannier middle line. The radical reformers in Parliament who would dismember the Church along Lollard lines in order to reendow the Crown have not been dismissed out of hand. Henry has shown himself willing to reach out to those of their heretical sect, if they will remain within the bounds of religion, the law, and public decency. He has tried to save them from their error. But he has also demonstrated publicly that for all his willingness to engage with opponents, he will brook no threat to traditional religion and public order. He has listened to his opponents, then made a clear, principled decision.

On the night of Thursday, March 6—the day after Badby is burned—it is said by Londoners that people who live in the houses around Smithfield are haunted by the dead Lollard's ghost and scared out of their wits by sudden gale-force winds. But Henry, we may guess, enjoys the easy slumber of a man who has played his part to perfection.

After the ashes of Badby's pyre are swept away from Smithfield and the excited crowd has gone away to repeat the story in London's streets and taverns, the political issues that prompted the poor tailor's burning remain. Henry has been firm in rejecting the Lollard-influenced bill calling for Church lands to be confiscated. But he and his council must still address the awkward central quandary of government in 1410. Put simply, there is never quite enough money and there are far too many things to spend it on.

When Parliament breaks up in May 1410, it gives Henry's new council its formal blessing, trusting them to "put the good decisions and ordinances made in this present parliament into effect."[11] Extraordinarily, it even places formal restrictions on the sickly king's ability to interfere with decisions taken in his own name. Yet the tax Parliament votes to support the prince's council in their mandate is only barely adequate, and scheduled to be collected and released in meager installments. At the same time, crucial government revenue from export taxes is falling precipitously due to a crash in the wool market, which is the powerhouse of the English export industry. It is plain that if Henry is to make any headway as the effective leader of his father's government, the only way to do so is by careful, inventive financial management.

Dull, painstaking, technocratic work seldom moves bards and chroniclers in the same way as battlefield victories. Yet the great triumph of Henry's leadership of the royal council in 1410–11 is that he realizes that nothing can proceed without it.

Henry's own top priority is securing Calais—a fact he makes absolutely clear when his uncle John Beaufort, earl of Somerset, captain of Calais, dies in March 1410 and Henry installs himself as replacement. Over the course of the next eighteen months, Henry's council gathers regularly to address its defense—and the realm's other problems. They meet in comfortable, private locations, often in London town houses such as Henry's smart Thames-side mansion at Coldharbour.[12] And once ensconced they try to work out how best to squeeze as much money as possible out of the available sources.

One short-term emergency measure is borrowing. The council writes begging letters and sends them out around England, bringing in several thousand pounds in private loans to the treasury from friendly nobles, including themselves. The councilors Bishop Bubwith and the earl of Warwick both lend money. So does the treasurer, Henry, Lord Scrope.

Even Henry's elderly grandmother, the formidable Joan FitzAlan, countess of Hereford, is persuaded to advance the Crown 500 marks.[13]

Loans, however, can only tide the government over in the short term. So Henry's council also seeks to slice away at the most bloated parts of the royal budget. The Crown spends heavily on payments known as annuities: cash pensions awarded to individuals in exchange for personal service. Annuities bleed the treasury of money. Easily granted as reward for (or incentive to) good behavior, they remain lodged on the books as recurring spending items for years and can add up alarmingly quickly.

Suspending or canceling annuities is a sure way to dismay the men who receive them, and when Archbishop Arundel was chancellor he was always loath to see them go unpaid.[14] The king feels the same way, for it is through annuities that he has rewarded many of the people who supported him during the revolution of 1399 and the turbulent years that followed. Henry, by contrast, does not fear people grumbling, and is secure in the knowledge that he owes his position not to an armed rebellion but to the fact of his birth and the public perception of his competence. Sheriffs are therefore ordered to freeze annuities and allow payments to go unmade. All wails of protest from annuitants themselves are ignored.

Meanwhile, Henry and the council look for other ways to boost income or slash expenditure. Sometimes it is painful. They trim the overall defense budget, ring-fencing an increased sum for the garrison of Calais but ordering savings everywhere else. They try a round of "distraint of knighthood": forcing men whose wealth means they are eligible to become knights to formally take up that position, and thereby qualify for heavier taxation. They commission a naturalized Italian known as Richard Garner to take command of the royal mint, with a view to "debasing" the money supply in England by making gold and silver coins with a significantly lower precious metal content.

Some of this will prove inspired policy in the long term—not least the appointment of Garner, whose reforms of the currency are the first attempted in sixty years, and long overdue. He will in time succeed in making the English currency more attractive to foreign merchants, while turning the royal mint into a moderately profitable business, which produces coin to a greater value than the gold and silver it melts down to make it.[15]

The immediate results of Henry's efforts at financial reform are, however, hard to discern. By March 1411, when Henry has had a year to prove his worth, the Crown remains in debt and is still running an alarming financial deficit. His brother Thomas continues to complain that he is underfunded in Ireland. There is not enough money to send an army to defend Guyenne, and there is little in the budget for defending Wales, beyond what can be collected in the principality itself. Unpaid annuitants are miserable. Henry's experience of rolling up his sleeves and taking charge of financial administration is a crash course in the unglamorous side of kingship. It is useful, but not always a lot of fun.

What is more, the challenges facing the realm continue to mount. Having had a taste for burning heretics in London, Archbishop Arundel decides that he wishes to root them out of England's most prestigious university, at Oxford. It has long been Arundel's belief that Oxford is a fertile breeding ground for Wycliffite abomination. He is correct, but his heavy-handed attempts to impose proper religious thought and practice on the university lead him into a bitter conflict with the university's chancellor, Richard Courtenay, and the dispute between them must eventually be settled by the king himself.

Elsewhere in England, disorder is physical rather than intellectual. In the Midlands and the southwest of England, gentry-led criminal family gangs terrorize their neighbors: ignoring the rule of law, pursuing violent private vendettas, kidnapping or murdering their enemies, and threatening royal officials with the same fate if they try to intervene. Troublingly—if perhaps understandably—the worst-afflicted areas are in or close to the duchy of Lancaster. Here, families who have long-standing connections with the king in his capacity as duke, or who aided the revolution of 1399, regard themselves as the most immune from the sanctions of his public authority.[16] They believe this because more often than not it is true. It is part of the usurper's curse, and while his father is still the king there is only so much that Henry can do about it.

Then there is trouble at sea. Piracy has been endemic in the Channel for many years. But during 1410 and 1411 the worst offender is a privateer called William Long, who combines a respectable tenure as the mayor of Rye, in Sussex, with a side career of terrorizing, robbing, and hijacking ships belonging to foreign traders. Long's behavior is doubly offensive to Henry: first because he himself is the warden of the Cinque Ports, of which Rye is one; second because the council is trying to negotiate the renewal of a trade treaty with Flanders, whose merchants are unamused by Long's raids.

Despite repeated warnings to desist, in the spring of 1411 Long steals a vast quantity of salt and wine from a fleet of Flemish merchant ships and proceeds to sell his plunder up and down the south coast, to customers including (it is alleged) the bishop of Chichester. Negotiations for the renewed trade deal—which must be signed off by none other than John the Fearless, duke of Burgundy, who is the overlord of Flanders—are very nearly scuppered. To prevent economic meltdown, Henry is forced to pay on his own account 1,000 marks to fund an expedition to apprehend Long, which is led by the chancellor, Thomas Beaufort, who also holds the office of admiral of England.

Navigating the kingdom through the upheavals of 1411 is difficult work, which must be pursued on many fronts with very little respite between crises. Yet as the months pass, it becomes clear that one issue is rising above piracy, heresy, gentry gang warfare, financial insolvency, and currency reform. That issue is England's relationship with France. It is the business that will dominate the rest of Henry's adult life. In 1411, it will lead to the collapse of his first attempt at ruling England.

14

BALLADS AND BRAWLS

Busy as he is becoming in 1410 and into 1411, Henry still finds time to enjoy one of his lifelong pleasures: reading.

Since he was a young boy he has been surrounded by books, from his mother's beautiful devotional works to the Latin primers bought for his schoolroom. As he grows into adulthood, concerning himself with the business of financing wars and chastising pirates, he maintains his love for texts as beautiful objects, deepens his interest in history and romance, and indulges a fondness for reading about the noble pursuits of the hunt.[1]

The bookish bent is a family trait, which goes back to the first duke of Lancaster, Henry Grosmont, and waxes strong in the youngest generation. By their late teens and early twenties Henry and his brothers are known as a brood of story lovers, and despite their youth, poets are beginning to think of them as both patrons and the recipients of good advice. To writers of a moralizing persuasion—which in this age is most of them—the promise of four young princes all with an interest in letters and language is too much to resist.

One of the most famous instances of literature being addressed directly to the young Lancastrian boys is recounted by the sixteenth-century antiquary John Stow. The tale is undated, but there are good reasons to place its events in around 1410 or 1411. Stow tells a story in which Henry and his three brothers are sitting together one evening at the London house of a Welsh-born wine merchant and aspiring politician called Lewis John, who is a business associate of Thomas Chaucer, the reliable Lancastrian parliamentary speaker.[2]

As the fine wines flow, one of Chaucer's and John's friends stands up to speak. Henry Scogan is a middle-aged gentleman poet from Norfolk, old enough to have once exchanged verse with Thomas's late father, Geoffrey Chaucer.* He addresses the four princes as "my noble sons and eke [also] my lords dear," before presenting to them a ballad, "written with my own hand full rudely."[3]

These verses will in time be remembered as Scogan's "Moral Ballad." At first, Scogan seems to be dispensing the timeless advice of the rueful older man addressing the bright-eyed youngster. "Sudden age" has fallen upon him, Scogan sighs, and as it does, he remembers his misspent "*juveneté*, the which is impossible again to call."[4] He laments having cherished vices over virtues for too long, then asks God to forget the ignorance of his youth and grant him perseverance to do holy works.

Then, however, Scogan slips neatly from confessing his own wrongs to explaining why he is addressing this complaint to the younger men, "all whom I love entirely." He wishes, he says, "for to warn you, as I can . . . that time lost in youthful folly, grieves a man ghostly and bodily."

Until this point Scogan's words have seemed to be a conventional imprecation to lordly virtue. But as his ballad develops, line by line, his words adopt the tone of a ticking-off, earned by young men who need to hear some stern advice from a trusted friend. "Lordship nor estate," says Scogan, "without virtue may not long endure . . . virtuous noblesse comes not to you by way of ancestry, but . . . through lawful business of honest life, and not by sluggardry."

Take heed, he says, "how men of poor degree through virtue have

---

* But not, as is sometimes claimed, the tutor of the four princes.

[been] set in great honor . . . Think also, how many a governor called to estate, has often been set full low through misusing of right, and for error." He quotes verses by Geoffrey Chaucer, in a poem known as "Gentilesse." He parses Chaucer for the younger men. See, Scogan tells them, "how virtuous noblesse, rooted in youth, with good perseverance, drives away all vice and wretchedness, [as well as] sluggardry, riot and distance."[5]

Are these platitudes? Perhaps. But two of Henry's brothers in particular may need to hear them. On midsummer's night in 1410, Thomas and John are embroiled in a brawl (described by a different writer as a "hurling") in London's nearby Eastcheap ward.[6] Out drinking way past midnight, they and their friends get into a row with another group of men. The fight escalates, lasting for an hour, and is only broken up when the mayor and city sheriffs are summoned. The king himself is called upon to admonish the boys for causing such mayhem though (maybe unsurprisingly since Thomas was involved) he lets them off.[7]

John Stow does not give a date to Scogan's "Moral Ballad," but it is possible—perhaps even likely—that it is written in 1410 or 1411 and, while addressed to all four of the princes, is intended particularly for Thomas and John. It may even be—though there is no evidence for this beyond speculation—that Prince Henry lies behind its composition. Scogan's advice on virtue, seemly behavior, and reflection on the heavy responsibilities they will all grow up to bear seems only barely applicable to Henry: the prince who long ago at Shrewsbury had good cause to consider the seriousness of his calling, and who has lately ordered the burning of a heretic, taken command of the royal council, and become deeply immersed in the intricacies of government and finance.

Much, much later, when the great drama of Henry's life is written up by William Shakespeare, "Hal" will be portrayed as a riotous youth, a drunkard, and an idler who fails to grow up until it is nearly too late. But in 1410–11 there is vanishingly little sign of any such high living in him. While his brothers brawl in the streets, Henry is wrestling with affairs of state. Scogan's "Moral Ballad" contains advice that Henry is already putting into practice. It is Thomas and John who need to hear it more than he does. And he who needs them to pay attention. Henry needs to know that his brothers will one day be behind him as he leads England along its difficult path.

Whoever's hand lies on Scogan's shoulder as he composes his "Moral Ballad," it is certain that this is not the only reading material Henry has to stimulate him in this time. He seeks out works that will serve as practical handbooks for politics and warcraft, as well as providing entertainment for its own sake. He is beginning to take a deep interest in the history of conflict—and is fascinated with the Trojan War. He is especially enthusiastic about works written in English, which has been flourishing as a language of romance, poetry, and intellectual treatises since the last decades of the fourteenth century. In the books he reads, receives, and commissions lie clues about the man he is becoming, and the ruler he hopes one day to be.

At some point in the decade after 1403 Henry acquires a stunning manuscript copy of Geoffrey Chaucer's English adaptation of *Troilus and Criseyde*. It is a gorgeous, lavishly decorated manuscript: the kind of which Mary de Bohun would have been proud. On the first leaf of parchment, little meadow flowers weave in and out of the neat lines of verse. Troilus and Criseyde (Cressida) stand facing each other inside the great curve of the letter *T* that begins the opening line, dressed in the latest fifteenth-century English styles. At the foot of the page is neatly inked Henry's personal heraldry: the king's quartered arms of England and France, overlaid with a three-pronged bar (known as a "label").

The poem that follows is perhaps Chaucer's best work. In just over eight thousand lines, adapted from an earlier version composed by the great Florentine poet Giovanni Boccaccio, the poet recounts the doomed love affair of the title characters, a passion that is created and then shattered by the pitiless events of a seemingly endless war.

Troilus is, like Henry, the vigorous son of a king—in this case Priam, king of Troy. During the Trojan War, the ten-year struggle that is believed to have occupied the ancient Greek world in the twelfth century BCE, he falls in love with Criseyde, with whom he strikes up an exchange of letters. Shortly after consummating their relationship, Criseyde is sent out of Troy to the Greek camp to join her father, who has defected to the enemy. Troilus is disheartened, but Criseyde promises to trick her father and come back to Troy. Unfortunately, once out of the city she changes her mind, has her head turned by a Greek named Diomede, and lets her correspondence with Troilus tail off until he realizes their affair is over.*

Chaucer's matter in *Troilus* is most obviously the tragedy of romance: the poet announces at the very beginning that he will show what "pain and woe Love's folk endure."[8] But there are any number of such stories in the world on doomed love. Commissioning an illuminated manuscript such as the one made for Henry is expensive. It requires hundreds of hours of scribal work. Ordering one is a decision that must be carefully thought through. So it may be that this particular account of love gone wrong is more than just a ripping yarn by a late family friend. *Troilus* also speaks to themes that Henry feels he has experienced in his life so far.

The setting of Troy is likely meaningful, for Henry has felt the grind of siegecraft for real, even if firing cannons at Aberystwyth lacked the dreadful glamour of a thousand Greek ships setting sail for Troy. But more than this, Henry has seen—and felt—enough to light up when he reads Chaucer's lines reflecting on the circularity of fate. Summing up his story, Chaucer laments the variability of Fortune, drawing on ideas he has picked up from the sixth-century philosopher Boethius. Henry can think here of all the times he has known Fortune's wheel to turn. He has seen his father lose his inheritance, win it back and take a crown, then be laid low, ravaged by disease. He has lived through Owain Glyndŵr's rise from obscurity to preeminence, and then seen the process happen in reverse. He knew King Richard at his mightiest, then saw his starved, dead face when that monarch was drawn through London's streets in his open coffin.

So Henry knows well what Chaucer means when he writes: "Forth her course Fortune [is going] to hold . . . In each estate [there] is little heart's rest. God [grant] us for to take it for the best!"[9]

---

* An early form of the modern method of escaping romantic obligation known as "ghosting."

There is much to admire in Chaucer's telling of *Troilus*. But it is not enough for Henry, whose interests in the Trojan War extend beyond the love lives of its heroes. The history of the war at large is beginning to grip him, and he begins to contemplate a project that will go much further than Chaucer did in *Troilus and Criseyde*. There is no satisfactory account in English of the war available to inspire those of his countrymen who cannot or will not read in Latin or French. So, in or around 1411, Henry makes up his mind to find a writer who can take on the task of writing one. It will be a project that demands astonishing stamina, patience, and dedication, but which will stir the warrior instincts of all Englishmen who share his desire to perform soldierly deeds and avoid the sins of sloth and idleness.[10]

In the meantime, there is plenty more to read. Henry's cousin Edward, duke of York, has been working on an English translation and adaptation of the *Livre de la Chasse*—a treatise on hunting originally written in French by the eccentric fourteenth-century count of Foix known as Gaston Phoebus. York's edition, known in English as *The Master of Game*, contains advice on trapping hare and hart, wild boar and wolf. It expands on the relative merits of mastiffs, spaniels, and greyhounds and provides practical instructions for kenneling them.[11]

The Master of Game is dedicated personally to Henry, "by the grace of God eldest son and heir unto the high excellent and Christian Prince Henry IV," and in the prologue York appeals to what he discerns as Henry's upright nature. "Hunting causeth a man to eschew the seven deadly sins," he writes. He expounds at length on hunting as a cure for sloth and idleness, an activity that offers a man the opportunity to wear himself out in the fresh air, enjoying nature's beauty and bounty before going home to bed to "sleep well and steadfastly all the night without any evil thoughts of any sins, wherefore I say that hunters go into Paradise when they die, and live in this world more joyfully than any other men."[12] Hunting, writes York, can even cure disease, for "men know well that the best way to terminate sickness that can be is to sweat. And when the hunters do their office on horseback or on foot they sweat often, then if they have any evil in them, it must [come] away in the sweating."

The laborious prose notwithstanding, the whole prologue of the book reads as though it is a rehearsal of conversations the two men have had at some point in their past—perhaps when York was one of Henry's companions during the campaigns against Owain Glyndŵr the previous decade. It seems that the duke is preaching to a convert, not admonishing his younger cousin Henry to amend his ways, as Scogan affected to do in his "Moral Ballad," but rather reflecting back to Henry thoughts that have already occurred to him, and that please him to see repeated by others in his extended circle.

Finally, there are books that deal not with the bloody business of the chase, but with the business on which Henry spends his working hours: politics and warfare. While he was still in Wales, an Oxford academic named Richard Ullerston composed a formal letter to him in Latin, concerning the high duties of leadership. *De Officio Militari* presents leadership conventionally: a prince ought to fight to protect his realm, the Church, and his faithful people; he ought to make laws and provide justice; he must be wise and he must be a credible leader.[13]

This is good advice, succinctly expressed. But Henry also receives a much fuller guidebook to governance, written in English verse by a civil servant from the office of the privy seal called Thomas Hoccleve. Known as *The Regiment of Princes*, Hoccleve's poem mines several sources to offer a handbook for good kingship. He offers Henry advice drawn from a letter supposedly written by Aristotle to Alexander the Great. He decorates this with anecdotes he has borrowed from a well-known text known as the *Chessbook*, a popular tract by a thirteenth-century Italian moralist, which uses the game of chess as a vehicle for moral sermons. But most of all, he translates and adapts an older "regiment of princes" by the Italian scholar Giles of Rome, who combined a career in the Church with an academic post at the University of Paris and a post as tutor to the eldest son and heir of the king of France: the future Philip IV (Philip the Fair).

Like every other writer who addresses Henry at this point in his life,

Hoccleve is explicit about his purpose in trying to help Henry prepare for the job of kingship, which will—he tactfully assumes—be coming his way before too long. In anticipation of "royal dignity," Hoccleve writes, Henry must beseech God to grant that he has developed the discipline and experience that will prove "profit to us" and beneficial to Henry's own reputation.[14] He must have "dread and awe" for God's punishment, "do right to great and small, and keep [the] law." He must be true to his word, pay his debts, dispense justice, avoid fornication, pursue wisdom, and be mindful of life's fleeting nature.

"This world's joy is transitory," writes Hoccleve, in support of his last point.[15] Like Chaucer in *Troilus and Criseyde*, he leans into the image of Fortune's wheel. Hoccleve warns his reader—Henry, in this instance—to beware the turn of the wheel and "the storm of descending." For when a man stands most steadfast, Hoccleve writes, "then is he next to his overthrowing." So fleeting is Fortune, the poet remarks, and so variant, that "after glad look, she shapeth her to sting."[16]

In one sense, this advice, and the metaphor of the wheel turning is so commonplace as to be banal. Yet in another it is extremely prescient, and not just because it touches on experiences Henry has had in the past. For in these years, as Henry absorbs the barrage of good advice being addressed to him from the pens of men like Chaucer, Scogan, and Hoccleve, he is closer to a turn of Fortune's wheel than he knows.

He has been in position as head of his father's council for nearly two years. He has expanded his realm of interests beyond defense of the seas, funding wars, and reforming the coinage to taking forward action in the lurching affairs of France, where Burgundian and Armagnac factions remain at each other's throats. He is beginning to feel so confident in his role, indeed, that he and others on the council are thinking of proposing abdication to the continually enfeebled king, so that Henry can take over the government of the realm in his own right.

Yet just as it seems that Henry—well-read and now unusually experienced in the business of government—is at the peak of his powers, the wheel turns and his own "storm of descending" breaks.

The late autumn of 1411 marks the onset of a period of crisis worse than anything Henry has experienced since Shrewsbury in 1403: a journey into the political wilderness from which it appears he may never emerge. It will be as low as his political stock ever sinks: a time when he will learn through bitter experience what Geoffrey Chaucer put nimbly into words in *Troilus and Criseyde*:

"At the last," Chaucer wrote, "every thing hath end."[17]

15

"THE STORM OF DESCENDING"

In the black of night, shortly after midnight on November 9, 1411, Henry's allies Thomas FitzAlan, earl of Arundel, Richard Beauchamp, earl of Warwick, and John Oldcastle, Lord Cobham, steal out of a southern gate of Paris. It is freezing cold and they have a long march ahead of them. But they, and the hundreds of English and Welsh archers who are at their backs, know the risk and discomfort are well worth accepting.

Since the murder of Louis, duke of Orléans, France has been spiraling toward civil war. These men have crossed the Channel to join the fray. They have all been lodged in the French capital for more than a fortnight: the ordinary troops billeted with citizens, the earls dining from time to time with the demented king Charles VI. They have joined armed bands making sorties out of the city every few days, terrorizing the people of the surrounding countryside and trying to drive off enemy units blockading the French capital.

Now a decisive moment has arrived. Arundel, Warwick, Oldcastle, and their allies are going to march through the cold night along the southern (or "left") bank of the river Seine until they come to a town called Saint-Cloud, where their enemies have built a makeshift wooden bridge and fortified camp around a stone tower.

When they arrive, they will use fireboats to destroy the bridge. They will bombard and storm the town. They will capture or kill as many of the defenders as they can. Then they will press on northward to farther enemy camps beyond—at Montmartre and the royal suburb of Saint-Denis. Their ultimate goal is to chase them away from all the approaches to Paris and secure the capital for the winter.

It is a bold plan. It is designed to use the element of surprise to cause maximum panic and confusion among the other side. Its success will then rely on speed of movement and brutal, bloodthirsty execution.

The plan bears all the hallmarks of its chief architect. This is the man who is the earls' leading ally in the French capital, and perhaps the person most at blame for the parlous state in which the realm finds itself.

He is John the Fearless, duke of Burgundy.

Arundel, Warwick, Oldcastle, and others of Henry's trusted lieutenants have been in France since early September, when they sailed to Calais with nearly two thousand men-at-arms and archers. This is the biggest invading army to have left England for France for thirty years.[1] But the lords departed amid some controversy, and the first signs of a significant political falling-out between Prince Henry and the king.[2]

The decision to send English troops to intervene in French affairs is not itself outrageous. Indeed, there is virtually no one in England who believes that strife between the Burgundians and Armagnacs represents anything other than a golden opportunity to wrangle from the French concessions on long-standing military and diplomatic issues. Played properly, the Burgundian-Armagnac conflict could be a way to get the French to refrain from attacking Guyenne and retreat to the borders of that southwestern territory that were agreed on with Edward III in the landmark Treaty of Brétigny in 1360. It could be the key to guaranteeing the security of Calais, forcing the French to punish piracy, and extracting a stable trade agreement made with Burgundian-controlled Flanders.

All are agreed, moreover, that military intervention is the right way to proceed, preferably on the side of the duke of Burgundy, given the importance of Flemish trade to the English economy. This is not just the preferred policy of young, ambitious men like Arundel, Warwick, and Prince Henry. Throughout the summer of 1411, the king himself has been planning to defy his ill health and lead an army to France in person, to plunge into the war on the side of the Burgundians. He has approved negotiations for a marriage between Henry and John the Fearless's eldest unmarried daughter, Anne.

Yet virtually on the eve of the campaign's departure—as ships were being loaded with pavilions and weapons, and knights were on their way to their summons point in London—Henry IV suffered both a relapse of his health problems and a major pang of guilt. John the Fearless is a self-confessed, cold-blooded murderer. He is the killer of Louis, duke of Orléans, who showed Henry IV great kindness during his exile in 1398–99 (even if he made a good deal of trouble for him thereafter). When King Henry is in particularly poor health, he likes to torture himself by stewing on his own wretched catalog of sins: usurpation and regicide high among them. The idea of adding to this list suddenly appalled him and he announced that the expedition was canceled.

By that time, however, preparations had been made. And it seemed to many around the king that it would be somewhere between wasteful and outright foolish to abandon them altogether.

Prince Henry was one such person. So he ignored his father's sudden reticence and ordered his men to go to Calais anyway, meet up with John the Fearless, and see what developed. Henry agreed to pay the initial costs of the campaign out of his own income.[3]

He openly defied his father's wishes. He did so because he believed that backing John the Fearless against the Armagnacs was the right policy.

He also did so because he has reached a point in his political career where he thinks that he knows best.

Shortly before dawn on November 9, Arundel, Warwick, Oldcastle, and their Burgundian allies draw up in view of the Armagnac encampment at Saint-Cloud. They have been marching all night, and now a fierce fight lies ahead of them.

Their plans have been changing on the move. John the Fearless's idea of sending in fireboats has failed: blazing boats filled with pitch and resin sent downriver have been easily put out by the defenders of the wooden bridge.[4] Nevertheless, there are only around fifteen hundred Armagnac troops defending the tower, town, and bridge. The Burgundians and English have lost the element of surprise, but they still outnumber the defenders two or three times over. So long as they keep their heads and seize the position before Armagnac reinforcements arrive from farther north, the day should be theirs.

When the thin autumn dawn breaks, the fighting begins. It is vicious from the start. The town's makeshift defenses—carts turned on their sides, wooden fences, and stone-filled barrels—present no serious obstacle. Charging behind a barrage of stone shot from catapults, the Burgundians and English batter their way through the fences and pour into the town, engaging the Armagnac troops at close quarter, seizing houses and using their upper stories as sniper positions to take out troops posted around the bridgehead on the riverbank.

Some of the defenders panic and shut themselves in the stone tower that is the only properly fortified defense. Others barricade themselves inside a church. Neither of these can hold off the invaders for long. Arundel leads the assault on the church, and though he takes large casualties, he eventually breaks in. This is a small mercy to the Armagnacs packed inside the church. The English are inclined to take prisoners for ransom. The Burgundians in the streets are driven by bloodlust.

By noon, the streets of Saint-Cloud are strewn with butchered men. A part of the timber bridge has collapsed under the weight of terrified troops trying to flee. Saint-Cloud has fallen, and as news spreads, it shifts the momentum of the civil war sharply toward John the Fearless and the

Burgundians. The Armagnacs abandon their positions around Paris and retreat.

In the days that follow, it becomes clear that John the Fearless is in full control of the mad king Charles, and has his sights set on destroying the Armagnacs for good in the new year. The English have helped him do it.

The earl of Arundel and the others stay for a while in Paris to enjoy the triumphant atmosphere, apply the city's finest medical ointment to their wounds, and reap their rewards.[5] There is some unseemly tussling over prisoners, whom the English wish to protect and sell for ransom. The Burgundians, however, "enjoy putting their traitors to death," and they prevail. Once they are finished maiming and slaughtering their captives and parading hunks of their flesh around the city, John the Fearless sends the English back across the Channel well rewarded for their contribution to his cause. "Our men had the victory, and came home again with great gifts," writes one chronicler.[6]

But by the time they reach England, they find that everything has been thrown into turmoil.

Henry's decision to overrule his father and send troops to help John the Fearless against the Armagnacs is the culmination of several months of rising tension between father and son. There is one deep-seated issue: Henry is beginning to look too much like a king for the real king's liking. But there have been several specific flashpoints.

The first of these concerns Archbishop Arundel, whose campaign to stamp out Lollard heresy has led him into a bitter dispute with Oxford University. Since July 1411 Arundel has been trying to carry out a formal inspection—or visitation—of the university, to see that heretical doctrine is not being taught. The university, keen to maintain intellectual decorum but jealous of its independence, has literally barred its doors against him.

In September, the chancellor, Richard Courtenay—who is one of Henry's old comrades from the Welsh wars—appeals to Henry directly to rein in Arundel. Henry tries to stand up for his friend. But his father takes the opposite side of the debate, and applies for a ruling from Rome confirming the university is indeed subject to the supervision of Canterbury.

Things have not improved from here. In October, six knights from Henry's household, including his steward, Roger Leche, are arrested and imprisoned in the Tower of London, apparently for their part in a long-running feud with retainers of Henry's brother Thomas. Henry is in no position to interfere on his men's behalf—not least since Thomas's men are arrested, too. But it is embarrassing nonetheless—and it highlights an increasing estrangement of Henry and his brother.

The tension between the brothers has not been helped by Thomas's latest scheme: to marry thirty-two-year-old Margaret Holland, the vastly wealthy widow of John Beaufort, late captain of Calais. Thomas has the king's backing for this lucrative union, and indeed the pope's—whose approval is needed, since Margaret is effectively Thomas's aunt. But the two surviving Beaufort brothers—Henry's closest allies on the council—have been trying to block it.

Matters come to a head in early November. While Arundel, Warwick, and Oldcastle are preparing to march on Saint-Cloud, a parliament opens in the Painted Chamber at Westminster Palace. But on the day it opens, the king immediately gives orders to postpone (or "prorogue") it, saying he cannot attend. He does not give a reason, allowing members to assume—if they like—that he is his usual sickly self.

Later, however, a different story will emerge. In fact, it is alleged, Prince Henry and his ally Bishop Henry Beaufort have been lobbying the other lords "as to which of them would ask the king if he was prepared to resign the crown of England [on grounds of illness] and allow his first-born son to be crowned."[7] Their concern seems to be that the king is not simply incapable of exercising power but that he is now dangerously obstructive to the good governance of his own realm.

Henry and Bishop Beaufort may well have honorable intentions and the best interests of England at heart. But they have badly misjudged the king. Henry IV knows better than anyone else alive that honorable intentions lay behind the revolution of 1399, when he asked his cousin Richard to "resign the crown." He may even think further back in English history to the revolution of 1327–28, when his ancestor Edward II was successfully persuaded to abdicate the throne in favor of his own eldest son, Edward III.

No amount of nice language can disguise these two resignations of royal power as principled transfers of power for the public good—not least because both kings were murdered shortly after giving up their crowns. Henry and Bishop Beaufort are in effect planning another coup—and this time it amounts to far more than simply restaffing the royal council.

Whether they take their proposal to the king or he summons the two men to him is not clear. But either way, it seems there is a showdown. Hot words are exchanged, the hottest of them coming from Henry himself. He tells his father it is plain that he can "no longer apply himself to the honor and profit of the realm."[8]

Thus the challenge is laid.

Yet it is a challenge without an ultimatum. And when Parliament reopens, it is clear that this king has no intention of doing as his eldest son wishes. Far from giving up his crown, he drags himself from his sickbed to make a brave demonstration of his own abilities.

By the end of the month, Prince Henry will have been removed completely from power.

Henry IV's return to the heart of his own government is not achieved with a single clean strike. But it is patient, methodical, and complete.

After his showdown with Henry and Bishop Beaufort, he allows Parliament to begin its business, but he makes it clear from the very start that he is in charge. When the commons elect Thomas Chaucer as speaker for the third time, Henry IV informs him sharply that he does not "under any circumstances wish to have any kind of novelty in this parliament."[9]

Two weeks into the parliament, he summons Richard Courtenay, chancellor of Oxford University, to meet him at Lambeth Palace, the London headquarters of Archbishop Arundel. There the king informs Courtenay that Arundel has every right to visit Oxford and inspect it for Lollard heresies, and unceremoniously sacks him as chancellor.

Then, on the last day of November, the king summons Henry and the rest of his councilors to the parliament and formally thanks them for their hard work over the last eighteen months. It is officially noted on the parliamentary record that they have "fulfilled their duty well and loyally in accordance with their oath taken."

There are no harsh or recriminatory words spoken. It is all passive aggression, but it is clear what is meant. The councilors' duty is done, and their services are no longer needed.

Henry tries to stall his father, telling the parliament that he and his colleagues have "done their duty with diligence and industry . . . to the best of their wisdom and knowledge." But the king only agrees, and then adds a patronizing barb: he is sure that if more money had been available to spend, then Henry and his councilors "would have been able to do their duty better in many ways than it had been done."[10]

Then the matter is closed. There is no grand gesture, no immediate sweeping of the boards, and no appointment of a new council. But on Saturday, December 19, when the parliament is brought to a close, the rules laid down in the 1410 parliament, obliging the king to follow the advice of his council, are scrapped. That weekend the king sacks virtually every member of his council, including Henry and the two Beauforts. He reappoints Archbishop Arundel as chancellor and installs one of the knights of his royal chamber as treasurer.

In the new year, the king and his new advisers begin a wholesale overhaul of royal policy. The most jarring change in direction they make is in foreign policy. Having formerly been committed to the Burgundians, Henry IV now strikes up diplomatic relations with the Armagnacs, who in their desperation are prepared to offer him almost anything they can think of: formal recognition of the Lancastrian kingship, which has thus far been avoided, and the restoration of Guyenne back to the borders laid down in 1360, with a few other choice estates thrown in as a token of goodwill.[11] Accepting these terms with delight, the king and his new council abandon the alliance with John the Fearless, sign a deal with the Armagnacs, known as the Treaty of Bourges, and prepare to send another army to France, this time to engage in the civil war on the opposite side.

This causes "many to marvel at the unexpectedness of the king's change of mind," writes one chronicler, adding that "in a very short space of time the English, as it were, were holding in their hands two opposites."[12] Prince Henry writes to the duke of Burgundy to express his acute embarrassment. But his father does not care whether he upsets John the Fearless or anyone else. Switching direction is, indeed, part of the point he aims to make.

Sending a new expeditionary force across the Channel will require money and another round of elaborate military preparations: thousands of pounds must be borrowed or raised for wages, ships chartered to carry ten thousand horses—and so on.[13]

It will also require leadership. The king is back in control and still harbors a delusion that he might one day regain enough strength to command an army in France himself. But that dream cannot survive very much exposure to reality. He can barely stand up, let alone mount a horse. So by the summer of 1412, he has accepted that he will have to send someone else in his place.

Unsurprisingly, the earls of Arundel and Warwick are not asked to reprise their roles of the previous winter. Instead, the king turns to his son to take his place at the head of a grand mission in which four thousand troops will be shipped to Normandy, marched south to join the Armagnac princes fighting John the Fearless in the Loire valley, then moved on to take possession of fortresses promised them by the Armagnacs in what will now once more be English-held Guyenne.

It is a serious military undertaking, and if the king cannot go it requires the prestige of a prince of the royal blood at its head. Unfortunately for Henry, the prince his father chooses to lead the army in the summer of 1412 is not him. It is his younger brother Thomas.

16

"SONS OF INIQUITY"

To prepare Thomas for his exciting new mission to assist the Armagnacs, Henry's brother is showered with offices, titles, and favors. It would be an exaggeration to say that Thomas has never experienced such largesse before—his stipend for representing the king in Ireland has been handsome. But in the first half of 1412 he is elevated to full princely rank, with the promise of riches as befit the status.

In the first instance, Thomas's marriage to his uncle's widow, Margaret Holland, which has been long resisted by her Beaufort brothers-in-law, is finally cleared; the ceremony takes place in May.[1] A few weeks later Thomas attends his father in a ceremony at Rotherhithe, where he is raised to the peerage as earl of Albemarle and duke of Clarence. He becomes the royal lieutenant in Guyenne,* where his military expedition is bound, and he is promised rich bounty if he performs his duties on

---

* A particular slight since Henry has been, since the beginning of their father's reign, duke of Aquitaine.

campaign there with distinction. A third of all plunder taken by the army on campaign will be his, as will the ransoms of the most valuable prisoners.

For a young man who has seemed a little bereft of purpose and at times outright allergic to his role in Ireland, this is a rapid elevation. Worse for Henry, it occurs at just the moment that their father seems finally to be succumbing to his long sickness: he is wizened and shrunken, barely able to stand, and he spends weeks on end at the shrine of Thomas Becket in Canterbury, either praying for life or preparing for death. The moment for a formal transfer of power is coming ever closer. Yet as a fleet of ships is assembled in Southampton, flags of St. George fluttering above them, ready to take Thomas to France, there is little doubt that the twenty-four-year-old is now the golden child of the Lancastrian family.

In the months that lead up to Thomas's departure, Henry lives under a double shadow—in part that of his ascendant younger brother and in part that of his own disaffection at having to live with the consequences of his mistakes. He feels sorry for himself. He has mistimed his charge at the throne, and as a result he has tumbled at alarming speed from his privileged position. Worst of all, it is his own fault. He overreached and has now been brought heavily down to earth.

No doubt it has been very frustrating to serve as an almost-king. His father's regular, unconsummated flirtation with death, which has put Henry so many times within a heartbeat of the crown, has tested the limits of his patience. It is barely a year since Thomas Hoccleve was flattering him as a new Alexander, and urging him to prepare for the moment that the crown will "honor you with royal dignity."[2] Now he is a political outcast.

As Thomas is catapulted forward in his father's estimation, just at the moment when this matters most, Henry grows sour and frantic. And in the summer of 1412, as Thomas prepares to sail for France, where he has a chance to prove himself the natural successor to the dying Lancastrian patriarch, Henry's instinct for political theatrics, combined with his first real taste of aimlessness, brings him as close as he will ever come to ruin.

The first sign of trouble following Henry's dismissal from the royal council comes at the end of May 1412, when he writes to John the Fearless, explaining the recent volte-face in English policy. Although in his letter Henry steers carefully away from outright criticism of his father, he lavishes praise on John the Fearless's upright diplomatic conduct, conducted "in the spirit of friendship." He reminds the duke, somewhat gratuitously, of the upright way in which both of them have gone about their business so far. He implies that John the Fearless has done nothing to deserve the betrayal but explains that the Armagnacs have made an offer too good for his father to turn down, and that it is in "the public good of the kingdom" to accept.

This is, on the surface of it, obedient and polished diplomacy. But there is no doubt from Henry's tone where his heart lies, and it is not with the Armagnacs. It is with the "noble and illustrious" John the Fearless to whom he writes.[3]

The duke of Burgundy will not have to read very carefully between the lines to realize that Henry is in poor humor. But in fact, it is worse than that. For what Henry does *not* mention is that around this time there is an apparent attempt on his life.

One night as he is sleeping in a room known as the Green Chamber at the Palace of Westminster, Henry and his attendants are woken by the yapping of one of their pet spaniels. They light the room and search it, to discover that the dog has been barking at an intruder, who is hiding behind a wall hanging, or "tapet."

The shock of the intrusion must be serious. Henry may indeed be reminded of the suspicions of Richard II, whose Cheshire archer bodyguard used to reassure him that they would keep him safe while he slept. Perhaps Richard was not as paranoid as was once thought.

In any case, the spaniel saves Henry. The intruder is marched out of the Green Chamber and taken to Henry's friend the earl of Arundel for interrogation. Under questioning, the man gives a bizarre story: he claims he has been hired by none other than Bishop Henry Beaufort, who has sent him to sneak into the Green Chamber "with orders to kill the prince there in his bed."[4]

Arundel gives no credence to this story, for it makes no sense: Henry has had few closer political allies in recent years than his uncle Henry Beaufort, and the two of them have been as one on every important issue, right up to the attempt to oust Henry IV from the throne. Marking the intruder down as a lone wolf, the earl has him tied in a sack and thrown in the river Thames to drown.

No further action is taken. But the incident, which will still be a political talking point nearly fifteen years later, can only add to Henry's unsettled state of mind.

Henry's grievances at his exile and his brother's emergence into the sunshine of their father's favor finally erupt in mid-June 1412, when Thomas marries Margaret Holland and it becomes public knowledge that the young duke of Clarence will also be leading the expedition to France to aid the Armagnacs: a campaign in which Henry will play no part.

This is a moment of high humiliation for Henry: a time when his demotion is plain to the whole realm. He decides that he needs to act to halt what seems to be a total freefall. On June 17 he is in his estates in the Midlands, near Coventry, when he issues an open letter, addressed not to his father but to the whole kingdom.

"Dear and sincerely beloved," he begins, "I am sure you are well aware of the widely publicized news that the serene highness, my most feared father, Henry, famous king of England and of France, has recently decided to go on a journey to lands overseas."[5]

This is an uncontroversial beginning, but from it Henry goes on to stitch together an extraordinary sequence of half-truths, exaggerations, distortions, accusations, and outright lies. When the invasion was first planned, Henry claims, his father asked him to serve, and "assigned me a fixed number of troops." (This is not true, but provides a basis for Henry's next claim, which amounts to that of military incompetence in his father's high command.) The number of men he was assigned, Henry states, was "so feeble a force that I was likely to be cut off from any chance of honorable service to my most feared father and lord or of making proper provision for the safety of my own person."[6]

Henry claims that he pointed this fact out to his father, who gave him permission to go to Coventry and raise a larger force "to further the general good of this kingdom, which is my fervent wish and desire above all else." However, he says, as he has been doing this, people around the king have started to whisper that he is planning an armed uprising: "that I was affected with a bloody desire for the crown of England, that I was planning an unbelievably horrible crime and would rise up against my own father at the head of a popular outbreak of violence, and that in this way I would seize his scepter and other royal insignia on the grounds that my father and liege lord was living a life to which he had no proper title and which relied on tyrannical persuasion."

Even without the narrative chicanery on which it is based, this is a grave accusation. Henry does not name the whisperers, but he does launch into an astonishing tirade against them: they are "sons of iniquity, nurselings of dissent, schism fomenters, sowers of anger and agents of discord . . . villains until the end of their days." Their aim is to strike at his innocence, and their desire is "with a serpentine cunning to upset the ordered succession to [the] throne."

Here, in the open, is Henry's deepest fear laid bare. Despite his "love, loyalty and obedience" for and toward his father, he hints that Thomas's appointment to lead the army in France is the prelude to his adoption as heir to the throne. Cut off for the first time in his adult life from privileged access to the king, Henry now suspects everyone around him of plotting against him. Exactly who the "sons of iniquity" might be is left to Henry's readers' imaginations, but it is not hard to guess whom he might mean: Archbishop Arundel and the rest of the new council, his father's household, and, very possibly, Thomas himself. There is a struggle afoot, Henry suggests, not only for the favor of "my most feared father and lord" but also for "the faithful hearts of the people, whose support I hoped was a sure source of strength."

Henry's anger at his sudden fall from grace has sparked his instinct for populist theatrics and diversion tactics, of the sort he has demonstrated more than once in the past: after the first failure of the siege of Aberystwyth and during the burning of John Badby.

Now he prepares for his riskiest performance to date. Within days of issuing his open letter, Henry and "a large crowd of friends and a retinue of servants bigger than any that had been seen before" leave Coventry and make their way south to seek an audience with the king.[7]

Henry's argument, hotly made in his open letter, is that he has been gathering men around him for the good of the realm, and that anyone who claims he is doing anything more than that is a liar, a snake, and a schismatic. But he is playing a very dangerous game. Gambling perhaps that his father is too weak, his brother too callow, and the rest of the political nation too nervous of the consequences to resist him, on June 29 Henry sweeps into London.

He comes, he says, to see that those who have slandered him should be brought to justice. He takes up residence in the house of Thomas Langley, bishop of Durham, a political neutral trusted both by his father and by him. Then he waits to be called to see the king.

Around July 3, 1412, Henry is summoned from Langley's mansion to an audience with his father at Westminster Palace. Exactly what each man feels at this moment is impossible to say for certain, but it is surely a moment of the highest personal and political tension. Ever since the prince has arrived in London, rumors have been circulating that he is to be charged with embezzling money intended for the defense of the English garrison at Calais—a claim that infuriates Henry and adds to his sense that dark forces are conspiring to destroy him.

According to an account written more than a century later, but based on the memories of an Irish lord who knew Henry and Thomas well and may have been a witness to the events, Henry arrives at Westminster Palace in the company of his huge retinue—making a wordless but unmistakable statement about the strength of his following, whether or not he is in office or favor. They are admitted to the palace, but Henry instructs his followers to wait in the public area of Westminster Hall while he goes alone to see his father.

When they meet, in a private chamber, attended by only three or four others, the men present contrasting figures. The king is a husk of the man who was once a jousting companion of Boucicaut, a glamorous pilgrim to Jerusalem, and a valiant combatant who defended his family's inheritance and took with it the English crown. Though only forty-five, he is a wasted shell, carried around his palaces on a litter. Henry, meanwhile, is not only the perfect figure of physical strength, but has arrayed himself in a quite striking outfit for the meeting: he wears a gown made from blue satin, decorated all over with little eyelets, from each of which hangs a needle on a silk thread.[8]

The symbolic meaning of this decorative pattern, if there is one, is now obscure, but the dash Henry cuts is unmistakable. And he matches his appearance with his actions, launching into a speech protesting his innocence, his eternal loyalty, and his determination to pursue anyone who has done the king ill. He asks that the king will bring to justice the rumormongers who are slandering him and presents papers he says will exonerate him of charges relating to the misuse of funds meant for Calais. At the height of his tirade, Henry falls to his knees in front of his father and presents him with a dagger. If the king doubts his loyalty for even a second, Henry says, then he should kill him on the spot, for "my life is not so desirous to me that I should live one day that I should be in your displeasure."[9]

Feeble as the king is, he can hardly resist such a performance, and he bursts into tears. The two men hug and the king tells Henry that he trusts him absolutely. So long as he is content to wait for the next parliament, then he will see his enemies disquieted and the rumors against him set aside.

A reconciliation has been reached. Or so it seems as father and son part company. Henry goes back to Bishop Langley's house with his crowd of retainers around him, and remains in London for another week.

Yet as that week goes by, it becomes clear that Henry has been subtly outmaneuvered by his father once more. He has been allowed his moment of flamboyance, felt the wizened old man's tears on his shoulder, and retreated from the meeting in apparent triumph. But now the moment has passed, very little has changed. Thomas is formally invested in his new title of duke of Clarence. His ships for France continue to be fitted out in Southampton harbor. The embezzlement accusations against Henry lead to a formal investigation, which drags on until October. And the parliament at which he has been told to expect exoneration never meets.

Henry leaves London on July 11. He avoids his brother's feting and does not go to Southampton in August to see the expedition to France depart. In mid-September he comes to London once more, again with a vast retinue at his back, and once again visits his father to rail about slanderers. Otherwise he has nothing to do but kick his heels.

If there is any truth in much later anecdotes about Henry's alleged drunkenness, fondness for low company, and involvement in the sorts of unseemly scuffles that his brothers Thomas and John pursued two years earlier, it may date from this time. An account of his life by an author known as the Pseudo-Elmham alludes to his "untamed youth" and makes various winking insinuations about Henry's sexual appetites that are inconsistent with most other descriptions of his character. This may be the one time when Henry, purposeless and disaffected, waiting for an uncertain future to arrive, has time to live out a carefree adolescence he otherwise bypassed.

The autumn of 1412 passes into winter without any clear advance in Henry's fortunes. In France, Thomas cuts a bloody path through the countryside, but is then confounded by the volatility of French factionalism. Almost as soon as he arrives in France the Armagnacs and Burgundians announce that they have come to terms with each other, and would very much like the English to go home. They announce themselves willing to pay the obscene sum of £40,000 to Thomas if he will retire back to England. In fact, Thomas goes to Bordeaux, the capital of Guyenne, and sets about trying to restore English control of the duchy, which he does in bloody fashion, remaining there well into the summer of the next year.

Henry IV, meanwhile, continues his slow but apparently endless decline. He spends Christmas in his palace of Eltham and begins to imagine that he has enough last reserves of strength to survive another pilgrimage to Jerusalem. He even orders oak trees to be felled in the royal forests for the construction of barges to take him.[10] In February 1413 a parliament meets in London, and though its records are lost, it seems the king makes a public appearance to announce that he is going to lead a crusade.

At this point, Henry may be forgiven for wondering if his father will ever die. But in March 1413 he hears that the king has gone to his bed in Westminster and is not expected to rise from it. Of course, Henry has heard this before. The king made his will four full years ago, but the self-described "sinful wretch" has remained on earth ever since.

This time, though, it is different.

On hearing of his father's decline, Henry visits him on now what is surely his deathbed. What passes between them will be preserved in different versions by several writers. Most agree that Henry IV expands on his favorite themes of contrition, repentance, and humility. He tells Henry to "behold thy father, who once was strenuous in arms, but now is adorned only with bones and nerves." He asks him to settle the Crown's debts. He advises him to employ upstanding religious men as his own confessors and to "be not fond of ease, but always engaged either about the things of God, or about the good of the kingdom for the sake of God, or about some of those pleasures and excellent sports, which have in them nothing of the foulness of vice."[11] He laments ever having snatched the throne from Richard. And he warns Henry against squabbling with his brother Thomas, for although they are both of "great stomach and courage," discord between them will spell "destruction and misery" for the realm.[12]

Having delivered this homily, on March 20, 1413, Henry IV crawls from his bed and tries to stagger to the shrine of Edward the Confessor at the heart of Westminster Abbey, which is surrounded by tombs of his Plantagenet ancestors: Henry III, Edward I and Edward III, and the double tomb in which Richard II's first wife, Anne of Bohemia, rests but Richard himself does not.

He never gets there. Collapsing on his way to the chapel, the king is picked up by his attendants and carried to the abbot's house, where he is taken to a warm room and laid in front of the fire. By and by, he regains consciousness, but cannot understand where he is. His servants tell him the room is known as the Jerusalem Chamber and he murmurs his satisfaction.

A Burgundian chronicler named John Wavrin gives the most picturesque version of what happens next, rolling up into a simple tableau all that has passed between father and son for the four years since Henry IV was last on his deathbed. In this version, Henry IV is lying so still and apparently breathless on his bed that his attendants assume he has died and cover his face, "as is the custom of the country."

The chronicler alleges that as soon as Henry is informed by the guards that his father is dead, he comes to the chamber "to seize the crown as heir" and duly takes it.

Yet his father is still not quite gone. He stirs on his gold sheets, then croaks to his servants that his crown is missing.

"Sire, my lord the prince your son has carried it away," comes the reply. So the king has Henry recalled to his bedside, and gives him one more improving lecture. Why, he wonders, did Henry assume the crown is now his? "Have you a right to it?" the dying man asks. "For I never had any."

"My lord, as you have held and guarded it with the sword, so is it my intention to hold, guard, and defend it all my life," replies Henry. This does not quite answer the question, but the king has no more energy to argue.

"Fair son, do now with it as shall seem good to you," he says. And at last, Henry IV asks for God's mercy and dies.[13]

Whether any or none of this account of Henry IV's last moments is true cannot now be tested. But one thing is unarguable. The death of the old king is the starting point for the accession of the new.

And although there has been a measure of uncertainty—in Prince Henry's mind at least—that he is guaranteed the crown, when Henry IV finally dies it is plain there has never been any other serious candidate for kingship.

Since 1399 Henry's life has been a journey toward this moment: the day when he takes the crown, not as a usurper like his father, but as a lawful heir. He was not born to do this job, but he has nonetheless expected to do it for all of his adult years.

His apprenticeship has been longer, more testing, and rounder in its demands than that of any other English king since Edward I inherited the crown in 1272. It has nearly killed him. It has exposed his faults and demanded that he recognize and learn to control them. It has hardened him.

But this long apprenticeship has also allowed Henry the freedom to make mistakes, to try on different political guises, to work out who to trust, and to grow as sure as he can be of how to approach kingship when it belongs to him in full.

In March 1413 Henry ascends to his father's throne better prepared for rule than any king in living memory. He arrives at a moment of extraordinary opportunity. Yet he succeeds with some doubts still remaining about his fitness for office; entrenched financial, religious, and political challenges; and lingering resentment of the Lancastrian dynasty at large.

That combination will make the years that follow some of the most dramatic and memorable in England's entire history.

PART 2

KING

1413–1422

Let us make wars so that we might have peace, for the end of war is peace.

BISHOP HENRY BEAUFORT

17

"A DIFFERENT MAN"

Henry V is crowned on a stage draped in gold cloth, set high in Westminster Abbey, on Sunday, April 9, 1413. Outside freezing rain lashes London, while elsewhere in England blizzards swirl.[1] It is Passion Sunday, two weeks before Easter, and late in the year for such a hard cold snap, let alone sleet and snow.* "Everybody was surprised by the severity of the weather," writes one chronicler.[2] Another writer notes that all over England, snowdrifts bury people, animals, and houses, "creating great danger and much loss of life."[3]

The whiteout strikes many as an omen, although no one can agree on what it means. Some say it shows the new king's reign is going to be austere: that Henry will prove a "man of cold deeds . . . severe in his management of the kingdom." Others, more optimistic, see in the snowfall a sign that Henry will freeze vice and allow the green shoots of virtue to emerge.

---

* But not wildly so. Much later in the fifteenth century the battle of Towton will be fought in a blizzard around the same time of year (March 29, 1461).

("See! Winter is now past, the rains are over and gone," quote the scripturally minded.)[4] Astute observers may realize that these two readings could both be true.

Certainly, the days leading up to Henry's coronation are busy, filled with practical business and great matters of state. Henry gives orders for a general keeping of the peace, and issues injunctions against rioting. He appoints important public officials, reconfirming his brother John as warden of the north and swearing in local judges—justices of the peace—to keep order in the shires. He makes some personal gifts: his stalwart servant Peter Melbourne is granted a pension to support him until the end of his days, as thanks for serving Henry unfailingly "from his youth up."[5]

Henry buries his father near Becket's shrine in Canterbury, as the old king wanted. This is a time-consuming process, requiring a detour away from London and Westminster at a time when Henry is needed there most. But he can do nothing else. For all their differences in the last years of the older man's life, in public Henry has consistently professed respect and love for his "mighty" father. That respect extends to the circumstances of his burial. So at the end of March, once the old king's shriveled corpse has been disemboweled, embalmed, stitched into a suitably regal outfit, then sealed in an elm-wood coffin, Henry and his brothers John and Humphrey accompany it by Thames boat from Westminster to Gravesend. They then follow it overland as it makes its way by carriage to Canterbury Cathedral. Five hundred marks is allotted for the ceremony—not a lavish sum, but enough to deck the funeral cortege out in gold and to provide a mass of blazing candles in the cathedral.[6] A much grander memorial service is planned for the summer. By then, Thomas will have returned from Guyenne.

As well as making funeral arrangements, Henry also takes care to keep up the traditions of coronation. Fourteen years ago, in the days before their father was crowned, Henry and his brothers were knighted with a group of other young men at the Tower of London. And so, on Friday, April 7, 1413, two days before his own coronation, Henry repeats the exercise, raising fifty young men up to knighthood. They experience, as he did, the sacred ritual of bathing, taking instruction on the duties of chivalry, and keeping an all-night vigil before their dubbing with a sword.

When these young men look around at one another, a few faces in the group may cause a surprise. Among the new knights Henry has chosen are Richard, Lord Despenser, seventeen, and John Holland, eighteen, sons of two ringleaders of the Epiphany Rising of 1400—heirs to die-hard Ricardians who once tried to kill Henry and his family. Even more startling is the presence of Edmund Mortimer, twenty-one, and his younger brother, Roger, the lads who have been touted since boyhood as alternative, anti-Lancastrian candidates for the throne: nephews of Owain Glyndŵr's late henchman Sir Edmund Mortimer, whom Henry has kept as his own personal prisoners since 1411.

Considering all that Henry has been through, and how determined these young men's families once were to see him removed from the succession or even killed, this is trusting and magnanimous—even to the point of naivety. But Henry has decided that one of the themes of his reign will be reconciliation.

There is no better time to start than now.

The rituals attending a king's coronation have been seen twice within living memory: in 1377 and 1399. But familiarity makes them no less grand.[7] The day before the ceremony, Saturday, April 8, Henry rides out of the Tower of London, processes through the heart of his capital city, then makes his way along Fleet Street to Westminster, at the head of a parade that includes all his new knights and many more old ones, the great lords of the realm, and a throng of ordinary Londoners.

This is a journey of just under three miles, and along the route there is plenty to stir Henry's memories. The great spire of St. Paul's Cathedral marks the spot where he saw his grandfather John of Gaunt laid to rest. Any drift of smoke from the north may recall the dreadful day John Badby was burned in a barrel at Smithfield. Fleet Street takes him past John Rote's mansion, where he and Thomas saw Richard II entertained by their father on the eve of the Revenge Parliament. Westminster itself holds the courtyard where they saw that grisly assembly first meet.

All these sights, and more, may give Henry pause to consider the eventful life he has lived to this point. But once the rites of coronation begin on Sunday morning there can be little time for reflection. Having spent the night at Westminster Abbey, Henry is bathed and dressed in silks. He is taken on a solemn procession around the abbey church, accompanied by clerics chanting anthems. Then he is led up to the glittering platform that stands between the high altar and the choir, to undergo the rites that will make him a king. He is invested with regalia including a cross, scepter, and rod. He is stripped to his tunic and anointed with holy oil—likely the same oil as was used in his father's coronation, originally presented to Thomas Becket by the Virgin Mary.[8] He is re-dressed in royal vestments, priestly in character, and ministered with the sacrament of Christ's body and blood.

Archbishop Arundel, who by ancient right conducts the ceremony, leads Henry to the shrine of Edward the Confessor, where he places one crown on his head, and shortly afterward, another. Arundel also guides him through the swearing of the king's oaths, by which Henry promises to uphold the laws and customs of the realm, to protect the Church, and to see that justice is done. There is much bearing around of swords and solemn singing of hymns and anthems, and the whole ritual takes hours to complete. But eventually it is done, and Henry can retire momentarily from the congregation. He is a king. Now he must break bread with his subjects for the first time.

The venue for the coronation feast is the great hall of Westminster Palace. And here, once more, Henry sits raised up above his people, this time on a dais, his throne covered with a canopy. It may not seem so long that he was here before, when, as a thirteen-year-old, he attended his father, holding the royal sword Curtana, with the kingmaker earl of Northumberland at attention by his side.

Unlike his father, he has no son to carry his sword yet. But, Henry may reflect, he has no Northumberland to worry about, either. He has arrived here all on his own.

So this is King Henry V. But who, exactly, is the new king that the hundreds of worthy guests at the banquet see?

He is twenty-six years old: in the prime of manhood. Inevitably, he presents a different figure than his father did during his last, agonizing decade of sickness. Henry is much more like his father in his younger years: lean, strong, athletic, and handsome. Beneath the coif in which his head has been wrapped to hold in the oil of anointing, he has a full head of straight brown hair, which matches his dark eyes. He has a broad forehead and typically thin, straight Plantagenet nose. His neck is long and slender, his cheeks are clean-shaven, and his lips are crimson.

Below his right eye Henry may well still bear the scars of John Bradmore's surgery to save his life in 1403. But he has worn the scar nearly ten years—time enough to grow into it. He is still young enough that one monk at Westminster describes him on this day as "residing in the appearance of an angel."[9]

The same monk records that as Henry sits angelic before his guests, who are feasting on courses of a huge variety of fish and fowl, he seems very happy. Yet others see in Henry something different. Some observe that Henry only picks at his food during the feast, and is stern of countenance.[10] Almost overnight, he seems to have assumed an exaggerated seriousness, as though any hint of levity has been squeezed out of his person as part of his transformation from prince to king.

"As soon as he was invested with the emblems of royalty, he suddenly became a different man," writes one chronicler. "His care now was for self-restraint and goodness and gravity."[11] One of his closest attendants, a chaplain associated with the royal household, writes that Henry seems to have undergone a religious awakening: "after he had first taken his seat upon the throne of his kingdom, [he] wrote out the first law of Deuteronomy in the volume of his breast."[12] A third, later, writer agrees: Henry has "reformed and amended his life and his manners," he writes, so that there is no hint left of any "youth or wildness"; all that remains of his former character is "gravity and discretion."[13]

It is as if he knows that this moment represents a great pivot point in his life.

Something profound has happened to Henry on the day of his coronation. But what? To some observers, it is a combination of a "born-again" religious awakening with a genuine moral reformation—a setting aside of the loose trappings of princely youth for the stern sobriety of kingship. It seems that as king Henry has decided he must physically embody the heaviness of his new royal office. His transformation will become the dramatic hinge of the stories—and legends—that are told about him for hundreds of years afterward. Yet what exactly it is—and means—is not easy to pin down.

In the cartoon history of Henry's life and reign, given dramatic rendering by a chronicler writing in the 1470s and crystallized into legend by Shakespeare nearly two hundred years after the events, what happens *is* straightforward. Before Henry is king he is Hal: a lightweight, flippant, sensuous gadfly; a lover of women and a charmer of men. He plays the fool for so long that he almost becomes the fool, until, at the moment of his father's death, he realizes he can cavort around no more. As this chronicler puts it, as Prince of Wales, Henry "intended greatly to riot and drew to wild company," but on becoming king he realizes "the great charge and worship that he should take upon him."[14] He sends away his former friends, whom in Shakespeare's rendering include Sir John Falstaff, and, just in time, knuckles down to the serious business of rule. This is an attractive story, and in Shakespeare's hands it is masterfully told. But it is a dramatic exaggeration drawn from a scrappy patchwork of evidence.

Some of the inspiration behind stories of Henry's "untamed youth" has already been encountered: the writer known as the Pseudo-Elmham claims he "seethed with the flames of Venus" during his days as prince.[15] From an Italian biographer called Tito Livio, writing a quarter of a century after the events he describes, we have the assertion that on his coronation, Henry put aside "youth and wildness" in favor of "gravity and discretion."[16] An Anglo-Irish nobleman called James Butler, fourth earl of

Ormond, who is a contemporary of the king and a military companion of Thomas, duke of Clarence, will one day claim Prince Henry and his friends enjoyed disguising themselves as highwaymen and robbing acquaintances, before later revealing the trick, then repaying handsomely those who fought back most fiercely during the mugging.[17] From gossip passed between generations of legal officials and written down in the sixteenth century will come a highly improbable account of a young Henry assaulting a royal judge called William Gascoigne.[18]

Henry's supposed abandonment of his bad company rests on another reminiscence of the earl of Ormond, who claims that on his accession Henry calls all his old friends to him and asks them to either "change their life and conversation" as he intends to, or else depart his company and "upon pain of their heads" never come back.[19] (This charge is elaborated by a chronicler who alleges that Henry sacks all but three sober and serious men in his household, whom he has hated but now comes to respect and even love.)[20]

All of this is alluring, melodramatic, and highly appealing as dramatic narrative. Some of it may be partially or even substantially true. But to roll all this together into the Shakespearean portrait of Henry as a roustabout, irresponsible tearaway before his coronation, who utterly changes his behavior after it, means setting aside everything else we know about Henry as a young man.

He has made mistakes, undoubtedly. He flirted with ruin during his father's last years. He underestimated his father and allowed his brother Thomas to surpass him briefly in the old king's estimation. But these are not the same charges as the garbled whispers of roistering that are scraped together to make Shakespeare's version of events. Henry has never been Hal, and his self-reinvention on April 9, 1413, has nothing to do with forswearing taverns and women.

In fact, it is best understood as a masterful demonstration of Henry's favorite tactic, which he has used at so many critical moments in his life so far—from his appearance at the Gloucester parliament during the Aberystwyth crisis, to Badby's burning, to his reconciliation with his father in Westminster in 1412.

It is the trick he learned first from Richard II.

Henry is performing.

And a well-judged performance it is, too. Henry may be only twenty-six years old, but he has been a familiar political figure in England for half his life. He has enjoyed a fuller, deeper apprenticeship to kingship than any other monarch since Edward I. His subjects know him, and have had a long time to anticipate his arrival. But he cannot allow familiarity to breed contempt. He understands that if he is to succeed as king he must free himself clearly and without delay from any obligations he has incurred as prince. He must present himself as an embodiment of justice—available to all his subjects and above the tug of faction. That is why as he sits in Westminster Hall, still greasy with the oil of anointing, and with the whole political nation assembled at his feet, he unveils to them a new demeanor. He is showing them himself not just as a new man, but a new political being entirely.

In truth, Henry's newfound seriousness does not require a wholesale changing of his ways, for gravity, religiosity, and intensity of focus are already essential parts of his character; adding chastity, economy of speech, and severity to the mix is hardly a radical departure from what exists already.

But Henry's transformation is real nonetheless, and it is best thought of as a hardening of his features into a mask that will never, from this day, slip. On both the night that his father died and the evening before his coronation, Henry spent time praying with and confessing his sins to a hermit of Westminster called William Alnwick. Now that he is king, he will seldom be seen without an entourage of priests, preachers, and professional praying men, as well as Carmelite friars employed to take further regular confessions.[21]

Piety, earnestness, sobriety, and the pursuit of justice and God's will: these traits will henceforth define who Henry is. They will not always make for easy company, yet they will serve him dreadfully, magnificently well. Unlike Richard II, he will be a king of substance as well as style. Two years after Henry's coronation a French spy will prepare a report that describes, in passing, the character of the king. Henry's ministers, writes the spy, think that the king has "the fine manner of a lord and a great bearing." But the spy notes that Henry has remained chaste since the day of his coronation, and adds his own opinion that this man sounds better suited to the Church than to war.[22]

Before very long it will be plain how partial a reading of Henry V this is. For one thing, despite his sincere devotion to religious ritual and prayer, Henry continues privately to enjoy secular pleasures such as watching wrestlers and musicians perform, and he enjoys the japing of a court fool called William.[23] He spends huge sums with wine merchants, and tailors who dress him and his friends in fine costumes on important occasions, and he immerses himself in tales of Arthurian knights for pleasure.

And Henry's personal piety is in no way at odds with his growing expertise in and enthusiasm for military campaigning and the martial arts. In time he will demonstrate that religiosity and pitiless generalship can very easily go hand in hand; if he is like any churchman, it is a warrior monk.

Nevertheless, in the moment, the spy's observation that Henry is a king of unusually straightlaced temperament speaks to the completeness of the mask that, on the day of his coronation, he has slipped forever over his face.

18

FALSE FRIENDS

Two days after Henry's coronation he leaves the Palace of Westminster and travels northwest to spend Easter at Kings Langley, in Hertfordshire.

It is a fine place to pass the holiday. The royal residence is an extended manor house, greatly enlarged in the thirteenth century and further modernized in the fourteenth. The public halls and suites of lavish apartments are large and brightly painted. There are huge kitchens and private bathhouses with hot, running water. The windows are glazed. Fires crackle beneath mantels carved from expensive stone, and the entertaining rooms are lit by candelabra fashioned from plaster of Paris.

Outside, a clock installed by Edward III strikes on the hour, the chime of its bell ringing across courtyards, beyond which are acres of vineyards and parkland. This is excellent ground for hunting game or even spotting exotic beasts. One hundred years ago a camel gifted to Edward II wandered the estate.[1]

But Kings Langley is more than just a comfortable country retreat. It is a symbolically charged place for Henry to have chosen for his first visit as king. Adjacent to the palace is a house of Dominican friars ("the Black Friars"), and in their priory church lies the tomb of King Richard II.

Henry was thirteen when Richard was laid to rest in Kings Langley, having been starved to death at Pontefract Castle. He witnessed the perfunctory public mourning Richard was afforded in London, its aim chiefly to persuade the citizens that the old king really was dead.

At that time the disregard for the dead king's will may have rankled with Henry, who knew Richard's indulgent, affectionate side as well as his violent caprice. Now, just a few weeks after he has laid his father to rest, the king of his childhood is on his mind again.

In Easter week, Henry carries out the customary royal duty of distributing Maundy Thursday alms to the poor, doling out more than £400 in charitable gifts to a crowd of three thousand paupers. He makes an even more significant donation the following day, when he donates 25 shillings to the Black Friars.

He makes this gift during the customary Good Friday ritual of creeping to the cross.[2] All the faithful at Kings Langley assemble to crawl on hands and knees to kiss the crucifix within the church: a humble journey that takes them past Richard's burial place. As they creep, Henry has made up his mind what to do. He will have the old king exhumed and moved to the place he wished to lie. There is another tomb, in Westminster Abbey, where the corpse of Richard's first wife, Anne of Bohemia, awaits his presence.

Before the year is out, Henry will send Richard to be with her.

Henry's concern for setting right some of the wrongs done to Richard has a reasoning of its own. Richard was no one's idea of a fine king. But he showed Henry some kindnesses and taught him some lessons. Henry feels, perhaps, that there is a personal debt to repay.

But atoning for his father's failure to honor Richard's will is not only a matter of conscience. It also satisfies Henry's political desire to make the start of his reign a time for reconciliation. He began that process on the weekend of his coronation when he raised to knighthood the Mortimer brothers and the heirs of the Epiphany plotters. In the weeks that follow, he continues to cultivate the sense of a fresh start.

The first parliament of the reign opens on May 15, 1413, exactly a month after the creeping to the cross at Kings Langley. By now Henry has begun reshuffling the personnel of government. In key posts he places men he has known for a long time and deeply trusts.

To lead the royal council and the central office of government, he appoints as chancellor his uncle and longtime collaborator Bishop Henry Beaufort. As treasurer he brings in Thomas FitzAlan, the earl of Arundel, whom he sent in charge of the 1411 expedition to France to help John the Fearless drive the Armagnacs from Paris. Richard Beauchamp, earl of Warwick, a veteran of that same campaign, as well as the battle of Shrewsbury, is also brought into the heart of royal affairs, with a roving role in diplomacy and government.

It is hardly surprising that Archbishop Arundel has been removed as chancellor and replaced by Henry's archloyalist Bishop Beaufort. Yet Henry takes care not simply to restore to high office everyone his father removed when he canceled Henry's mandate as regent in 1411. Elsewhere he shows himself willing to rely on men who are of his father's world as well as his. Sir Thomas Erpingham, a sixty-year-old knight, courtier, and diplomat who was a close confidant of his father, is appointed as steward of the royal household—a job he performed for Henry IV at a similar stage of his reign. As chamberlain, Henry appoints Sir Henry FitzHugh, an upstanding Yorkshireman of a similar vintage to Erpingham who has also done many years of loyal service to Henry IV; the old king trusted FitzHugh enough to send him aboard the ships that took Henry's sister Philippa off to her Scandinavian wedding back in 1406.

This pattern of appointments, by which Henry is blending men who have served him well for many years with others who have shown themselves longtime stalwarts of his father and the house of Lancaster, will be repeated at every level, from the council and household down to royal representatives in the shires of England.[3]

With this tone having been struck, when Parliament opens, Bishop

Beaufort gives his opening speech, laying out Henry's intended philosophy of kingship. He draws his theme from the book of Ecclesiastes. "Let reason go before every enterprise, and counsel before every action."[4]

The king, Beaufort promises, is committed above all to three things: "the proper and effective support of his high royal estate . . . good governance and the upholding of his laws within the realm . . . [and] the nurturing of his foreign allies, and also the resisting of his enemies outside the kingdom."

This is a direct continuation of the theme Beaufort introduced when he addressed Parliament for the first time during Henry's princely tenure as quasi-regent in 1410, speaking of the pillars of justice.* But now Beaufort also explains to his listeners that the guarantee of Henry's good intent is his newly intensified religious demeanor. As the chapter of Ecclesiastes he has selected continues: "The countenance is a sign of changing of the heart."

This message of open ears and goodwill toward all men finds a receptive audience, and Henry's first parliament agrees to a generous grant of taxation. The need for money is, as usual, acute, and with the situation in France volatile, it may well stay that way. Parliament therefore agrees to give Henry a tax on wool exports for four years along with an income tax (known as a fifteenth-and-tenth). The taxation is granted, say the commons, "for their great love and affection, for the good of the realm, and for good governance in future."[5]

The king assures his people that this money will be well spent: he spells out a plan to settle his father's debts and promises to fund the royal household before paying out annuities to his personal followers. He listens with sympathy to complaints about continuing violence and lawbreaking across the country. When the commons grumble about clerics laying fines on adulterers instead of giving them a good old-fashioned whipping, he agrees to look into it. When they rail against the flooding caused by rivers being re-coursed to make artificial fishponds and mills, he agrees that the loss of life is intolerable.[6]

---

* See chapter 12.

Finally, as a gift to the realm, and a further demonstration of his commitment to a new beginning, Henry grants a general legal amnesty. He announces a pardon for almost all crimes committed in England up until the day of the parliament's opening. Immunity is on offer for almost anything, from stealing animals and firewood out of royal forests to paperwork offenses relating to illegal land leases.* To claim the benefit of the pardon, one simply has to apply by Christmas for a charter, and pay the appropriate fee. The cost is steep, at 16 shillings and 4 pence. But it is cheaper than a long lawsuit over a land deal gone wrong—and it certainly beats a hanging.

As the parliament disperses, Henry must hope that his early efforts to promote harmony over discord—to balance rewarding his supporters for their loyalty with embracing reliable old Lancastrian servants—will buy him some respite from plotting of the sort that bedeviled his father's early years. This is a critical—even an existential—issue. As one poet who writes around the time of coronation puts it, the king's crown is a symbol of "lords, commons and clergy . . . all at one assent . . . If we among ourselves debate, then ends the flower of chivalry. All other lands that do us hate, our feebleness will aspy."[7]

But despite his best efforts, Henry will not enjoy total relief from schemes against him. In fact, the first plot against his crown and his realm—and his life—is already being hatched.

It will come from a source worryingly close to home.

In June 1413, as his first parliament is closing, a group of bishops led by Archbishop Arundel—recently ousted as chancellor of the royal council—comes to visit Henry in his palace at Kennington to complain about one of his friends.

---

* The only exemptions from the general amnesty are for officials "who have formerly been officers of the mint, and ministers of the mystery of money, coinage, or of the exchange in the Tower and City of London and the town of Calais."

Kennington is a comfortable manor house set in parkland a couple of miles from the south side of London Bridge. Its spiral staircases and grand chimneys were installed by its most enthusiastic owner, Richard II's father, the Black Prince. It has been one of Henry's regular haunts ever since he was awarded it as a teenager in his capacity as duke of Cornwall. As such, Kennington has hosted many of his longtime associates from his younger days. It is one of these youthful acquaintances of whom the clerics have come to make their complaint. He is John Oldcastle, Lord Cobham.

Oldcastle is around ten years older than Henry. He comes from a respectable family of Herefordshire gentry and has a long and distinguished military record fighting for the Crown. In 1407, during the wars against Owain Glyndŵr, Oldcastle helped blast Aberystwyth Castle out of rebel hands. The next year he married Joan Cobham, through whom he claimed his baronial title. In the autumn of 1409 he represented England with distinction at a high-profile jousting tournament held at Lille, and in 1411 he was alongside the earls of Arundel and Warwick as one of the captains in the mission to assist John the Fearless.

So Oldcastle is known as not only an associate but a friend of Henry. But there is one matter at least on which Oldcastle and the king sharply part ways. That issue is heresy.

For at least three years (and probably much longer) Oldcastle has been a promoter and protector of Lollardy. Even at the time of John Badby's burning in 1410, it was common knowledge that Oldcastle had a Lollard preacher living with him in Kent—protected behind the walls of the Cobham family's fortified seat of Cooling Castle. Oldcastle is said to have sponsored this preacher, and others like him, to go out into the country railing against the "false" teachings of the Church: the presence of Christ's real body in the Eucharist, the legitimacy of popes, and much more.

One chronicler records that Oldcastle has been "present in person during their wicked sermons" and has "put down any hecklers . . . by terrifying threats of what the power of the secular sword would do to them."[8] And this is not all. Besides running a preaching stable, Oldcastle exchanges letters with the most dangerous radicals in Europe, based in Bohemia. He collects heretical books.

The specific complaints about Oldcastle in June 1413 are prompted by a raid on the London premises of a book illuminator and suspected Lollard, during which an unbound sheaf of heretical essays is confiscated. The illuminator identifies the papers as Oldcastle's. By the time Arundel and the bishops visit Henry at Kennington they have already questioned Oldcastle, who has batted them away nonchalantly, admitting the papers are his but saying breezily that he has not yet read them. The bishops politely urge Henry to rein in his friend. They acknowledge Oldcastle's long-standing association with the Crown, and his knightly status, but insist on the grotesque nature of Oldcastle's heresies, which are so jarringly at odds with Henry's regal, ultrareligious demeanor.

Henry agrees. Or so it appears. He admits that the heresies expressed in Oldcastle's papers are among the most disgusting things he has ever heard.[9] He asks for some time to bring Oldcastle back to his senses. The bishops go off, hoping he is serious. But this will not be the last that any of them have heard of the matter.

During the summer of 1413, Henry shows little urgency about effecting Oldcastle's religious reeducation. In July he advances Oldcastle 400 marks to settle a debt. In August Oldcastle pays for a troupe of twenty-six wrestlers to perform in Windsor Forest, where the king is busy hunting deer with his crossbow. Oldcastle knows his man: wrestling is Henry's favorite spectator sport. But he is also cocky, and at Windsor he overplays his hand. He presumes to lecture the king about finance, religion, and politics, telling him that for every friar in the country whose head he cuts off, his treasury will swell.[10]

This is essentially a rehash of the Lollard petition to the 1410 parliament that demanded wholesale land confiscations from the Church as a means of reendowing the Crown. It is also tone-deaf and rather stupid. It stirs Henry into action: he rounds on Oldcastle and berates him for his impudence. Oldcastle is shocked. He takes umbrage and then he takes flight, leaving Windsor, riding home to Cooling Castle, and barricading the doors.

In abusing Henry's friendship, particularly on an issue where he has long ago made his position clear, Oldcastle is asking for trouble.

After the argument at Windsor, Henry realizes that he has "wasted a lot of time to no purpose" in trying to bring Oldcastle back from his errors, and sends word to Archbishop Arundel that he may proceed against him for heresy.[11] In due course, royal officers appear before the tall, round, crenelated gates of Cooling Castle with a warrant for Oldcastle's arrest. The baron, who has been defying Archbishop Arundel's summons to a clerical hearing until this point, sees that resisting arrest will lead to very serious trouble, so he hands himself in and is taken to the Tower of London to await trial.

The hearing takes place in late September at the London house of the Black Friars, whose heads Oldcastle so recently advised Henry to chop off. Oldcastle is to be examined on a number of points, which he tries to preempt by presenting the court with a statement of his beliefs, written in English. This document describes Oldcastle's opinions on the true presence in the Eucharist, the necessity of confession, and the value of pilgrimages.

On paper, Oldcastle presents his views as reasonably as he can, but over the course of several oral examinations, he becomes contrary, testy, then outright rude. Matters reach a head when he describes the pope as "the true antichrist," then sweeps his arms wide and tells all listening in the court to beware Arundel and his fellow clerics, for they are "leading both you and themselves astray, and are taking you down to Hell."[12]

Archbishop Arundel, presiding, is by now shedding tears of exasperation and pity, as he realizes he has little choice but to proceed to judgment. He declares Oldcastle a heretic, excommunicates him from the Church, and condemns him as "a son of wickedness and darkness" who has "so hardened his heart that he does not listen to the voice of his shepherd."[13] He formally hands him over to the secular authorities to face his punishment.

Like John Badby before him, Oldcastle is to be burned.

Notwithstanding Oldcastle's abuse of their friendship, this is a blow to Henry. It is also a test of the hardness of his resolve. Knowing Oldcastle as he does, and having some practical experience of Lollards, he cannot be surprised that his friend has proven stubborn. But he still hopes to convince him to save his skin. There is a convention by which convicted heretics can be allowed an extended period to consider whether they really want to be burned to death. Henry and Arundel grant Oldcastle this reprieve. Unlike Badby, who was allowed a year to brood on his opinions, Oldcastle is given forty days' imprisonment in the Tower.

But once again, Oldcastle shows that he is not just incorrigible in his heresies. He is also entirely unthankful for Henry's grace. He is sent back to the Tower on September 25, 1413. Three and a half weeks later, on the night of October 19, he escapes.

Broken out of his cell by a die-hard Lollard called Richard Wrothe and a sympathetic bookmaker named William Fisher, Oldcastle disappears into London's underground network of Lollard radicals to conspire "in holes and corners against the power of both Swords, as he had done previously."[14]

From the shadows, he begins stirring up like-minded religious dissenters behind a campaign of armed resistance. Oldcastle's target is not only the organized Church, but also a king whom he now nicknames "the Prince of Priests."

Like Hotspur ten years before him, Oldcastle has transformed from a friend of Henry's into a mortal enemy.

During the same months that Oldcastle is causing Henry such irritation, the king is also continuing to make arrangements for the bodies and souls of his ancestors and predecessors.

Between May and July 1413 he orders a new tomb for his mother, Mary, topped with a copper effigy, to be raised in Leicester Cathedral. In June, on the holy weekend of the Trinity—which his father particularly revered—he hosts a grand service of remembrance for the old king in Canterbury Cathedral. This time his brother Thomas attends, having returned at last from France. Banners representing all the kings in Christendom are arrayed around the cathedral, which is lit by thousands of torches and candles.

The next month, Henry goes back again to Canterbury, this time to present a sumptuous gift to Becket's tomb: a golden head decorated with pearls and jewels, along with two matching gold candlesticks. This is lavish royal patronage indeed—but Henry is saving his noblest gesture for the end of the year.

On December 4 a royal body is brought to Westminster Abbey for burial. It is Richard II's. Released from his grave in the friary church at Kings Langley, this old king is borne south very slowly on a horse-drawn hearse, lying in a new coffin, draped all over in black velvet. In keeping with Richard's will, he makes this progress with torches burning all around the hearse and a large crowd of ecclesiastics and nobles walking behind.

When Richard reaches Westminster, Henry is waiting, and there a service designed deliberately to match his father's interment and commemoration takes place. The same royal banners of Christendom used in Canterbury are displayed, and a comparable number of lights blaze around the coffin. Richard is lowered into the tomb where his first wife, Anne of Bohemia, has lain since her death in 1394. Thus he is "buried and put in his own sepulcher, that he [made] himself," remembers one Londoner.[15]

Thomas Hoccleve, who wrote Henry his fullest treatise on kingship in 1411, writes a poem to commemorate the occasion. He praises Henry's "benignity" and "loving heart." For, he says, "our king Richard that was, ye may well see, is not fled from his [i.e., Henry's] remembrance away. My wit sufficeth not to [describe] with what honor he is brought to this town, and with his queen at Westminster in th'abbey, Solemnly in tomb laid a-down."[16]

With this ceremony, Henry's mission to honor Richard's memory and right some of the wrongs of his deposition is almost complete. The last steps are two building projects. The first is secular: Henry commissions works to rebuild the manor of Sheen, which Richard had torn down on

Anne of Bohemia's death. He plans to spend heavily on it: bringing stone for the gatehouse from Yorkshire, using Kentish ragstone for the walls, and having window glass specially made in London. He plans suites of offices and living apartments, a kitchen decorated with a giant wooden antelope and carved ceilings, pillars and roof beams throughout.[17] The antelope is a Lancastrian symbol and personal flourish, but otherwise this is a design and construction project Richard could have admired.

Henry's second building works at this time are religious. To Thomas Hoccleve, Henry's reinterment of Richard II springs from his natural instinct toward unity in the realm; and that same instinct has made him an opponent of Lollardy and a defender of traditional Catholicism. ("Our liege lord, the king, is Champion for holy church—Christ's knight is he!" writes Hoccleve. "Look up, thou Albion! God thank, and for thy Christian prince pray! . . . He, of thy soul's health, is lock and key!")[18] Channeling exactly this spirit, Henry makes plans for the construction of three separate religious houses, in fulfillment of a penance imposed on his father by Pope Gregory XII as punishment for deposing Richard II and executing the rebellious archbishop Scrope in 1405.

The foundations Henry establishes to fulfill this charge are a Carthusian charterhouse opposite the new manor at Sheen; a nearby dual house for men and women at Syon, to be seeded with Brigittine sisters following a rule popular in Sweden, where his sister Philippa is queen; and a Celestine house, somewhere in the same region.

Only the first two of these religious projects will come to fruition, but Henry will take a keen interest in the progress of his monastic foundations in the years to come. This, rather than Lollardy, represents his interest in religious reform: whereas Oldcastle dreams of ripping up the fabric of English religion, stripping away Church property, and purging the Church of doctrine and liturgy that does not suit his tastes, Henry is of a far more traditional reforming bent. He would see monasticism reorganized and revived: the Church bolstered and refreshed, but in a conservative manner. This is an approach that has a far more orthodox pedigree—for monastic reform has been a recurrent trend in Catholicism for nearly one thousand years.

Yet Henry's bid for political reconciliation and religious renewal is not allowed to proceed smoothly. For shortly after he has laid Richard to rest and made the first tentative steps toward revitalizing English monasticism, he finds his crown under urgent threat. The escaped prisoner Oldcastle and his Lollard allies make one last attempt to put Henry from the throne and install the ghost of Richard, or the nearest man they can find to him, in his place.

As 1413 draws to a close, Henry plans to observe the Twelve Nights of Christmas at Eltham, the palace that was once his father's favorite. All three of his brothers are to be there, and a large order for French and Portuguese wines has been placed for the many revelers.[19] Actors known as mummers have been hired to come to the palace and entertain, with one company booked for an appearance on Twelfth Night.

As Christmastime approaches there is no specific cause to worry. But security is still tight. John Oldcastle has not been seen since he disappeared from the Tower two months earlier. It is known that his followers have been sending notes around the realm encouraging sedition. The new jailor at the Tower of London has reported suspicious visits to other Lollards held there. Henry, Thomas, John, and Humphrey may remember that it was at Christmastime fourteen years earlier that they had to flee for their lives from Windsor Castle, during the Epiphany Rising. So although the royal household is making ready to celebrate, they do so with a degree of caution.[20]

On the day of Twelfth Night itself—January 5—news of a plot finally breaks. Two carpenters from London lose their nerve and turn themselves in and, in exchange for a cash reward, spill the details of an imminent attempt on the lives of the king and his brothers. The mummers who have been hired to entertain the court will include kidnapper-assassins, charged with seizing the king and princes, before a large-scale rebellion descends on London in the following days.

Instead of finishing the Christmas celebrations with a flourish, Henry swings into action. He leaves Eltham and moves to Westminster Palace.

The mayor of London organizes raids and arrests in a series of pubs known to harbor Lollard networks: the Axe in Bishopsgate and the Wrestlers on the Hoop in Smithfield. Royal agents are sent to keep watch on a safe house where Oldcastle is said to be holed up. And orders are sent out to sheriffs all over England to keep a watch for all illegal assemblies.

In the days that follow, the potential scale of the uprising becomes clear. Henry learns that as many as twenty thousand Lollard sympathizers are planning to march on London, to assemble on January 10 on a patch of open ground west of the city, known as Fickett's Field. Around five thousand Londoners are expected to come out from the city and join them.

As one breathless chronicler puts it, "at every path, street and crossroads you could have seen crowds of people flocking together . . . brought to London by the extravagant promises of the Lollards."[21] The most extravagant reports of the rebels' plans suggest that they intend to vandalize St. Paul's Cathedral and Westminster Abbey, rob every friary in London, and put Oldcastle in charge of the realm.

On January 9, therefore, Henry has an urgent decision to make. He can wait and see if the rebellion turns out to be as serious as the government's spies and informants are telling him.

Or he can strike early.

Henry chooses to act. On the evening of January 9, he assembles his closest advisers, led by his three brothers and the earls of Arundel and Warwick. With them he leads as many troops as he can muster from his household out to St. Giles' Field, a little way north of the rebels' planned muster point. They order the gates of London to be barred and guarded by armed men. Then they lie in wait.

The tension, undoubtedly, is high. ("Oh!" exclaims one of Henry's chaplains, remembering events a few years later. "What amazing, lamentable and bitter madness!")[22] Even the heavens seem to feel it: as Henry and his comrades march out to face down the rebellion, above them, a meteor streaks through the night sky. But as the night wears on, something remarkable starts to happen. In small groups, Lollards clearly from far out of town, unfamiliar with London's geography, start appearing from the darkness. Confused and disorganized, many of them mistake the royal troops for fellow plotters and ask which way they should go to find Oldcastle. All Henry's men need do is grab them as they appear, and haul them off to prison.

As daybreak approaches, the rebels' numbers begin to swell a little. But by this time it is becoming clear that the king is ahead of them. Any Londoners who planned to join the rising are stuck behind the barred gates and the city walls. Meanwhile, both inside and outside those walls, further raids are taking place.

Those Lollards who have their wits about them turn and start making their way back toward their distant homes. Those who do not are rounded up to face summary trial and execution.

Oldcastle, frustratingly, is nowhere to be found when his rumored safe house is raided. He slips the net and disappears once more into the Lollard underworld. But when January 10 dawns, the rebellion is over.

19

THE ROAD TO WAR

Within hours of the Lollard rising's collapse on January 10, 1414, justice is being served. Several dozen prisoners seized by the king's men have been put on trial in the Tower of London and sentenced to die.

Three days later, gallows stand grim on St. Giles' Field, and the guilty are strung up, with those who refuse to recant their Lollardy being burned after they are dead. The sight will remain lodged in folk memory for generations. Woodcuts depicting the Lollard hangings made many decades later, during the sixteenth-century Reformation, will show rebels roasting on fires at the same time as they choke in the hangman's noose.

Most of those killed in January, and during the two months of judicial inquiries that follow, are ordinary artisans, tradesmen, and servants. Their violent deaths are designed to show how the new king intends to deal with "these cursed superstitious heretics," as well as those who presume to threaten the peace.[1] In his first parliament Bishop Beaufort promised that Henry was committed to "good governance and the upholding of his laws within the realm." He needs to show that these were no empty words.

Yet there is at least as much mercy as retribution in Henry's response to the Lollard rising—particularly where those accused or convicted are knights and gentry. He has never squirmed in the face of dispensing justice. But neither does he forget that he began his reign nine months earlier in a spirit of reconciliation. There is no need to jeopardize this by making needless martyrs.

So although several hundred rebels are arrested, only sixty-odd are convicted, and around half of those executed. Many of the rest are committed to prison, where conditions can be foul but are not deliberately deadly. Others are pardoned outright. Suspects arrested for heresy rather than treason—among whom a significant number are women—are bounced back and forth between the secular and clerical courts.[2]

A bounty, naturally, stays on John Oldcastle's head.

Meanwhile, Henry puts on a positive show of orthodoxy to remind his subjects what true religion looks like. He commands "litanies to be performed and processions to be made throughout the kingdom, saying that it [is] well pleasing and grateful to God for thanks to be given to the Most High Sower after the destruction of so great a crop of evil, and the cutting off of the vilest tares from the good grain."[3]

Those loyal to Henry at this time emphasize how unruffled the new king seems by the experience. "Amid the storms and stresses cause by these painful experiences, the mind of the king remained firm and was unshakable,"[4] writes one of his chaplains. However, not everyone may enjoy quite the same confidence.

A French diplomatic embassy is visiting England at the height of the Lollard crisis. Its members have been sent to visit Henry by the Armagnac dukes who are currently in power in Paris, to discuss terms for a treaty between the two realms. They arrive in December and depart in February 1414, so they are in England to witness the uprising from start to finish.

No matter how calm and collected Henry has been in facing down Oldcastle and his fellow radicals, this has not been the ideal time for an important foreign delegation to visit. The kingdom's reputation as a land of regicide, insurrection, and revolution is one that Henry is trying his best to shake off, yet thanks to John Oldcastle, that impression is exactly the one the ambassadors take with them back to Paris. It is inconvenient and embarrassing, to say the least.

If things are messy in England, however, affairs are far worse across the Channel. For the French, 1413 has been another dreadful year. The summer saw Paris convulsed by a new round of rioting and murder, stirred up by John the Fearless. In league with a powerful faction of butchers, the duke encouraged a populist rising known as the Revolt of the Cabochiens. Thugs wearing white caps took control of the streets of Paris for many weeks, storming the Bastille, and even breaking into the royal residence at the Hôtel Saint-Pol. After four months of bloody mayhem, the revolt was eventually put down by the Armagnacs. But John the Fearless escaped the capital and is now holed up in Flanders, plotting his next move.

Meanwhile, in the south, things are little better. The duchy of Guyenne has been overrun since 1412 by the English expeditionary army originally sent under Henry's brother Thomas, duke of Clarence. Thomas has returned to England, but many of the troops who went out with him have not: they are lodged in and around Bordeaux, under the command of Thomas Beaufort.

During their time in Guyenne, the English have repeatedly ravaged the countryside, extorted huge cash payments from the Armagnac dukes, and captured valuable prisoners. The soldiers who have enjoyed eighteen months robbing and plundering the pleasant southwest are coming to view France as a place where an enterprising English soldier might go and make a fortune. They share this realization with the hundreds of independent English mercenaries who are elsewhere in the French kingdom, hiring themselves out to both sides of the civil war.

Finally, Charles VI, whose insanity lies at the root of all France's calamities, shows no sign of either regaining his wits or dying. His eldest surviving son, the dauphin Louis, turns seventeen in January 1414, and is coming to be seen as an alternative figure around whom a stable government can rally. But he alone cannot bring an end to the violent hatred that exists between the Burgundian and Armagnac factions. In fact, he is personally torn between the factions. Although he is married to John the Fearless's daughter, he is coming to fear and even hate his father-in-law. Yet he does not share the Armagnac leaders' unquenchable thirst for revenge on John the Fearless at any cost. In early 1414 Louis is ensconced in Paris among the Armagnac dukes. But over the course of the year he will test the limits of their trust as he tries to broker a peace deal.

All of this presents a situation that, if agonizing for the French, promises significant opportunity for Henry. French politics is certainly changeable, and it is hard to know where one stands from one month to the next. But at the same time, vast amounts of French military resources are being wasted every month as the king's subjects fight among themselves, and there are two alternative courts in France whom the English can play off against each other. As a boy Henry saw Richard II come tantalizingly close to achieving a long-term settlement to the Hundred Years War. That was nearly twenty years ago. Henry may have only one chance of his own to make peace. There may never be a better time to act than now.

Since diplomatic protocol holds that truces and treaties between realms should be thrashed out anew whenever there is a change of ruler, there has been a regular exchange of ambassadorial missions between Henry's court and the two French factions since the start of his reign.* During the course of these meetings various demands and proposals have been tested.

The English goal, in essence, is to turn the clock back to the year 1360, and to seal such an arrangement with a marriage. This means forcing the French to observe the concessions made to Edward III in the Treaty of Brétigny: giving England control of an expanded Guyenne, plus the counties of Poitiers and Ponthieu, amounting in total to approximately one-third of all French territory.

---

* In summer 1413 a grand English embassy of more than two hundred dignitaries, led by the experienced diplomats Richard, earl of Warwick; Henry Chichele, bishop of St. Davids; and Henry, Lord Scrope, crossed to Calais and held talks with both the Armagnac dukes and John the Fearless. Then (as we have seen) French envoys came to England between December 1413 and February 1414.

In return for this Henry could agree to surrender the English claim that Plantagenet kings are also, by bloodright, kings of France. And he most likely *should* seek to take a French princess in marriage—either the one remaining unmarried daughter of Charles VI, twelve-year-old Catherine, or a daughter of the duke of Burgundy.

Perhaps unsurprisingly, neither the Armagnacs nor the Burgundians have yet agreed to make this raft of lopsided proposals the basis for a long-term peace treaty: the Armagnacs because they will not and John the Fearless because he cannot. The best the Armagnacs can agree to at the London conference that concludes in February 1414 is a truce lasting one year, renewable in similarly short increments.

But Henry is not discouraged. During the course of the year he will make it his mission to—as his chaplain puts it—"secure a perpetual peace" by whatever means necessary.[5]

At the end of April Henry goes to the Lancastrian stronghold of Leicester. There is much family history here. He takes up residence in the castle where his grandfather John of Gaunt died. He has the opportunity, if he wishes, to visit his mother, where she lies buried beneath her fine new tomb effigy in the family mausoleum at the Church of the Annunciation.[6]

Nostalgia, however, is not the purpose of his visit. Henry goes to Leicester because Parliament—originally called for January but delayed by the Oldcastle rising—is meeting there, its members assembling inside a huge temporary wooden shed built for the purpose alongside the city's friary. Henry has promised that this, his second parliament, will legislate firmly on law and order: a long-standing source of grievance, particularly in areas like the English Midlands, which are plagued with gang violence. He has already shown his intention to begin this kind of work in Wales and the Marches, where he has sent the earl of Arundel, along with a panel of senior judges, to make sure that there is no revival of the disorder that dominated his father's early years. Owain Glyndŵr has been quiet for many years, but he is still supposedly at large.

Wales and the Midlands, however, are only parts of a bigger task: that of restoring confidence in royal peacekeeping throughout the realm. In Leicester, laws are being drafted that will allow central government to intervene wherever local officers such as sheriffs are deemed to have lost their grip. Further acts are planned introducing harsher sentences for piracy and the Lollard heresy. England's foremost Lollard-hunter, Archbishop Arundel, dies aged sixty-two after suffering a stroke during the course of the parliament. (His last political act is to issue a clerical ordinance ordering that Lollards should as a matter of course be hanged as traitors, in addition to being burned as heretics.)[7] But Henry does not intend to go easy on those who would subvert orthodox religion or the serenity of the realm. As Bishop Beaufort says when he makes the opening speech on the first day: "a kingdom cannot be in a state of well-being without our omnipotent lord God being praised and honored . . . and his laws and the Christian faith guarded, exercised and well preserved."[8]

To show he is serious, Henry brings with him to Leicester the whole staff of the most senior court in the land—the Court of King's Bench—with a mandate to start the crackdown right away.[9] Royal judges will spend the whole summer of 1414 touring the most troubled counties in England, investigating hundreds of backlogged cases of felony, trespass, and even treason.

There is an inevitable cost to this judicial surge: the roving judges will generate so much work for the legal system that by the end of 1414 it will be teetering on the brink of collapse. Henry will have to announce another general pardon, similar to the one he granted in the first parliament of his reign, in order to cope with the flood of cases. But it is not as chaotic a policy as it seems. Henry understands that an overworked justice system is far preferable to an underworked one, and that being seen to be tough on crime and its causes is really what his people want from him.

Since the Leicester parliament marks the start of Henry's drive to bring a harder edge to royal justice and peacekeeping in England, the majority of the business that takes place in the great temporary hall is concerned with this matter. Yet in between the parliamentary sessions, Henry has other, equally important things on his mind. As a local chronicler called John Strecche will recall, "in this parliament, many other things were discussed secretly, which only became known later."[10]

Those secret things pertain to France, for while Parliament is sitting, rival ambassadors sent from both the Armagnacs and the Burgundians arrive in England at the same time. Henry spends more than £2,000 on entertaining these two sets of diplomats. This is a very generous entertaining allowance, but it is money invested, not frittered. While feting his guests, Henry learns that the civil war in France is as dire as ever. Troops are in the field and Burgundian cities are under siege. The Armagnacs are dragging the confused king around at the head of their army, but he has only the faintest idea of what is happening from day to day.

The time is surely drawing near where full-scale English military intervention on either side—or even the threat of it—could unlock all sorts of generous concessions.

The difficulty, as ever, is knowing which of the sides in the civil war to back. Henry has traditionally favored Burgundy, and he seems to be of the same mind now. The Burgundian envoys have an interesting—if not perfect—proposal to put to Henry. John the Fearless is under extreme pressure in Flanders and, as another chronicler describes it, urgently wishes "to be strengthened for his war."[11] For this he is prepared to enter into a full and reciprocal military partnership with Henry.

The Burgundian envoys suggest that if Henry sends five hundred men-at-arms and a thousand archers to help John the Fearless drive Armagnac forces away from his territories, the duke will in time throw his men behind an English conquest of greater Guyenne. After this is done, the two men can even consider a joint attack on parts of Normandy held by Armagnac nobles.

There are many holes in this plan, not least the question of what the duke of Burgundy—who claims to be a loyal servant of the mad Charles VI, fighting to purge his court of traitors—will do if the king orders him to lay down his arms. How will he be able to help Henry if Henry decides to lay siege to a castle not held by an Armagnac lord?[12]

These are not easy questions to answer, but they do merit more discussions. So the diplomatic shuttling continues. In June 1414 two English embassies leave for France. One goes to Ypres, in Flanders. Another heads for Paris. Both delegations pass through a seething realm, in which Frenchmen are fighting Frenchmen, siege engines are drawn up outside blockaded cities, and trust between the warring factions is nonexistent. Understandably, in this chaotic environment, they have a mandate from Henry to be bold.

The diplomats who visit Paris are led by Henry's trusted allies Thomas Langley, bishop of Durham, and Richard Courtenay, the former chancellor of Oxford University, who is now bishop of Norwich. These clerics are treated to the finest entertainments Paris has to offer, then invited to state their case to the most senior nobleman currently resident in the French capital, the elderly duke of Berry.

The case they state is jaw-droppingly brazen. Richard Courtenay tells the French councilors in Paris that Henry wants everything Edward III had been promised in 1360, every other territory that has ever been held by any Plantagenet king going back to Henry II's reign in the twelfth century, and 3.6 million ecus, which he calculates as fair payment for the long-overdue balance on John II's ransom and an appropriate dowry for agreeing to marry Princess Catherine. Not surprisingly, the duke of Berry declares himself regrettably unable to agree to anything like these terms. The best the English can hope for, he says, would be a restoration of some lands, which would be held only at the pleasure of the king of France, not in full sovereignty, and a much smaller dowry.

The talks break up without agreement. So do the talks being conducted simultaneously with the duke of Burgundy in Flanders. By September both English embassies are on their way back to England to report to Henry on their progress. On the face of things, there is not much to say. But Henry cannot be very surprised to find that his aggressive demands have been rebuffed. He cannot have expected anything else. His demands to the Armagnacs have been so outlandish that they can only have been meant to be impossible for anyone bar perhaps the deranged Charles VI to consider.

A sea change is sweeping through English policy toward France, and it bears the marks of the bold instincts Henry has shown since he was a teenager cutting his teeth in Wales. A second parliament of the year is due to open in Westminster in November. And when it does, Bishop Henry Beaufort opens it with an address that is far more aggressive than any he has delivered before.

Just as a tree has a time when it germinates and a time when it flowers, says Beaufort, so too do men's lives have a rhythm that they must follow. "Man is given a time of peace," he says, "and a time of war and of toil."

King Henry has decided that now is the time to fight.

During the first two years of his reign, Henry faces many moments at which he is called upon to prove himself. More often than not, when such moments arise, he follows his instinct for performance and meaningful spectacle. This will in time mean that the story of his life and reign as told by chroniclers proceeds almost in a sequence of staged, dramatic scenes. This is perhaps his intention.

One such vignette of Henry's approach to rule is recorded by the author of the so-called Brut chronicle, and it dates from the early years of Henry's rule, when he is demonstrating his determination to provide law and order at home, in exchange for support for his aggressive, expensive plans in France. The story concerns a pair of knights from northern England: one from Lancashire and the other a Yorkshireman. These two gentlemen have been pursuing a bitter private feud, which has spiraled into open gang warfare between their many supporters.

As the chronicler recounts the tale, Henry summons the two lords to his presence at Windsor to discuss why they have "skirmished together" to the detriment of the peace. They find him sitting at his dinner, eating a plate of oysters. "Whose men are you?" he asks them.

"Your liegemen," they reply.

"What authority or commandment had you to raise up my men or my people to fight and slay each other?" continues Henry.

The knights have no good answer, so Henry swears to them "by the faith he owes to God and St. George" that if they do not make peace by the time he has finished his oysters, then they shall both be hanged.

Predictably, the knights make peace, and Henry sends them packing with a warning that if they ever quarrel violently again, they will both die. "After that, no lord dared make party or strife," writes the chronicler, "and thus [Henry] began to keep his laws and justice, and therefore he was beloved."[13]

This story is rather too neat, and its homiletic conclusion too simple, to be read as literally true.* But Henry really did call individual troublemakers to his presence at times, and was unafraid to demand that even his most loyal lieutenants—including such close allies as the earl of Arundel—put down huge cash bonds as a guarantee for their own followers' peaceable behavior. The oysters story is best understood as a parable. It is evidence that Henry's campaign to present himself as a king who personally stands for a tough, uncompromising, interventionist law-and-order monarchy has worked.

This matters, because it is the bedrock of Henry's policy in France, which is now all about preparing for war.

The members of the Westminster parliament of November 1414 respond to Henry's call to arms enthusiastically—and generously. Rewarding him for addressing their concerns about public order (as well as his self-restraint in not asking for a grant of taxation at Leicester earlier in the year), they listen receptively to his requests at Westminster for a war chest. Bishop Beaufort explains to them precisely what the king means.

If Henry "has a greater increase in his patrimony, it will be possible to reduce the burdens on his lieges, and when these things have been accomplished, great honour and glory must indeed necessarily follow from them," he says.

Beaufort spells out the deal Henry is offering. "Because our said lord the king wishes that true and impartial justice should be done to all his lieges, to the poor as well as to the rich," he says, "if there is anyone who

---

* It riffs, most obviously, on the biblical story of the Judgment of Solomon (1 Kings 3:16–28).

wishes to complain of any evil or wrong done to him which cannot be remedied by the common law, he should deliver his petition."

The test of all this, of course, lies in the result. Beaufort asks the parliament for a "generous subsidy": a grant of taxation big enough for Henry to start assembling an invading army to take to France. And the commons, who are asked to vote through the taxation, fall into line. After three weeks of debate, the members sign off on a "double" subsidy of two fifteenths-and-tenths. Officially, through the veteran speaker Thomas Chaucer, they advise the king that this is money they would like to see spent on "the defense of your realm of England and for the secure and safe keeping of the sea."[14]

This is hardly a war cry. But no one in Westminster in 1414 can delude themselves that Henry plans to spend this generous grant of taxation on anything but a major military expedition on French soil.

Even so, no one at the parliament can possibly imagine just what a return Henry will provide on this investment. It will be a year before another parliament is called. By that time, Henry will have transformed himself from a bold, unproven new king into a warrior in the first rank of European princes.

20

"FICKLE AND CAPRICIOUS FORTUNE"

In the early months of 1414, just before his law-and-order parliament meets at Leicester, Henry passes some of the lean days of Lent in Kenilworth Castle. The palatial fortress remains one of his favorite places, despite—or perhaps because of—the memories of his miraculous medical ordeal at the hands of John Bradmore after the battle of Shrewsbury.

Henry is so fond of Kenilworth that in 1414 he is making plans to develop a whole new site on the estate, where he can escape the pressures and scrutiny of royal office. The castle's main buildings are huge and staggeringly impressive, but they have not been updated in forty years, since a young John of Gaunt remodeled the castle in regal fashion with a vast great hall and reception chamber and new towers, kitchens, and luxurious suites of apartments. Now Henry intends to leave his stamp on the place just as his grandfather did. And he knows exactly where he wants to do it.

For more than two centuries Kenilworth Castle has been surrounded by a large man-made lake, known as the Mere, beyond which stretch hundreds of acres of mature parkland stocked with deer and other beasts of the chase. On the far bank of the lake lies a patch of ground about four acres in size, currently overgrown with brambles and overrun by foxes. Henry has decided to turn this into an artificial island. The island will be circled by a set of double moats, and the bridge across them will be accessible by barge or rowboat from a jetty on the Mere. On the center of the island Henry plans to erect a large structure, which will come to be called the Pleasance. Wooden buildings and four large stone towers are to enclose a landscaped private garden.[1] It will serve as an all-in-one manor house, hunting lodge, and luxury retreat.

The Pleasance is not an entirely original idea. Henry may have been inspired by Richard II, who in the mid-1380s had a lodge known as "la Naight" built at his riverside palace of Sheen, on an island in the river Thames.[2] He must know that his friend and ally Richard Beauchamp, earl of Warwick, has a double-moated pleasure house called "Goodrest" at his ancestral seat of Warwick Castle, very close to Kenilworth. And he may well have heard that John the Fearless enjoys the use of a place called "the house on the marsh" at the famous Burgundian ducal castle of Hesdin.

Yet even if there is precedent to follow, the Pleasance is an ambitious and, for Henry, a very personal project. It is no simple garden folly. Henry is building a palace within the palace, where he can go to live in meditative isolation when he feels the need. As a monk called Thomas Elmham puts it in a verse biography of Henry, the tangled briar patch "now becomes peaceful marshland; the coarse ground is sweetened with running water and the site made nice." Here, says the monk, Henry is making a place where he can think, reflect, and puzzle out the great challenges that lie ahead of him. The Pleasance will be where "the king considers how to overcome the difficulties confronting his own Kingdom. [Here] he remembers the foxy tricks of the French both in deed and in writing and is mortified by the recollection."[3]

This is more than mere poetic fancy. For around this time, while he is staying at Kenilworth Henry is allegedly the subject of one of the most notorious "foxy tricks" in all England's medieval history. The trick will become known as the tennis ball incident.

The tennis ball incident, as told by the same monk who describes the building of Henry's Pleasance, unfolds as follows. During Lent in 1414 Henry is at Kenilworth Castle, when he receives ambassadors sent from the French court. They come bearing gifts, along with a message from the seventeen-year-old dauphin, Louis. The gift consists of a set of Parisian tennis balls, and the message of "some very jesting words," informing Henry that the balls are sent so that he can "play with his young men, as [is] his wont."

Unfazed by this impudence from a prince a decade his junior, Henry dismisses the gift with a quip. He promises very soon to send back to the dauphin *London* balls—that is, cannonballs—which will smash down French houses. Thus, Henry says, he will bring profit to England and send the French packing from their own country.[4]

This, at any rate, is the story that the monk tells—and that is picked up and repeated by other writers, eventually to be written into national legend by Shakespeare. Whether it happened in exactly this way is another matter. A different account of the event lacks the tennis balls themselves, but has Henry being told that he is openly ridiculed in Paris. Diplomats at the French court, in this version, have been taunting their English counterparts, "vomiting venomous words" and saying that since Henry is so young, they'll send him tennis balls to play with, along with some pillows to sleep on until he has grown up a bit.[5] Henry replies that if the French wish to talk about lying around in bed, then he will show them the dangers of doing so, by "hammering on their doors at dawn" to rouse them from their slumbers.

It is difficult to say which of these versions—if either—represents the truth. But perhaps it does not much matter whether the insult Henry perceives from the French court comes in the form of a prank gift, secondhand gossip, or simply his own growing belief that French occupation of lands that ought to be English is a personal slight. In 1414 Henry worked successfully to persuade the English political nation to finance and back an invasion of France. By early 1415 preparations are well underway. French diplomats in contact with their English counterparts are reporting that Henry's mobilization ought to be taken seriously. They may think what they like about Henry's abilities as king, but they should not doubt his determination to come and fight them.

The message seems to find its mark in Paris in February 1415. At the end of that month, a fragile truce is brokered between the Armagnacs and Burgundians, in the hope that this will dissuade Henry from his conviction that a divided France represents a soft target. A few weeks later, the dauphin, now eighteen, launches a coup in which he dismisses Armagnac princes from their leading roles in government, packs off his wife, Margaret of Burgundy—John the Fearless's daughter—to live in miserable separation from him in the Parisian suburbs, and declares himself regent of France with full royal powers during his father's interminable sickness.[6] These powers are to include the personal duty to defend the French realm against the English.

The dauphin knows, as does everyone else with an eye on international affairs, that the current truce between France and England expires in May 1415. After that, he must accept that the "London balls" could start raining down on the kingdom at any moment.

By the time the dauphin Louis makes his bid to take personal control of France, England is indeed in an advanced stage of war preparedness. As members of a final French embassy sent to Henry's court to parlay for peace in the late spring of 1415 discover at first hand, the king is set on trying his claims to French territory by combat, and coldly hostile to any offers of peace that do not include impossibly vast grants of territory and a marriage to the French king's daughter. Henry is intransigent, and the ambassadors need only look around them to see that he is not bluffing.

For months, Henry's officers have been stockpiling weapons and goods, hiring men and transports and beasts of battle and burden. Above everything, they have been raising huge sums of money. Henry's career since the age of thirteen has been an applied lesson in the first principles of warmongering: it must be paid for, and it will always cost more than it should. To lose one's grip on finance risks political crisis. What is more, to Henry's mind, to be broke is unkingly, even shameful. Henry wishes to depart for France, as one report produced by his treasury officials to illustrate the state of the royal finances puts it, "as a well ordered Christian prince" with a "clear conscience."[7] With this in mind, he throws himself into the details of financing his expedition to France with an urgency unmatched by any king in living memory.[8]

The taxation agreed on by Parliament in 1414, generous as it is, will fund only a part of the campaign Henry has in mind. To make a mark in France, he knows he needs far more than the country has already promised him. Indeed, the treasury report that alludes to his clear conscience lays the situation out in detail: Henry must raise at least twice as much again by any means he can find.

This is a huge task, requiring both fiscal discipline and personal determination. It means squeezing every last penny out of sources like Henry's personal landholdings in Wales, Cornwall, and the duchy of Lancaster. It means slashing outgoings on his annuities to royal retainers. It means bolstering confidence in his government's creditworthiness by preventing royal officials from paying debts and wages "on assignment": that is, by issuing IOUs in the form of wooden treasury tallies to be claimed against future revenue.[9] It means grossly inflating the traditional fees the Crown charges to noble men and women for buying royal pardons or licenses to marry.[10] It means threatening, flattering, cajoling, and bribing anyone who seems that they might be parted from their wealth: convincing them by whatever means possible to believe in him and share in his vision of a righteous war.

For much of 1415, therefore, Henry is a king with a begging bowl and a menacing stare. He borrows large sums of money from nobles, churchmen, foreign bankers, and native merchants in the City of London. Bishop Beaufort, as chancellor, sets an example by lending more than £2,000 from the revenues of his diocese of Winchester. The citizens of London are prevailed upon in person by Henry's brothers John and Humphrey to make a collective loan of 10,000 marks. Oligarchs like Sir Richard

Whittington* make huge personal contributions in tacit—or sometimes blatant—exchange for personal power. (Henry hands Whittington complete control over all London planning and building licenses as thanks for a cash advance of £1,600, though he makes it plain he wishes to see London looking smarter when he returns from campaign than when he leaves.)[11] When Italian financiers fail to show immediate enthusiasm for plowing money into an invasion of France—remembering, perhaps, that in the 1340s, Edward III all but bankrupted several of the most respectable banks in Europe by defaulting on loans advanced for a similar enterprise—Henry jails their managers until they cooperate.

Of course, Henry understands that loans must be secured by collateral as well as optimism. Some are backed by the promise of future revenues from the wool tax. Many more are secured on handouts of royal treasure. To the mayor of London Henry pledges a fabulous collar of Lancastrian "SS" symbols made of gold. To his cousin the duke of York he hands over a prized alms dish from the royal chapel known as the "Tiger nef."†[12] To lesser lenders all over England, Henry's agents pawn anything they can lay their hands on, from swords and spurs to rosaries and holy relics—even pans from the royal kitchen. They hawk a jeweled sword set with ostrich feathers that belonged to Richard II's father, the Black Prince, and a necklace Henry wore while he was Prince of Wales, which is studded with rubies and pearls. A jewel-embroidered tunic from the royal wardrobe is unstitched into three parts to be given to three different creditors.[13] Henry's father's favorite crown is given to Thomas, duke of Clarence, who will be taking the biggest band of troops of any lord on the campaign. Thomas dismantles it and hands it out to his followers in sections.

The scramble for cash to convert into war wages and machinery is hardly dignified, but now Henry has committed to war, he is focused on

---

* This extraordinary London merchant is the character on whom the British pantomime character "Dick Whittington" is (very) loosely based. It is a quirk of British historical tradition that this super-merchant and philanthropist is better known today as the owner of a prodigal cat than as one of the men who made the Agincourt campaign possible.

† So called because it is in the shape of a ship of the sort known as a nef, and is decorated with golden tigers at prow and stern.

it with solemn intensity. He is telling everyone who will listen that his war is a righteous one, justified by monstrous wrongs done to him and his ancestors by the French. It is as though he has finally landed on the reason God has saved his life on so many occasions. Now nothing will hold him back.

One week after Easter in April 1415 Henry summons a great council of English nobles and explains to them what he plans to do.

A general order has already gone out demanding that every ship of any significant size, in every major English port, is to be pressed into service for transporting an army either to Guyenne or to northern France.

When added to the royal fleet, the ships of the Cinque Ports on England's southeast coast, and around seven hundred ships hired in Flanders, this will amount to an enormous armada, crewed by at least ten thousand mariners.[14] It is big because it needs to be. Contracts are being drawn up with war captains, who will be responsible for recruiting nearly ten thousand troops—mostly longbowmen—to serve under them. There will be more than two thousand men-at-arms; a large corps of engineers, medics, clerics, and servants; as many as twenty thousand horses and pack animals; and a mountain of supplies, including food, weapons, arrows, animal fodder, and tents. Anticipating sieges against walled cities and castles, Henry also packs a dozen fat cannons and expert gunners to operate them.

No army of this size has left England in generations, since the glorious days of Henry's great-grandfather Edward III in the 1340s and 1350s. And as in Edward's most famous campaign of 1346–47, which culminated with victories at the battle of Crécy and siege of Calais, the army will be led in person by the king, attended by dozens of his most senior noblemen: forty-three of them in total.[15]

Two will be his brothers: Thomas, duke of Clarence, and Humphrey, who has been raised in 1414 to the title of duke of Gloucester. Thomas already has valuable experience fighting in Guyenne, and although his leadership of that campaign was the cause of much friction between him and Henry, the two have settled all their differences since Henry's accession and Thomas has been nothing but supportive and loyal. Humphrey, now twenty-four years old, does not have much experience of military combat. Indeed, although he is a learned and artistically inclined young man, Humphrey does not have much experience of anything. A French campaign will belatedly begin his military education.

Henry's other brother, John, who has also recently been ennobled, as duke of Bedford, will not be accompanying the king. But this is in no sense a sign that Henry does not trust him. Quite the opposite: John has served a long apprenticeship in northern England and understands the politics of border defense better than anyone else. England's neighbors in Wales and Scotland are sure to see Henry's absence on French campaign as an opportunity to make mischief. John is to serve as lieutenant of England and see that their plotting gets nowhere.

John's job will begin when the great invasion fleet sets sail. The council of April 1415 is told that this will take place "at Lammas": the height of summer.[16] Troops will muster in Southampton on July 1. The ships will weigh anchor on August 1. They will be gone for up to a year. While they are away, John, duke of Bedford, will have to be ready for challenges to England's borders and Henry's crown, which could come from any direction.

If any proof of this were needed, it arrives before the war fleet even sets sail. For as the English army makes its way to Southampton, Henry learns of a fresh challenge to his rule. As with the Oldcastle rebellion of eighteen months earlier, it will come from a source worryingly close to the throne.

When Henry made his brothers John and Humphrey dukes in 1414, he also raised another member of the extended royal family to the peerage. Richard of Conisbrough is a thirty-year-old son of the house of York. His elder brother—a dozen years his senior—is Henry's longtime military comrade and cousin Edward, duke of York. Since Edward has devoted more of his attention to his great passion of hunting than he has to the dynastic obligation of reproduction, Richard of Conisbrough is also the heir to the duchy. In the meantime Henry has granted him the title of earl of Cambridge.

Unfortunately, while Henry has granted Richard titles, he has been unable to bestow on him good sense. In years gone by Richard has fought in the wars against Owain Glyndŵr. He accompanied Henry's sister Philippa to Scandinavia when she went to be married. Yet he has never really distinguished himself as a servant of the Crown. In ennobling him Henry has therefore set his cousin a challenge. The earldom of Cambridge does not come with any land or revenue. Henry has suggested that Richard should earn his fortune by way of plunder on the impending campaign in France.

To Richard, this feels rather too much like hard work. So, rather than proving his worth in a war against the French, he decides to turn his hand to the somewhat more difficult task of bringing down his own king.[17]

His plot is as ludicrous as it is complicated. With the connivance of two other lords in the royal circle, Cambridge aims to announce a general rebellion; burn the warships in port at Southampton, Portsmouth, and elsewhere around the Solent; cause the army waiting to go aboard to desert; flee to Wales with that perpetual vehicle of dynastic intrigue, Edmund Mortimer, earl of March; invite a fake Richard II said to be at large in Scotland to meet them there; summon Henry Percy, twenty-two-year-old son of the late Hotspur, who has been living in exile in Scotland since childhood; drag Owain Glyndŵr out of hiding; and make contact with the renegade Lollard leader John Oldcastle.

This ragtag coalition of every anti-Lancastrian enemy, alive, at large, or otherwise, will then bring Henry V to battle and kill him, capture and murder all three of his brothers, and finally put someone else on the throne: one of the fake Richard IIs; Edmund, earl of March; or Richard's four-year-old son and namesake, who also happens to be March's nephew.*

---

* Richard, earl of Cambridge, is married to Anne Mortimer, the sister of Edmund, earl of March. This four-year-old is the future Richard, duke of York, from whom the Yorkist faction in the Wars of the Roses springs.

It is undoubtedly a grand conspiracy, but not a very clever one. And as with any complicated scheme, there are more ways for it to go wrong than right. It is improbable, for example, that Henry Percy will help undo Henry V, given that negotiations are underway to restore him to his family's earldom of Northumberland. The phony Richard II, meanwhile, is now as dead as the real one. Oldcastle has not broken cover since his rebellion, and reports from Wales say that Owain Glyndŵr is also dead and has "been buried by his followers in the darkness of night."[18]

But Cambridge's most obvious miscalculation is to assume that his brother-in-law Edmund Mortimer, earl of March, actually wants to be king. March has recently been fined the vast sum of 10,000 marks by Henry for getting married without a proper royal license. But he seems to have accepted his punishment with good grace, and is tightly involved in the war preparations: so tightly, indeed, that on July 24 he is one of the men who signs his name as a witness to Henry V's will. So although March indulges Cambridge, meeting him and his co-conspirators several times for dinner, his heart is not in the endeavor. Since infancy, March has been the focus of other men's plans to destroy the house of Lancaster. Despite this, he has found the Lancastrians uncommonly lenient toward him, and as a result he has far better cause to support Henry V than to try to replace him.

Around a week after witnessing Henry's will, therefore, March comes to the king in Portchester Castle and reveals that Cambridge is at work on some elaborate treachery and has pitched him a leading role. He informs Henry of the various strands to the plot, and he tells him he must act right away. It is July 31. The coup is due to take place in less than twenty-four hours. If Henry wishes to stop it, he must confront and arrest its ringleaders. Chief among them is, of course, Richard, earl of Cambridge. One of his busiest collaborators is a northern knight called Sir Thomas Grey of Heaton, an old Percy loyalist whose son is engaged to Cambridge's daughter, Isabel. But the third—and by some distance the most shocking—is one of Henry's most trusted advisers, a trusted diplomat, an ally and council member from Henry's days as prince, and a knight of the Garter: Henry, Lord Scrope.

Like John Oldcastle before him, Lord Scrope is one of the relatively few men whom Henry V counts as a friend and intimate. He has been approached by the conspirators in the hope that he is bitter about the memory of his uncle, Archbishop Scrope of York, beheaded by the old king, Henry IV, for his part in the 1405 northern rising. Although Scrope has never shown any sign that he is brooding on this, he has attended meetings with the rebels and knows the full extent of their plans. He seems, in these meetings, to have been trying to destroy the plot from the inside, by pointing out the folly of its various parts to the other members. Yet he has breathed no word of it to Henry. Most fatefully, perhaps, he has been heard to speak skeptically of Henry's wisdom in attacking the French, claiming that he is "undone" whether he goes to France or stays.

As soon as Henry hears March's confession, he acts. Even if it were in his nature to ponder trouble before facing it, which it is not, he has no time. Twelve thousand troops are under orders to be ready to embark the ships the next day, August 1. Many thousands of sailors are standing by. Henry summons all the lords in Southampton to an emergency council to discuss with him rumors of a plot. By the time it meets, Cambridge, Grey, and Scrope know that they have been betrayed, and all three are ready to confess. They are taken away to prison to await their trials.

They do not have long to wait. On Friday, August 2, a local jury finds Grey guilty of treason and sentences him to death: he is beheaded outside Southampton's walls. On the Monday following, a special panel of twenty lords convenes to judge the peers, Cambridge and Scrope. With the earl of March and Cambridge's brother, the duke of York, sitting loyally in its ranks, this jury too passes the death sentence. In the case of Cambridge, this is entirely deserved: he has nothing to plead but his manifest guilt. Scrope, however, is unfortunate. Under the law, his actions have not met the threshold of treason: he denies that he knew of the part of the plot that involved actually killing Henry and his brothers. He has a plausible explanation: he was trying to bring down the plot from within. And he may hope that his long-standing good service to the Crown and personal friendship with Henry might count for something.

Yet for Henry, the circumstances outweigh everything else. As a loyal friend, Scrope of all people should have known how much Henry has invested in preparations for this campaign—and how much he stands to lose if it is disrupted. That he allowed the plot to develop without saying a word may not qualify him for death under English law. But his duplicity offends Henry V's sense of God-given justice, and his reported pooh-poohing of Henry's prospects in the field is unforgivable. Once sentence is passed on the two lords, Cambridge is walked to the execution spot to lose his head. But Scrope is dragged there behind a horse. His last wish, that he should be buried with dignity in York Minster, is ignored. Only his head ends up in that city, set on a spike above Micklegate Bar.

In dealing so ruthlessly (and, it is decided many decades later, illegally)* with a former friend, Henry has shown what mood he is in on the eve of his departure for France. According to one account of the episode, Scrope's only words on his condemnation are "I have sinned," which drives Henry to "weeping and sighing," but not to mercy.[19]

An account written many years later claims that Henry delivers a long and rousing speech to the condemned men, in which he expresses his sadness that there is no friendship nor bond that lust for power will not destroy. "I have often experienced in others, and lately in myself, how fickle and capricious fortune can be," he says, echoing Richard II's lament in the Tower of London following his deposition in 1399.

Unlike Richard, however, Henry does not dissolve into self-pity. Instead he segues into a condemnation of the perfidious French and restates his determination to march into France—which he is now doubly determined to seize as "our glorious and magnificent trophy."[20]

Writers closer to the events record no such speech. But they are nevertheless struck by Henry's apparent commitment to justice, if not the letter of the law. One chronicler remarks that verses written by Ovid of the first Roman emperor, Augustus, would be equally fitting for Henry:

---

* When Edward IV, Yorkist grandson of Richard, earl of Cambridge, usurps the throne in 1461, his first parliament declares the proceedings against the Southampton plotters spurious and illegal.

Our prince is slow to punish, quick to reward,
And when compelled to toughness, a man of grief.[21]

Two days after the failure of what becomes known as the Southampton Plot, on Wednesday, August 7, Henry boards his newly refitted flagship, the *Trinity Royal,* at Portsmouth harbor. At three o'clock on the following Sunday afternoon this magnificent vessel, decorated at the prow with a carved English leopard wearing a copper-gilt crown, and elsewhere with French fleurs-de-lis, sails out in pride of place among hundreds of others, raising its flag to half-mast as a sign that the expedition has begun. Hours later the whole fleet is cruising past the Isle of Wight on toward the French coast beyond. One of the newest ships is painted with a motto Henry has taken to heart: *une sanz pluis* ("one and no more"). It is a cryptic phrase, but on this day it could be read to mean that there is one God, one king, and one mission.[22]

At the head of the fleet a flock of swans paddles around the *Trinity Royal* just before it heads into open water. One of Henry's chaplains, aboard, will later remember this being spoken of as "a happy augury for the task we have undertaken."[23] That task is the invasion and conquest of the kingdom of France, and it will now occupy Henry from this day until the moment of his death.

21

"FIRES OF HELL"

A beautiful summer dawn breaks over the coast of Normandy early on Wednesday, August 14, 1415, to reveal Henry's great armada sitting at anchor in the mouth of the mighty river Seine.[1]

The English have been there all night. The first vessels sighted land the previous evening, but Henry has forbidden his troops from disembarking until he gives the command. He knows he has just one chance of sending his army ashore for the first time. He wants it to be as powerful a statement of his intent as possible. He does not want his troops scattering, giddy at their first sniff of plunder.

The only men he permitted to leave the ships overnight, therefore, belonged to a small reconnaissance party led by his cousin John Holland, knighted on the eve of his coronation and lately raised to the title of earl of Huntingdon. They went out under the cover of darkness with instructions to "explore the countryside and find somewhere to quarter."[2] From their report he has learned—or confirmed—several useful things.

The first is that this part of the Seine estuary will not be a straightforward place to unload more than ten thousand men with all their animals and supplies. Although it is more hospitable than the coast below the cliffs that loom away to the north, the waterline is still studded with large, sharp boulders that could wreck landing vessels. The beach is littered with smaller stones that French defenders can use, along with conventional weapons, to pelt the invaders and drive them back into the sea.

The second thing is that Henry's planned point of attack, the large town on the northern bank of the estuary known as Harfleur, does not present as an easy target, either. The town proper is ringed with walls between ten and twenty feet thick, punctuated by towers with evocative names such as Dragon, Swan, Snail, and Stork, each topped with a brightly painted statue of the appropriate beast.[3] In front of its three great gates stand earth-and-timber barbicans with sniper holes cut out. The river Lézarde, which flows through the city into the Seine estuary, can be dammed so that the northern approach to Harfleur floods. Although there are two promising areas of thickly forested high ground to Harfleur's east and west, its south is protected by a mile of soggy marshland, through which ditches have been cut and earthworks raised.

So the town cannot be rushed or stormed. The deep man-made channel through the marsh, along which ordinary shipping passes to reach the harbor inside the city walls, has been blocked with wooden stakes and chains. Merely landing on the shore will be a major undertaking. Even a few defenders with "manly hearts," writes a royal chaplain who stands watching the sun rise that morning, could keep Henry's army "at bay certainly for a long time and perhaps indefinitely."[4]

Yet there is a third piece of intelligence brought back by Holland's reconnaissance patrol, which puts everything else into perspective. Although Henry has made no secret of his departure for France, and his expected destination has long been Normandy, there is no French army or even a local militia standing guard on the shore to oppose him. Inside Harfleur lurks a force of a few hundred professional soldiers and crossbowmen and between six and eight thousand ordinary townsfolk. Otherwise, the coast lies undefended.

It is almost too good to be true. Do the French expect Henry to land elsewhere—on the long, soft, sandy beaches of the Cotentin Peninsula, maybe, where Edward III came ashore in the 1340s? Are they still so wracked by their internal strife that they cannot raise an army to defend their own soil? Are they so rattled by his aggression that they fear meeting him too early, and hope to let his army blow itself out before engaging?

Aboard the *Trinity Royal* on the morning of August 17 Henry cannot answer any of these questions with certainty. But he *can* see that Harfleur, long a bolt-hole for pirates and foreign merchants alike, is defended more by the landscape than by human hands.

He can confirm with his own eyes what he has suspected all along: if captured, this town could become an English forward base at the mouth of the Seine, threatening Rouen and Paris upriver. It could be an English enclave superior even to Calais, the very first town on mainland Europe he visited as a boy, and the focus of so much of his political attention as prince.

And he can feel in his heart what he is starting to believe with every fiber of his being: that God wants him to succeed.

At around six a.m. Henry sends the order to his men to begin their landing. Barges and skiffs are lowered into the salt water. Sailors begin carefully rowing them between the deadly rocks. Minutes later the first Englishmen are wading onto the land Henry claims for his own. The king and his brothers Thomas and Humphrey are among them. Henry's first action once he comes ashore is to drop to his knees and pray. As the sharp pebbles of the beach press into his knees, he asks God that "by the honor of his divinity he [will] give him justice of his enemies."[5]

In his last letter to Charles VI, sent at the end of July 1415, Henry warned the French king that he intended to direct his war according to the ancient laws of Deuteronomy. He would "fight to the death for justice," he wrote. But before he wreaked vengeance against any town that defied him, he would offer peace.[6] On Monday, August 19, with his army now fully ashore, he makes good on this promise. He sends messengers to the citizens of Harfleur, offering to treat them well, "if freely and without coercion, they would open their gates to him and, as was their duty, restore that town, which was a noble and hereditary portion of his crown of England and of his duchy of Normandy."[7]

Henry positions this as a fair transaction: he is their rightful lord, and it is their duty to obey him. But he frames his offer in scriptural terms, and when the defenders reject it, he lets them know that they can expect biblical vengeance. A herald is sent to the city walls to inform them "of the penal edicts contained in the [Deuteronomic] law, which it would be necessary to execute upon them as a rebellious people should they thus persist in their obstinacy to the end."[8] As specified in Deuteronomy, this means that Henry will now attempt to pound the city into submission, and if he succeeds he will "put to the sword all the men therein" and take all the women, children, and livestock as plunder.[9]

By the time this exchange is underway, Henry has taken up residence on the hill called Mont Leconte, to the west of Harfleur, where he is lodged in the elegant priory of Graville, whose Romanesque buildings were built long ago on war bounty taken in England by a comrade of William the Conqueror. It is a long time—seven years—since he has personally taken part in a siege. That was the long, grinding struggle to take back Aberystwyth from Owain Glyndŵr. At Harfleur he is camped in much greater comfort: the priory has been transformed into a luxurious palace. A full staff including heralds, priests, medics, and even half a dozen painters scurry around dressed in scarlet uniforms, and cooks prepare delicious meals served at a high table set with gold and silver cutlery.[10] Yet a siege is a siege, and when Henry looks out from the priory to the town below, what he sees will seem familiar.

From his vantage point he can see Harfleur boarded up against him—its gates obstinately shut, some of its abandoned suburbs burned by his own men, others flooded with dammed river water by the citizens themselves. On a hill to the east, known as Mont Cabert, there is another substantial English position, commanded by his brother Thomas, who has dragged several thousand men and a number of cannons on a ten-mile march around the floodwaters of the Lézarde to reach this advantageous spot. Elsewhere, spread out over the two hills and on the marshland to the south of Harfleur the rest of the English army are camped, their tents and pavilions so numerous that they resemble "a right great city."[11]

Down in that mass of canvas, men with the red cross of St. George emblazoned on their tunics are busily digging trenches, assembling stone-throwing catapults, and erecting protective screens from behind which gunners can operate their bombards. Engineers are studying the walls and towers to plan the course of mines that will be dug to weaken their foundations. Troops are tying together long bundles of sticks, which they will use to fill up the town's defensive ditches. Priests are hard at their own labor, offering "holy prayers to honor God, and [saying] their accustomed service as they used to do when they were at home in England in time of peace."[12]

English discipline is holding strong. Henry has issued the customary strict ordinances against looting, robbing, rape, or murder of civilians and the desecration of holy buildings. He has reminded his army that they are here because this land of Normandy is rightfully his, and its people are therefore his subjects. He must hope that their good behavior holds.

Meanwhile, the defenders of Harfleur—who do not seem to appreciate that they are in fact Englishmen true and loyal—are also busy. On the town walls Henry can see—and perhaps smell—soldiers and citizens readying themselves for the coming assault. Some are filling tubs with hot pitch, sulfur, and quicklime to hurl at anyone who comes near. Others are lining up guns and catapults behind the barbicans at each gatehouse. And inside Harfleur, where the great steeple of the Church of St-Martin rises elegantly above the jumble of rooftops, citizens are covering the pavements with clay and animal droppings, to deaden the impact of the impending barrage and lessen the danger of shrapnel.

It is an impressive sight. Harfleur is held by only a few hundred experienced men-at-arms, under a tough Armagnac crusading veteran named Raoul de Gaucourt. This force has arrived at the town so recently that Raoul has not been able to organize a mass expulsion of useless mouths—women, children, the elderly, and other noncombatants. But they have otherwise done a fine job of shoring up defenses. It is the view of Henry's chaplain, perhaps echoing the king's own, that no besieged people could have prepared themselves "more prudently or with greater security to themselves."[13] All the same, Henry may reason, in a contest between prudence and cannonballs, the advantage is typically held by the side with the biggest guns.

The roar of the English cannons that open fire on Harfleur once peace has been rejected will be remembered with dread for many years afterward. "From every side," writes Henry's chaplain, "our king with his guns . . . pounded the barbicans and the walls and the towers."[14]

Over the years, the guns in the English royal artillery have been given dainty names like "Messenger" and "King's Daughter."[15] But in reality, they are brutes: monstrous, gaping-mouthed iron beasts mounted on hardwood platforms, weighing several tons each and capable of blasting forth hunks of rubble and masonry several hundred pounds in weight. If they overheat or otherwise malfunction, they can explode, maiming or killing their operators. A monk in Paris calls them "machines of extraordinary and unaccustomed coarseness" that belch out millstones "with such a terrible noise and crash that they seem to come from the fires of Hell."[16]

Once his guns start firing, Henry has no intention of allowing them to stop, for the damage they do to the citizens of Harfleur is psychological as well as physical. There is plenty of military knowledge and no shortage of willing pairs of hands in Harfleur, so that even as the English cannons blow holes in Harfleur's walls, shattering the timber barbicans outside the gates, collapsing rooftops, and even wrecking the steeple of the Church of St.-Martin, the defenders are able to make running repairs and keep up a barrage of fire and shot of their own. However, as Henry learned during the bombardment of Aberystwyth all those years ago, no man can stand the mental torment of a ceaseless booming and hail of sharp stone forever. All the English need to do is keep it up. So as his gunners get to work, Henry comes down from his hilltop priory and walks among his army, personally urging them to throw themselves into their hot, smelly, dangerous, difficult work.

His chaplain later recalls him staying awake "night and day," positioning siege engines and cannons to his liking.[17] Another writer states that he "daily and nightly in his own person visited and searched the watches, orders and stations of every part of his host, and whom he found diligent he praised and thanked, and the negligent he corrected and chastised."[18]

And as he tours his men's stations, Henry shows that for all the austerity of the kingly persona he adopted on the day of his coronation, when it comes to the smoke and grime of a siege he can still project an earthy, soldierly bearing. In one of his first addresses to a group of captains at Harfleur, he tells them to "be of good cheer, and blow you and cool you well, and come up all-with your ease,* for with the love of God we shall have good tidings."[19]

This is by no means a one-man show. Among the dozens of senior men in his army, Henry can rely for advice and command on his brothers Thomas and Humphrey, his uncle Thomas Beaufort, his cousins John Holland and the duke of York, and his old friends the earl of Arundel and Richard Courtenay, bishop of Norwich.

His brother Thomas in particular shows how well he deserves his reputation as a soldier of extreme, even reckless bravery, leading direct attacks on the town's moat and its battered walls, with men-at-arms and archers inching their way toward the town's defenses under the cover of wooden shields and shelters known variously as "cats," "sows," and "weasels." Thomas is also in charge of operations below the city walls, where a fierce game of mining and countermining is taking place, with a network of tunnels under the marsh becoming a subterranean combat ground for "the exercise of knightly acts."[20]

At the start of September, a few weeks into the siege, Henry sends word to the wealthy wine merchants in Bordeaux, the capital of English-held Guyenne, to update them on progress. Harfleur has not yet fallen, they are told, but it is blockaded, bombarded, and surely only days away

* Literally: "a-blowe yow and be-kele yow wel, and comyth up all with youre ese." Loosely: "take a few deep breaths, keep cool, relax." As the modern American military idiom has it: "stay frosty."

from capitulation. Soon their ships will be able to pass this stretch of the coast unbothered by the pirates who have for too long used it as a lair. Henry asks the winemakers to send, as a token of their gratitude, several hundred barrels of their wares.[21] This may suggest that supplies are running low. But it also shows Henry's tail is up. He is already starting to look beyond Harfleur to the wealthy towns that lie farther up the right bank of the Seine, which include the Norman capital, Rouen, and beyond it, Paris.

By the time Henry writes to the vintners of Bordeaux, the grim details of Harfleur's plight have reached the dauphin Louis and his royal government in Paris. English agents are spreading the story that Henry is well-enough supplied to stay on the marshes of the Seine estuary through the winter if he must—just as his great-grandfather Edward III did in 1347 when he seized Calais from the dauphin's great-great-grandfather Philip VI.

This is not true, but it does not need to be. As Louis knows from his own sources, Harfleur is a couple of weeks away from starvation. If it is not relieved it will fall, and the blow to his young pride will be almost as severe as the bloody sanctions Henry has promised to visit upon the citizens. If Harfleur is to be saved, an army must march on it immediately.

The problem is that there is scarcely any army to march. All summer Louis and his council have been paralyzed by a general tax strike among the French people, whose resources and morale have been wasted almost to nothing by the horrors of the civil war. Rankling mistrust between the outwardly reconciled Armagnacs and Burgundians means Louis can scarcely contemplate leaving Paris without fear of a coup taking place in his wake.

Only at the end of August does an order go out for all able-bodied warriors in the kingdom to take up arms and join Louis in relieving Harfleur. On September 10 the befuddled Charles VI is guided to the royal abbey of Saint-Denis and handed the oriflamme: the sacred crimson French battle flag supposedly once raised by Charlemagne as he marched against the Saracens.* Marshal Boucicaut, the most famous warrior in France, and a one-time jousting partner of Henry's father, is appointed captain of Normandy. But by this time, it is too late.

Five days after Charles VI takes the oriflamme, with no army but Henry's anywhere near the Seine estuary, the defenders of Harfleur ask for a parlay under a flag of truce. Their offer, made to Henry's brother Thomas on September 15, is a typical chivalric proposal: they ask Henry to quiet his cannons for three weeks, until October 6. If the dauphin and Boucicaut have not relieved the city by then, they will open the gates.

When the message is relayed to Henry, he replies in bracing fashion. Days earlier one of the huge barbicans defending the city gates was captured and burned. Reeking smoke from burning dung used in its foundations clouds the siege camp. To the north, the English have diverted the river Lézarde and are draining the land it has flooded. Harfleur is on the brink.

After some back-and-forth, Henry grants the defenders a week to make provision for their relief, and allows them to send messengers to Paris to relay the details of the deal: if Louis has not arrived by September 22, Harfleur will surrender. On the morning of that day, the messengers arrive back with a doleful report. The dauphin is not coming. The game is up.

That afternoon, Henry reverts to one of his favorite guises of kingship: the theatrical performer. In a silken tent pitched outside Graville Priory, on top of the hill overlooking Harfleur, he ascends a throne draped in cloth of gold and fine linen, flanked by the greatest English lords and knights present, sitting, as one observer puts it, "in his estate as royal as did ever any king."[22] Harfleur's commander, the grizzled veteran Raoul de Gaucourt, leads a delegation of the leading citizens to Henry to present him with the keys to the town.

Haughtily, Henry keeps Raoul and his companions waiting on their

* But in fact not quite three hundred years old, having first been raised by Louis VI in the twelfth century.

knees in a separate tent to his own for some time. When they are finally admitted to his presence, he lectures Raoul on the Deuteronomic laws of war, telling him that by rights all the citizens' lives are now at his whim. Since the start of the siege he has warned what would happen if he were resisted in his efforts to take the town.

Yet then Henry changes tack. Because the townsmen have come out to surrender in peace, "even though tardily," he says, "they should not depart entirely without mercy."[23] Rather than an apocalyptic slaughter in the streets, Henry gives orders for the English flag to be raised over Harfleur's walls, the soldiers to be taken as prisoners of war for ransom, and most of the citizens to be expelled, taking with them nothing but a few coins each from his treasury and their souls. Just as Edward III did with Calais in 1347, so Henry aims to do with Harfleur in 1415: it is to be resettled with English merchants, garrisoned with English soldiers, and established as a military forward base and economic colony.

In the short term, Henry appoints his uncle Thomas Beaufort, earl of Dorset, as warden and captain of Harfleur. He assigns twelve hundred of his men to remain in place as a garrison, and sends for workmen from London to come and repair the damage to the town's walls and buildings. He makes a fine show of walking barefoot to the half-collapsed Church of St.-Martin, where he gives thanks to God for his victory. He writes in grandstanding fashion to the dauphin, reminding him that wars cause "the death of men, the destruction of the countryside and the lamentations of women and children," and offering to "submit our quarrel, by the grace of God, to a trial between our body and yours."[24] The prize will be the French crown itself. He gives Louis eight days to consider this proposal of trial by single combat.[25] He orders his army to rest and recover from the exertions of their siege on the marsh.

Then he turns his mind to a very difficult question, which must be answered in very short order. Where should he go next?

Since setting sail from England six weeks earlier Henry has done much as he said he would: he has come to France and begun his quest for justice, to be satisfied by conquest. Harfleur has shown what he can do, given men, guns, money, and time. Just a few weeks ago he was dreaming of a push up the Seine to continue his conquest. But already things are starting to look different.

It is growing late in the year—too late, realistically, for a tilt at another town of Harfleur's size, let alone a regional capital such as Rouen, some fifty miles inland. The dauphin is highly unlikely to gamble the French kingdom on the sort of one-on-one dogfight that Richard II long ago ordered Henry's own father to contest at Coventry—not least since he is belatedly gathering an army that will be larger and fresher than Henry's own.

What is more, Henry's own army has been terribly depleted outside Harfleur. Living on waterlogged land in sweltering heat, eating sun-rotted food and unripe fruit pilfered from the countryside have led to an epidemic of disease. Dysentery and other fluxes of the gut have killed at least two thousand of his troops, and many more have been invalided back to England. Henry's brother Thomas is among the sick. His longtime counselor and confidant Richard Courtenay, bishop of Norwich, has died. So too have Thomas FitzAlan, earl of Arundel, Henry's old comrade and one of the most capable generals in England, and Michael de la Pole, earl of Suffolk, a faithful servant of Henry IV and the house of Lancaster.

Some of these men have been at Henry's side since he was prince, and losing them grieves him deeply. Courtenay often slept in Henry's own tent at night, and Henry was with the bishop when he died, wiping his friend's feet and closing his eyes before having his body shipped back to England to be buried with honor among the royal tombs in Westminster Abbey.[26]

In these circumstances the cautious course of action is to follow Courtenay's body home and to regroup, restock, and come again next year, if Parliament will grant the funds. Yet a doubt nags Henry. He has come to France proclaiming himself its rightful ruler and the defender of its people from the tyranny of its warring nobles. He has gambled his reputation and almost all the political capital of his new reign on the outcome of this campaign.

If he returns to England now, will those who were not here to hear the cannon bark and see the walls of Harfleur crumble consider the English flag fluttering above one more French town justifiable return on the huge investment in Henry's army? God has spoken in his favor, no doubt. But has he spoken loudly enough?

This is the dilemma on whose horns Henry sits. If he goes home, he risks grumbling at the lack of progress, perhaps even another rebellion. But if he remains in France, he risks being wiped out either by disease or by the first army he faces. The alleged words of Henry, Lord Scrope, the friend he executed, may ring bitterly in Henry's ears: he is undone whether he stays or he goes.

In early October Henry gathers his council at Harfleur and asks them for their recommendations. A majority of them tell him to go home.

Henry considers their words. He thinks about their arguments. Then he sends his ships back to England and orders his army to make ready for a march into the unknown.

22

"HIS LITTLE BLESSED MANY"

Of the twelve thousand fighting men who came to France with Henry on his righteous quest for justice, perhaps only six thousand (and no more than eight and a half thousand) are alive and in any fit state to follow him when, on Tuesday, October 8, 1415, he rides out of the battered but newly English town of Harfleur and sets off in the direction of the only other English port on the northern French mainland: Calais.[1]

His depleted army—"so very small, yet arrayed bravely enough"—has provisions for an eight-day march.[2] They will be taking the straightest possible route to Calais, by roads that follow the coastline of Upper Normandy northeast into Picardy. Along the way they will cross several rivers: the widest of them the Somme, which can be forded near Abbeville by a crossing known as the Blanchetaque.

The men will move fast: the distance from Harfleur to Calais is more than 150 miles, which means they must cover around 20 miles a day, every day that they are on the road. But they will have no time to break things. As the army sets off, Henry reissues his strict ordinances on behavior. "Under pain of death, no man should burn and lay waste, or take anything save only food and what [is] necessary for the march."[3]

As they leave, Henry affects to be in good spirits. He has written home to the City of London, whose merchants have invested so handsomely in his campaign. "We are in very good health," he tells them, before summarizing the events of the siege and adding that he hopes "by the fine power and good labor and diligence of our faithful people overseas to do our duty to achieve as soon as possible our rights in this area."[4] For the march he has brought several treasured keepsakes that speak to his determined, devout frame of mind. Although he has commanded his men to leave behind absolutely everything that they can do without, his own servants carry a crown, a jeweled sword of state said once to have belonged to King Arthur, a glittering golden crucifix, and a six-inch fragment of Christ's own True Cross.[5]

Yet if Henry is confident, his men—and even his noble companions, including his brother Humphrey and cousins John Holland and Edward, duke of York—may wonder what on earth they are all doing. It is Henry's prerogative as king to ignore their advice to go home from Harfleur. But to drive his men on what amounts to an eight-day sprint through enemy territory seems aggressive to the point of recklessness. It also seems out of keeping with the meticulous, ordered planning on which Henry has based his military campaigning so far.

Henry, too, must know that he is taking a huge risk. Yet ever since he was a young prince burning down Owain Glyndŵr's house, he has understood the value of deploying bursts of extreme and unexpected aggression. He is taking a big risk, but a calculated one. The arguments will not change, however many times they are rehearsed. To go home directly from Harfleur will encourage disparagement of a costly campaign fought for poor reward. To overwinter at Harfleur will invite the dauphin to come and try his own hand at besieging the town—a task that will be much easier now that Henry's cannons have leveled so much of it. (It will also incur huge payments for wages to troops who are not engaged in fighting.)

Henry needs to show that he can do more than take a single town. He

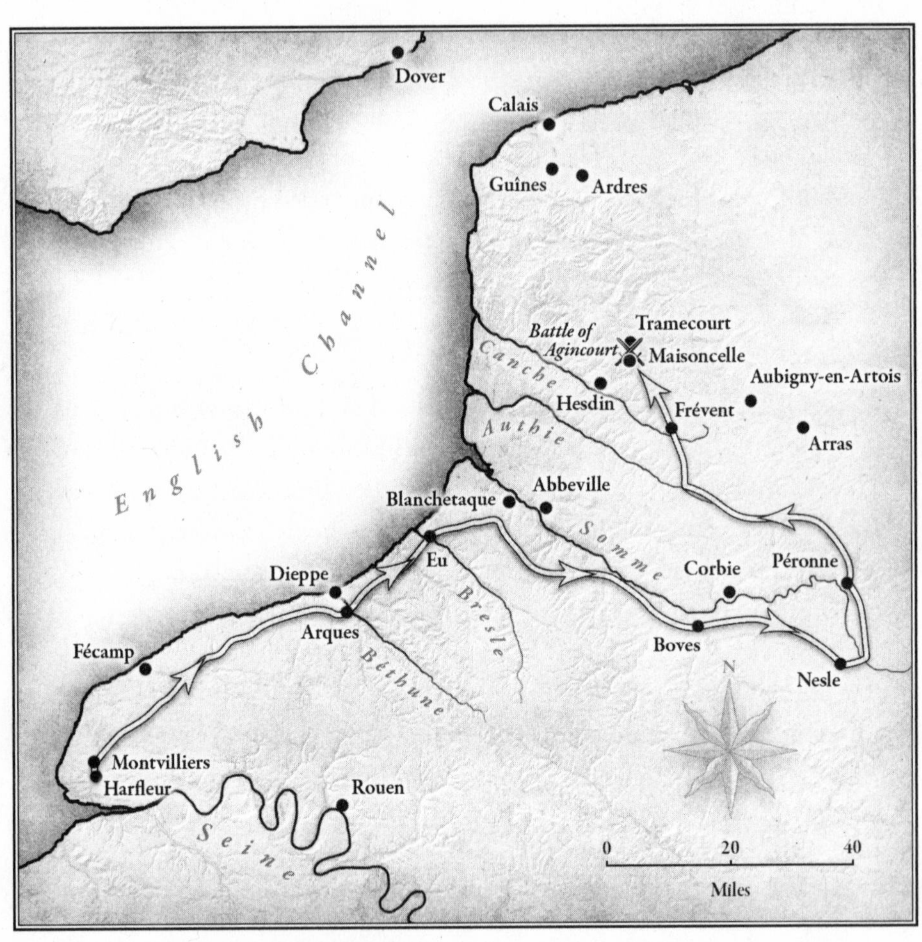

The Agincourt Campaign of 1415

needs to distract the dauphin from any thoughts of taking Harfleur back before it has been repaired. He needs to show his face to the people of Normandy, which he claims as his own realm. But more than anything else, he needs to demonstrate that God remains on his side. A quick triumphal procession from this new Calais to the old will meet all those objectives. If everything goes to plan, the march will be done by October 16. By November they will all be back in England.

The only thing Henry must avoid is being intercepted by the French.

The first days of the march pass relatively smoothly. Henry leads his men past the towns of Montivilliers and Fécamp in peace. His troops—of whom about three-quarters are archers—obey his injunctions against looting and arson. They overnight in the open. During daylight they keep their pace up. They do not hit their daily target of twenty miles' advance. But they are not far off it.

On Friday, October 11, three days after departing Harfleur, Henry faces his first challenge. Some way inland from Dieppe, near the town of Arques (Arques-la-Bataille), his men enter a valley where three rivers flow together.* These are passable by a network of bridges, but the town is barricaded shut, the river bridges are guarded by a large stone castle on a hilltop, and the mood of the castle's garrison is not hard to judge. As the English come into view, cannons boom in warning. If Henry wants to cross the water here, his troops will have to run a gauntlet of gunshot.

Approaching what ought to be the halfway stage of his dash for Calais, Henry is still bullish. He sends a messenger to the castle and offers a deal. The garrison can either hold their fire and let his men pass unharmed—or Henry will suspend military discipline, and give the people of Arques a taste of how an English army on the road in France traditionally acts.

It is not a hard decision for the garrison to make, and the messengers soon return with good news. Henry has been granted "free passage and a

---

* The Eaulne, Béthune, and Varenne combine to form the river Arques, which empties into the sea at Dieppe.

fixed amount of bread and wine with which to refresh the army, in order to ransom [the] town and neighbourhood from being burned."[6] The route is clear. The extra provisions are welcome. Henry has demonstrated a reliable lesson of warfare: often as not, extortion works.

It works again the next day, Saturday, October 12, when the English encounter the town of Eu. This is the last major Norman settlement the men will pass before they enter Picardy, but they find its inhabitants less pliable than those of Arques. Rather than laying down warning fire, the citizens send out an armed sally against Henry's lines. There is a short but fierce engagement, with injuries on both sides, before the French are driven back inside the town walls. After this flurry of violence, Henry is able to cut the same deal as he did the previous day: freedom to pass by the city, and a consignment of bread and wine in exchange for calm heads.

Yet as the English leave Normandy behind them, a worrying rumor starts to spread among the ranks. Sunday, October 13, will bring them close to Abbeville, on the southern bank of the river Somme. This is the last great natural barrier they have to overcome. But according to captives taken during the skirmishing, it is also where the English adventure is doomed to end.

Henry has been planning to lead his men across the Blanchetaque, a wide, natural causeway revealed when the Somme ebbs at low tide, over which Edward III's army made a famous charge during the Crécy campaign of 1346. It is not hard for the French to guess that this is where he will head. So, as Henry and his men have been heading north from Harfleur, enemy troops have been racing just as hard in the same direction. And they have won the race. A large force led by the constable of France, Charles d'Albret, and the famous Marshal Boucicaut is now assembled on the north bank of the Somme. They have broken all the bridges for miles upriver and mined the Blanchetaque, which is now "fixed with sharp stakes" and completely impassable.[7]

Even worse, back in the Norman capital, Rouen, an even larger French army is assembling under the dauphin. In a matter of days it could be ready to ride north and attack the English from behind.

Suddenly, things appear bleak. Ahead of Henry's army lies the wide and now unpassable obstacle of the river Somme, guarded on its northern bank. To his rear is gathering a large, fresh enemy army, fired by indignation at what the English have done in Harfleur. To his left lies the sea.

Unless Henry can summon a miracle, he and his men are trapped. His chaplain, writing a little while later, remembers the sickening feeling that sweeps through Henry's army as the hard reality of their predicament sinks in.

"[We] looked up in bitterness to Heaven," he writes, "seeking the clemency of Providence, and calling upon the Glorious Virgin and Blessed [Saint] George to intercede . . . [and] deliver us from the swords of the French."

Perhaps the only man among the English who does not despair as they reach the river Somme is Henry. Persuaded by his captains that he cannot risk fighting his way across the Blanchetaque, he turns his men east. They now begin a hard slog upriver, in search of a bridge across the Somme that has been missed by the breakers, or a shallow point in the waters where they can wade. It is an intimidating journey. But Henry, who has been in dire trouble in war before now and survived, does not lose hope.

Even so, it is hard to see how he will wriggle out of the trap in which he is caught, for every day he and his men spend on the south bank of the Somme seems to bring worse news. The bridge town of Abbeville is shut up and heavily guarded. The crossing at Saint-Rémy has been destroyed. By October 15 the English are at a little town called Boves. They bully the inhabitants into giving them bread and wine, to replenish food stocks that are running so low that men are grinding up walnuts to make flour for their bread. But when dawn breaks on Wednesday, the sixteenth, the situation is desperate. This was the day they were due to arrive in Calais. Instead, they are one hundred miles away and traveling in the wrong direction.

Discipline and morale are now threatening to break, and Henry can sense it. On Thursday, the seventeenth, his men are attacked as they pass the town of Corbie. They win the engagement, but dissent is spreading in the ranks. Henry decides to strike hard against it. As the army rests at Corbie, he brings before the men one of their own: an archer accused of stealing a pyx from a nearby church. After a perfunctory hearing, Henry finds him guilty and has him hanged from the branch of a tree. Next, he addresses a rumor that the French are planning cavalry assaults against the English archers, ordering every one of his bowmen to equip himself with a "stake or staff, either square or round, but six feet long . . . and sharpened at both ends," which he can drive into the ground in front of him if necessary, to guard against a horse's approach.[8] And the following day, when they pass the walled town of Nesle, make the customary request for provisions in exchange for peace, and are rebuffed, Henry does not negotiate. The townsfolk in Nesle have hung red flags on their walls as a symbol of their defiance. Henry orders all the hamlets surrounding Nesle to be burned to the ground. If the south bank of the Somme is where his march to Calais is to end, Henry is at least determined to go down fighting.

On the morning of Saturday, October 19, as smoke billows up from Nesle, providence finally smiles. Outriders going ahead of Henry's army report an area of marshland through which the Somme and tributaries run low and slow. There lie two causeways across the water that are only partially destroyed and can be repaired. Even better, the French on the far bank have not yet tracked this far upriver. If the English hurry, they can cross.

Henry wastes no time. Men rush to the crossing points and start filling in the gaps in the poorly hacked-up causeways with anything they can find, pulling down abandoned houses in the nearby countryside for timber. A little after midday the causeways are back in service, and the army is picking its way across. By the time the French on the far bank of the river hear what is happening and send a detachment of cavalry to try to oppose the crossing, it is too late.

As his men splash across the water of the Somme, Henry stands at one of the crossings and watches them pass. He has kept his nerve, and his men have followed his lead. They are still a very long way from Calais, with little left to eat or drink. One French army is in the field and another must soon be coming to join it. This is not how he wanted the march to proceed. But he and his men are alive, and amid the jubilation at having forded the river, they are increasingly confident that the French will be "disinclined to follow after us to do battle."[9]

On that score, however, the English are dead wrong.

In Rouen on Sunday, October 20, a French royal council votes overwhelmingly in favor of ordering Constable d'Albret and Marshal Boucicaut to block Henry's path to Calais and take on his men in battle. Charles VI is enjoying one of his occasional periods of lucidity, but for understandable reasons his noble advisers decline to send him north to lead his army. Neither do they risk sending the dauphin. The prospect of either man being captured by the English does not bear consideration.*

Command of the army will therefore be shared by d'Albret, Boucicaut, and a number of mostly Armagnac dukes, of whom the most senior is Charles, duke of Orléans, an inexperienced twenty-year-old nephew of the king. He will join the army as soon as he can. John the Fearless, duke of Burgundy, however, will be going nowhere near it. He is considered by many around the king and dauphin to be as serious a menace to the kingdom as Henry V. So this is a partisan army with a top-heavy command structure—yet what the French lack in tight leadership they more than make up for in weight of numbers. As paid troops and volunteers flood into Picardy to join the French army, its numbers swell to somewhere between twelve and fourteen thousand, of whom two-thirds are men-at-arms.

As this formidably large force starts coming together near the town of Péronne, its leaders send three heralds to Henry to inform him of their

* The memory of the battle of Poitiers (1356), when Richard II's father, the Black Prince, captured Jean II of France, must haunt Charles VI's counselors. This is a point noted by a contemporary chronicler writing at the abbey of Saint-Denis.

intention. They are ready to fight and ask him to name a time and place to do battle.

Exactly what Henry replies will be disputed in the retelling. It seems that a location is discussed: Aubigny-en-Artois, roughly halfway between the present camp and Calais. The date proposed is Thursday, October 24. But whether this is a fixed plan in the mind of either side is open to question. Each side must suspect the other of negotiating in bad faith and planning another, more advantageous moment to fight. So Henry also tells the heralds what they already know. He is heading through the countryside toward his town of Calais. He is neither hiding nor running scared. If the French want a battle, all they have to do is come and find him.[10]

This fighting talk is no bluff. After all Henry has been through in the summer of 1415, and all he has learned in his career of the importance of facing down one's enemies, he means what he says. As his chaplain puts it, Henry is very calm and "heedless of danger."[11] After the heralds depart he puts on armor and tells his men to do the same. From now on they must expect to give battle at any moment.

The following day, as the English march in battle order past Péronne, where the French were recently encamped, they see the roads churned up as if by a force "many thousands strong." The sight terrifies many of the men, who are by now hungry, thirsty, tired, and living on the ends of their nerves. Some begin wailing, asking God to "have pity on us and, of His ineffable goodness, turn away from us the violence of the French."[12]

But they keep marching. They do not catch sight of this vast French army for three more days. Only on Thursday, October 24, as they cross the river Ternoise and come up onto high ground not far from the villages of Maisoncelle and Azincourt, do Henry and what one English writer calls "his little blessed many" finally see what scouts have been reporting for some time.[13]

No more than half a mile away across a small valley are the French cavalry, "filling a very broad field as if they were an innumerable multitude of locusts."[14] They are standing directly between the English army and the last fifty miles of road that leads to safety in Calais. They show no inclination to get out of the way.

Henry's men have now been marching, sleeping rough, and scavenging whatever they can find to eat for sixteen days and around 250 miles. And now, what Henry planned as a brazen show of his own military strength has turned into a long-overdue expression of French chivalric might: "the fairest sight of armed men that ever any man saw in any place."[15] A ripple of fear spreads through the English ranks, which one of Henry's closest advisers, Sir Walter Hungerford, betrays as he stands beside Henry looking at "grim-looking ranks of the French." If only, says Hungerford, they had ten thousand more of the best English archers.

"That is a foolish way to talk," snaps Henry. He swears by the Almighty that "I would not, even if I could, have a single man more than I do. For these I have here with me are God's people, whom he deigns to let me have at this time. Do you not believe that the Almighty, with these his humble few,* is able to overcome the opposing arrogance of the French?"[16]

Hungerford's reply is not recorded. Perhaps there is nothing to say. By now the sun is setting. It is too late in the day for battle to be joined. But whether the English have ten men or ten thousand, one thing is certain. The next day, there will be blood. God will show his hand. Henry V's "little blessed many," his "humble few," will meet their fate.

Henry spends the night of Thursday, October 24, in a house in the hamlet of Maisoncelle. His troops camp in the open air, on ground made sodden by a heavy downpour of rain. The French are camped so close by that the English army can see the lights of their fires and hear the laughter of men playing dice and imagining the fortunes they will earn when they each capture an English lord.[17]

The French, however, cannot hear the English. Henry has ordered that they camp in eerie, monastic silence. Any lord or man-at-arms who breaks this rule will lose his horse and armor. Any archer who makes a sound

* This account, of course, provides the inspiration for Henry's most famous Shakespearean soliloquy: "We few, we happy few, we band of brothers" (*Henry V*, act 4, scene 3).

will lose an ear. They sit in the wet and the dark so quiet that some of the French think they must have run away.

Needless to say, Henry is not for running. By dawn on Friday, October 25, he has risen, heard three masses in his full armor, and is out lining his men up. The French have chosen the battleground, which lies between two areas of woodland: one of which extends away from Henry's billet at Maisoncelle and the other near a hamlet called Tramecourt. Henry places his men between them. His center consists of little battalions of men-at-arms, commanded by him, the duke of York, and Thomas, Lord Camoys, a veteran nobleman who has been fighting in France and Scotland since the 1380s. (By chance, Lord Camoys is married to Elizabeth Mortimer, who was widowed in the last battle Henry fought: her first husband was Hotspur.)

On either wing, and in little "wedges" between his battalions of men-at-arms, Henry places the bulk of the army: the archers. Each of them drives into the ground before him the six-foot-long sharpened stake that he has been carrying since Henry gave the order to make them, back at Corbie. Farther away in Tramecourt's woods Henry sends a detachment of a couple hundred more longbowmen, hidden so that they can shoot into the flanks of French cavalry as they charge past. To the very rear, near the small collection of luggage that passes for the army's baggage train, priests are positioned with instructions to pray as hard as they ever have for victory.

It is not a complicated battle formation. Indeed, it is virtually identical to the one Henry's great-grandfather Edward III deployed at Crécy in 1346. It relies on the French charging the English center, and being mown down by deadly longbow shot from the flanks as they come forward. And it is exactly what the French think Henry will do. Their plan, drawn up by Marshal Boucicaut a fortnight earlier, is to send initial waves of cavalry directly into the archers, knocking them out of the fight before a second wave of riders heads straight for Henry's center and crushes them through sheer weight of numbers.

Both sides, in effect, know exactly what the other will do—or at least, what they intend to do. But if Henry recalls anything from his experience twelve years ago at Shrewsbury, it is that once a battle is begun, there is very little way to know how it will unfold. By the early morning of Friday, October 25—the feast day of St. Crispin and St. Crispinian—Henry has set everything up. All that is left for him to do is rally his troops' spirits, and give the order to fight.

What Henry says to the men as he rides before his army—looking as theatrical as he ever has, mounted on a gray-and-white horse, dressed in mail and plate armor, wearing a dazzling surcoat emblazoned with the quartered lions of England and French fleurs-de-lis and a bascinet-style helmet topped with a gold crown*—will be the subject of much embroidery and exaggeration in the centuries that follow.

Those who are there bring away from the field strikingly different recollections. A writer from London has Henry gesture to the heaving French lines a few hundred yards distant on the other side of the clearing between the woods and say: "Sirs and fellows, yonder many will let us of [i.e., stand in] our way, and they will not come unto us. But now let every man prove himself a good man this day and advance his banner in the best time of the day and year."[18]

A monk writing in St. Albans imagines Henry quoting the Roman poet Lucan, saying, "Look! Here is that very day which your valor has so often asked for. 'So put forth all your strength' and see what lance, ax, sword and arrow can achieve in the hand of the powerful."[19]

A French monk writing in Paris hears that Henry gives his men a detailed appraisal of the battle situation and sums up the tactics he expects them to follow, concluding: "Now is the occasion to use all your intrepidity. The needs of the moment should boost your courage. Rather than being scared of doing business with so many princes and barons, be of firm hope that their large number will turn, as in the past, to their shame and their eternal confusion."[20]

Another English chronicler, writing half a century after the fact, has Henry "charging every man to keep himself wholly together." He asks

---

* Unlike his father at Shrewsbury in 1403, who cautiously deployed several lookalikes on the field as a hedge against being captured by his enemies.

what time of day it is, and when he hears it is Prime (the first hour of daylight) he remarks that "now is a good time for all England to pray for us, and therefore be of good cheer and let us go to our journey."[21]

It is easily possible that Henry says some or even all these things, for he cannot possibly address his whole army in its three divisions all at once. He likely gives several sets of final words, each tailored to its audience, and each spun and polished as it is repeated in the war stories later told.

Yet of all the reported versions of Henry's speech at Agincourt, there is one that speaks most clearly to the simplicity of the situation, the apparent state of Henry's mind, and the severe public image he has tried to project since the day of his coronation. The army, for all that the men are weak, hungry, wet, cold, and tired, is prepared to fight. The troops are lined up as well as they can be. Henry has shown his men over and over again what he expects from them, and has tried to instill in them his own belief that God wants them to defeat the French. So the time for grandstanding is over. One London chronicler gives Henry the briefest but most believable three-word speech as he sends his men into the fight.

"Fellas," he says, "let's go."[22]

Each man's experience of battle is his own. At the battle of Agincourt there are twenty thousand or more such experiences, of which almost all are lost to history.

Some who write about the battle afterward will wax poetic: "The air thunders with dreadful crashes, clouds rain missiles, the earth absorbs blood, breath flies from bodies, half-dead bodies roll in their own blood, the surface of the earth is covered with the corpses of the dead," writes one. "This man charges, that one falls, this one attacks, that one dies, this one recovers, that one vomits forth his soul in blood, the killer is enraged, the dead crushed in grief; the living desires to surrender, the charge of the victors does not allow the time for withdrawal, cruelty reigns, piety exults, the brave and the strong are crushed, and mountains of corpses are piled up, a vast multitude is yielded up to death, princes and magnates are led off as captives."[23]

Other writers will try to present more factual accounts, summarizing the various movements of the several parts of the two armies as they engage. They will tell how the two armies stand and regard each other warily across a wet and muddy field for several hours, neither wishing to advance and cede any advantage. They will recount how the English make the first move—the men-at-arms and some of the archers in the center moving forward to goad the French into making their charge.[24] Eyewitnesses will remember the English commander of archers, Sir Thomas Erpingham, giving the cry to begin this advance, throwing a baton in the air and bellowing, "Now strike!" (*Nescieque!*)[25]

Then they will remember the trumpet blasts from the French, as they rise to the challenge, "completely confident that, given their great number, the English could not escape from them."[26] They will recall the thunderous charge of the French cavalry through the thick mud of the field, the knights giving their ancient war cry of "Montjoie" as they gallop; and then the near-silent onslaught of the English longbows: thousands of them drawn and released together, thousands of arrows set in a deadly swarm to rain down on the French riders and horses alike.

Each volley of arrows shot by the English longbowmen, trained from childhood to operate that difficult, deadly weapon, kills or cripples hundreds of men and animals. Those French knights who manage to charge through the arrow-storm either run straight into the sharpened stakes of the longbowmen who have been shooting, or else see the spikes, shy away, and cause chaos as they flee into their own men, who are still advancing on hoof and foot. Soon, thousands of confused, enraged, terrified French are being funneled into a killing zone between the woods, a space too narrow to contain them all: a space from which they cannot escape.

"The loud war cries of our men struck the stars on high," writes an English monk, describing the French falling prey to the relentless arrowshot. "The French fell in great numbers as the arrows pierced them: here fifty, there sixty."[27] Henry's chaplain, who is on the battlefield, praying with all his might, remembers seeing English archers finally running out of arrows and "seizing axes, stakes and swords and spear-heads that were lying about [with which] they struck down, hacked and stabbed the enemy." Soon French bodies are piling five feet high in front of the English lines. But still the gory frenzy continues. "[Never], it seemed to our older men, had Englishmen ever fallen upon their enemies more boldly and fearlessly or with a better will."[28]

Where, in all of this, is Henry? This is his war, and his battle: the direct result of an insult he feels is personal to him, and a pattern of events that he has driven forward with every fiber of his being. He sets the battle order. He gives Erpingham the instruction to order the first advance. From this moment, many kings would have retreated to watch events unfold from some high point on the field, as Edward III had done at Crécy.

Henry chooses a riskier path. For the two or three hours that the fighting goes on, he is in its midst, trusting perhaps that just as God saw fit to spare him at Shrewsbury, so he will save him again today.

Indeed, two French chroniclers attest to his presence in the thick of the battle. They record that "eighteen gentlemen banded together and swore that when the two sides came together they would with all their might get as close as possible to the king of England that they should knock the crown right off his head, or else they would all die in the attempt. They did indeed do this. When they found themselves close to the king one of them [some accounts claim this is the duke of Alençon] with an axe in his hand struck on the king's bascinet such a heavy blow that it knocked off one of the fleurons of his crown."[29]

Just as an arrow to the face nearly accounted for a sixteen-year-old Prince Henry, so an ax to the head nearly spells the end of the twenty-nine-year-old adult king. But nearly was not good enough for the Percys at Shrewsbury, and it will not do for the French at Agincourt, either.

Others are not so lucky. In the press of the fighting, Henry's cousin the duke of York is killed: "his bascinet to his brains was bent," recalls one account.[30] So too is the twenty-one-year-old earl of Suffolk, who has enjoyed his title for only seven weeks, after his father died of dysentery at Harfleur. Henry's brother Humphrey is knocked to the ground right beside him, and Henry saves his life by throwing himself on top of him, using his body and armor to deflect a death blow.

Henry survives. Humphrey is seriously wounded, but he also survives.

Indeed, the English lose vanishingly few men across the whole army. And as the French attack breaks up in chaos, with bodies heaping everywhere and survivors taking flight, it becomes clear that this has been an astonishing victory for Henry. For a king to have put himself in the face of such peril for so long speaks to his physical aptitude for fighting and his willingness to gamble everything if he detects the faintest scent of victory. That Henry has inspired his small and weak army to overcome the larger, fresher, more confident, and more glamorous French one is not just the basis for a dramatic legend: it is a military fact.

As the battle winds down, however, there is one more tough and bloody decision for Henry to make. The French have taken flight and the English archers are combing the enormous piles of French dead, which include some of the greatest lords and knights, looking for high-born survivors to take as prisoners of war. As they do so, a shout goes up that fresh French troops have been spotted riding toward the field. Several leading French noblemen—such as the duke of Brittany—have not arrived at Agincourt in time to join the main battle. Now it seems they, together with the remnants of the army scattered from the field, may be returning to fall upon the exhausted English.

This is a deadly serious situation. Already during the battle a band of peasants has robbed the English baggage positioned at the rear of their lines, stealing Henry's sword of state and his crown. Danger still lurks everywhere.

His tired soldiers are raising up Frenchmen in their midst to take them captive. If they are about to fight again, these prisoners will be at best a distracting burden and at worst a lethal threat within their own ranks.

A few of the most valuable survivors dragged out from the corpse piles have been identified and taken away: among them are Marshal Boucicaut, the duke of Bourbon, and the count of Eu. Henry orders all the rest to be killed on the spot.

This pitiless order to slit the throats and beat in the skulls of vulnerable men will in time be counted as a great stain on Henry's character: a prized piece of evidence for those who would cast him as a blinkered, heedless warmonger bereft of conscience and ambivalent to the values of chivalry. It is made worse by the fact that, in the end, a second attack does not materialize—whoever is approaching the field thinks better of trying their luck.

And doubtless, it *is* harsh and cold-blooded generalship. It certainly affronts his own men, so many of whom blanch at the order that Henry has to send around a death squad of two hundred archers to see the job through. Convention holds that prisoners should be treated properly according to their rank and ought not to be summarily executed when they have surrendered. Economic theory suggests that prisoners are worth more alive than dead. Basic humanity might be expected to give a man pause before ordering a massacre.

But Henry has made cold choices about men's lives since he was fifteen years old and he hanged the Welsh rebels who hijacked Conwy Castle. He burned John Badby in a barrel to make a political point. Just months before Agincourt he had his dear and hitherto loyal friend Lord Scrope decapitated for being too slow to show his unwavering loyalty.

Henry is no saint. But nor does he presume to be. He is by his own advertisement a king who has imprinted the laws of Deuteronomy on his heart, and a commander who would rather not see his own men slaughtered like hogs. In the moment, he does not know that the sight of banners on the horizon is a false alarm. Nor is he minded to wait and find out.

His contemporaries understand this. What's more, they allow it. The French had, after all, brought the oriflamme out of Saint-Denis Abbey—an explicit statement that they were prepared to show no mercy and give no quarter on the battlefield.[31] And in the aftermath of Agincourt, many writers do not even see fit to mention the killing of the prisoners. Instead, they express great shock at the numbers of French killed—more than three thousand noblemen, knights, and squires, including three dukes and five counts, and nearly the same again in ordinary men. They write woeful laments about the "great pity and damage" done to the kingdom.[32]

But even on the French side, writers do not castigate Henry for his inhumanity. To a writer called Jean Le Fevre, the massacre of the prisoners was a calamity the French brought on themselves. It was "most pitiable" to see, he writes. "For, in cold blood, all those noble Frenchmen were killed and their heads and faces cut." But it was "the wretched company of the French [apparently returning to the battlefield] who had caused the death of these noble knights."[33]

Henry himself agrees with this assessment. After he has left the blood-soaked field of the battle he christens Agincourt, heading finally toward Calais, he is told that among the prisoners who have not been butchered is Charles, duke of Orléans. The twenty-year-old—who has until now led a relatively charmed life, entertaining himself by having lines of the poetry he writes stitched onto his robes in pearls—is so downcast by his fate and that of his uncle's realm that he has gone on hunger strike.[34]

Henry goes to the young man and tries to cheer him up. "Noble cousin," he says, "be of good heart. I realize that God has given me the grace of having a victory over the French, not because I am worthy of it, but I believe in full certainty that God wanted to punish the French.

"If what I have heard said is true, it is no wonder, for they say that there has never been seen such a great disarray or disorderly behavior in excesses, sins and wicked vices as has reigned in France at present.

"It is pitiful to have it recounted, and horrible to those who hear of it. And if God is angry at it, it is no wonder, and no one can be surprised at it."[35]

Charles of Orléans can do no more than listen to Henry's homily and accept his misfortune. Though he does not yet know it, he will remain an English prisoner of war for the next quarter of a century, during which time the full and awful legacy of Henry V's victory at Agincourt will be revealed.

23

TRIUMPHS

On Saturday, November 23, 1415, almost a month after his great battle, Henry rides the short distance from Eltham Palace to Blackheath, the large common that lies southeast of London. He has a small party of his household officials beside him and a choice selection of prisoners of war at his back. Some of Henry's captives are destined for long spells in prison, others for remand to await ransom, and some for lives of menial service in lords' mansions. Today, however, they are to be given a tour under armed guard of England's jubilant first city, so that they may look upon the splendor of their conquerors' capital and the capital's inhabitants may rejoice.

Henry and his companions arrive at Blackheath at ten o'clock in the morning, but long before they get there Henry can see a crowd that is nearly as large and no less grandly arrayed than the French army he defeated at Agincourt.

As many as twenty thousand of London's citizens have come four miles down the Thames from the suburb of Southwark to receive the king "worthily and royally."[1] All are dressed in their finest clothes. The mayor and aldermen wear furred scarlet gowns with black-and-white-striped hoods, while the members of the wealthy merchant guilds, many of whom have invested personally in the king's war, come out in cloaks emblazoned with the symbols of their crafts.[2] Their hearts, says one writer, are "leaping with joy."[3]

As this colorful scrum escorts Henry to the city for his formal entry, it becomes clear that no cost has been spared in devising the welcome. It is twenty-five days since news of the miracle at Agincourt was brought to London—overturning earlier rumors that the king and his army had been wiped out on their way to Calais—and all of that time, it seems, has been spent on putting up decorations and rehearsing pageantry.

In Southwark, London's clergy greet the king in procession, singing *Te Deum* as they lead him onto London Bridge. Standing guard over the bridge are the effigies of the giants Gog and Magog: he a monstrous warrior holding a spear and ax, and she "so huge that her bulk [is] in truth fit not only to spawn gigantic demons, but to bring forth the towers of hell."[4]

Beyond these ogres, where the drawbridge marks the midpoint of the viaduct, await a lion holding a lance and an antelope bearing the royal arms; past them, at the gates to the city proper, looms the equally massive figure of St. George, in full armor. A banner above the gates declares London to be "the city of the King of Justice."[5] Inside the gates, little boys dressed as angels, wearing white gowns, gold makeup, and laurel leaves in their hair, peer down from the windows and rooftops of the houses, singing, "Blessed is he that comes in the name of the Lord."

Henry surveys this heavenly scene and responds approvingly. "Hail to the royal city," he says, adding that he hopes Christ will take good care of London and her people forever. Then he sets off on a tour that will last until the middle of the afternoon. As he passes from street to street, he is shown all manner of astonishing performances, any one of which would have met the high standards for public spectacle set by Richard II. Fountains gush wine. Actors dressed as ancient prophets sing psalms as they release flocks of tame sparrows, which circle the royal party and settle on Henry's shoulders. The famous cross at Cheapside is disguised beneath a huge mock castle, built of timber and covered in linen painted so that it looks "as if the whole work had been made by the art of masonry." Maidens dance around this fortress singing, "Welcome Henry the fifth, king of England and of France," while more angel-boys stand on its ramparts tossing out golden coins and laurel leaves as the parade passes by.[6]

As Henry takes all of this in, he is pleased to see that the citizens have mostly followed his instructions concerning the nature of the celebrations. Though he understands their excitement about his victory, he is not Richard II: he is adamant that this cannot be all about him. He therefore carries himself with "quiet demeanor" and at "gentle pace." He refuses to show off his armor from Agincourt or to display his mangled battle crown.[7] A popular song has been written to describe his achievement: known as the "Agincourt Carol," it recounts how "Our king went forth to Normandy . . . In Agincourt field he fought manly; He had both field and victory." But its chorus is all piety: "*Deo gracias Anglia, redde pro Victoria!*" ("Give thanks to God, England, for the victory!")[8] Henry has forbidden jingoistic songs that merely taunt the French. Praise, he insists, should be given only to the Lord.

So although the day is magnificent and memorable for the vast crowds who line London's streets and the noble men and women who watch from the upper windows of houses along the route, the highlights for Henry are most likely not the pageants but rather two church services at which he offers his own thanks to the Almighty for delivering him home safely.

The first of these takes place at St. Paul's Cathedral in the heart of the City, where Henry kisses the relics of Erkenwald,* London's patron saint. The second, an even grander ceremony, takes place upriver at Westminster Abbey, where Henry prays at the shrine of Edward the Confessor, before finally retiring to Westminster Palace.

It has been his intention all day to show his people that he is "rendering thanks and glory to God alone, not to man."[9] As he retires for the night in

---

* The seventh-century Saxon abbot and bishop Erkenwald died in or around 693 CE. He has long been venerated by the citizens of London and is the subject of a fourteenth-century alliterative poem, likely written by the so-called Pearl Poet, whose other works include *Sir Gawain and the Green Knight*.

the relative quiet of the palace he may reflect that he could have done little more to state his case.

The glorious procession through London is a fitting end to what has been a month-long triumph for Henry, which has taken him from Agincourt to the abbey and palace where his reign formally began two and a half years earlier. Even before arriving in London he has been feted in several other towns and cities, in equally excited fashion.

The celebrations began at the castle of Guînes, in Picardy, where in the days after Agincourt he dined with his highest-born French captives and lectured them on his favorite topic of God's wish to punish sin and correct the wayward. They continued when he entered Calais on October 29, to be met by his old comrade Richard Beauchamp, earl of Warwick, and a phalanx of clerics singing hymns.

After making a rough crossing of the Channel, during which almost every English and French passenger except for Henry was violently seasick, he was feted on the beaches of Dover (where the barons of the Cinque Ports waded out to meet his boat in driving snow and carried him ashore on their shoulders), at Canterbury (where the new archbishop, Henry Chichele, greeted him in person and escorted him to pray at Becket's tomb), and at every stopping point thereafter on his way to the capital.

The warm reception has no doubt been much more enjoyable than the hard march that earned it, and outpouring of pieties, rather than simple crowing, is pleasing. It is also splendid to learn that Henry's brother John, duke of Bedford, has kept a steady hand on government during the royal absence, and is busy turning the realm's celebratory spirit into promises of more funding for government and war. While Henry was still at Calais, his victory known but his future plans still uncertain, John and Bishop Henry Beaufort eased from an excited parliament held at Westminster Palace the grant of a large subsidy, and the promise of import and export duties on wine, wool, and other high-volume commodities, guaranteed every year for the rest of Henry's life.

This is one of the most lavish, openhanded tax grants in England's history, rendered all the more remarkable because it is made in the spirit of gratitude rather than fear. (Richard II managed to extract a lifetime grant of wool taxes from Parliament only at the height of his tyranny in 1398; Henry's father was never granted any such thing.)[10] The flood of funds allows plans to be rushed forward for the repayment of loans and the return of the plate, jewels, trinkets, and saucepans that were pawned in the summer to pay soldiers' and sailors' wages. It makes the defense of Harfleur, as well as Calais and Guyenne, feasible. It permits the plotting of another expeditionary campaign.

It is also, frankly, very flattering. Less than four months earlier, when Henry sailed for Harfleur, he was an unproven king against whom dynastic plots were still actively being raised. Now his right and fitness to rule, and the legitimacy of the house of Lancaster, is all but impossible to gainsay. It is the result of a fearsome gamble, which it would not be wise to repeat too many more times. Nevertheless, Henry has shown the English people what he can do for them. Now the people stand ready to show what they can do for him.

As Bishop Beaufort puts it during the opening of the November 1415 parliament that cuts loose the realm's purse strings (and also declares the executions of the Southampton Plot ringleaders as legally sound), the English "should honor the king, because he himself honors God Almighty above all others." As ever, Beaufort has a line from scripture to support his argument. "As he did unto us," he says, "so let us do unto him."[11]

Welcome as praise and tax are, however, Henry is not ready to sit back and bask in his achievement. Harfleur and Agincourt were glorious. But they are only the first steps toward the higher goals Henry has set himself in France. There is more—much more—to be done before he can consider that justice has been served. And away from France lie other huge challenges. Henry cannot neglect his duty to provide law, order, and good governance in England. He is increasingly interested in the wider politics of Europe, where efforts are afoot to bring to an end the damaging papal schism, which has torn the western Church apart since 1378. After that could lie the noblest task of all: a crusade.

So while England celebrates, Henry knows he has only just begun his work. Around this time a letter is addressed to him from the English clergy, who have, like Parliament, voted to award him generous taxes in recognition of his success so far. Probably written by Chancellor Beaufort, the letter counsels Henry to avoid the sins of "pride, vainglory, boasting, swelling words, cruelty, rage, and the fury of revenge; all of which are enemies greatly to be dreaded by conquerors." Better, says the author, to praise God for his mercy, and then look to the next tasks at hand. "No man putting his hand to the plow, and looking back, is fit for the kingdom [of heaven]," he goes on, "but continued effort usually leads to success . . . it is fitting that your royal highness should not boast of the past, but be anxious for the future."[12]

This is advice Henry scarcely needs to hear. He spends most of December in Westminster and London, dealing with the last great and urgent matters outstanding from the year's campaign. He and his three brothers attend a vigil and memorial service at St. Paul's for their cousin the duke of York, who was killed at Agincourt. Also present at that service is Thomas Beaufort, earl of Dorset and captain of Harfleur, who probably lobbies Henry for urgent funding to repair the defenses his cannons tore chunks from in the summer; at any rate, in mid-December Henry licenses a stonemason from Essex to press-gang all the "carpenters, tilemakers and tilers" he needs to go and do the work.[13]

After this he goes to Lambeth for Christmas. Once the festivities are over, he applies his mind seriously to the big question: what next? As part of the answer he decides to go on a journey similar to the one he took in 1403, when he was recovering from his injury at the battle of Shrewsbury. Then, he went on pilgrimage to Walsingham and Canterbury. Now he takes himself off on another holy tour, to St. Winefride's Well, in north Wales.[14]

The seventh-century Welsh princess St. Winefride lived a pious life, and a calm one, taking religious instruction from a tutor and setting her heart on a life of chastity and devotion to Christ. But her tranquil existence was shattered one Sunday morning when a prince called Caradog broke into her home and tried to rape her. Winefride escaped the house and fled toward the safety of her tutor's church, where he was celebrating mass, but just as she reached it, Caradog ran her to ground and cut her head off with his sword.

The tutor, understandably vexed, laid a curse on Caradog that killed him on the spot, the ground swallowing up his miserable corpse. He then prayed for Winefride to be brought back to life, which she was, bearing only a thin, white scar on her neck to show where the sword's blade had struck. Winefride grew up and followed her dream of becoming an abbess. In the meantime a well burst forth on the spot where her head had originally landed.[15]

It is to this well that Henry goes in early 1416 to give thanks for God's grace. Whether he sees any parallels in his own recent experience of flight, a chase, and a miraculous deliverance we cannot know. But certain more obvious similarities with his journey must strike him as he takes the road into north Wales through Shrewsbury.

This is the part of his realm where he cut his teeth as prince and nearly lost his life for the first time. The well itself was dear to the heart of Richard II, who visited it in 1398, assigning funds for a chantry chapel near the well and a hostel for pilgrims visiting the site. Henry's own father went there after the battle of Shrewsbury, and saw that this work was completed.[16] The chapel, which now encloses the well on three sides, with a metal grate allowing pilgrims to bathe in its waters, is enduring proof of his father's gratitude at having come through the awful trial of 1403—and perhaps his relief at Henry's life having been saved by his surgeon John Bradmore.

As Henry puts his hands into the cold water that springs up from the rock below, he may consider—as he has had cause to so many times in his life—how lucky he is. In a few months he will be thirty years old. It is little short of a miracle that he has made it this far.

Henry cannot linger in north Wales as he once did at Canterbury and Walsingham, for the new year has already brought shocks and challenges. Over Christmas, reports have reached England that Louis, the dauphin, eldest son of Charles VI, has died in Paris, aged eighteen.

15. Several pivotal moments in Henry's life took place at Kenilworth Castle. His life was saved by John Bradmore here, after the battle of Shrewsbury. He built his "Pleasance" on the Mere (now drained). The "tennis ball" incident supposedly happened at Kenilworth, and Henry VI may have been conceived here.

16. The battle of Agincourt in 1415 was a tactical master class aided by a healthy amount of good luck. Henry's deployment of longbowmen against French cavalry canceled out huge French superiority in numbers. His order to kill French captives after the battle was logical at the time but has blackened his reputation since.

17. The Painted Chamber in the old Palace of Westminster (since destroyed by fire) was a regular gathering place for parliaments. Only with the country's consent could Henry raise the taxation he needed for his wars. He was a master of managing his domestic political agenda in order to earn his subjects' approval for foreign adventures.

18. Henry married Catherine de Valois, the youngest daughter of Charles VI of France, in 1420, concluding the Treaty of Troyes, which gave him the right to be regent of and heir to France. The treaty committed Henry to a long war of conquest in France which would test English resources and commitment to his cause.

19. Most of Henry's greatest sieges—from Aberystwyth to Harfleur and Meaux—involved heavy deployment of cannon. The siege of Rouen, capital of Normandy, combined an artillery bombardment with a blockade, during which many poor townsfolk were left to starve in the city ditch.

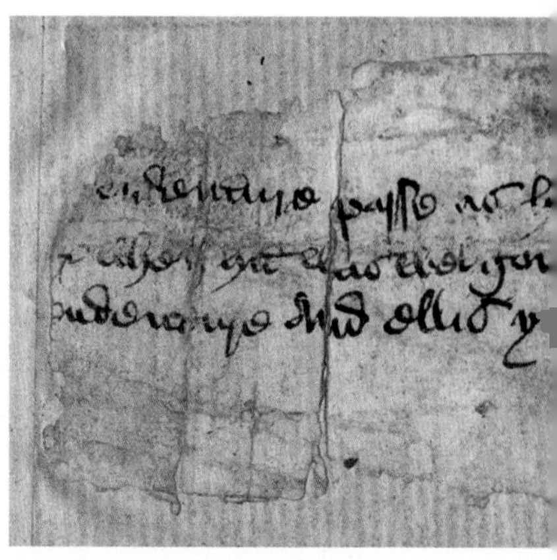

20. (*above*) An example of Henry V's handwriting, in a note concerning contracts for military service before the Agincourt campaign. Henry pored over his paperwork, often annotating it in his own hand. He was also an enthusiastic user of English.

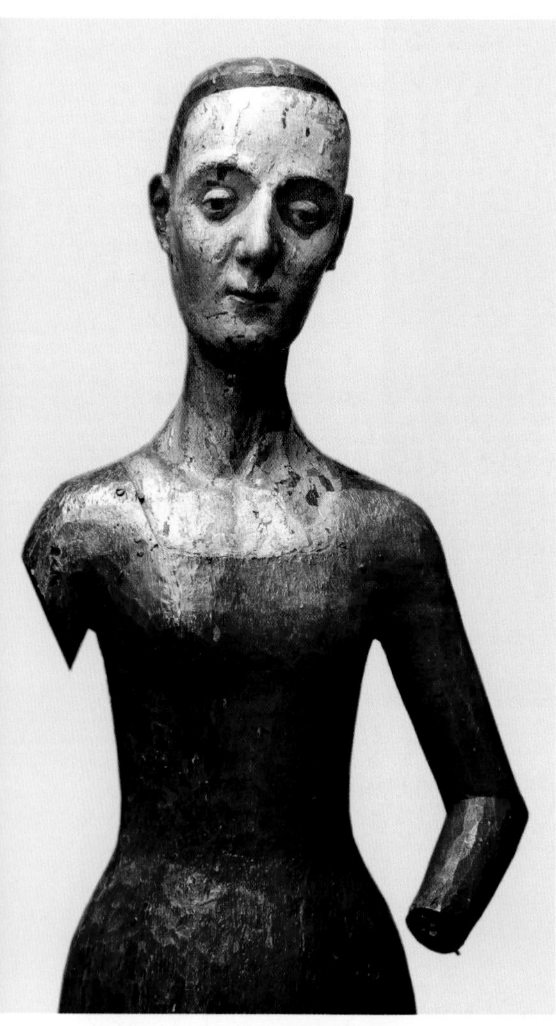

21. (*above*) Henry set his heart on marrying Catherine de Valois early in his life, and saw his ambition through. Catherine is represented here in her funeral effigy. After his death, she married a Welsh gentleman called Owen Tudor, whose descendants eventually became the rulers of England in their own right.

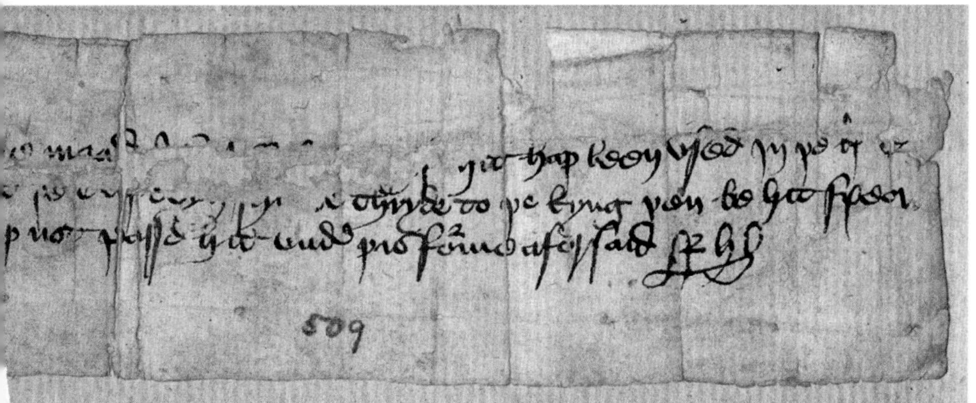

22. (*left*) John the Fearless, duke of Burgundy, was the arch-instigator of the civil war that tore France apart during Henry's lifetime. John's murder by the Armagnacs in 1419 was the key to Henry's capture of the French Crown.

23. (*above*) After contracting dysentery, Henry died in the Chateau of Bois-de-Vincennes in 1422. His death at the age of thirty-five was a terrible shock, but the English kingdom of France he had established outlived him by more than a decade.

24. John, duke of Bedford (kneeling), was a capable deputy for Henry V, and perhaps the brother most temperamentally like him. John's training ground had been the north of England during their father's reign and he often served as regent in England during Henry's long campaigns in France.

25. The treaty of Troyes, agreed in 1420, disinherited Charles VI's last remaining son, the dauphin Charles, and confirmed Henry as the "heir and regent of France." It was the most significant peace deal signed in the Hundred Years War since the Treaty of Bretigny in 1360.

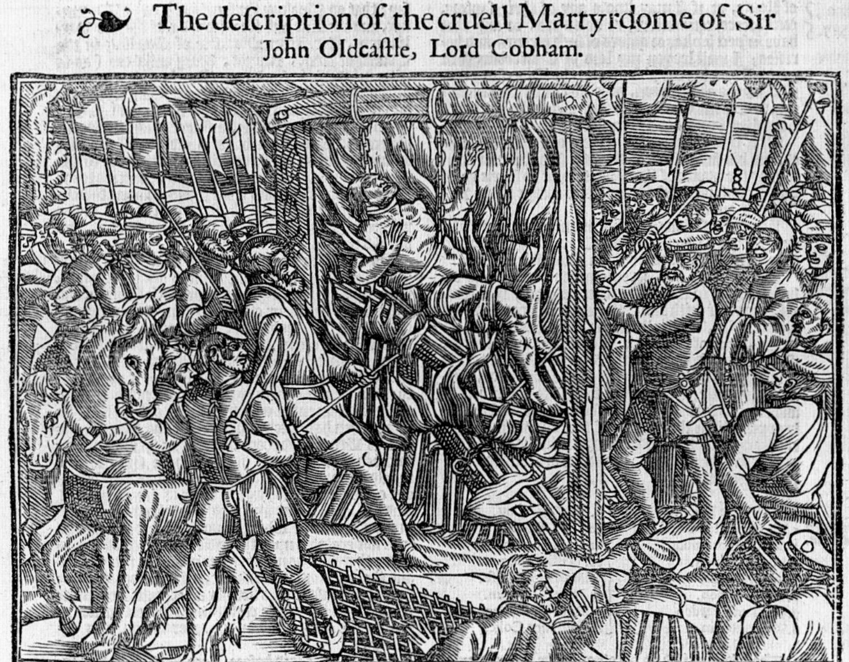

26. John Oldcastle, Lord Cobham, was a confidant of Henry, but his commitment to Lollard beliefs made their friendship untenable. Oldcastle proved a stubborn heretic and his plots against the Crown eventually earned him an agonizing death on a Lollard gallows: a device on which he was hanged and burned at the same time.

27. Laurence Olivier plays Henry V in a 1944 film adaptation of Shakespeare's play. The story of Henry's life has been doubly overlaid by Shakespeare's preoccupations with the themes of a king subsuming his self for the good of the kingdom and the national mood of the 1940s.

28. Henry's tomb effigy in Westminster Abbey is carved from oak and was completed in the 1430s. (The replacement head pictured here was produced in the 1970s.) The inscription on Henry's tomb declares: "Virtue conquers all" and exhorts its readers to "flee idleness."

Early in December 1415 Louis was gripped by an attack of dysentery. Twelve days later he was dead.

Louis is not mourned long by those who knew him well. A chronicler at Saint-Denis, the mausoleum of French kings dating back to Clovis, writes a scornful obituary notice, calling the dead boy "a good looking prince with a pleasant exterior and a robust constitution, but little taste for the profession of arms." He accuses Louis of disrespecting the French nobility and of indulging an incorrigible idleness that led him to sleep all morning, to eat at unsociable hours, and to spend more time playing the harp with his servants than attending to affairs of state. Louis would tolerate no criticism of his misbehavior, frittered far too much money and attention on wine, clothes, and women, and was beastly toward his wife, John the Fearless's daughter Margaret, whom he banished from his presence.[17]

Such was the judgment of a pious and well-connected chronicler who saw the worst in the dauphin Louis and implicitly blamed him for the catastrophes of the year in which he died. Yet had this account been repeated to Henry, he might well have noted that it also happens to read as a direct vindication of everything he has done to reshape his own public image since his transition from prince to king. His abandonment of lightness and ease and his adoption of a monkish mien have protected him from critiques like this.

The only charge from Louis's sheet that could be leveled at the adult Henry is a taste for music. He has been a keen harpist since childhood, and has become an accomplished composer, too: around this time he will write beautiful settings for the religious hymns known as the Gloria and the Sanctus. But such an austere hobby as this could hardly be thrown in his face as time wasting. Whatever may be the burdens of treating his royal office with such heaviness, it appears that both God and man approve.

More immediately, the dauphin's death is a reminder that events in France will not stand still. Louis's seventeen-year-old brother, John, is the new dauphin, and his promotion will surely shift the currents of French politics, as will Henry's evisceration of the ranks of French nobility at

Agincourt. But whether it brings advantage to John the Fearless's Burgundian party, the Armagnacs (now led by Count Bernard of that territory), or some other faction that will arise from the morass of ambition and self-interest around the mad king Charles VI remains to be seen.

What Henry does know is that his first task must be to defend Harfleur from recapture. His second must be to formulate a strategy to take another bite out of French territory. Both of these tasks come into focus in their different ways in March 1416.

Before Christmas, as we have seen, Henry answered a plea from his uncle Thomas Beaufort, earl of Dorset, for help rebuilding Harfleur's walls by ordering a gang of Essex tradesmen across the Channel to saw planks and lay tiles. By the time spring arrives Dorset is all but screaming for full military reinforcement of the town. Bernard of Armagnac, as constable of France, has sent troops overland to blockade the roads leading into Harfleur, and ships around the coast to close off access to supplies by sea.

Although Dorset has led brave and successful sorties out of Harfleur, in which he and members of the large garrison have killed many Frenchmen, the situation there looks dire. They have eaten the horses. People are starting to die of hunger. Dorset's frustration fairly leaps from the page when he writes to Henry to complain of a lack of flour, meat, weapons, ammunition, and other basics, without which it will become impossible to hold the town.[18]

Henry understands the problem, and doubtless sympathizes. He was once captain of Calais, and used to making such peevish addresses himself. He sends out orders for an army of 7,500 men-at-arms and archers to assemble that summer in Southampton for three months' active duty: a tour that he will lead, flanked by his brothers John and Humphrey. This will be a naval campaign. Henry has not fought one of these before. But as he proved on his way home from Calais the previous winter, he does not suffer from seasickness.

As preparations begin for this adventure, Henry calls a parliament to pay for it. But after only a few weeks he cuts its business short to devote his attention to a prestigious guest who has arrived in England in the guise of peacemaker. His name is Sigismund of Luxembourg, king of the Germans.

Nearly twenty years older than Henry, Sigismund presents a curious figure. He is grand but perpetually broke; full of energy but not always subtle in its deployment.[19] He has old links with England—his sister Anne of Bohemia was Richard II's first queen. What's more, he is a crusading veteran of high rank if not glorious track record, having led the combined Christian forces at the notorious battle of Nicopolis of 1396, at which God's troops were routed by the Ottoman sultan Bayezid I. Since then, Sigismund has become obsessed with reconciling Christendom's divided peoples, so that a united international army might one day be raised once more and sent to chastise the Turks. Three critical steps toward achieving this are to heal the papal schism that has wrenched Europe apart since 1378, to stop the Burgundian-Armagnac civil war, and to make peace between England and France.

To achieve just one of these goals would be a triumphant act of statesmanship, but Sigismund is doing his best. To address the schism he has convened a Church council in the city of Constance in southern Europe; Henry's capable representatives there have been his friend Richard, earl of Warwick, and Robert Hallam, bishop of Salisbury. The task of the delegates at the Council of Constance is to wheedle or force the resignations of all three men who currently claim to be pope: Benedict XIII in Avignon, Gregory XII in Rome, and a piratical gangster from southern Italy who rules as John XXIII* from Pisa. But to do this also requires a whole secondary round of international diplomacy, for each of these holy fathers has his own adherents, who must formally withdraw their backing from their preferred pope if Sigismund's plan is to work. Sigismund is determined to do the required lobbying in person, and along the way to see what other diplomatic coups he can achieve.

So it is that the German king lands in England on May 1, 1416, arriv-

* Not to be confused with the much-admired twentieth-century pope John XXIII, who took this regnal number considering the medieval pope mentioned here to have been illegitimate.

ing from Paris, where he has been afforded only lukewarm hospitality, and where he has been dismayed to see rioting between Burgundians and Armagnacs, whose differences he has been utterly powerless to patch up. Henry is a great admirer of Sigismund and is keen to give him a fittingly regal welcome. The earl of Warwick escorts Sigismund from Calais to Dover. Henry's brothers, Thomas, John, and Humphrey, bring him to London, where Henry rides out to meet him with five thousand aristocrats and gentlemen in his entourage. He invites Sigismund to make Westminster Palace his own, inducts him as a member of the Order of the Garter, and gifts him a jeweled sword used at his own coronation, which, he tells the emperor, "we received from the altar for the defense of church and faith."[20] He fetes him and his large train of servants and companions at every turn.

Fortunately for Henry, Sigismund proves entirely susceptible to flattery. He agrees to host at Westminster a sham Anglo-French peace conference, at which the French are represented by prisoners of war from Agincourt, who are confronted with demands even more extreme than usual: Henry still wants the clock turned back to 1360, making him master of a third of France; he still wishes to marry Charles's daughter Catherine, with a massive dowry; but he also now wants Harfleur recognized as his own, legitimately conquered, colony.

Unsurprisingly, even the presence of the great would-be peacemaker Sigismund cannot persuade the captive French to dismember the kingdom from which they are exiled. When negotiations stall, Sigismund offers to take Harfleur into his own hands until an agreeable solution can be reached over its future. Both sides refuse this, too. Meanwhile, French troops under the count of Armagnac are mustering to storm the town.

Despite Sigismund's best efforts, it is clear that the only way Harfleur's future will be resolved is through another recourse to arms. In mid-June the German king is invited to enjoy an English summer in the beautiful castle at Leeds in Kent. Henry heads to the south coast to inspect the naval force that is assembling there, supervised by his brother John, duke of Bedford. And English ambassadors travel to France, where they are met by deliberate obfuscation and heel-dragging, as the French attempt to buy time for their naval and land blockade to reduce Harfleur to helplessness. It is obvious that fine words alone are not going to save Harfleur from starvation and possible reconquest. Henry decides to set sail at the end of July to remind the French what he is made of.

Yet when late July arrives, Henry changes his mind. He does not take command of his navy after all. According to more than one writer of the time, this is down to Sigismund. "The emperor* discounselled him from that," writes one chronicler, "saying that the king, in whom the common wealth rests, ought not so lightly to submit himself to every peril." The French assault on Harfleur, Sigismund argues, can be just as easily beaten back "by some of his princes of his commandment as by himself."[21]

So Henry is in Southampton in the last days of July to see thousands of troops board the fleet that lies at anchor in the Solent, cramming onto ships with names like *Holy Ghost, Petit John, Swan,* and *James.*[22] But he does not board the flagship himself. Instead he appoints his brother John as "leader of his naval force and the one responsible for relieving the siege, re-provisioning the town and overthrowing the enemy."[23]

With contrary winds blowing in the Solent, it is a fortnight later when John finally leads his fleet out into open waters, toward the mouth of the Seine and Harfleur. Henry does not wait to see them go. Unable to do any more than he already has, he goes back to London, lodging in Westminster Palace and asking the hermit resident at the abbey—the man to whom he confessed his sins on the night of his father's death—to pray especially for his brother and the thousands of men aboard the ships, "continuously and untiringly."[24]

The battle that is fought in the Seine estuary on August 15, 1416, between the English armada of John, duke of Bedford, and an enemy fleet composed of French ships and huge, hired Genoese carracks, is every bit as bloody as Agincourt. It lasts nearly seven hours, during which the

* As king of the Germans, Sigismund has a claim to be Holy Roman Emperor, a title that is eventually bestowed on him in 1433.

captains of the ships try to outmaneuver one another, sailing side by side so the soldiers on board can shoot longbows and crossbows, pelt one another with stones and lumps of metal, then use grappling hooks and ladders to board one another's vessels, where they commence vicious hand-to-hand fighting.

The towering "castles" at the fore and aft of the Genoese ships cause great bloodshed on the English side, for they give a vantage point for their crews to shoot and hurl missiles downward. Yet ultimately the advantage lies with the smaller and more agile English ships, and as the battle rages, John's men manage to board, ground, wreck, or capture the core of the French fleet, scattering the rest. Losses on both sides are terrible: the English lose roughly 2,500 men (around a third of their fighting force) and twenty ships; the French and Genoese almost as many themselves. For days the mouth of the Seine bobs with bloated corpses, "being carried back and forwards on the ebb and flow of the tide as if seeking other interment than the fishes would provide."[25]

For all the horror and the loss of life, however, it is an English victory, which shatters the French sea blockade and makes the presence of the count of Armagnac's land army pointless. John, who is hurt in the fighting, leaves half of his surviving fleet at Harfleur and brings the rest home to England.

News of John's victory reaches Henry at an auspicious moment. He is in Winchelsea, overseeing the building of a new ship called *Jesus*, on Friday, August 21. The previous week—in fact, on the very day that the sea battle outside Harfleur was being fought—he and Sigismund have agreed on a personal peace treaty and military alliance, which binds England to Germany and condemns French stubbornness, arrogance, and two-facedness. The Treaty of Canterbury is both a mark of Henry's rising reputation as a European statesman and a shot across the bows of the French—or at least, the Armagnacs who hold sway around Charles VI and the new dauphin, John.

Taken together with the providentially timed relief of Harfleur, this makes it a fine summer for the king of England. It is all "a great source of joy to him" says his chaplain.[26] Henry gives thanks to God for continuing to smile on his struggle for justice. Then he sets up an exploratory conference with the Armagnacs' bête noire, John the Fearless, duke of Burgundy, and summons an English parliament to ask it for another huge grant of taxation.

The next year he is going back to France, to try once more to seize his birthright. Selling this plan to the parliamentary commons, who meet yet again in October 1416, Chancellor Beaufort quotes Cicero, whose orations Henry read in his Latin lessons when he was a little boy.

"Our said sovereign lord [i.e., Henry] is again of necessity obliged to have recourse to the issue of the sword if he wishes to achieve an end, peace and termination of his just aim and quarrel," Beaufort tells the parliament, summoning all the solemn bombast he can muster, "thereby fulfilling the words of the wise man, who says: 'Let us make wars so that we might have peace, for the end of war is peace.'"

24

"FEARED BY EVERYBODY"

Among the fine gifts that the German king Sigismund leaves Henry following his state visit of 1416, perhaps none has greater symbolic value than the pickled heart of St. George.

In life St. George was a Greek-speaking Cappadocian who served in the personal bodyguard of the emperor Diocletian, before being martyred for his Christian faith in 303 CE. In death he has watched over Englishmen at war ever since the heyday of the crusades. George was recognized as the patron saint of the realm by Edward III, and now occupies a special place in the annual cycle of royal pageantry.

The chapel of St. George at Windsor, the spiritual home of the Order of the Garter, into which Sigismund is sworn during his visit, already contains some valuable pieces of the saint's person: an arm bone and a fragment of skull. Sigismund enhances this collection greatly by the addition of George's heart, enclosed in a beautiful gold reliquary.[1]

This fine relic will remain a prized ceremonial possession of the chapel for generations. But in the immediate circumstances of Henry's reign, with another invasion of France planned for the early summer of 1417, its protection is going to be vital. Successful as the Harfleur and Agincourt expedition was, Henry is now setting his sights on a far bigger and more difficult campaign. Pinching ports and chancing his arm in battle is not enough. Henry means to go further. His aim is the full conquest of Normandy.

Grand as this plan sounds, Henry is starting from a strong place. His victories of 1415 have persuaded Parliament, and its clerical equivalent, convocation, to be lavish with their tax awards. The Treaty of Canterbury with Sigismund has given Henry a powerful foreign ally. Exploratory talks with John the Fearless, duke of Burgundy, held during the autumn of 1416, do not produce a formal alliance, but John agrees to do as little as possible to oppose Henry, and actively to assist him if Henry appears to be on the verge of some significant breakthrough.

The first calls for archers, men-at-arms, and ships to make their way to Southampton, ready for a campaign that will last up to a year, are sent out in the first days of 1417. By late April, Henry is impatient to set sail, for news has arrived from France that yet another prince of the royal family has died: the dauphin John has succumbed to an abscess, and been replaced by Charles VI's fourth and last son, the fourteen-year-old Charles, count of Ponthieu. As it transpires, English ships will not leave port to take advantage of this French misfortune for nearly three months. Nevertheless, Henry formally departs London on April 27, making offerings at St. Paul's Cathedral, before crossing London Bridge with the mayor to give further donations in Southwark, at a church dedicated to St. George.

"And in this way," notes one writer, "he gave his farewell to every man, praying them all to pray God for him."[2]

Henry's preparations for his second invasion of France ask as much from his realm as the first. Ten thousand fighting men are contracted for the expedition, along with a multitude of engineers, medics, priests, and support staff. Thousands of sailors are required to take them across the Channel. The need for livestock as transport and haulage is as great as ever. So once more the royal jewel-house is raided for treasures to pawn for loans: a crown is pledged to Bishop Beaufort, who personally lends the king the massive sum of £14,000; a collar and a sword to the citizens of London. Large ships are impounded in every major port,* to sail alongside ships of the royal fleet, which is expanding, year on year. (Henry's own vessel for the expedition is the brand-new, thousand-ton clinker-built *Jesus,* whose construction at Winchelsea he was inspecting during Sigismund's visit.)[3] Grain and cured meat are sought from anyone who will sell them, in England or abroad. Every sheriff in the land is ordered to take stock of the geese in their shire, and have six long feathers ripped from the wings of each, to make arrow fletchings.[4] Clog makers are forbidden to make shoes from aspen, which is the favored wood for arrow shafts, on the grounds that their use of the wood is "to the great and perpetual detriment of archery."[5]

All this amounts to another huge logistical undertaking, and Henry's hand is present everywhere in it. He writes personally to the provost of Saint-Sever, in Gascony, asking to borrow two weapons masters renowned for their skill in making crossbows. He pores over government documents more intensely than any king of England before him, annotating them and sometimes even writing them in his own hand.[6] He concerns himself minutely with the timetable for departure, corresponding with his brothers to let them know when there are delays. The siblings already know their duties: Thomas and Humphrey will once more accompany him to France, while John, duke of Bedford, stays at home to oversee government. This is becoming Henry's preferred use of his brothers' talents: the proud and hyperaggressive Thomas makes an excellent comrade in the field, while Humphrey is showing an aptitude and appetite for warfare despite his injuries at Agincourt. John, meanwhile, is the closest to Henry in character, combining levelheaded political judgment with a warlike but analytical temperament.

When Henry realizes he needs more money than he already has from the City of London, he makes sure that the phrase "Our most dear and faithful and good friends" is scribbled on the outside of his begging

---

* These even include Venetian merchant vessels, much to the irritation of their Venetian owners.

letter.[7] He is understandably guarded about the exact nature of his invasion plans, keeping his intended destination "secret from his company, except . . . to such persons as was his pleasure."[8] Yet he still manages to conjure a feeling of common purpose behind his mission.

Of course, personal courtesies and polite flourishes cannot win a war on their own. But they matter. Since his days as prince, Henry has been absorbing the lessons of military organization under budgetary constraints. He is by now as adept in the laborious arts of financial planning as any ruler England has had. But he also has a sharp sense for the need to stir public opinion, never to take support for his wars for granted, and to foster a sense of participation in this faraway conflict among the overwhelming majority of his subjects who will never set foot in France. Henry's insight as a warrior king is that public morale and public finance go hand in hand.

In one sense this is a matter of fostering the spirit of Agincourt as expressed in the joyous words of the "Agincourt Carol": "Almighty God he keep our king, his people and all his well-willing, and give them grace without ending." To ensure that there are plenty of occasions for the English people to thank God for his protection, Henry has Archbishop Chichele decree that the feast day of St. Crispin and St. Crispinian (October 25) should be marked with particular reverence every year. Chichele also orders that religious processions across England should be increased in number and vigor during the course of the campaign. In London, the mayor and aldermen are encouraged to take action to ensure public decency is maintained: brothels and bathhouses are closed and citizens banned from harboring people known to be of "evil and vicious life." These laws are passed explicitly so that the populace may avoid incurring "the great abomination and displeasure of God."[9]

Yet if orders for the English people to go about unbathed and undersexed can be policed, it is not so easy to force them to be cheerful. Henry realizes that morale is also a matter of policy itself, which must be made with public prejudice and public confidence equally in mind. He understands, for example, the hostility of English taxpayers to the idea of novelty. His grandfather John of Gaunt attempted to reform the tax system in the 1380s by imposing poll taxes, and in doing so sparked the great rebellion of 1381. Henry's father provoked howls of complaint in his parliaments whenever he tried to impose unusual forms of income tax. So while Henry demands more taxation from the English people than has been raised in generations, he is careful only to raise it through traditional forms. There is no meddling with the system, just a determination to make it work.[10]

Similarly, Henry strives to demonstrate that the English crown under his stewardship is good for its debts. When the question is raised in a royal council of how much pay is due to the families of Agincourt veterans who died on campaign—should they be paid up until the day their loved one died, or receive wages to the value of their original contract?—Henry decides on the more generous award.[11] Not only does this do away with the need to haggle with thousands of bereaved families over back pay amounting to shillings and pennies, it also frames Henry in the minds of his subjects as a king who may be demanding but is also generous and fair. Later, when Henry realizes just a few weeks prior to his departure for France that he needs an advance on funds promised for later in the year by convocation, he writes to the English bishops appealing not to his own needs but to those of his men. "Our voyage requires great haste," he writes, "but the men of our retinue cannot go with us unless they have their wages paid in hand."[12]

Finally, as Henry prepares for his second French campaign, he offers up policy and action that will remind his subjects of his commitment to law and order at home. He extends the general pardon that was granted to the country in 1414, by which immunity from prosecution can be bought from the Crown for a steep but fixed sum. But at the same time the royal law is trained hard on notorious evildoers.

Henry sends out panels of judges far and wide across England to investigate crimes and try criminals. In London a Lollard preacher who has been distributing tracts "full of errors, over a wide area" is hanged, drawn, and beheaded.[13] In Sussex and Surrey a special judicial commission is sent out to pursue a criminal who goes by the name "Friar Tuck," whose gang stands accused of committing "divers murders, homicides, robberies, depredations, felonies, insurrections, trespasses, oppressions, extortions, offenses and misprisions"; Henry demands to have this Friar Tuck brought before him and his council in person.[14] At Lynn in East Anglia, meanwhile, three men have been on a serial killing spree, mutilating children: one boy has had his eyes gouged, another his back broken, and both have had their tongues cut out. The murderers are run to ground and hanged.[15]

There remains, of course, one notorious criminal—and heretic—who has not yet been dealt with as Henry would wish. John Oldcastle is still alive, at large, and alert to all opportunities to spread Lollard doctrine and agitate against Lancastrian rule. Oldcastle represents an irritating piece of unfinished business as Henry prepares to depart once again for France. But for the time being, there is nothing that can be done about him.

Due to the scale and complexity of preparations, Henry's departure for France is significantly delayed from his original target of May 1417. It is stalled further when a small fleet of French and Genoese ships puts into the mouth of the Seine outside Harfleur, and has to be driven away by a detachment of the English navy under the command of Henry's cousin John Holland, earl of Huntingdon. But by the end of July all is ready. Henry has revised his will, formally reappointed his brother John as keeper of the kingdom, and is carrying out government business in Portsmouth harbor, from his cabin aboard the new ship *Jesus*.

On August 1 Henry and his army land in Normandy, about twenty miles south of Harfleur, on the opposite, southern side of the Seine. The town closest to their landing point is called Touques, and at the first sight of the English, its citizens surrender without a fight. They act, says one French writer, as though the English army is composed not of men but of giants or wild beasts.[16] In reality they know there is no prospect whatever of either surviving a siege or being rescued: the new, teenage dauphin, Charles, is in Rouen with an army around a quarter the size of Henry's, and his advisers have a bogeyman even more terrifying than Henry to worry about. John the Fearless, duke of Burgundy, is once again threatening to march on Paris. The dauphin and his Armagnac advisers must decide which part of their realm to defend. They choose the capital.

So this is as easy a start to the campaign as Henry could have wanted. He accepts the surrender of Touques, dubs two dozen knights on the beach, makes his brother Thomas constable of the army, then issues a formal challenge to Charles VI. In this he says nothing he has not repeated many times before, but he warns Charles that he now knows exactly what to expect if he continues to deny Henry. "If you still refuse to do us justice, greater evils will follow," he writes.[17]

And so they do. By the middle of August, several more small towns and castles near Touques have also surrendered, and Henry is taking aim at his first major target. This is Caen: the effective capital of Lower Normandy and a wealthy mercantile city that has easy access to the sea via the river Orne. In 1346 Caen was thoroughly and bloodily sacked by Edward III. In 1417 its citizens hope to avoid such a horrible experience, but unlike their compatriots in Touques they are not willing simply to hold up their hands to Henry's band of ogres. They fall back behind Caen's network of thick stone walls, ditches, towers, and gatehouses and prepare to wait out a siege.

Henry brings up to Caen enough men, guns, and equipment to prosecute a siege on the scale of Harfleur. But he scarcely needs it. As the leaders of the city's garrison retreat behind the walls, they give orders to destroy every building in the suburbs, so that the English may not use any of them as bases for attack. The buildings marked for demolition include two huge and glorious abbeys founded by William the Conqueror: a nunnery known as the Abbaye aux Dames to the east of the city, and a monastery known as the Abbaye aux Hommes to the west.* Mines have been dug under the abbeys' towers to weaken them so much they are unsafe for use as positions for archers and gunners. But before they can be brought down, an appalled monk sneaks into the English camp and betrays the plan to Henry's brother Thomas, offering to help him break into the

* Or, more properly, the abbeys of Saint-Étienne and Trinité.

Abbaye aux Hommes. Thomas, quicksilver and always interested in escalating a fight, needs no second invitation. In short order his men have taken both abbeys and are dragging cannons up onto the towers to aim down into the barricaded city.

Once the bombardment begins, Caen holds out under round-the-clock fire for two weeks. By September 4 the streets are a wrecked tangle of shattered wooden houses and the walls have been broken in several places. Henry judges that the time has come. To clarion blasts and the squawk of trumpets his men rush the walls on his side of the city, while the defenders try to stop them "armed with weapons, swords and missiles, spears and stones." Amid fierce hand-to-hand fighting, a well-known English knight called Sir Edmund Springhouse slips on top of the walls and is run through by the defenders, who then set fire to him as he is dying and hurl his burning body from the ramparts. This horrifying tale makes its way back to England as pro-war propaganda, where it hardens hearts against "those inhuman French scum."[18]

Grisly and agonizing as Springhouse's death may be, however, it is only a small setback. As Caen's defenders scramble to the city's breached western walls, the king's brother Thomas hurls his own troops into action on the eastern side. Screaming "À Clarence! À Clarence! St. George!" they rampage through the broken streets, bypassing the churches but ignoring Henry's injunction to spare women and children and butchering everyone who stands in their way. As many as two thousand citizens are killed in a frenzied sack.[19] By the time the day is done, only Caen's citadel holds out. Henry sends cannons up to the foot of the walls to blast away from close range, and the thunder of gunpowder and broken stone rapidly persuades the garrison to negotiate surrender. They ask for reprieve until September 18, hoping in vain that the mad king or callow dauphin will abandon Paris to save them.

Needless to say, no such succor is coming, and for good reason. At the same time as Henry is blowing Caen to smithereens, John the Fearless's armies have been seizing towns along the Somme valley and are camped in Beauvais, two days' ride from Paris. The duke of Burgundy is inveighing against the incompetence of Charles VI and, with remarkable if not admirable brio, claiming that he is the only person who can save France from King Henry V. In fact, Burgundian brutality is easily as grotesque as that of the English. As John the Fearless plows remorselessly toward Paris, he decorates the countryside with the bodies of Armagnac soldiers, beheaded and hung up from the trees.[20]

On September 20, Caen's garrison surrenders. Henry lets them leave, along with anyone else who declines to swear fealty to him. Then he moves briefly into the castle and sets about organizing a new government of occupied Normandy, of which Caen will be the headquarters. To replace the thousands of citizens who have fled or been killed, Henry sends summonses to England for merchants and settlers. He appoints trusted advisers—including his father's veteran treasurer Sir John Tiptoft—to key positions in the new administration, orders coins to be minted for circulation in the conquered territories advertising himself as king of France, and promises to cut taxes—an offer anyone who has followed his recent policy in England may not entirely trust. He calls a meeting of his senior military officers to remind them that the people of Normandy are his subjects and, unless evidently contumacious, are to be treated properly.

Henry also writes home, sending a letter to the citizens of London, informing him of his deeds to date, and giving thanks for God's grace in sending "unto our hands our town of Caen, by assault, and with right little death of our people; whereof we thank Our Savior . . . praying you that ye do the same, and as devoutly as ye can."[21] Unlike his days in Wales, when he wrote to his father to report his battlefield successes in French, Henry now uses English wherever he possibly can, to be sure that as wide an audience as possible can understand him, and assuring them that no matter how hard his eyes are trained toward Rouen and Paris, he will always in his heart and mouth be one of their own.

According to one chronicler of Henry's reign, once Caen has fallen "the fame and virtue of our prince" wins Henry "many friends."[22] A stronger motivating factor, perhaps, is the desire of most ordinary Normans not to die. But whether it is terror or admiration that floods the hearts of the people, once Henry marches into the Norman countryside at the start of October 1417, he meets precious little resistance.

His army fans out, and within two weeks they have taken a clutch of other towns and cities by doing no more than knocking on the gates and ordering those who answer them to surrender. By the end of the month Henry's men have captured the great cathedral settlements of Lisieux and Bayeux. They have taken the walled city of Alençon and Argentan and almost every other important town and fortress in the notionally powerful duchy of Alençon, as well as most of the major strongholds in the neighboring county of Perche.

The duke of Alençon at this time is a fourteen-year-old boy, whose father was killed at Agincourt. (This is, supposedly, the duke who delivered the blow that dented Henry's crown in the thick of the fighting.) The lad's uncle is the duke of Brittany, a lord who is regarded as a power broker in French politics, since Brittany is an independent realm, whose rulers have long been entangled in the Hundred Years War. In early November Henry holds a meeting with John of Brittany at Alençon Castle. He forces the duke to wait for his attention on bended knee, before gracing him with a conference at which they agree on a nonaggression pact, banning all enemies of England from Breton lands and ports. A similar deal is done with the duchess of Anjou, whose lands border Normandy to the south.

Thus protected from attack along two of Normandy's frontiers, when winter sets in, there is a sense of inevitability about Henry's conquest. Rather than closing down military operations for the winter, he decides to press ahead. On December 1, he takes the bellicose Thomas and enthusiastic Humphrey to begin a siege at Falaise, the birthplace of William the Conqueror. Falaise is heavily fortified, and defended by a garrison of several hundred professional soldiers commanded by some of the most experienced soldiers in the kingdom. It ought to be impossible to take. Yet after two weeks of heavy cannon bombardment, the defenders' nerves fail, for, as one writer puts it, they cannot endure "the awesome volleys of stones, feared by everybody, which they [see] launched into their midst time after time."[23] Though the defenders of Falaise's huge castle remain obdurate for several months, the defenders of the city proper give up before the year is out.

Henry accepts their surrender, and keeps going. In January 1418 he splits his army, with the aim of wrapping up the conquest of Lower Normandy in short order: sending Thomas in one direction and Humphrey in the other. They encounter barely any more resistance than before. Only when Humphrey appears before the soaring walls of Cherbourg in March does a garrison have the nerve and resources to defy the English—and then only temporarily. Henry summons ships from England to blockade Cherbourg by sea while Humphrey organizes a siege that will last six full months. But other than Cherbourg and the unassailable island fortress of Mont-Saint-Michel, by the time summer 1418 arrives the whole of Lower Normandy is Henry's. He can turn his attention to Upper Normandy, to the north of the river Seine, and the duchy's ancient capital, Rouen.

Occasionally in the midst of all this campaigning Henry takes short breaks. He keeps up his lifelong habit of reading: he has claimed as his personal prize from the fall of Caen a historical chronicle on a subject that is no longer known, but that clearly grabs his attention.[24] He also pauses to observe religious festivals. He spends Christmas at Bayeux and Easter at Caen. And he is there again for the feast day of St. George, April 23, 1418. Although he is unable to celebrate the day at Windsor, where George's skull and arm bone and heart lie, Henry makes sure England's martial protector is honored in "solemn festival" nonetheless. He holds jousting matches and banquets. He dubs several new knights in honor of their robust service to his crown, then sends them off to assist with the various military operations going on across the invaded land.

A few days after these celebrations, an elderly preacher arrives at Caen. He is named Vincent Ferrier and is famous for the sweetness of his voice and his penchant for giving sermons many hours in length. Ferrier impresses Henry by performing a miracle in which he restores good health and the power of speech to "a dumb youth whom it was said had not eaten or drunk anything for two years."[25]

Then Ferrier tells Henry that the year to come will bring him great fortune and the discomfiture of his enemies. One of the most powerful lords in the kingdom of France, says Ferrier, is shortly going to die.

These are tantalizing words, which seem to promise even more opportunity for Henry as chaos sweeps through France. There is no way of telling who is marked for death or when. All the same, Ferrier is good at what he does.

Before the summer is out, the preacher's words will come true.

25

"WHO IS THE GREAT LORD?"

While Henry and his army roll through Lower Normandy in the winter of 1417–18, back in England his brother John, duke of Bedford, is guiding domestic government with the same steady hand he used in 1415. Now twenty-eight years old, John is as statesmanlike as Henry himself. He is powerfully built, with a distinctive beaked nose and strong arms and legs. He has proven himself as a general many times on land and at sea, but like Henry (and, indeed, Humphrey, duke of Gloucester) he also has a cultured, learned interest in art and literature. John collects books and tapestries and cultivates a princely bearing through his love of fine clothes and jewels.[1] Henry is blessed to have a brother made so closely in his own image, whom he can empower to deputize for him without fear that he will become charged by jealous rivalry. What is more, he needs him. There is much in England to keep John occupied.

In the north of England the Scots take the opportunity presented by Henry's distraction in Normandy to storm the borderlands, in an expedition that becomes known as the Foul Raid. They besiege the towns of Berwick and Roxburgh, and Bedford is compelled to travel north in person to persuade them of their error. He joins forces with his and Henry's uncle Thomas Beaufort—whom the king has rewarded for his long service with promotion from earl of Dorset to duke of Exeter—as well as Hotspur's son, Henry Percy, now restored to the family title of earl of Northumberland, and Ralph Neville, earl of Westmoreland. Together they break the sieges, deploying an army of troops whom Thomas Beaufort declares to be equal in "courage and spirit" to any man in Normandy.[2]

After this, John returns south to manage a parliament summoned to keep money flowing to Henry in Caen—or wherever else he might be. Bishop Henry Beaufort, who normally gives the opening sermon to parliamentary gatherings, is preparing to visit Sigismund at the Council of Constance, where wrangling to reunify the papacy is reaching a critical stage and Henry wants an experienced representative in place. He has resigned the chancellorship in preparation for his new mission. So this time Bedford is assisted by Thomas Langley, bishop of Durham, another longtime ally whose years in royal service extend back to Henry IV's reign.

Once Bedford and Langley have the parliamentary gathering seated in the Painted Chamber at Westminster Palace, they expect business to be done quickly. They need a large tax grant, but since Henry is spending his subjects' money well, there is no obvious reason for it to be withheld. Langley reminds the parliament of Henry's distinguished track record: fighting Glyndŵr in Wales, foiling the "dreadful evils and most dangerous treasons" of English rebels, trouncing the French at Harfleur and Agincourt. Taking as his theme an injunction from the book of Samuel, Bishop Langley urges the assembly: "Take courage, be men,* and you shall be glorious!"[3]

The members in the Painted Chamber do as they are bid with barely a quibble. They grant the tax—another double subsidy—and set a schedule for its collection. Yet they do not dismiss immediately. For as they are sitting, in early December 1417, news arrives from the Welsh borders that sends a crackle of excitement around Westminster. A skirmish has taken place near Welshpool, where tenants of a peer called Edward, Lord

* To be understood in the sense of the modern injunction "Man up!" (1 Samuel, 4:9)

Charlton of Powys, have captured the most wanted man in the realm: a jailbreaker, absconder, renegade, and rabble-rouser who has been at large from the law since escaping from the Tower of London nearly four years ago.

He is none other than "that boastful ancient of evil days, Lollard leader and prince of heretics, John Oldcastle."[4]

Oldcastle's capture is a boon for the Crown, for his freedom was a blot on Henry's drive to create an ordered realm in which orthodox religion is observed and troublemakers are brought to justice. Glimpses of him have been reported over the years in Warwickshire and Oxfordshire, Shrewsbury and Oswestry. He is rumored to have consorted with a roll call of the most notorious enemies of the Lancastrian crown: the fake Richard II, the real Owain Glyndŵr, and the treacherous Richard, earl of Cambridge.[5]

Until now, though, no one has been able to lay a hand on him. So John, duke of Bedford, has made it a priority of his tenure as England's keeper to track Oldcastle down. Passing through the Midlands on his way home from scattering the Scots, he has rounded up and imprisoned all the Lollards he can lay his hands on. Oldcastle's properties in Kent have been belatedly seized by royal agents, his wife has been thrown in jail, and his known associates have been squeezed for intelligence concerning his whereabouts.[6] This, it seems, is what provided the information that led to Oldcastle's arrest.

News of Oldcastle's capture reaches Westminster around December 1, 1417. It is understandably electrifying, so Parliament remains in session while the treacherous heretic is brought south under heavy guard. He arrives nearly a fortnight later on a horse-and-cart, still carrying injuries sustained during the fight that produced his arrest, including a painful shin where a woman in the arresting posse hit him flush with a footstool.[7] On December 14, 1417, he is brought before Parliament for trial. His crimes are rehearsed at length: his "various heretical beliefs and other manifest errors repugnant to Catholic law," his plans to overthrow the monarchy and "to kill our lord king, his brothers, the prelates and other magnates," his "numerous other evil and intolerable deeds."[8]

Asked what he has to say to all this, Oldcastle responds as is his wont: earnestly and at length. When he is told by the most senior judge present to keep his comments brief, he says that "it means absolutely nothing to me that I am being judged by you," then declares his allegiance to "King Richard, who [is] still alive in the kingdom of Scotland."[9]

In saying so, Oldcastle passes his own death sentence. No man could utter such words in a parliament loyal to Henry V and hope to live, and Oldcastle surely knows it. It is possible that he speaks like this because he realizes the game is up, and prefers to face a traitor's death—some variation on hanging and beheading—rather than being fed to the fire as a heretic.

But if this is Oldcastle's hope, he is to be swiftly disappointed. His old enemy Archbishop Arundel's provision that Lollards should receive double punishment remains in place. So as soon as his appeal to the pseudo–Richard II has left his lips, Parliament proceeds to judgment. It decrees that "the said John [Oldcastle] should be confirmed and adjudged as a traitor to God, and a notorious heretic . . . and as a traitor to the king and his realm . . . he should be taken to the Tower of London, and from there drawn through the city of London up to the new gallows in the parish of St. Giles outside Old Temple Bar in London, and there hanged and burned [while] hanging."

So Oldcastle is to pay "the penalty of both swords."[10] St. Giles' Field is the place where in January 1414 Oldcastle tried to raise the rebellion that would have overthrown the king. Now, four years on, he is taken back there, to find awaiting him a gallows of wicked novelty. For his treachery he is hung up in chains, with an iron collar around his neck. For his heresy a fire is lit below.

It is as hideous a sight as the Lollard John Badby's death-barrel once was. And just as Henry V entreated Badby to renounce his unbelief at the last, so John, duke of Bedford, now steps forward to offer Oldcastle a late reprieve, if he will confess his sins to one of the many priests in the crowd that has gathered to watch him die. Oldcastle retorts that even if St. Peter and St. Paul were before him, he would keep his mouth shut. The only person to whom he will speak is Sir Thomas Erpingham, once a Lollard himself, and more recently commander of the archers at Agincourt.

Oldcastle asks Erpingham to keep a watch over his bodily remains, and to make it known to his followers if he is resurrected. "The bigot was so far gone in his craziness that he actually thought he would rise again from the dead after three days," writes one, punctiliously Catholic, chronicler.[11] But if Oldcastle is mad, he is also strong, firm in his belief, and, at the end, very brave. The fire is lit, the flames lick up, and Oldcastle finally holds his peace, as the inferno devours him and the wooden gallows he is chained to.

The punishment visited on John Oldcastle in London at the beginning of 1418 is hideous. But one theme of Henry's reign is that things can always be worse in France, and that this usually redounds to England's advantage. At the end of May 1418 another spasm of violence in Paris reminds everyone of the grave dysfunction that haunts the French political realm, fulfills the prediction made at Caen by the visionary preacher Vincent Ferrier, and lays open Henry's path to completing his conquest of Normandy.

It is, as usual, the work of John the Fearless. Throughout May 1418 the duke of Burgundy engages, with his usual bad faith, in talks to bring about a new truce between his faction and that of the count of Armagnac, so that the French might oppose the English as one. By the last days of the month a draft deal has been thrashed out, on terms that will effectively give John the Fearless mastery of the kingdom, with full access to Queen Isabeau and her last remaining son, the teenage dauphin Charles. This deal is so objectionable to the count of Armagnac that he prevents its ratification, bringing the peace process to a stalemate. Meanwhile, Henry's armies are dismembering the kingdom virtually unopposed. A mutinous mood sweeps the streets of the French capital.

The gathering storm breaks in the early hours of the morning on May 29, when several hundred Burgundian troops are secretly let into the city, beginning a fortnight of lawlessness, chaos, and running street battles between partisans of each side. The king and queen fall into their hands. But Armagnac loyalists snatch the dauphin Charles and smuggle him out of Paris beneath a bedsheet, eventually taking him to the cathedral city of Bourges, 150 miles south of Paris, below the river Loire. The count of Armagnac himself, however, is caught hiding in a basement and carted off to prison in the Conciergerie. He does not remain there long.

On June 13, the Parisian mob, excited by rumors of an Armagnac army approaching to take the city back, break into the Conciergerie and other prisons. With axes and clubs they beat and hack to death all the leading Armagnacs they can find, including the count.

The slaying of the Armagnacs is not quick or clean. Bodies and faces are mutilated. One English chronicler records a lurid account of the count of Armagnac's death. In this version he is flayed alive and hung up by his bootstraps; feathers are glued to his exposed flesh using his own drying blood, which are then plucked out one by one, causing him to suffer hundreds of exquisitely agonizing miniature deaths before his last.[12] This horror story is untrue, but its circulation reflects the depravity into which France is thought, quite rightly, to have sunk. When Henry writes another letter to London around this time, detailing his military progress, he skirts briskly past "the death of the earl [sic] of Armagnac, and the slaughter that hath been at Paris, for we trust you have full knowledge thereof."[13]

Paris remains at a boiling point throughout the summer of 1418, by the end of which much of its population has died or run away. The young dauphin is establishing his alternative capital in Bourges. Henry, meanwhile, is well on his way to battering through the walls of the Norman capital, Rouen.

Henry arrives at Rouen on the night of July 29, 1418, with an army that has been called in from everywhere else in Normandy, and bolstered by fresh troops brought from England under his tireless uncle Thomas Beaufort, duke of Exeter. He has thousands of men at his disposal: the majority of them experienced, skillful, battle-hardened veterans whose morale is sky-high after a year of fighting that has produced nothing but victories. (They will be reinforced in time by a force of fifteen hundred native Irish warriors under James Butler, earl of Ormond; these troops cause a general sensation thanks to each man's bare legs and feet, the little ponies they ride without a saddle, and their exotic arms and armor, consisting of a round "targe" shield, a sharp knife, and a handful of short spears.)[14]

Just to get to Rouen Henry's men have already achieved the extraordinary military feat of crossing from the left to the right bank of the Seine, in the face of united opposition from the garrisons of two dozen towns who do not wish to see the English anywhere near their walls. But as Henry surveys Rouen at sunrise on July 30, it is plain that this will be his biggest challenge to date. As he writes in a letter shortly after his arrival, Rouen is "the most notable place in France, save Paris."[15] It is a large city, with a population of twenty thousand or more inhabitants; a garrison of around fifteen hundred professional soldiers; a network of walls, defensive towers, and deep ditches; a castle; and a smoking hinterland of suburbs burned and torn down in panic in response to the news of Henry's approach.[16] Every citizen has been told to lay down supplies to survive a six-month blockade.

Henry is determined to reduce it, but he must know that, as one member of his large army later writes in a famous poem, "a more solemn siege was never set, since Jerusalem and Troy was got."[17] The last time Rouen was successfully taken was more than two centuries earlier, when the mighty French king Philip II "Augustus" snatched it from Henry's ancestor King John in 1203.

Henry, however, has learned and achieved more in siegecraft during the thirty-one years of his life than almost any other English king since Richard I, whose heart, preserved after his death in 1199, lies entombed in Rouen's cathedral. He understands that success will depend in large part on his ability to keep his own army supplied while completely stopping the flow of food and reinforcements to the besieged. Guns and mines will play their role. But in a city of this size, the deadliest weapon is hunger.

To that end, on arriving in Rouen, Henry splits his army into four camps connected by communications trenches. The divisions block the main entrances to the city and are commanded by himself, his brother Thomas, his uncle Thomas Beaufort, and the highly capable Thomas Montague, earl of Salisbury, a veteran of Harfleur and Agincourt. Other positions around the city are held by John Mowbray, earl of Norfolk—the twenty-six-year-old son of the duke whose aborted duel against Henry's father in 1398 began his peculiar journey to the crown—and John Holland, earl of Huntingdon, who keeps guard of the southern, right bank of the Seine. Henry enacts his usual strict code of discipline and makes regular rounds of all the camps, inspecting the guns, adjusting his troops' positions, and hanging those who disobey his orders for good behavior. To keep morale high and dehydration low, he also sends to London for fine wines and one thousand pipes* of ale and beer.

To ensure that no French shipping can run relief expeditions to Rouen's citizens, Henry has the river blocked by wooden posts driven into its bed, with chains strung across them. A bridge prefabricated in England is erected for English military use. Troops on barges cruise up and down the Seine, sniffing out trouble. At the river mouth—where Harfleur stands—Henry posts ships borrowed from the Portuguese, allies of his kingdom since John of Gaunt's day.

Thus every conceivable means of saving the people of Rouen from starvation is blocked off. All that remains is for Henry's army to stay alert, healthy, obedient, and in position, ready to defy every sally made from the city gates and any attempt to relieve Rouen from outside. The responsibility for organizing the latter lies with Charles VI's government in Paris, eighty miles away upriver. It is now led by Henry's sometime ally but a man he now describes as "our full enemy": John the Fearless, duke of Burgundy.[18]

* Roughly half a million pints. The English have earned their reputation as enthusiastic beer drinkers over many centuries.

As guardian of the king of France, John the Fearless can no longer observe his promise to stand by while Henry carves up the realm. However, the political situation in France during the summer of 1418 is so dire that it is the middle of October before he can even begin to contemplate coming to Rouen's aid, issuing a summons for men to join an army he can march downriver. By this time Henry has had the city in a stranglehold for two and a half months, and hunger has set in. Despite the orders given before Henry's arrival, the citizens are nowhere near prepared to endure half a year of want, and the autumn has seen dogs, cats, rats, and mice hunted for meat, which is traded at black-market prices.

From time to time droves of women, children, the elderly, and the infirm are shoved out of the city gates to reduce the number of starving mouths inside the walls. In the past Henry has allowed such wretched victims of his strategy to pass his lines unmolested. Now he orders that they should remain in no-man's-land: sleeping rough in the broad ditch that runs around the city in front of its walls. "It was pity to see them," writes the eyewitness poet. "Women come kneeling on their knees, with their children in their arms to succor them from harm; old men kneeling by them, making a doleful cry, [saying] 'Have mercy upon us, Englishmen.'"[19] From the ditch these emaciated citizens cry out to their English guards that they would rather die than go back into the hellish city. Mothers give birth in the ditch, and hoist their babies up to the city ramparts so that they may be baptized by starving priests inside. The softer-hearted guards throw down crusts of bread. But this is as far as mercy is allowed to go. As winter approaches and the weather turns, the ditch-folk begin to die of exposure.

Before they die, says the poet, many of the expelled citizens are heard to "curse their own nation." This is exactly the effect Henry wishes to achieve. In the course of his wars he is becoming accustomed to authoring great cruelties. In part this is his duty as God's scourge of the sinful French. But the sight of Rouen's citizens starving and freezing in their own ditch has a political purpose, too. Henry wants to be accepted as the ruler of Normandy. For this to happen, he must convince the population that their existing leaders cannot keep them safe.

This strategy is hardly a secret. At the end of October, Henry allows a group of messengers to leave Rouen and go to Paris, to describe to John the Fearless the nightmare through which they are living. The messengers weep and beat their breasts and foretell the loss of Normandy in its entirety if they are not rescued. They also promise John the Fearless that if he abandons them to the English, those who survive will never forget it, and will wreak vengeance on him and his children: he will have "no bitterer enemies in the world."[20]

John the Fearless promises to act. But in his heart he knows he cannot. He has neither the money nor the men, and it will be a grave risk for him to leave Paris undefended with the Armagnacs now thirstier for his blood than ever before. He must also know that Henry has diplomats negotiating with the dauphin Charles for a peace that would surely include a mutual agreement to hunt him down and annihilate him. The risk of antagonizing the English to the point that they will side against him is real and perhaps existential. He is trapped between enemies. Worse, this situation is clear to everyone around him. Although John the Fearless sends out urgent summonses for troops in the king's name, and takes Charles VI to Saint-Denis to receive the oriflamme, the popular response is lackluster. Not until late November does he have anything like the numbers he needs to make a credible attempt to relieve Rouen. And even then he dithers and refuses to march.

Inevitably, then, by December Rouen is on its knees. Its people have been without fresh food or other supplies for nearly five months. As Christmas approaches and the prospect of help from either the Burgundians or the Armagnacs vanishes, the only question is whether the city's garrison will negotiate surrender or risk a breach of the walls and a massacre.

This is as well for everyone, for by now there are signs that their resistance, the winter weather, and the grind of the cruel and cold campaign are starting to tell on Henry's nerves. In late November he writes to his brother John in London to nag him about a fairly routine government matter. Henry has heard that Englishmen have been breaking the terms of the nonaggression pact he agreed to the previous year with the duke of Brittany. Reparations are due to the Bretons, but John has been slow in dealing with this.

Henry's tone as he upbraids his brother is tart and sarcastic. He supposes, he writes, that John has forgotten his repeated demands for the reparations to be made. He orders him to make good this oversight, and to send to Rouen a list of all the truce breakers' names. He signs off by telling John to stay on top of his work in future, so that he has no cause to write in like manner again, "seeing how busy he is otherwise."[21]

Only under extreme stress does Henry write in such terms to his reliable brother. But John is not the only recipient of a tongue-lashing. On New Year's Day 1419 Henry receives representatives of Rouen's garrison, who have finally given up hope of salvation, at his siege headquarters in a charterhouse east of the city. The garrison's first request is that Henry deliver proper care and relief to the refugees shivering in the city ditch.

"Fellas," snaps Henry, "who put them there?"[22] When a knight among the representatives speaks of Henry "winning" Rouen, he is even more abrasive. "Rouen is my own land," he says, adding that if he is further resisted, then "the men within will speak of me until Doomsday."[23]

He is in no mood for charity. The garrison will surrender, and that will be that.

On January 13, 1419, Rouen does surrender, under strict terms brokered by Archbishop Chichele of Canterbury. A big fine, total disarmament, and a commitment by the citizens to clean up their filthy, stinking streets are the conditions Henry demands. In return he offers peace and property rights for all those who recognize him as their rightful lord.* The official handover of keys happens six days later, and Henry

* Or almost all. The captain of Rouen's crossbowmen is executed, after the city surrenders, for crimes committed during the defense. He is accused of having hanged captured Englishmen from the walls of Rouen and tied others in sacks with live dogs, then drowned them in the river Seine.

appoints the indefatigable Thomas Beaufort, duke of Exeter, as governor of the newly captured city, just as he did at Harfleur three and a half years earlier. Then his men go in, blowing trumpets and shouting, "Saint George!" to take control of the streets.[24]

The sight that greets them when they enter Rouen is described with chilling clarity by the eyewitness poet. Most of the townsfolk are "but bones and bare skin, with hollow eyes and visage sharp," he recalls, "unlike living men but the dead." Some women hold dead children to their breasts, while elsewhere filthy babies whimper in the laps of their dead mothers. Orphaned toddlers aged just two or three go about begging for bread.[25] Despite the cleanup operation Henry has ordered, corpses still lie everywhere, and people are dying faster than carts can take them away.

When Henry makes his own formal entry into Rouen, he does so with his now-customary sobriety. For him, there are no clarions. He approaches the city gates flanked by bishops and abbots holding crucifixes, each of which he kisses in turn. Then, mounted on a dark horse adorned with black damask and a golden breastplate, he trots through the city to the great Cathedral of Notre-Dame, where he makes offerings and hears a mass. Behind him a page holds aloft a lance with a fox's tail dangling from it. This was, the most astute observers note, a favorite symbol of Henry's father.

As the singers of Henry's personal chapel sing *Quis Est Magnus Dominus?* ("Who is the great lord?"), Henry can reflect that he has achieved another astonishing military feat. It has come at appalling human cost, yet it is becoming ever harder to doubt his claim to be the man that God wishes to rule Normandy—and perhaps all of France. Rouen will prompt a rash of defections of other towns in the region to his rule: so many that his thoughts must turn now to government as much as to further conquest. It will not be long before Paris is in his sights.

26

"THIS UNLUSTY SOLDIER'S LIFE"

At three o'clock on the afternoon of May 30, 1419, Henry paces in slow, stately fashion toward a post set at the center of a meeting ground in a meadow on the banks of the river Seine and kisses the hand of Isabeau of Bavaria, queen of France.

Large bands of noblemen, counselors, attendants, and guards watch from both sides. It is an extraordinary sight: the austere English king greeting and embracing the short, tough, long-suffering French queen.[1] Yet the mood among the onlookers can only be tense. This meeting, not far from the town of Meulan, has been a good while coming. It has taken much fraught diplomacy to arrange, and the security measures around it are formidable.

The meadow at Meulan has been divided into a French and an English zone, each fenced off with tall wooden palisades and—on the French side—wicker screens to defend against longbow shot. Between is a neutral zone, also ringed with more huge fences, with armed guards posted at each of its three entrances.[2] The negotiating pavilion is at the heart of this bristling compound, accessible only to the most senior delegates; on

Henry's side, these include his brothers Thomas and Humphrey, his uncle Thomas Beaufort, Archbishop Chichele, and Richard Beauchamp, earl of Warwick. In the camp beyond, strict ordinances forbid any tomfoolery on the part of the ordinary soldiers: brawling, wrestling, and even the use of foul language are punishable by death.[3]

Security is tight for good reason. The last personal summit between English and French royalty took place more than twenty years ago, in 1396, amid a field of bright pavilions at Ardres. Henry was there, then: a little boy brought across the sea by his father to watch Richard II take away Queen Isabeau's eldest daughter, Isabelle, as his wife. Now Henry is a thirty-two-year-old man, come to stake a matrimonial claim of his own. If terms can be struck with Queen Isabeau, then Henry will conclude his war of conquest and marry Isabeau's youngest girl, the seventeen-year-old princess Catherine.

The prize is huge and the bride close at hand. Catherine arrived at Meulan with her mother in a train of luxurious carriages just one hour before talks began. She is a poised, elegant, willowy girl with large round eyes, a small mouth, and a slender neck. Her willingness to do her dynastic duty, if called upon, is not in doubt. All the same, as Henry and Queen Isabeau progress arm in arm toward the tent where they will sit on gold-draped thrones and listen to their lawyers argue, both sides are wary. Since the fall of Rouen, Henry has ostensibly held the upper hand in diplomacy. But already this spring Henry has seen peace negotiations with the dauphin's rival court collapse amid ill feeling on both sides. His demands are vast. He will give up his hereditary claim to be king of France, but in return he wants the French to yield to him everything once held by Edward III under the 1360 Treaty of Brétigny, along with all he himself has conquered in Normandy—to be held, as one attendee at the conference puts it, "of God only, and not of none earthly creature."[4] The dowry he asks for taking Catherine as his queen is 1 million ecus.

Even among the Burgundians who surround Queen Isabeau at the French court there is no consensus that these are acceptable terms. Then there is the awkward fact that the only man who ought to be able to make such an agreement is absent from the conference. Charles VI was supposed to be brought up to Meulan from his lodgings at Pontoise for the first day of discussion. But that morning he suffered one of his mental lapses and has been judged too mad to be seen in public.

So there is little trust and not much love between the two sides, as well as a nagging sense that the dauphin Charles is likely to try to find a way to wreck the negotiations, unless they can be completed in haste. Henry charges the earl of Warwick with making this point to Queen Isabeau. Warwick does so in brusque fashion, announcing in his opening speech that the English wish to have everything agreed on and formalized before a week is out.

Unfortunately for Henry, there is no hope whatever of such a timetable being met. On the third day of the talks Henry and Catherine are introduced in person and spend a little time in private conversation. (Watching gossips are transfixed by the princess's expensive clothes and her perfect performance of virginal shyness.) But after this, the first week of the conference passes in a combination of leisurely feasting and obtuse debate over protocols and terms, and the princess does not return to the meadow to see Henry again.

There are many stumbling blocks in the discussions, which cannot possibly be resolved in seven days: the scale of Henry's demands, his desire to hold lands in France "of God only," which would permanently alienate French territory from any control by the French crown, disputes over costs deductible from Catherine's dowry, and many other, pettier matters besides.

The greatest problem of all, however, is the fact that the person who is really in control of negotiations on the French side is not the mad king Charles or the forbearing Queen Isabeau, but John the Fearless, duke of Burgundy.

Henry has known John the Fearless long enough to realize that the duke, while resourceful and on occasion useful, is not a man to be trusted. At Meulan John lives up to his reputation, dragging out discussions, avoiding firm commitments, and, all the while, maintaining a line of communication with the dauphin's circle in an attempt to double-cross the English. He does this because his objective is as it always has been: to be the moving force in French politics, whichever way he can. And for all that Henry seems to be in a dominant position, John can smell on the English a hint of weakness.

There is no doubt that Henry's military achievements in France have been extraordinary. Between the fall of Rouen in January 1419 and the opening of the peace conference at Meulan in May, his armies have effectively completed the conquest of Normandy, with only the island of Mont-Saint-Michel holding out against them. Henry has recently taken delivery of a consignment of much-needed gold and silver coin—around £40,000 of it—shipped to France from England following the latest round of tax collection.[5] He has begun to organize the administration of occupied Normandy, overseen by one of his most trusted diplomats, the Welshman Philip Morgan, whom he has appointed as Norman chancellor. Morgan's task is to see that Normandy can one day pay for its own government and military defense. Henry has invited English settlers to come and take up new lives in conquered cities, and he has granted great estates to his brothers and other English noblemen, with the aim of giving English taxpayers and war captains a personal stake in defending the land they have won. Nothing like this has been seen since the heyday of Edward III.*

Yet exhaustion is setting in. Henry and his men have been away from home at war for more than eighteen months—an unprecedentedly long and expensive tour of combat. The army's wage bill swallows gold and silver even faster than John, duke of Bedford, can ship it over. Some men are deserting as payments go into arrears. Finding competent troops to rotate in for those who are injured or unwell is proving impossible, and those who have been in the field from the start are starting to gripe. One weary

* Henry seems to envisage the re-creation of an Anglo-Norman landholding class of the sort that was created after the Norman Conquest; persisted into the first two generations of Plantagenet rule under Henry II, Richard the Lionheart, and King John; and destroyed when Philip Augustus conquered Normandy in 1203–4.

soldier writes home around this time, asking his friends to pray that he may "come soon out of this unlusty soldier's life, into the life of England."[6]

So for all that Henry affects confidence at Meulan, John the Fearless knows the English position is a little more precarious than Henry can admit. He works his diplomatic angles accordingly. And as the first week of talks gives way to a second, and then a third, Henry and his team realize they are being stalled and perhaps even strung along.

It is not hard to work out why. The Burgundians are making progress with the dauphin. John the Fearless is now shuttling between meetings with the English and the Armagnacs, keeping Henry on the hook while at the same time trying to broker terms that would unite France against the English devils—and preserve his own position as the most powerful man in the realm.

In mid-June, Henry sees John the Fearless for a private meeting and confronts him with his double-dealing. "Fair cousin," he says, according to one French chronicler, "we wish you to know that we will have the daughter of your king, and all that we have demanded with her—or we will drive him out of his kingdom, and you as well."

John the Fearless replies coolly that Henry can say whatever he likes, "but before you drive my lord and I out of the realm, you will have grown very tired, and of this we have no doubt."[7]

As Henry's reign has progressed, there have been fewer and fewer people who have dared speak to him so defiantly. But John the Fearless knows Henry of old and, true to his nickname, he is not intimidated. Henry tries several tactics to break through the duke's insouciance. One morning he attempts to bully the French as they arrive for talks by arraying his troops as though ready to fight. On another occasion he tries to dazzle them with largesse: treating the entire rival delegation to a delicious feast.[8] But by the end of June the French negotiators are scarcely engaging with their English counterparts. In the first week of July it is clear that talks are over.

Queen Isabeau writes to Henry to explain, as delicately as she can, what has happened. Although Henry's proposals for peace were perfectly acceptable to her, she writes, "there was nevertheless great difficulty in the way of accepting them and concluding with you." Her counselors, she continues, have all along been urging "that we should incline to our son." Had she and John the Fearless agreed to peace with Henry, "all the lords, knights, cities and good towns [in France] would have abandoned us and joined with our said son; whence even greater war would have arisen."[9]

The queen may well be sincere. She is probably right. But this is of no comfort to Henry. At the core of his strategy in both war and diplomacy is keeping the two factions in French politics more hostile to each other than to him. Now he has overreached. His tireless military campaigning has led him to a position where he felt he could force on one side or another a lasting peace deal weighted heavily in his favor. Yet he has been too successful: the boom of his guns and the terrors he has visited on the inhabitants of Normandy, followed by his demands for half the kingdom as the price of peace, have finally scared the French into each other's arms.

On July 11 a long-awaited peace treaty is agreed upon outside the castle of Pouilly. But the English are nowhere to be seen. After just three days of discussions, John the Fearless and the sixteen-year-old dauphin exchange gifts and kisses and announce their intention to put aside all old hatreds in the name of hustling Henry V out of France for good. Eight days later, Burgundian diplomats pass the details of the peace of Pouilly to Henry via the earl of Warwick. With chutzpah worthy of their master, the Burgundian ambassadors ask for another month of truce, so that John the Fearless may use his influence with the reunited royal family to establish terms for a peace treaty with Henry. When the report of the meeting is communicated to Henry, he reacts with the cold pragmatism to which he usually reverts in time of crisis.

In a newsletter written in English to the citizens of London on August 5, 1419, Henry explains his position bluntly. There will be no more truce. Notwithstanding the weariness of his men and the depletion of his treasury, he still intends to have the justice he has always sought. "Forasmuch as our adverse party will have no peace or accord with us, but finally have refused all means of peace, we be compelled again to war through their default," he writes. "The which we recommend to your good prayers with all our heart."[10]

By the time Henry writes this letter, he has already recommenced his war, and in brutal fashion. On the night of July 30, around three thousand English troops move quietly under cover of darkness from Meulan up to Pontoise, the town where, just a week earlier, Charles VI, Queen Isabeau, and John the Fearless were keeping their court. They hide in ditches around the town walls until just before sunrise. Then, as the night watchmen come down from their posts to give way to the guards on the day shift, they pounce. Men run tall ladders up against the town walls, scramble up them, storm down into the streets, and break open a gate.

Whatever orders for restraint Henry may have given his troops in the past are now suspended, save for his command not to plunder churches. Screaming "St. George!" and "The city is taken!" the English pour wild-eyed into Pontoise. They fight running battles with the surprised garrison, many of whom are still in their nightshirts. They kick down shop doors and loot houses. They cut down soldiers and civilians without discrimination. They drive terrified townsfolk skittering from their homes, pouring onto the roads toward Paris with nothing more than they can carry in their arms. Many of the refugees lose even this, as they are set upon later that day by undisciplined mercenaries in the pay of John the Fearless.

The plunder the English take from Pontoise is rich and welcome, and the town itself, says Henry in his letter to the Londoners of August 5, is so profitable that he asks his people to give special thanks to God for its capture.[11] He takes up residence in the castle and refuses any overtures for terms of surrender under which the ejected citizens might return to their homes. Pontoise is not part of Normandy, and in any case he is no longer governed by terms of truce with either the Armagnacs or the Burgundians. Henry sends his brother Thomas out on the sort of job Thomas likes best: taking raiding parties to lay waste to the countryside, destroying the harvest and spreading panic among the ordinary people. Then he allows the shock waves of this latest victory to ripple outward. Pontoise lies only twenty miles from the walls of the French capital. As Clarence himself writes in his own letter to the citizens of London, its capture represents a "passage to Paris."[12]

As word of Pontoise's fall reaches Paris, carried by the pitiful columns of homeless who stagger there, shocked, bloodied, and sunburned, the capital is gripped by terror. Food shortages from Clarence's destruction of the harvest send prices spiraling and the popular mood plummeting. Law and order start to break down. It is said, accurately, that the king, queen, and John the Fearless have abandoned the city and barricaded themselves in the royal residence at Lagny-sur-Marne, twenty miles to the east. They are imploring the dauphin to join them so that the resistance to Henry's terror can take shape.

Once more it seems Henry has the French at his mercy. Yet for all the chaos his return to war causes, he must also know that time is running out. The farther east he pushes, the more he stretches his supply lines, which run all the way back to Harfleur. His conquests near the coasts are growing vulnerable to raids to seize them back, and his manpower is thinned by the need to garrison every new castle and city he takes. Money is no more abundant than it was in the spring. And intelligence is reaching him that the dauphin's Armagnac advisers have struck a deal with the governors of Castile and Scotland to ship a Scottish army to France to join the war.

What is more, Paris may well be roiling with discontent, but its citizens are not exactly begging Henry to ride in and take command of the city for himself. Henry sends Thomas riding up to the walls to taunt the populace. But a siege is out of the question: it would be a bigger undertaking than Rouen, beginning from a far weaker position.

So as August passes, Henry finds himself in a bind. It is not as obviously deadly a crisis as he faced in October 1415 before Agincourt. Yet for all his unwavering belief that he is doing God's work, with God's favor, he must ask himself how on earth he is going to secure an exit from this campaign that will allow him to go home to England and regroup. He has perhaps just weeks to figure something out.

But as things turn out, Henry does not have to think about it very long at all, for on September 10, the French answer his questions for him. On that evening, a meeting is scheduled between John the Fearless and the sixteen-year-old dauphin Charles, at which the two men are to come face-to-face once more to make a reality of the peace they agreed to at Pouilly and begin rebuilding Charles VI's war-torn realm.

The meeting is fixed for a secure spot: a fortified bridge joining the town of Montereau to an island fortress at the junction of the rivers Seine and Yonne. John the Fearless and his men are granted the use of the castle; the dauphin and his advisers and bodyguards are lodged in the town. Despite the supposed rapprochement, there remains deep mistrust between the two camps. Only ten men, armored but unarmed, are allowed to accompany their masters onto the bridge, which will be locked at either end to prevent foul play. The men allowed onto the bridge must be named in advance, and they must take an oath to conduct themselves with honor.

Honor, however, is a virtue that has been in short supply in France for many years. At five o'clock on the appointed evening, John the Fearless receives a signal in the castle that the dauphin is ready for him to proceed onto the bridge. He emerges cautiously and finds the teenager sitting on the far side.

Ever since John the Fearless orchestrated the murder of his rival Louis, duke of Orléans, in 1407, he has been paranoid about his own safety. He has wavered over whether to take this meeting at all, knowing that no matter how much trouble is taken over security, when dealing with the Armagnacs, there is always a heavy element of risk.

And so it proves.

John the Fearless steps onto the bridge and approaches the dauphin, greeting him politely and kneeling in respect. Charles raises him cheerfully to his feet. But then he gives a nod to one of the men in his party, named Tanneguy du Châtel. Forgetting his oath to keep the peace, Tanneguy whips out an ax from beneath his cloak and screams that John the Fearless is a traitor.

On the town side of the bridge, the dauphin's men see their signal. They throw over the barricades and storm forward, yelling bloody murder. As they do, Tanneguy du Châtel swings his ax—first at one of John the Fearless's attendants and then, powerfully, into the duke's back.

John the Fearless tries his best to protect himself with his hands, but he is helpless. Another of the dauphin's men sets about him with a sword, cutting through his wrist and slashing his face, bellowing that this is sweet revenge for the death of Louis of Orléans. Tanneguy du Châtel hits John the Fearless once more in the face with the ax, crushing his jaw. Finally, as the duke falls to the ground, a third man stabs him through the belly with a sword.[13]

Pandemonium erupts. The Burgundians in the castle see what is going on, and try to rush the bridge to save their master. But they are too late. The dauphin's men have it under their command, and in any case, John the Fearless is unconscious, fatally battered and rapidly bleeding out. His body is robbed of its jewelry and disrobed, and the next day it is slung in a rough grave in a nearby church.

For a brief few hours the dauphin's supporters—many of them diehard Armagnacs who never truly accepted the peace of Pouilly and whose hatred for John the Fearless outweighed all other political goals—are triumphant. They have slain the beast whose murderous actions in Paris in 1407 have tormented them for more than a decade. And they have done so with the blessing and connivance of the heir to the French crown.

Yet their jubilation does not last long. Blinded by their loathing for John the Fearless, they have made him a martyr, ensured that the Burgundian-Armagnac rivalry will continue with the fury of a blood feud, and opened a path for Henry V to not only escape the riddle of his military predicament but bring himself to the brink of mastery over northern France.

A century later the duke of Burgundy's skull, half shattered by the sword and ax blows dealt that grim night on the bridge at Montereau, is shown to the French king Francis I. The monk who presents it points out a large gap in the skull, and remarks to his monarch that it is through this hole the English entered the noble kingdom of France.

27

"THINGS ARE DIFFERENT NOW"

On the first day of October 1419 Henry is with his army at Gisors, a Norman frontier town dominated by a large stone fortress, founded by his ancestors more than four centuries ago. The castle's glowering octagonal keep and thick walls, into which jail towers are built, is a reminder of just how long this land has been fought over by kings of France and England.

If Henry has his way, that ancient contest could soon be decided for good. Yet just for a moment, his mind is not here in Normandy. It is in a different stronghold, more than four hundred miles away: Pontefract Castle in northern England. Henry is composing a letter to his English chancellor, Thomas Langley, bishop of Durham, ordering him to see that security there is tight.

As well as having been the death-place of Richard II, Pontefract holds some of the high-value captives taken at the battle of Agincourt nearly four years ago, among them Charles, duke of Orléans. Henry is still mindful that he in particular should not make a bid for freedom. "See and ordain that good heed be taken unto the secure keeping of our French prisoners," he tells Langley. "For their escaping, and principally the said duke of Orléans, might never have been so harmful nor prejudicial to us as it might be now . . . which God forbid."

Chancellor Langley is a diligent, experienced royal servant, but Henry spells out what he wishes him to do all the same. He must tell the jailer at Pontefract to be on his guard against "fair speech" and "promises." He must ensure that he is not so "blinded by the said duke that he be the more reckless of his keeping."[1] Henry does not spell out to Chancellor Langley what he will do if his orders are flouted. He does not need to.

Even for a detail hawk like Henry, this caution might in normal times seem excessive. Charles, duke of Orléans, not quite twenty-five years old, has hardly been a problem inmate so far. He has decided to pass what will be a very long detainment in England writing poetry in English and French, on themes that range from courtly love to the misery of confinement.[2] All the same, Henry has experience with high-value inmates escaping and causing him difficulties: John Oldcastle was one.

Now, as Henry points out in his letter, would be the very worst moment to have a man such as Charles of Orléans—the nephew of King Charles VI, with French royal blood running richly in his veins—on the loose. Three weeks have passed since the murder of John the Fearless, and France is in uproar. The senior peer in the land is dead. The dauphin Charles's hands are stained indelibly with blood. The two factions in French politics have gone from the brink of reconciliation to a mutual hatred deeper than ever.

Henry has been in France for more than two years and now he has a golden opportunity to snatch the greatest prize of all.

During his summer negotiations at Meulan Henry was on the verge of trading in his hereditary claim to the French crown for a large, independent settlement of land, and Princess Catherine's hand in marriage. He had concluded that he was at the limit of his bargaining potential, and his goal was to force an exit on the best possible terms.

With John the Fearless dead, he believes he can do much better. "I shall now surpass all my ambitions," he is said to have exclaimed, when he was told of the murder at Montereau.[3] So long as there are no serious mishaps—such as the poet-duke Charles of Orléans escaping—Henry believes he can take everything. Not just Normandy, the Brétigny territories, and a fine bride with a big dowry, but France itself.

Around the time that Henry writes to his chancellor ordering him to keep the duke of Orléans under close guard, he is also spelling out his ambition to French royal ambassadors who visit him in camp at Gisors. The diplomats are sent by Queen Isabeau in Troyes and will report back to a shell-shocked royal council in Paris. Henry therefore treats them to the sight of his kingship in the round. They arrive to see his army blasting away at Gisors Castle, battering the garrison into submission. But they leave having been treated to the most gracious hospitality the king in his siege camp can muster.

When it comes to discussing the ongoing crisis and Henry's attitude toward it, he does not sugarcoat his demands. He tells the ambassadors plainly that he sees himself as the rightful master of the realm. He says he will not seek to depose Charles VI, but he wishes to rule as his regent until the older man dies. He then intends to succeed him as king, establishing a dual monarchy in which England and France remain independent realms, governed separately but by the same monarch. Henry explains what the French can expect when he completes this takeover. He will give France the good governance it deserves—just as he has in England. He will protect the French people and defend the realm's borders. He will still marry Catherine, although now, since he intends this to seal his takeover of the entire French realm, he will forgo his request for a dowry.

When it is put to him that this is a long way from the settlement he proposed only a few months earlier at Meulan, his reply is curt. "Things are different now," he says.[4]

This is not to say that Henry does not understand how much he is asking for. He shows the ambassadors he possesses regal style as well as military muscle. He feasts the diplomats generously in his grand tents, hung with tapestries of Arthurian heroes and conquering Roman emper-

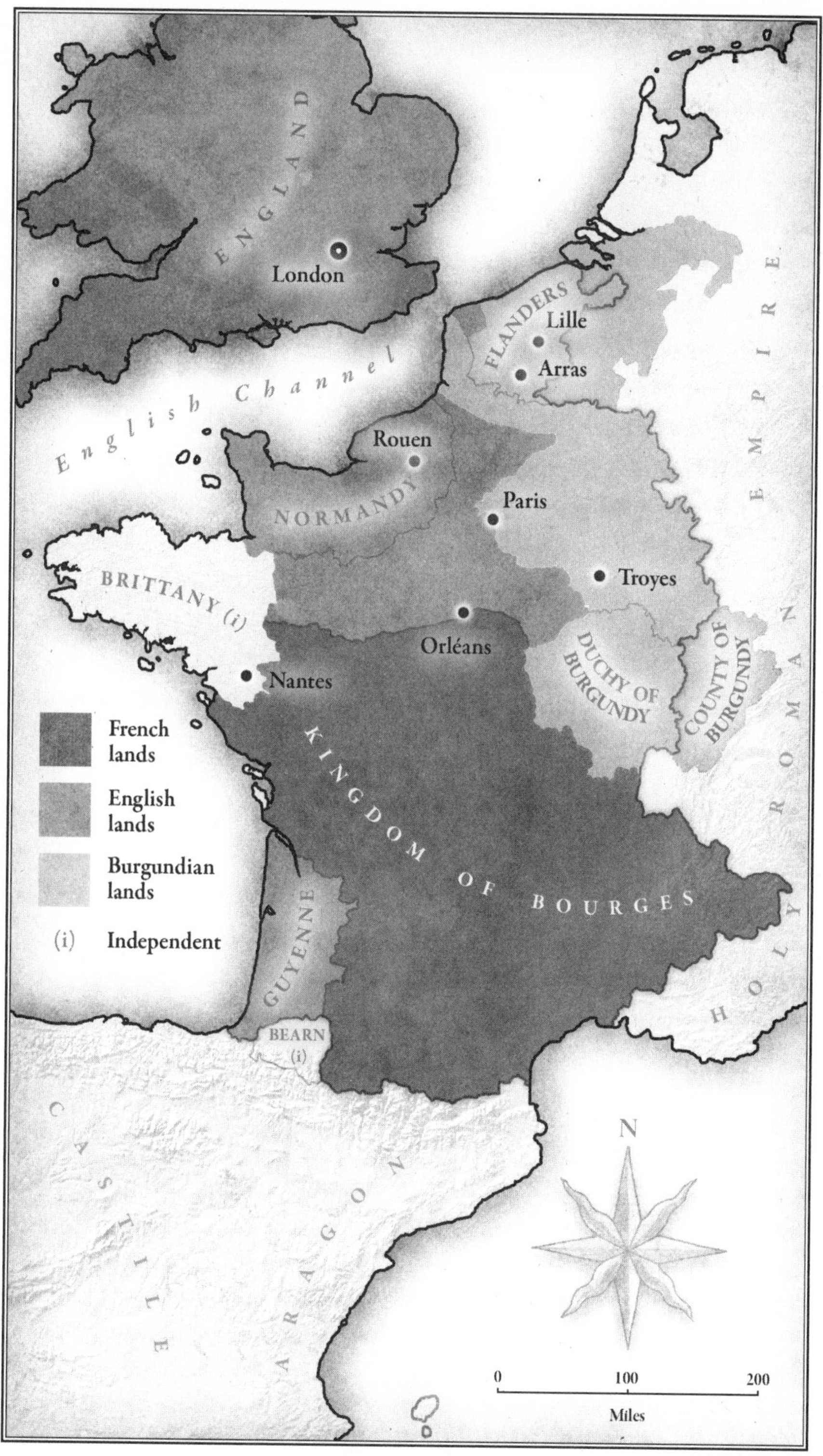

France Following the Treaty of Troyes (1420)

ors, while wearing jewels that are typically emblazoned with slogans such as "Without Fail" and "To Love and Serve."[5] He tells them more than once that he expects "some people [will] call me reckless for undertaking something so difficult and so perilous." He acknowledges that the dauphin will be filled with "boiling ardor" and try to ruin his plans, but insists "he will end up approving . . . when he no longer has around him the slanderers and perfidious seducers who constantly push to divert him from the path of reason."[6]

The effect is dazzling. The ambassadors go back to Paris full of unexpected admiration for this uncompromising but openhanded warlord. They speak of Henry's "affability, benevolence and courtesy" and show off the rich gifts he has given them. They report on his easy manner with the great and lowly alike. ("A scrupulous observer of justice, he knows how to spare the humble and humble the proud.") They note that he values economy of speech, getting straight to the point and replying directly to proposals with simple phrases like "It's impossible" and "It will have to be like this." They report—with approval—that there are no prostitutes in the English camp. Yet they also see that while military discipline is insisted upon, so too is the belief that hard work pays off. "If [Henry's] troops experience some setback, he always tells them: 'As you know, the chances of war are variable; but if you want to secure the favors of fortune, always maintain the same courage.'" Henry learned the value of political theater and the occasional big gamble at a young age. He has forgotten none of it now that he is auditioning publicly for the role of king of France.[7]

Having made his pitch for regency followed by kingship, Henry delegates the task of persuading the French to accept it to Richard Beauchamp, earl of Warwick, who shuttles between the English camp and the French council in Paris, spelling out Henry's demands and responding to objections.

This is no small task, not least because there are so many people who have a stake in the decision. There are the king and queen in Troyes, their advisers in the capital, and, in Flanders, a new duke of Burgundy: John the Fearless's twenty-three-year-old eldest son, whom history will come to know as Philip the Good.

Philip is, in his own way, as singular a figure as his late father: a budding patron of the arts, a practical joker with a zany, childlike sense of humor, and an enthusiastic womanizer who will in time father several dozen bastards. In 1419, however, he is also young, uncertain, and grief-stricken. What is more, he has a claim of his own to be the next king of France, if the crown should turn out to be up for grabs.* Henry does not know Philip the Good well. But he knows he needs him to forget his own royal claim and fall into line. So while the earl of Warwick leads diplomatic negotiations, Henry concentrates minds on all sides by moving his army up from Gisors to threaten Paris.

In the second half of October English troops seize the Seine bridges closest to the capital, allowing them to control access to the city. They overrun Charles VI's residence at Saint-Germain-en-Laye, a modern building only recently rebuilt after it was burned to the ground by Edward III in 1346. They stop all deliveries of food and provisions into the capital. Thus positioned, Henry announces his deadline for the French to accept his demands. If he does not have satisfaction by November 11, he will take what is his by force.

The notion of storming Paris has long lain beyond Henry's capability. But conditions in the capital are by now abysmal, and the ordinary people are on the verge of despair. The ravaged countryside around Paris, overrun by English soldiers and drenched by relentless, freezing rain, yields little food or fuel. What little can be harvested stinks of rot and mildew. Black-market prices mean "eggs, butter, garlic, onions, firewood and meat, in short all the things on which people and animals and children could live" are traded for outrageous sums. Infants have no milk to drink. On All Saints Day, November 1, the traditional day for commemorating the dead, no bells are rung and no fires lit.[8] A citizen of Paris who keeps a

* Philip the Good is Charles VI's first cousin once removed. Henry V is Charles VI's fourth cousin once removed.

journal throughout these dark days finds it hard to decide who deserves the greater curses: the dauphin Charles, corrupted by his Armagnac advisers, who wants nothing more than to waste his own father's land "with fire and blood," or Henry's English troops, "who are doing as much harm as the Saracens."[9]

In the end, the distinction does not matter much. News of Paris's plight is sent to Philip the Good, with a recommendation that he make up his mind about Henry V as soon as possible. The young man surmises correctly that he has no time and little choice. He can either go along with Henry's hostile takeover of France and try to extract as much from the deal as possible, or else bear the responsibility for a period of bloodshed that could be worse than anything yet seen, the end point of which may be the wholesale destruction of the realm.

Just before Henry's deadline of November 11 expires, he hears from Philip the Good. The Burgundians have agreed to enter an alliance with the English. Philip will recommend that Charles VI and Queen Isabeau bow to the inevitable, disinherit the dauphin, marry their daughter to Henry, and accept him as their heir and regent. There will be plenty more ambassadorial wrangling to agree on the fine points of the deal. But the headline is straightforward. Henry can have what he wants. He extends his truce and agrees not to march on Paris until it is ready to welcome him as its ruler.

Henry spends Christmas 1419 at Rouen. On Christmas Day he seals a formal alliance with the Burgundians, in which he agrees to love Philip the Good "sincerely and affectionally as long as he lives," and to work to "make a suitable punishment of Charles the dauphin . . . and his accomplices, guilty of the atrocious homicide committed against the person of the illustrious deceased prince, the last duke of Burgundy."[10]

Philip is tasked with taking troops to Troyes, where he must see to it that Charles VI and Queen Isabeau assent to the decisions that are being taken on their behalf. A timetable is set for a full treaty to be agreed upon, ratified, and confirmed with a royal wedding between Henry and Princess Catherine. By the summer of 1420, Henry expects to be the regent of France, and a married man.

Four and a half months are required to draw up the terms of the treaty that will put France into Henry's hands at last. But he has plenty to keep him busy.

He spends at least some of his time reading—or being read to. Henry borrows from one contact a six-hundred-page copy of *Guiron le Courtois,* an Arthurian romance set in the generation before Arthur is king.* This long and tangled epic spins out a plot of marital rivalry and knightly adventure, combining action and humor, while posing ethical questions about love, loyalty, and chivalry. It has long been popular among nobles and knights, and is structured to be read aloud in short sections, discussed, debated, and laughed over in company. Henry may well borrow the book with the aim of entertaining the men around him as well as himself, as their time in the field stretches ever longer before them.

Enjoying adventure stories, however, is only a distraction from the continuing grind of the military campaign. Since this will now extend at the very least into the first quarter of 1420, Henry needs to refresh his army with an injection of manpower, to guard against the possibility of treachery on the Burgundian side, or the dauphin moving against him. To that end, he decides to bring his brother John over from England, at the head of as many fresh troops as he can muster. Henry hopes this will be somewhere in the order of five thousand men, though in the end John can raise little over one thousand.[11] It is not perfect. But it must suffice.

In John's place, Humphrey is sent back to England to take up the reins of domestic government. This is a considerable promotion for him, and a sign of Henry's faith in his youngest brother, who was under-occupied and inexperienced before the Agincourt campaign and is now one of his ablest companions. But Humphrey will have to draw on all he has learned at Henry's side, for England is on the cusp of war-weariness. The most recent parliament held in Westminster has granted Henry continued fund-

* Prequels and origin stories are as essential a part of the medieval Arthurian canon as they are of the modern-day Marvel Cinematic Universe.

ing in the form of direct taxation, but members have warned that the flow of money from England to France cannot continue forever, not least because it is causing deflation through sheer scarcity of coin. Inventive new ways of squeezing out war finance will soon be required, along with assurances that there is an end in sight to the war, and that the newly conquered lands in France will soon be self-sufficient in paying for their own defense.

In the meantime, the parliamentary commons suggest Henry buy English wool wholesale and sell it in Normandy, and use the profits he makes to fund his war. This is certainly one possibility, though Henry sees other, more opportunistic, avenues of war finance as well. His stepmother, Joan of Navarre, has recently fallen out with a friar in her household, who has made noisy and public accusations against the dowager queen, claiming that she has been practicing witchcraft and necromancy, "for the death and destruction of our said lord the king in the most evil and terrible manner imaginable."[12]

This is almost certainly either baseless or a gross exaggeration of Joan's innocuous dabbling in the arts of divination. All the same, it presents a possibility. When Henry hears of the charges made against his stepmother, he orders that she be arrested and her extensive lands taken into royal possession, so their revenues can be diverted into the war chest.

Henry does not enjoy giving this order—or at least, he will later admit that it nags at his conscience once he has made it. But he cannot afford to pass up the promise of easy money. Joan's lands yield thousands of pounds of profit annually, at a time when every shilling and penny that can be brought into the treasury counts. Henry can also console himself with the knowledge that despite the inconvenience to her liberty and her landed estate, the queen is treated as well as a prisoner can be. Far from languishing in a dungeon, or even facing formal legal proceedings for her alleged sorcery, Queen Joan lives under relaxed house arrest in royal manors including Rotherhithe, Dartford, and Leeds Castle—the latter a residence of such opulence that it was recently judged fit to house the German emperor Sigismund.[13]

When Humphrey gets to England and has a chance to interview Joan over dinner, he finds the queen is living in the extravagant luxury to which she has long been accustomed as the widow of Henry IV: even as a prisoner she dresses in expensive furs and gold jewelry, and her shopping accounts include outgoings on strings for her harp, a new cage for her pet songbird, and three dozen pairs of shoes. Whether she is mollified by these comforts or indignant about the insult to her good name is ultimately of little consequence. Henry has a war—and a peace—to win.

On May 8, 1420, Henry leaves his lodgings in the town of Pontoise, where he has spent much of the spring, and travels with his army at his back to the abbey of Saint-Denis, to the north of Paris. That evening he prays inside the abbey church and makes offerings at its shrine. Saint-Denis is a charged and sacred space. Around Henry as he moves through the great Gothic building are the tombs of dead French kings, lying cold and silent in the night.[14] He is not one of them yet, but his time is nearly upon him.

Over the course of the next eleven days, he marches his men 115 miles southwest from Saint-Denis to Troyes. They keep up a brisk pace, constantly on guard against attacks by any Armagnac bands looking to spoil the procession. Henry periodically detaches troops to stand guard over bridges, to see that he is not ambushed from behind. When he sweeps past Paris, he makes sure that he is recognizable to the citizens who crane their necks over the city walls to see him: he has a war helm topped with a gold crown carried before him. This represents wisdom, writes one onlooker—but it is a reminder, too, that the road to this point began on the field of Agincourt, four and a half years earlier.[15]

On May 20, Henry finally arrives at Troyes, where Charles VI and Queen Isabeau have been staying, effectively prisoners in their own realm, for the past year. The first figure to greet them on the road is Philip the Good. Henry appraises for the first time the slender-faced, slightly lugubrious young duke, who greets him elegantly from horseback, "reverently, not too much and not too little," as one writer later remembers.[16]

The two men strike up a cheerful rapport, and Philip leads Henry into the city, showing him to an inn by the market square, which is marked by the sign of the Crown and has been "magnificently furnished" for his stay.[17] After settling in, Henry gives orders for his troops to find lodgings in the villages around Troyes—cautioning them not to overindulge in the powerful local wine.[18] Then he goes to the palace of the counts of Champagne to visit the king and queen and his bride-to-be, Princess Catherine.

Henry has not seen Charles VI in person for twenty years, and has never spoken to him directly. There is little to dazzle him now. The French king cuts a shambolic figure, sitting on a throne beneath a canopy of fleurs-de-lis in the great hall of the palace, vacant and unrecognizing. He has no idea who Henry is. Henry approaches his throne, bows courteously, and greets him—but the best Charles can do is to mumble: "It's you! You're very welcome now you're here . . . say hello to the ladies."[19]

There could scarcely be a more sharply contrasting vision of kingship to the one Henry has cultivated for the past seven years. Turning from Charles, he greets both Queen Isabeau and her daughter with deep bows and kisses. He speaks briefly with Catherine for the first time since their audience at Meulan. Then he takes his leave of the royal family and goes back to his rooms at the Crown. He has been a long time on the road, and he remains in his rooms for the rest of the day. Tomorrow the real business begins.

On Tuesday, May 21, Henry, Queen Isabeau, and Philip, duke of Burgundy, seal the Treaty of Troyes in a ceremony held at the city's cathedral. It is an extraordinary agreement, conceived according to a vision grander and more consequential even than Edward III's landmark Treaty of Brétigny, which it now supplants. Drafted in the voice of Charles VI (who is, as one onlooker puts it, "not well disposed" and is therefore unable attend its ratification), it laments the "great and irreparable evils and enormities" produced by the division of the kingdoms of England and France, then sets out the terms under which these are to be resolved.

Divided into thirty-one clauses, the treaty lays out the conditions for Henry's impending marriage to Catherine. It disinherits the dauphin and appoints Henry as the regent of France, providing that he does not "disturb, disquiet or impede" the king for the rest of his natural life. It explains how, on Charles's death, the throne of France will pass to Henry and his heirs, never to be relinquished. It makes provision for Normandy to be restored to the kingdom of France once Henry rules that realm, but reminds its readers that while England and France are to be ruled by one monarch, putting an end to all "disputes, hatred, rancor and resentment," the two kingdoms must never be united. It nevertheless establishes the basic terms of a mutual defense alliance and free trade agreement between the two realms and, finally, forbids any party to the treaty from entering into any negotiations with the dauphin and his Armagnac supporters.[20]

The treaty's terms, which are written in Latin and French, are read out in the cathedral to an audience of nearly one thousand onlookers, who include Henry's trustiest lieutenants: his brother Thomas, his uncle Thomas Beaufort, and Richard Beauchamp. After the formal reading, the affixing of seals, and the administering of oaths to observe its terms, the crowd remains in place for Henry's formal betrothal to Princess Catherine.

It is a truly pivotal moment in the history of England and France, as Henry reflects when he writes a letter to his brother Humphrey the next day, asking him to have the terms of the Treaty of Troyes proclaimed in England. "We signify unto you that, worshipped be our Lord, our labor hath sent us a good conclusion," he writes. He explains what has been agreed on with "our mother the Queen of France and our brother the duke of Burgundy" and tells Humphrey that in the next few days he is going to be married.

He also asks Humphrey to see that a new royal style is used on all official paperwork. In English, he now wishes to be known as "Henry, by the Grace of God, King of England, Heir and Regent of the Realm of France, and Lord of Ireland." He has clearly been agonizing over whether this title accurately sums up the role he will now be playing in French royal government, but assures Humphrey that for the time being it will do: "It seemeth that this word REGENT [serves] well enough."[21]

And so it does. On Trinity Sunday, June 2, at around midday, Henry attends to the final ceremony required to turn his regency into reality. At the Church of St. John in Troyes, he and eighteen-year-old Catherine are married. It is a lean, unadorned soldier's wedding, shorn of overblown pageantry and excess. Catherine arrives in a carriage drawn by eight white English horses—a gift Henry has given her. The duke of Burgundy attends dressed head to toe in black. A band plays, of course, for even when he adopts his most austere public persona, Henry can seldom do without music. But otherwise the ceremony is conducted, as one Englishman puts it, "with great solemnity."[22]

The same English writer tells friends back home that in "Paris and all other towns that are turned away from the Armagnacs' party, [people] make great joy and mirth every holiday in dancing and caroling." But that is not the case among Henry's army. It is customary for a royal wedding to be accompanied by a day or two of tournaments and jousting. Henry declines to honor tradition. Although the Treaty of Troyes is, as an English ambassador puts it, "mighty and virtuous, fair and gracious, sweet and amorous," it also commits Henry to a new mission, far more daunting than anything he has attempted before.[23]

The dauphin and the Armagnacs have been disinherited and abused in the terms of the Treaty of Troyes. But they have not been written out of existence. They still hold half of France, which as regent of the kingdom Henry now has a responsibility to bring back to obedience. So there is no time to waste. Two days after his wedding Henry marches his army back out of Troyes in the direction of the city of Sens, obstinately held by his enemies.

"There we may all joust and tourney," he says, "and demonstrate our prowess and toughness, for there is no finer deed in the world than to serve justice on evildoers so that poor people may live."[24]

28

"A LONG BATTLE"

Following Henry's marriage, the summer at first proceeds in straightforward fashion, as his army sweeps through the countryside, smoking dauphinists from their dens. Henry now travels at the head of a most regal delegation, which includes Charles VI and Queen Isabeau; his new wife, Catherine; Philip, duke of Burgundy; his brothers Thomas and John; Thomas Beaufort; and, as one chronicler puts it, numerous "other lords, barons, knights and esquires of noble birth and strong in battle."[1] The columns behind them include English veterans, Burgundian troops, fresh recruits shipped over the Channel by John, and German mercenaries, captained by Louis, elector of the Rhine, the widower of Henry's long-dead younger sister Blanche.

One new face among this esteemed party is that of King James I, king of Scots, who has been an English prisoner since 1406, when he was captured by pirates at age eleven. James is now a grown man: short, strong, and boundlessly energetic, a talented wrestler, archer, jouster, and poet. His interests and talents overlap conspicuously with Henry's, although this is not why he has been brought to join the English war machine. Scottish soldiers have been flooding into France to join the dauphin's cause, and Henry hopes that if he confronts them with their liege lord, he can make traitors of them, and so convince them to stand down.

The first city Henry targets after leaving Troyes is Sens, where his men find the garrison in hopeless mood. Ready to submit after barely a week of bombardment, they come out of the city wearing St. George crosses and tugging subserviently at their beards. The archbishop of Sens, who wedded Henry to Catherine at Troyes, has been exiled from the city as a Burgundian supporter, so on June 11 Henry escorts him personally back to his cathedral, telling him, "You gave me my bride, now I give you yours."[2]

Five days after this, Henry is at Montereau, the scene of John the Fearless's horrible murder. Its defenders put up more of a fight than those of Sens, but it does them little good. Henry's artillerymen take a week to smash through the town walls. They enter the city and exhume the mangled corpse of the old duke of Burgundy, which is a "pitiful thing to see."[3] Henry and Philip of Burgundy honor him with a requiem mass, then send him off to his family's mausoleum near Dijon to be laid to rest. After this they turn their attention to the island fortress into which the garrison have fallen back.

Between Henry and Philip, the army has more than enough cannons to inflict serious damage on Montereau's castle. But Henry would rather not spend the gunpowder or the days on doing it. So he takes a different approach. When his men storm the city walls of Montereau, they capture ten soldiers who are too slow in finding their way across the bridge to the river fortress. Henry sends word to the garrison captain inside that castle that unless they all surrender immediately, he will kill these prisoners to a man.

Unfortunately for the captives, the garrison's captain, Guillaume de Chaumont, lord of Guitry, demurs. He was on the dauphin's side of the bridge at Montereau when John the Fearless was murdered and may well consider that his cause is lost whatever he does. In any case, when Henry puts the hard bargain to him, he exhibits more bravado than common sense. The prisoners are brought out and made to kneel in view of the castle's battlements, with a gallows erected behind them. The captain, unmoved, sends down word that this is war and tough things happen. The best he will do for them is to let their wives and friends come onto the castle walls to wave them good-bye.

So this is what occurs. A group of forlorn women are fetched up to the walls of the fortress to sob their farewells, and a little later, every one of the prisoners kicks his last at the end of a rope—a fate which contemporaries blame squarely on the obstinate Guillaume de Chaumont rather than Henry. To show his absolute commitment to justice, Henry hangs on the same gibbet one of his own grooms, who has fallen foul of his harsh camp discipline by killing a knight in a fight. Then the firing of the cannons and the pounding of the trebuchets begin.

After little more than a week of bombardment, on July 1, the garrison gives up. Henry accepts its surrender and, once again, moves on. His next target is Melun, a city on a curve of the river Seine, about thirty-five miles south of Paris. Its capture would strike another blow against Armagnac positions near the French capital. But Melun will prove a far tougher place to crack than either Sens or Montereau. In fact, Henry and his Anglo-Burgundian army will find themselves trapped, frustrated, outside its defenses until nearly the end of the year.

The siege of Melun is, in some ways, like so many of the other long sieges Henry has already conducted in his campaigns in France. There are trenches and pontoon bridges, road and river blockades, trebuchets and ladders. Catapult operators hurl rotting animal corpses and camp filth over the walls to spread disease.[4] Just as at Harfleur and Rouen, Henry makes considerable use of cannon bombardment. The citizens of his English capital have sent him the gift of a gigantic bombard nicknamed "London." This joins an arsenal that pounds the city so thoroughly that the citizens cower in their cellars to dodge collapsing buildings and falling masonry.[5] ("London" eventually explodes, either through a flaw in its engineering or from sheer overuse.)

Beneath Melun's walls and ditches, meanwhile, miners and counterminers dig a warren of cavernous tunnels so wide that knights from inside and outside the city sometimes meet in them, doing battle hand to hand in a dank, rocky underworld. It is said by more than one chronicler that Henry and Philip of Burgundy both go down into these tunnels to take part in the fighting. According to one much later account, Henry joins "right mightily . . . a long battle" against the captain of Melun, an Armagnac officer named Arnaud-Guillaume de Barbazan, neither of them revealing their identities until a long way into the tussle.[6] Even if this story is polished up in the retelling for chivalric effect, it conveys the deep personal investment Henry and his fellow commanders feel for the course of the war, even after more than three unbroken years in the field.

Yet in other ways Melun is unlike all the other sieges Henry has directed. For one thing, he now has the king of France at his command. The shabby Charles VI is presented to the defenders of Melun shortly after the town is surrounded, and made to call on his people to let him in. The rather more vigorous James I is then produced for the same purpose. In neither case do these compromised kings' words melt the defenders' hearts or open the town gates. But Henry at least has the propaganda value of their presence on his side.

He also, of course, now has a wife. At first Catherine does not stay in camp with Henry, but resides around ten miles away at Corbeil, lodging with her parents; Henry's brother Thomas's wife, Margaret Holland; and other English ladies assigned to her household. Henry tries his best to see that her experience is not entirely dull. When it is clear that the siege is going to drag on for more than a few weeks, he has a house built for her near his own tents at Melun. Then he finds things for her to do.

When the men of the army are not manning guns, digging tunnels, or beating back sorties from the town gates, they while away their hours playing cards and a form of tennis. These pastimes will not do for a queen of England. Henry hires musicians to entertain his wife for an hour every morning and every evening, and in early October he pays the considerable sum of £8 13s for a pair of harps for them both to play.[7] Thus Catherine has a chance to get to know her husband as he is: a man whose military, religious, and artistic inclinations cannot be separated. He is a harp-playing aesthete and a pious patron of writers, who in the first year of their marriage commissions the poet John Lydgate to write a long, meditative verse biography of the Virgin Mary (known as the *Life of Our Lady*). Yet he is also a single-minded conqueror, who at one point during the siege of Melun forgets the careful provisions of the Treaty of Troyes and tells local people that before long he will be the master of their entire kingdom, and they will be no longer French but English.[8]

At the end of the siege, Catherine sees Henry at his most uncompromising. It is mid-November and while the army outside Melun is diseased, heavily depleted, tired, hungry, and homesick, conditions inside the city are worse. The people are shell-shocked from the relentless bombardment, and they are starving, having "barely any substance they can turn into food." Every horse, dog, and rat in Melun has been eaten, along with "all the most repulsive of nature's beasts," so that the city resembles a wasteland, "utterly scoured by the madness of hunger."[9] When the dauphin makes it clear—very belatedly—that he cannot relieve Melun, its garrison finally surrenders. But Henry is in no mood to let them all go free.

Several hundred men-at-arms, including Captain Barbazan, whom Henry allegedly fought with in the tunnels, are sent off to prison, where some, including Barbazan, are tortured by their jailers. Twenty Scotsmen among the garrison are hanged as traitors for having defied James I's order to surrender. And when one of John the Fearless's murderers is picked up among the prisoners, but manages to escape, Henry vents cold and righteous fury on the man he blames for this lapse in security.

The culprit is a captain from Guyenne and veteran of Agincourt named Bertrand de Caumont. Until now he has shown Henry faultless loyalty. But so, once, had Henry, Lord Scrope. Bertrand is accused of having taken a bribe to let the murderer go free. When Henry hears of this, he becomes "as angry as it is possible to be," and commands that Bertrand be executed with no delay.

To many of the men, including some of Henry's closest comrades, this seems excessive. As Bertrand is hauled before the army to face his death no lesser a figure than Henry's brother Thomas tries to intercede. Thomas falls to his knees and with "personal and very heartfelt prayers" implores Henry to spare the man.

Henry will hear none of it. "By Saint George, brother," he says. "If you had done the same thing, we would act in the same way, for by our power, we do not want, and will not have, any traitors near us."[10] Bertrand's head is struck off, with the whole army watching.

Henry leaves the siege of Melun with his reputation as a severe disciplinarian intact and the next challenges of his campaign on his mind. The time has come for him to go to Paris, to show the citizens the face of their regent and next king. After that, he must go home.

On December 1, 1420, Henry enters Paris for the first time, bringing with him Charles VI and the other male members of the royal entourage. Queen Catherine and the women make their own formal entrance the next day; Henry is (and will remain) pedantic about demonstrating that he owes his position as heir and regent of France to his own conquests, God's will, and Charles VI's free decision, not right of marriage.[11]

Inside Paris, the royal party find that conditions are still desperately hard. Staple foods such as flour, bread, peas, beans, and wine remain scarce and costly, and scrums form outside the city's boulangeries when they open at eight o'clock each morning, as customers scramble for what little is available before it sells out. Abject poverty is rife. "On all the dung-heaps of Paris in 1420 you could find ten, twenty or thirty children, boys as well as girls, dying from hunger and cold; no one was hard-hearted enough not to feel pity when one heard them cry out in the night: 'Alas! I am starving to death!'" remembers one diarist.[12]

Despite the hardship, however, the Parisians have their pride and do what they can to put on a fine welcome. The people line the streets and shout, "Noël!" The leading citizens all dress in red. Priests sing solemn anthems, and church officials bring the choicest holy relics out from their collections for Henry and Charles to kiss. Buildings are draped with fine cloth and somehow enough wine is found to set a fountain gushing. A Passion play is performed, telling the story of Christ's death and afterlife, and Charles and Henry go to Notre-Dame to make prayers and offerings at the high altar. Thus the citizens of Paris do what they can to retain their civic dignity, making "great jubilation" over the peace between the two kings, even as the night hours are rent by the wails of famished and freezing infants.[13]

Henry absorbs all this pageantry, wearing the aloof expression he typically adopts at moments of public celebration focused on himself. Then he gets down to business. With Charles and Philip he opens a meeting of the Estates-General—an advisory gathering of clergy, nobility, and commoners. It is a weak and partial assembly, representing only the half of the realm under the command of Henry and Philip of Burgundy (excluding Normandy, which Henry continues to treat as a political entity in its own right). But it does what it must: the Treaty of Troyes is declared good, taxes are levied, a recoinage is discussed, plans are made to boost the sluggish French economy, and the dauphin's name is cursed. Legal proceedings against John the Fearless's killers begins, and the dauphin himself is formally summoned to answer the charges against him. Needless to say, he does not appear, so he is officially found guilty of the "damnable crime," outlawed, and exiled from the realm.[14] This is in theory a stiff sentence, although the truth, obvious to all, is that the dauphin has suffered nothing much more consequential than that which was done to him at Troyes. At some point he must be either comprehensively defeated or, more likely, bargained with.

This business takes Henry all of the month of December. He is still in Paris at Christmas, so he and Queen Catherine host a lavish party in the Hôtel de Louvre, attended by his brothers Thomas and John. "No one would be able to recount the great state, pomp and splendor," writes one chronicler, describing the crowds of French subjects who appear at the Louvre to "honor and exalt" him. The same writer notes that it is all in sad contrast to the feeble Christmas celebrations hosted at the Hôtel Saint-Pol by Charles and Isabeau, who are "poorly and pathetically served" and attended only by a few old, faithful servants and "people of no consequence."[15]

If Henry were the sort of man to bask in his own achievement, now would be the time for him to sit back and consider just what an astonishing thing it is he has done. But he is not, and neither can he afford to be.

While he has been in Paris, an English parliament has been sitting in Westminster, having gathered, like the Estates-General, to ratify the Treaty of Troyes. The English members of Parliament were expecting Henry to be in attendance, to explain to them his achievement and lay out his vision of the future in person. By tarrying in Paris he has missed his first opportunity to explain to the English how and why they are to be expected to continue to contribute to his war effort, now that it is no longer a campaign of conquest in pursuit of ancient English right, but a French civil war. The parliament has petitioned Humphrey, duke of Gloucester, presiding in Henry's absence, "to request, encourage and persuade our most sovereign lord the king and the most gracious lady the queen, his wife, to return and come back to this kingdom within a very short space of time, as best suits his most gracious lordship."[16]

Behind the genteel language lies the sound of a realm desperate to see its king and meet its queen. Henry knows he can keep them waiting no longer. As soon as Christmas is over, he sets off for home. He makes detailed arrangements for the administration of France in his absence: leaving his brother Thomas as his overall deputy, his uncle Thomas, duke of Exeter, as the captain of Paris, and other of his most trusted men—the earl of Salisbury and Sir John Fastolf—in key positions elsewhere. He pays a short visit to Rouen before heading for Calais, whence he takes ship to Dover.

He arrives back in England on February 1, 1421, in a party whose noble core includes just the queen; James I of Scotland; John, duke of Bedford; Richard Beauchamp, earl of Warwick; and the earls of March and Norfolk. This is a notably small household, but Henry is traveling deliberately light. "Everyone else," writes one chronicler, is "left behind overseas, to guard his gains."[17]

But even as he leaves, Henry is looking back over his shoulder. One of his last acts before taking ship is to order a consignment of bows, bowstrings, and arrows to be sent to the men attending Charles VI, to see that the French king is properly protected.[18]

29

"À CLARENCE!"

Three and a half years have passed since the English people last saw their king, and on his return in February 1421 the country fetes Henry accordingly. One chronicler writes that he is hailed as "the angel of God."[1] Another notes that he is met with "solemnity and joy" beyond description.[2] A third records that "a great multitude of the country" comes to the Kentish coast "in good array on horseback" to welcome Henry and Catherine "with all honor and reverence."[3] The barons of the Cinque Ports follow tradition by rushing into the water at Dover to carry the new queen ashore.

As he did in 1415, Henry spends a little time progressing through the countryside, pausing at Canterbury and Eltham, where he leaves Catherine momentarily, before heading on alone to London. When he approaches the capital, it erupts in dutiful celebration. "The highly delighted clergy and people [staged] plays and shows of different kinds," recalls one chronicler.[4] Musicians dressed in newly embroidered gowns are sent to pipe Henry in from Blackheath, and once again model giants are built to stand guard over London Bridge.[5] There are "many diverse showings and sights through the high streets in the city," and "many other presents and gifts [for] both king and queen."[6]

Much of this has been signed off on by Henry before he arrives, for he is as meticulous about arranging his reception back into England as he has been in organizing the defense of France. But he takes care to see that the loudest cheers are reserved for Catherine, who is to make her own entrance to the city.

This is not just a show of courtesy toward his nineteen-year-old bride, or a desire to convince her of the charms of her new realm. It is a matter of practical necessity. There has been a marked change in England's political atmosphere between 1415 and 1421. The delirious triumphalism of the months following Agincourt has given way to nagging uncertainty about what the years of conquest have let them all in for. Henry must somehow rally his people behind a war against the dauphin, which will cost more than ever before, in pursuit of gains that stand to avail England of nothing very obvious. Henry understands that before he tries to sell this prospect to his people, he must give them something to cheer about. That something is the new queen.

Catherine is crowned in Westminster Abbey on the last weekend of February, in a ceremony that Henry arranges but does not attend. On Friday, February 21, the young queen comes up from Eltham and moves into the Tower of London. The following day she parades through London to Westminster, "in a fitting procession with horsemen at its head."[7] Angels serenade her and warriors shake their swords from fantastical castles as she passes through the city, escorted by citizens and merchant guild members on foot: "every craft in their best clothing, with all their melody and minstrelsy."[8] Every street along the route is hung "with rich cloth of gold and silk and of velvet and cloth of arras, the best that might be gotten."[9]

On Sunday Archbishop Chichele of Canterbury conducts the coronation ceremony itself, and this is followed by a feast over which Queen Catherine presides in splendor and around which Henry's brother Humphrey strolls, alert, seeing that protocol is observed. James I of Scotland sits to the queen's left; the earls of March and Norfolk kneel on either side of her, holding scepters; the countesses of Kent and Norfolk sit together under the table, one beside each of her feet. Most of the English bishops attend, and with them gather as many lords and ladies as can be summoned from that portion of the English nobility that is not still in France. Since late February belongs to the meatless season of Lent every course consists almost entirely of fish and seafood. There are lampreys and eels, trout and salmon, halibut and gurnard, great crabs, red shrimps, and even roasted porpoise.* The tables are set with "subtleties"—inventive confections made by talented pastry chefs. Those served at the coronation include a pelican accompanied by St. Catherine holding her wheel, "a painter and a maid before him," and "a tiger with Saint George leading it."[10]

And so the day proceeds with "all the great solemnity and royalty that might be done and ordained." Once it is over, Henry leaves Catherine at Westminster with a household of ladies and servants appropriate to her status. He arranges to meet her again in a few weeks' time, to celebrate Easter. Then he sets off on a progress around England, to give thanks at some of his favorite shrines, present himself in person to his anxious subjects, and ask for money.

Henry's tour of England in the spring of 1421 follows a great jagged loop, beginning in St. Albans, then taking him west to Bristol before he turns north through the Welsh Marches. He brings with him government officials, including the chancellor, Bishop Thomas Langley, so that he can work as he travels.

Henry rides his officials hard around the land. He visits Hereford and Shrewsbury, where he cut his teeth for so many hard years as Prince of Wales, and where he settles the outstanding ransom owed to the men and women who captured John Oldcastle four years earlier in 1417.[11] With Easter approaching, he then heads into the Midlands. When he reaches Kenilworth Castle, Queen Catherine joins him, and he is able to show her

* A porpoise is, of course, a cetacean, but this taxonomic distinction is seemingly not appreciated when the menu is drawn up.

his Pleasance—the tranquil private retreat on marshland reclaimed from the Mere, which he planned around the same time that Catherine's now long-dead brother Louis taunted him with gifts of tennis balls.* It is likely here that this story gains a coda of sorts, for soon after her visit to Kenilworth, Queen Catherine discovers that she is pregnant.

From Kenilworth, Henry visits the Lancastrian strongholds of Coventry and Leicester, before going north to Yorkshire, an area where he has reason to be concerned about general reluctance to provide troops for his campaigns. He and the queen visit Pontefract Castle, where Catherine's brother-in-law Charles of Orléans now lives, scribbling his poems to while away the years. They stop awhile in York, and Catherine—perhaps sick in the first stages of pregnancy—stays there, while Henry makes pilgrimages to the shrines of John Thwing at Bridlington and St. John of Beverley, who was said to have been especially helpful in interceding for Henry's victory at Agincourt.

Bridlington marks the most northerly point of Henry's tour, and after he has been here he sets a course back toward London via the major towns and shrines of England's eastern flank: Lincoln, where he sees a new bishop consecrated; Lynn, whence his sister Philippa once departed to become a queen of Norway; and Walsingham, where he last came in the months that followed his survival of the battle of Shrewsbury.

All along the way he remains hard at work, keeping pace with events in the two kingdoms for which he is now responsible. At Saint Albans he orders repairs to the castle of Pontorson, in Normandy, which has fallen into ruin, telling his officials to examine a particular bridge at the town if they wish to see the standard of work he expects. "And hasteth that it be done," he adds.[12] (This is a typically brusque, impatient turn of phrase of the sort Henry often uses when giving instructions; another favorite is "see that ye faileth not thereof in no wise.")[13] At Leicester he responds to news that the dauphin's allies in Castile are planning a naval assault on the Isle of Wight. If the constable of the island needs men or anything

---

* See chapter 20.

else to safeguard the coast, Henry writes that he must "notify us or our council in London as soon as possible."[14] He takes care to listen to the petitions of the poor.[15] And of course, he states and restates his urgent requirement for money, in the form of individual gifts and loans.

This is no easy ask. As one French chronicler concedes, Henry is a man of "discretion and good speech." He needs to be, as he travels from city to city, handing out alms, meeting local dignitaries, listening to their grievances and complaints, recounting "the boons that have come to him through his great labor and pain" in France, but also speaking of the many tasks "which remain still to be done."

Henry appoints commissioners of serious political standing—including his old ally Thomas Chaucer—to seek out wealthy individuals who have not yet contributed personally to the war effort, brace them for loans, and report back to him with a list of names.[16] But the onus is still on him, as king, to lead the drive for cash. When Henry tells his people of the situation facing him in France, he lets them know with typical bluntness that he needs two things: "finances and men-at-arms."[17] He knows he is asking a lot, for there exists in the country an existential worry about what more success in France may bring. The parliament that was held in Westminster before his return to the realm expressed its deep concern that Henry was sleepwalking the realm into a permanent cross-Channel union, in which Englishmen and their children would one day be ruled from Paris. Henry is all too aware that when his next parliament meets, in May, its members might easily revert to the mood of his father's reign and refuse him the tax he needs.

Yet around halfway through Henry's fundraising tour, it suddenly becomes a lot easier for him to make his case. The reason for this surge in his subjects' generosity is, however, far from a pleasant one. Shortly after Easter, while Henry is on the road between Beverley and York, a messenger—probably a man called William Kent—catches up with him carrying shocking news from France.

The facts are these: On Saturday, March 22, the day before Easter, an English army has been defeated in a major battle in France for the first time since the start of the long war nearly eight decades ago. They have lost around one thousand men, with "many lords slain and many others taken prisoner."[18]

In some ways the outcome could have been worse—for thousands more men managed to escape slaughter and are regrouping, awaiting orders for how to proceed. But who is to give these survivors their orders is not immediately clear. Chief among the dead is Henry's brother and lieutenant in France: Thomas, duke of Clarence.

Those who must pass on to Henry word of Thomas's death at the age of thirty-three realize straightaway that it touches "intimately against the king's advantage."[19] One well-informed chronicler writes that it "afflicts him intensely."[20] Henry has led a grueling life, in which he has lost many close friends and comrades: Hotspur and Oldcastle to rebellion, the duke of York in battle, the earl of Arundel and Bishop Courtenay to disease. But never has he lost a brother. He allows a day to pass before he discloses the news to those around him, and while this delay is in part, no doubt, to calculate the political consequences of the loss, it is likely also to give himself time to assimilate his grief.

There is much to feel sorry about. Thomas was a tough, brave soldier—too brave, perhaps—but nevertheless a general Henry trusted to stand in for himself. He was also the boy who once stood beside Henry, both of them wearing new gowns, when their father threw a party for King Richard on the eve of the Revenge Parliament in 1397. He was a teen who, like Henry, was once sent off to assume command in a strange part of the British Isles in the difficult early years of Henry IV's reign. And he was a warrior who, like Henry, spied weakness in the French and had the will to turn it into opportunity for England.

Thomas was never much of a politician, and there was a point at which their father's preference for him created what could have been a lasting crisis in his and Henry's relationship. Yet once Henry assumed the Lancastrian crown and leadership of the family, those things never came between them. Thomas, like John and Humphrey, has been as loyal a brother as any man could have asked for—and this is of huge consequence to Henry, who values loyalty above all else.

Among the last public words he spoke to Thomas was his reminder, as his brother pleaded for a man's life outside Melun, that "we do not want, and will not have, any traitors near us." Thomas was sometimes rash but never false. And now he is dead, in circumstances that should never have been allowed to come to pass.

Thomas's death was, regrettably, all his own fault, as the stories that are pieced together of his death soon reveal. Having been left in charge of the Anglo-Burgundian part of France in Henry's absence, Thomas spied what he thought was an opportunity to enlarge it through fast, aggressive action. In the early spring he drew together an army of around four thousand men—amounting to roughly half the English force available—and led it south toward the dauphinist county of Anjou, on an old-fashioned chevauchée. He rode his men as far as the city of Angers, found its ancient walls well defended, so turned away and allowed his archers to fan out into the countryside to seek food and plunder.

On March 22, Thomas's scouts told him that a large force of Scottish and French troops were in the field very close by, camped around the town of Baugé. "Unreasonably excited by the news," Thomas decided to engage, but chose not to wait for his archers to reassemble.[21] Despite the protestations of his fellow captains—who included the vastly experienced earls of Salisbury and Huntingdon—Thomas detached around fifteen hundred men and tried to surprise the enemy. Back in 1415 he missed Agincourt through sickness. This, perhaps, was his chance to make up for it.

Catching the Scots and French at Baugé unawares proved easy. Defeating them was not. The English were heavily outmanned and without longbowmen. Thus the battle that ensued was no Agincourt; it went according to simple weight of numbers. Clarence was killed almost as soon as fighting began, his jeweled and crowned helmet wrenched from his head as a prize for one lucky Scotsman. Several other famous captains also perished, including one of Henry's most trusted lieutenants, Sir

Gilbert Umfraville. The earl of Huntingdon was captured, as were two of Thomas's stepsons by his marriage to Margaret Holland: seventeen-year-old John Beaufort, earl of Somerset, and his younger brother Thomas Beaufort, aged fifteen.

The death toll and list of captives would have been far worse, had Thomas not left the earl of Salisbury behind in charge of the rest of the army. Salisbury rounded them up and marched them back to Normandy, pursued all the way by jubilant Scots.

It is hard to overstate the scale of this disaster. Besides the loss of Thomas himself, the wasteful sacrifice of around one-tenth of the English expeditionary army, and the cash value of the prisoners who are now on their way to the dauphin's prisons, Henry's late brother has handed the dauphin a huge boost in morale. It is no wonder that, as one chronicler writes, Henry is "heavy and wroth."[22] In one afternoon at Baugé, many months of his own patient and minutely considered work has been undone. Rumors are already flying around Europe that Baugé has proven such a devastating setback to the English cause that the dauphin is on his way to Paris to dictate the terms of a peace settlement, and that Henry himself has been killed.[23] So while Thomas's death makes it easier for Henry to put the case to his subjects that their financial assistance is essential, it is clear that he can spare little more time on his tour before he goes back to France in person.

He may also be nagged by the sense that Thomas's death suggests an awful conclusion, and perhaps the fatal weakness in English strategy since 1413.

It may be that God wants Henry alone to succeed. This may not be England's cause—but his alone.

Awful as the news of Thomas's defeat and death at Baugé is, Henry does not panic. He sees his fundraising tour through to its conclusion. When Thomas's broken body—recovered the day after the battle at Baugé by his only son, a bastard called John—is brought home, Henry has it buried near their father's, in Canterbury Cathedral, with one hundred bright torches burning around the hearse. (A grand tomb, later raised by Thomas's widow, Margaret, will bear carved effigies of both him and her first husband, John Beaufort.) With this done, Henry returns to London, where on May 2 a parliament is ready to open at Westminster.

There is no avoiding the matter of Thomas's death, so when Parliament assembles on its first day in the Painted Chamber, Chancellor Thomas Langley seeks to use the crisis as proof of Henry's enduring qualities as a monarch. First he rehearses an old theme of Henry's rule, pointing out that the king does not wish to "attribute or ascribe anything to himself, but all to God alone, following the habit of the most valiant emperor Julius Caesar, who did not wish to hear of his own deeds, through fear of pride." He credits Henry with the forbearance of Job, saying that when Henry "first heard and knew of the death of the honorable prince the duke of Clarence, his very dear brother, and of the other valiant knights and other persons killed and captured in his company, [he] praised God, and thanked him for his visitation of that affliction, just as he had had reason to do because of his earlier successes,* saying with the prophet, 'I will call upon the lord with praise.'"[24]

Were it not for the fact that Henry has for the last seven years and more made impassive determination the hallmark of his kingship, all this might smack of desperation. But Henry has been consistent in his approach to rule and his public bearing, even under these testing circumstances. What is more, when Parliament opens he proves that he is also still inventive and politically supple.

All at the parliament must expect Henry to ask them for a substantial grant of war finance. This has after all been the point of his tour throughout the spring. A public report has shown the royal balance sheet to be a wreck: Henry is spending almost every penny of his annual revenue on warfare, leaving almost nothing for the ordinary expenses of government and the royal household. The Treaty of Troyes, which is ratified before

* An early version of Rudyard Kipling's injunction in "If," to: "meet with Triumph and Disaster / And treat those two impostors just the same."

the rest of the parliamentary proceedings begin, theoretically absolves the English from paying for a French civil war. Be that as it may: if further humiliating disasters like Baugé are to be avoided, the Crown needs money.

Yet Henry does not demand a subsidy. Instead he strikes a deal. Despite the looming threat of insolvency, he makes it known that if Parliament will grant him taxation at its *next* meeting, he will hold off requesting one now. So rather than discussing the king's poverty, the members are given the luxury of three weeks to spend considering domestic government and the petitions of the people.

The result is a parliamentary schedule tightly focused on English affairs. Henry grants the legislation needed for a recoinage, which will restore the gold currency in England to its proper weight. He approves a bill clamping down on unlicensed doctors—or "meddlers in physic and surgery." He agrees that rowdy students at the University of Oxford can be threatened with charges of outlawry if they continue harassing the townsfolk and villagers of the nearby counties. He responds to complaints from fishermen working the Thames that fish traps below the water surface are proving a menace to shipping and are "made of such narrow mesh that a large part of the fry of salmon, trout, mullet, and other fish is . . . caught in the same and wasted, or given to pigs to eat." He agrees to send special royal commissions to the Scottish borders to try to restore order to a war-torn region where the royal writ does not run. He responds favorably to requests from wool merchants to lobby the duke of Burgundy over protecting the English trade with clothworkers in Flanders against cheap imports of Spanish and Scottish wool.

Almost all these issues are inconsequential to Henry's adventures in France. Yet by tackling them, he shows he has not forgotten what being king of England means. If he ignores the concerns of ordinary taxpayers, there is little hope of earning their backing for his campaigns. No matter how great his need, the contractual, transactional aspect of kingship is sacred.

Of course, fine sentiments such as these do not pay soldiers' wages. One reason Henry is able to act with such empathy and generosity toward his taxpaying subjects in May 1421 is because he has managed to secure a single, enormous loan that will go straight into his treasury. It comes from his uncle Henry Beaufort, bishop of Winchester, who raids his bishopric's ample cash reserves to put an astonishing £17,666 into Henry's war treasury—a sum that represents almost half the total value of all loans yielded by his fundraising tour (£36,840).

Beaufort, the former chancellor, has good reason to be so openhanded. He has been absent from English politics for as long as Henry, although for markedly different reasons. On resigning his position as chancellor in 1417 he went, as intended, to the Council of Constance, where he helped the emperor Sigismund resolve the papal schism through the election of the universally recognized Martin V as pope. As reward for his diplomacy, the new pope made Beaufort a cardinal, but rather than requiring his presence at the papal court, allowed him to remain as bishop of Winchester, so long as he reported directly to Rome and not Canterbury. Pope Martin also offered Beaufort legatine powers to enact church reform in England in the name of the papacy.

This apparent shift in Beaufort's loyalties from his king to the new pope has earned him Henry's withering displeasure, and since returning to England in 1419, Beaufort has been living in political disgrace in his diocese. His massive loan in 1421 serves two purposes. It means Beaufort can keep his cardinal's hat while being readmitted to the council and rehabilitated into political life.[25] It also means Henry can afford to return to France and try to sort out the mess left by his brother's untimely demise. In May 1421, as Parliament dissolves, this is the only thing that seems to matter.

Once the main business of Parliament is at an end, in late May Henry holds belated Garter Day celebrations at Windsor Castle. He has postponed them by a month from their usual date of St. George's Day, April 23, but there is a somber tone to some of the festivities. The barge that carries Henry and Queen Catherine from Westminster to Windsor is draped in black, with animated models of armored men on it striking bells with hammers.[26]

As in all things, the fine details of the visual spectacle have been personally approved by Henry, who has demanded to see cloth samples of the velvet and furs proposed for his household's gold-trimmed ceremonial robes even when he is on the road, miles away from London. But his mind is almost certainly more exercised by his simultaneous preparations for departure to France. Reports coming back from the continent grow more alarming each week: the military situation has deteriorated sharply in the five months he has been away, and it will take a huge effort to bring things back to the way he left them after Christmas 1420, let alone to take the fight back to the dauphin.

The pressure, the relentlessness of the war, the promise of hardship beyond anything his men have yet experienced might have broken a less determined king. But Henry is resolute. On June 10 he sets sail from Dover to take back command of the hard-pressed army.

He does not know—nobody can possibly know—that he will never set foot in England again.

30

TO JERUSALEM

Henry lands at Calais on the night of June 10, 1421. He leaves behind in England Queen Catherine, who is three months pregnant, and his brother John, duke of Bedford, in whose capable hands government has seldom gone awry. He brings with him Humphrey, James I of Scotland, the earls of March and Warwick, around four thousand fresh soldiers, and a pile of books.

Henry has been taxed hard by the multiple demands of politics, war planning, and formally mourning Thomas. More strenuous work lies ahead. Following the disaster at Baugé, Normandy is being competently held by the earl of Salisbury, who welcomes Henry back to France with a feisty status update, assuring him that the duchy "stands in good plight and never so well as now," and that "all the captains here do well their diligence, as well in sure-keeping of their places as in stirring and annoying of your enemies."[1]

In other areas, however, the outlook is less encouraging. The duke of Brittany, hitherto a cautious ally, has defected to the dauphin. The duke of Burgundy is distracted and hard up. The dauphin's armies have surrounded the city of Chartres, just sixty miles from Paris, and have also been harassing the citizens of the capital with raids up to their walls. Conditions in Paris are somehow even worse than when Henry was there at Christmas. Poor people have been reduced to eating pig slops and dog tripe scavenged from furriers' waste heaps. Starving wolves have been seen digging up human graves.[2] Henry has much to occupy his attention, and it is difficult to know which way to look first.

He knows he will be in France for at least six months—since this is the length of the contracts he has struck with the troops he brings. Experience suggests the campaign will be much longer. This may be one reason that he is in a bookish frame of mind. His travel library includes volumes from the royal library at Windsor, some of which are repaired and rebound before being sent to Dover for the journey. One of his recent commissions, which may be among this collection, is his edition of the devotional text *Meditations on the Life of Christ* by the anonymous writer known as the Pseudo-Bonaventure, which he has had translated into French. Another is a book Henry has borrowed from his aunt Joan Neville (née Beaufort), countess of Westmoreland: a history of Jerusalem that splices the adventures of mythical Arthurian knights with a chronicle of the First Crusade and the deeds of its leader Godfrey of Bouillon, who in 1099 became Jerusalem's first crusader ruler.[3]

A few months after arriving in France, Henry also sends to London to order a set of twelve books on hunting—perhaps copies, for gifting, of his late uncle the duke of York's magnificent treatise *Master of Game*.[4] And he decides that as well as the recorders and flutes he has brought on campaign, he needs a new harp, together with strings and a case: an order is placed in London for this, too.[5] Henry's tastes are eclectic, but one thing he has learned in his years of campaigning is that he enjoys and perhaps even needs relief from the long, boring, unsanitary business of marching and siegecraft.

There is to be plenty of this, and it begins with an advance south, to relieve Chartres, where the dauphin is besieging the Burgundian-held city. Henry decides to lead this expedition in person rather than delegating it to Humphrey or another of his captains. So after a short visit to

Paris to check up on Charles VI and judge for himself the scale of the civil unrest and destitution, on July 9 Henry joins his army mustering at Mantes, and prepares to ride out. Yet as he does, news arrives that the dauphin, unwilling to risk facing Henry in battle, has abandoned his siege and fled south across the Loire.

This is good news and bad. It saves Henry a job, and when he writes to the citizens of London to tell them about it, he projects confidence: "we trust fully unto our lord that through his grace and mercy all things here that we shall have to do with shall go well from henceforth," he says.[6] Yet the dauphin Charles's flight denies him the chance to take immediate revenge in kind for Thomas's death at Baugé. What's more, it is a reminder of just how much of his army's strength rests on his own reputation as a commander.

Instead of going to Chartres, then, Henry takes the army to the dauphinist town and castle of Dreux. This does not trouble him long. After a month, Henry's men are close to breaking into the castle, and the garrison treats for peace. By now it is the middle of August. Henry still hopes to engage the dauphin in battle if he can, so he leads his men as far south as Orléans in the hope of provoking the young man into a foolhardy response. Charles, however, does not take the bait. He has settled on a strategy of impertinent nonengagement. He sends out letters insulting Henry, deriding him for lacking the "power to torment the good towns under our obedience."[7] But on no account will he commit to the lottery of a battle.

When Henry gets to Orléans, he allows his men to plunder the suburbs and raid the citizens' wine cellars. Yet he realizes he cannot play the game by the dauphin's rules any longer. Autumn is coming. His supply lines are stretched and failing. His men are hungry and ill. Many of them are suffering from an outbreak of dysentery so severe that the folk of the countryside find "Englishmen dead on the roads and in the middle of the fields."[8]

Plagued in their bellies, perhaps one thousand men die on the march: an intolerable rate of loss. Henry does not harbor a scrap of fear for the young man he calls the "pretended dauphin."[9] But he has no weapon in his armory that can defeat the bloody flux. In late September he returns north, to a target closer to his own territory.

His object is the city of Meaux, which sits on the river Marne, twenty-five miles northwest of Paris. It is a dauphinist bolt-hole, the capture of which ought to relieve the sufferings of the capital's miserable citizens. Meaux is close by. It makes good sense to attack it. Nevertheless, securing its submission will keep Henry and his men pinned down and frustrated for the next seven months.

During all his time in France, Henry has seldom had such thin resources, nor faced such stubborn opponents, as he does at the siege of Meaux. The place sits across a loop of the Marne, with the walled city and its suburbs on the north bank and a smaller, heavily fortified area known as the Marché inside the riverbend, joined to the rest of Meaux by a single bridge.

Inside the Marché is a garrison of one thousand die-hard dauphinist troops. They are commanded by a singularly vicious lord known as the Bastard of Vaurus, whose despicable crimes include tying a heavily pregnant woman to an elm tree—his favorite execution spot—so that as she gave birth her screams attracted wolves, which ripped her to pieces and ate her newborn.[10] The bastard lacks humanity, compunction, and fear in roughly equal measure, and he has no intention of giving up easily. Within weeks of the English arriving at Meaux it is clear this is sensible policy.

Henry and his fellow commanders—the earls of March and Warwick, and Thomas Beaufort, duke of Exeter—are better versed in siegecraft than almost any men alive. They seize the suburbs of Meaux and blockade the city by land and water. They dig trenches and mines and set up cannons and catapults. They detach troops to go out into the surrounding area and reduce other outposts of enemy troops. But even they cannot force a fast victory, for circumstances are stacked against them.

The city is, as one chronicler puts it, "well vittled and also manned."[11] Henry's troop numbers are threadbare and not easily reinforced from Normandy, where every man available is needed for defense. The duke of

Burgundy is occupied fighting dauphinists on his own doorstep in Picardy. He cannot—or will not—contemplate coming to Meaux, even to meet Henry in person, for many months. So when winter sets in, the siege camp is a miserable place. Henry's habit has typically been to walk around his positions each day, directing his men's efforts and keeping morale raised. But that task has never been more difficult—as a lone trumpeter on the walls likes to remind him, by blaring out an irritating tune whenever he sees Henry among the men below.[12]

When winter arrives the change in seasons brings sleet and snow in such torrents that the Marne floods and the whole siege camp has to be moved. Disease continues to spread. The defenders of Meaux keep up a sapping campaign of raids out of the city's gates and well-directed cannon fire, which claims some prominent victims. One is a seventeen-year-old cousin of Henry's named John Cornwall, "a fine and valiant squire" who has his head blown off by a cannonball, to the distress of his father, a knight of the same name who is standing beside him when he is hit. In his anguish, the older man is heard to bellow that Henry's war is now proceeding "contrary to God and reason," for while the English originally came to reclaim Normandy, they are now trying to "deprive the dauphin of the realm that is rightfully his own."[13] Swearing an oath never to fight again, the elder Cornwall leaves the camp and goes home to England. Trudging the same path are other disillusioned Englishmen, deserting as they come to the end of their contracts or their wits.

The going, then, is grueling. But Henry does not panic, nor does he amend his belief that his war is going in the right direction. He sets up his headquarters in the elegant cloistered abbey of St. Faron, where he attends as usual to the fine detail of government business, while also sending out letters and envoys to sympathetic European allies, asking them to contribute to his cause. He answers a letter from Queen Catherine, who asks him to find a salary for her personal physician, who is attending her as she nears the end of her term of pregnancy.[14] He hears from England that a parliament assembled by his brother John has voted him a tax subsidy, the receipts of which are sorely needed.[15] He writes several times to the royal officers at Caen and Harfleur, asking them to send him ten thousand pounds of iron for cannon manufacture, as well as gunstones and "all the saltpeter, coal and brimstone" they can lay hands on. (As always he demands urgency: "faileth not thereof in no wise," he says.)[16] He briefs diplomats who are going to visit the emperor Sigismund and other German magnates, including his late sister Blanche's widower, Louis, elector of the Rhine. He tells these messengers to stick to the diplomatic line that he is "now in the point and conclusion of his labor, and through God's Grace, and help of his allies and friends, shall soon have an end of the war."[17]

And still he reads. The books he has brought with him do not seem to satisfy his wandering mind, for around the time he is at Meaux Henry also orders a copy of a volume about chivalry, a book by the eighth-century scholar Bede—likely his *Ecclesiastical History of the English People*—and a collection of sermons appropriate for Sundays.[18]

From time to time he may wonder about the progress of the most exciting literary commission he has made in recent years. Just before leaving England, he sent a Burgundian adventurer named Gilbert Lannoy on a journey to the Holy Land, with instructions to survey the "towns, ports and rivers" in Egypt and Syria and write a practical handbook based on his travels.[19] Lannoy—a storied knight with experience fighting in Spain, in the Baltic, and on the French side at Agincourt—departed in May 1421 armed with gifts of jewels, longbows, reams of cloth, and gold clocks, and letters of introduction to Christian and Muslim rulers alike. The intelligence Lannoy gathers, along with the largesse and diplomatic courtesies he is expected to distribute everywhere from Poland and Lithuania to Constantinople and Cairo, will be the basis for the next great project of Henry's life: a crusade to win back Jerusalem for the armies of Christendom.

Few other men would dare to dream of launching such an expedition, least of all amid a project as all-consuming as Henry's war in France. But Henry has always possessed extraordinary ambition, allied to an appreciation of the detailed planning required to bring dreams to reality. No matter how challenging the task at hand may be, he looks relentlessly to the future: to the next thing that he alone, with God's grace, can achieve.

On December 6, 1421, while Henry is directing the siege of Meaux and dreaming of a crusade, the bells of London ring out to announce that Queen Catherine has given birth to a baby boy.

The child is delivered at Windsor Castle, his arrival blessed by a relic Henry has borrowed and sent for the occasion.[20] This is the Holy Prepuce—or foreskin of Christ—removed at Jesus's circumcision and now kept safe by the brothers of the abbey of Notre-Dame de Coulombs, halfway between Dreux and Chartres.* The foreskin is believed to protect mothers in childbirth, and in this instance it does the job perfectly. When the news reaches Henry that his wife and son are doing well, he is "glad" and "thanks God."[21] He sends word to the queen that she should hear a mass dedicated to the Holy Trinity: his father's favorite subject of praise and thanks, and, as he gets older, increasingly his own, too.

Henry may reflect, as one English chronicler does, that the birth of this "fair son, a lord and prince," who is named after him, will bring "ease, profit and worship" to the realm—indeed, to both his realms.[22] At thirty-five years old, he is late to parenthood—nearly twice as old as his own father was when he was born. But now, however belatedly, he has an heir of his body. This bolsters his dynastic claim to the French crown—and it also helps secure the Lancastrian hold on the English throne, which was so precarious until just a few years ago.

Henry does not leave Meaux to attend the boy's christening, which takes place at St. George's Chapel in Windsor, with his brother John, Bishop Henry Beaufort, and the Flemish noblewoman Jacqueline of Hainault† standing as godparents. But he is delighted enough to want to

---

* This is far from the only known relic of the Holy Prepuce—at least a dozen churches in Europe claim to have the authentic one, which is especially revered since it is the only physical remnant of Christ's body left on earth.

† Jacqueline's presence in England in 1422 is controversial. She is the widow of the late dauphin John of Touraine (d. 1417), has been entangled in complex disputes over inheritances within the Low Countries, and has fled to England in the course of these to escape her second marriage, to John IV, duke of Brabant. Henry has granted her honorable asylum, but it

see his wife as soon as he can, to congratulate her and perhaps to repeat the trick. As soon as the queen has recovered from the birth, in early February 1422, Henry makes arrangements for a fleet of ships and mariners to be chartered at Southampton and other ports "for the passage of the Lady Catherine, Queen of England, and Duke of Bedford, in her retinue" to come and join him in France. His wife and brother do not hurry—it will be late spring by the time they arrive. But that gives Henry time to push as hard as he can toward a conclusion to the siege of Meaux.

The keys to the reduction of Meaux are Henry's determination, his captains' experience, and the dauphin's unwillingness to ride to the city's rescue. The alternative court Henry's young rival has established at Bourges is war-drained, deep in debt, and still wedded to the strategy of avoiding battle with Henry in person. Without ever saying as much, therefore, the dauphin leaves Meaux to its fate. The defenders are effectively sacrificed to sap Henry's manpower and resources. The only question is how long they can resist, and how much damage they can inflict as they do.

As it turns out, the walled part of Meaux on the north bank of the Marne holds out until March, when word leaks out that the starving, demoralized citizens are willing to open the gates. When they do, Henry sends men rushing in to prevent the garrison's soldiers—who have not surrendered—from burning the town as they fall back to the fortified Marché for a last stand. The earls of Warwick and March move the English cannons up close to the Marché's walls. It seems as though the end to the siege, laid all the way back in October, is now in sight.

But in fact, it takes another two months for Meaux to surrender, a period during which the English casualty list continues to rise. The dead now include Warwick's cousin the earl of Worcester, who is shot with a cannon, and Thomas, Lord Clifford, a veteran of Harfleur and Agincourt, who is killed by a crossbow bolt.[23] Meanwhile, disease continues to wreak its own havoc, and the brazen trumpeter on the walls keeps up his infuriating blare.

---

is a touchy subject, not least with the duke of Burgundy. Jacqueline will go on to marry—controversially, recklessly, and possibly bigamously—Henry's brother Humphrey.

Only on May 10, under threat of a rebellion among his desperate men, does the callous Bastard of Vaurus agree to surrender, on terms stacked heavily against him. Henry grants some of the citizens amnesty, but for the Bastard and his fellow garrison leaders, there is no mercy. The Bastard is drawn through the streets of Meaux and butchered beside the tree where he executed so many others. Hundreds more of the garrison are sent off in chains to serve years of hard imprisonment in Paris, London, and the remotest castles of England and Wales. The trumpeter who mocked Henry from the ramparts is finally silenced when Henry has his head chopped off.

So at long last, Meaux falls, yielding magnificent plunder, which makes up in some small part for the atrocious difficulties Henry and his army have suffered in breaking it. Henry's share of the spoils includes more than one hundred books, mostly Latin works concerning religion and law. These represent more than even he at his most bibliophilic can digest, but he can see a use for them nonetheless: the Carthusian monastery he founded in 1414 at Sheen needs a proper library. Since he first gave orders for its construction, Henry has been sending books (and money to buy books) for its collection. The rich literary pickings he acquires from Meaux will go a long way to stocking the monks' shelves.[24]

No doubt this gives Henry some satisfaction. But the relief at simply leaving Meaux must be even greater. As the prisoners are being taken away, the siege camp dismantled, and the citizens' wealth picked over, Henry can finally go back to Paris, where his wife is due to arrive at the end of May, in time to celebrate the festival of Whitsun. There he will be able to enjoy the comforts of the Hôtel de Louvre and, a little way outside the walls, the palatial forest chateau at Bois de Vincennes. He can take counsel with his leading generals about next targets, how to address the ongoing crisis in recruitment, and the ever-pressing matter of war finance. He will have a chance to speak covertly with the papal intermediaries he has asked to make the very first, discreet inquiries with the dauphin about a settlement that could bring the war to an end. The summer ahead does not promise to be a time of relaxation. But it marks the shift to yet another phase of his campaign, and a chance to see somewhere other than the obstinate walls of Meaux.

As summer arrives, however, Henry begins to feel unwell. He sees that Catherine is welcomed to Paris in regal fashion, with "a very fine company of knights and ladies," and two ermine gowns carried before her, to represent her status as queen of England and queen-in-waiting of France.[25] He watches as the citizens put on a performance of the martyrdom of St. George. He gives dinners at which he and Catherine sit "gloriously and pompously" wearing their crowns as they eat.[26] And he ensures that Catherine settles into Bois de Vincennes, to enjoy the comforts of the chateau there, set in hundreds of acres of woodland, out of which bursts a central tower taller than any other in Europe.

But the summer is blisteringly hot, and disease is everywhere. An epidemic of smallpox in Paris infects more children than anyone can count, as well as a large number of adults. In mid-June, Henry moves the whole court to Senlis to escape the spread. But when they arrive, it appears he has moved too late. At Meaux he had already been suffering some of the symptoms of camp sickness, which troubled him sufficiently then that he brought a doctor from England to attend on him. The "flux of the intestines" has proven impossible for him to shift, and may be worsened by an attack of the Parisian pox.[27] According to one account, he is afflicted by "an acute fever and overpowering dysentery," which leaves him so weak that his doctors do not dare give him purgatives or other "internal medicines" for fear that they will kill him.[28]

This is all highly inconvenient, for just as Henry is languishing on his sickbed, the dauphin Charles has made a move that opens the possibility of the battle Henry has yearned for since Baugé. One hundred and fifty miles south of Paris, dauphinist troops are ravaging the county of Nevers, which owes obedience to the duke of Burgundy. They have besieged the town of Cosne, which guards a river-crossing of the Loire. A deal has been struck with the garrison of the sort Henry is accustomed to making with the dauphin's castellans: if Philip of Burgundy or his allies do not come to the rescue by August 12, the soldiers can surrender with their lives.[29]

Ill as Henry is, this is too good an opportunity to miss. He and Philip of Burgundy meet and agree that they must strip every man they can spare from whatever duty they are engaged in and march them to Cosne to strike what could be a fatal blow against the "pretended dauphin." Preparations begin immediately, and by the third week of July an army of more than ten thousand men has assembled around Paris and is fit to march. Henry hauls himself from his bed and places himself at the head of the troops. He is still so weak that he must be carried in a litter. But he is there.

Once the army moves out, however, it is clear that Henry is in no condition even to be carried. He orders another doctor to be summoned from England. Public prayers are said in Paris and other towns of the Seine. The army marches on to Cosne under his brother John and the earl of Warwick. Henry himself is carried to Corbeil, just to the south of Paris, where he arrives on July 25. He stays there for two weeks, trying to rally his strength.

On August 12, John, duke of Bedford, and Philip of Burgundy line up their troops to do battle at Cosne, as has been agreed on with the dauphin. But the dauphin does not turn up. He has never wanted to fight an army commanded by Henry. Now it appears he will not even fight one assembled by him. Once more English hopes to strike a decisive field victory—a second Agincourt—are frustrated.

On the day his brother John is staring at an empty battlefield at Cosne, Henry has gathered enough strength to feel he can travel back to Paris, albeit slowly, and by barge. On August 13 he reaches the outskirts of the French capital once again. Here he attempts to ride. But the effort of even climbing into the saddle is too much for him. His horse has barely picked up its hooves before he has to be helped back down once more and placed back into a litter. His servants take him back to where he began this painful journey a month earlier: the chateau at Bois de Vincennes.

They all know that he is going there to die.

Henry has always been a clearheaded, detail-focused leader, and even as he realizes that he is not going to survive the summer of 1422, his approach to problem solving does not change. From his chamber at

Bois de Vincennes, he pays careful attention to both pressing government business and the arrangements for his own demise.

This is not the first time he has contemplated his own death. He made his first will before his Agincourt campaign, and revised it in 1417. Before setting out in 1421 on this—his last—adventure, he made a second, superseding will. Now as he lies on his deathbed, surrounded by his servants, doctors, and attendants, he tweaks its terms, to reflect his new circumstances as a father. The amendments are drawn up in a legal document known as a codicil.

The will itself begins with a lavish religious flourish, as Henry commends his soul to the protection of the Holy Trinity, the archangels, and a list of saints that proceeds from the Virgin and John the Baptist, to specifically English saints such as St. George, St. Alban, and Edward the Confessor, and on to lesser, local saints whose shrines he has visited in the course of his life: St. John of Bridlington and St. Winefride, whose well gushes near Shrewsbury, where his life was first saved.

After thanking almost the entire heavenly host, Henry prays that the English people will be delivered from "divisions, dissensions and every kind of heretical fallacy"—it would not do for Lollardy to rear its head or another John Oldcastle to appear. He insists that his most valuable French prisoners—the duke of Orléans chief among them—are not released unless strict conditions are met. Then he asks to be buried at Westminster, near Richard II and his other Plantagenet ancestors, rather than with his father and brother at Canterbury. Just as Richard once did, Henry gives minute details about the tomb, chapel, and program of Masses he expects to be set up for his body and soul, though he is vague about his funeral, merely detailing the number and type of candles he wants to surround his hearse. It is as though, despite his detailed planning, he also does not quite believe the worst will happen. He survived Shrewsbury and Agincourt. Perhaps he will beat this, too.

The rest of his will amounts to a list of donations. Henry makes personal gifts of favorite possessions: all the gold and silver ornaments in his chapel for Catherine; a pair of beds to his brother John; vestments to his uncle Henry Beaufort; a thousand pounds of gold to his uncle Thomas Beaufort, along with a bed decorated with hawking motifs, which once belonged to Henry, Lord Scrope. He leaves a gold cup to the earl of Warwick, all his furred cloaks to his chamberlain, Lord FitzHugh, and the choice of his best horses to John and Humphrey, saving one, the very best of all, which should go to his master of horses, Henry Noon.

Henry makes arrangements to pay his debts. He makes a long list of all the people whose wages must be settled. He arranges for life annuities to be paid out for eleven minstrels of his chamber, whose music has given him so much pleasure and distraction during his years in the field. And he bequeaths his books, which, with a small number of exceptions, are to be divided between his nunnery at Syon and the Carthusian priory at Sheen. Among the volumes kept back from this donation is the great Bible he inherited from his own father: this he wants to go to his infant son, little Henry, who in August 1422 is still not quite nine months old.[30]

His son's extreme youth, along with the fact that Henry himself is abroad in France, fighting a war unlike any contested by any English king before him, is the most difficult challenge to occupy him in the days that he lies wasting away at Bois de Vincennes. Verbally Henry tells his brother John that either he or the duke of Burgundy must take up the leadership of the war in France; and that no settlement can ever be made that abandons the English hold on Normandy.[31] The codicil he writes to his will deals specifically with England. In it Henry imagines a careful division of powers. He wishes the governance of the boy who will soon become Henry VI to be split several ways: his brother Humphrey taking charge of the boy's realm, Thomas Beaufort taking charge of his upbringing, and two trusted men of his household, Lord FitzHugh and Sir Walter Hungerford, supervising at all times. Henry must surely remember the challenges of his own youth, when he was guided by steady old hands like Peter Melbourne. He tries to do what he can to ease the path of his son, who will be smaller than he ever was when he is thrust to the front of royal rule, while having a more difficult job than anyone before him.

After this, Henry can do no more. He puts the finishing touches to the codicil to his will on August 26. His doctors continue to attend him, but with every day that passes he worsens, and the only advice the physicians will give him is that God sometimes changes his mind.

On the last day of August, Henry tires of being given hopeful assessments, and asks to be told "the pure truth."[32]

The bravest of his doctors kneels before him and says, as gently as he can, that they all suspect he has just a couple of hours to live.

At this, Henry summons his confessor, his chaplains, and his family members, and they hear "the seven penitential psalms"—solemn and confessional verses that have been sung together for hundreds of years at times of extreme penitence.*

At the end of the fourth of these, his chaplains call on God to "be favorable to Syon and build the walls of Jerusalem." Henry asks them to pause, and says that were it not for the death he is now expecting, it was his intention "to put the kingdom of France at peace, then go to conquer Jerusalem."[33]

This is no delirious fantasy. For at least a year, Henry has been reading and thinking about crusading. Even as he lies dying, Gilbert Lannoy is somewhere in the east, drawing up preliminary reports on how Jerusalem might be taken. Henry is as serious about this holy war as he ever was about France—where he has achieved more than any Englishman that ever lived. So there is, perhaps, no more appropriate subject for him to contemplate as his life ebbs away. A little over nine years earlier Henry's father passed away in the Jerusalem Chamber at Westminster Abbey, comforted to hear at the end that this was where he was. It is strange and fitting, then, that in a very different sense, the Holy City is on Henry V's mind, when, in the early hours of the morning on August 31, 1422, he too dies.

When he takes his last breath, Henry is a few weeks away from his thirty-sixth birthday. Many of those who knew him feel that he is irreplaceable. The group at his side when he dies includes John, Richard Beauchamp, Thomas Beaufort, and a long-serving household knight,

---

* Psalms 6, 31, 37, 50, 101, 129, and 142.

Louis Robesart. Now they, and their countrymen, must carry on without him.

"He did not leave his like on Earth among kings and princes," writes one admiring chronicler, "so that not only the people of England and France, but all Christendom mourned his death as he deserved."[34]

EPILOGUE

"VIRTUE CONQUERS ALL"

In death Henry is just meat, and liable to rot in the late summer's warmth. So once his eyes have closed for the last time, his body is taken from his chamber and cut open. His guts and organs are hauled out, and buried not far from Bois de Vincennes, at the splendid fortified abbey of Saint-Maur-des-Fossés. The carcass of fat, gristle, muscle, and bone that is left is boiled, embalmed "with all kinds of spices," and sealed in two fitted coffins of wood and lead, on top of which are placed "an image like unto him": a physical approximation of the dead man, an effigy made from boiled leather, a dummy with a crown placed carefully on its head.[1]

During his life Henry planned three kings' funerals: Richard II's, his father's, and his. He has been surprisingly vague about his own, yet it will be the most elaborate of the three, and not only because his deeds were the greatest and his demise the most untimely. His corpse also has the furthest to travel, the most cities to visit, and the most acclamation to receive. It is roughly three hundred miles from Bois de Vincennes to Westminster Abbey, and it takes nearly three months for Henry to get there. But in many ways, this long, slow, somber procession is the perfect realization of a Henrician triumph. The king himself is literally an unseeing statue, present but impassive, in absolute counterpoint to the outpouring of human emotion through which he travels. The acclaim that is rendered to him cannot be separated from the reverence due to God.

His funeral procession does not pass through Paris, but instead goes north of the French capital, to the abbey of Saint-Denis, where on September 15 Henry is honored with a service for the dead at the French royal mausoleum, where he so nearly earned himself the right to lie. From here he is put on a hearse and drawn slowly down the Seine valley, through Mantes and on to the Norman capital, Rouen. Here, in the city he starved half to death in 1418–19, he lies in state while the bells of the cathedral chime and monks chant psalms all through the night.

In the coming days his twenty-year-old widow, Catherine, arrives at Rouen to join the procession. Behind her is pulled an immense train of two dozen black-draped wagons, carrying her dead husband's personal effects, including a haul of treasure plundered recently from the siege of Meaux: gold rings, brooches and bracelets, coronets, cups, collars, rosaries, and fine silk belts.[2] Catherine and the funeral party stay at Rouen until October 5, then they set out for the coast. Ships have been summoned to Calais in the name of the new king, Henry VI, "for the conduct of the funeral of . . . our deceased father, and the queen, our mother."[3] There are none of the old king's terse injunctions to "see that ye faileth not." Already the voice of government is changing.

At the end of October, Henry, his mourners, and the hired ships are all at Calais, from where they sail to Dover, bringing the late king home for the final time on the last day of the month. One more time he goes to Canterbury, then along the old road to London, to be met outside the city by a delegation of clergy, merchants, and crisply dressed citizens, waiting to do their duty as they welcome him home. Just as he was after Agincourt and Troyes, he is honored at St. Paul's Cathedral; he is then led through the silent city, the streets lined with the black-clad mourners and the river teeming with black-draped barges, before finally, on November 7, he is taken to Westminster to be buried.

"The furnishing of the dead king's funeral, if you would like to know about it, was as follows." So begins one chronicler's careful account of the obsequies. "On the coffin containing his corpse was placed a figure very like to the dead king in height and appearance, clad in a long, loose-fitting purple cloak edged with ermine, with the scepter in one hand and a round, golden ball with a cross affixed in the other hand, and with a golden crown placed on its head over the royal cap, and slippers on its feet."[4]

Candles blaze as the bier is laid in state, the light glinting off the gold cloth draped over Henry's coffin. Three knights wearing the arms of England, France, and St. George, carrying banners of the Trinity and the Virgin, ride warhorses into the abbey and up to the high altar, where they are ceremonially stripped of their armor, to symbolize the final laying down of Henry's arms. Then, watched by a great crowd of nobles, administrators, city dignitaries, and household companions, Henry V is finally laid to rest, "between the [shrine] of Saint Edward and the chapel of the Holy Virgin in the place containing the relics of the dead."[5]

The tomb that will eventually be erected over his burial spot, topped with an effigy of the king in parliamentary robes, his hands and head and royal regalia all made of silver, will be the special project of the queen mother, Catherine. A later inscription, which runs around the tomb platform, will advertise Henry as the "hammer of the Gauls," and it will give readers two typically blunt pieces of advice, characteristic of the king inside the grave. "Virtue conquers all," reads one. "Flee idleness," says the other.

The advice is superfluous. In 1422, there is no room at all for idleness. Indeed, there is urgent business to be done. Two days after the funeral, in the Palace of Westminster, the first parliament of Henry VI's reign opens. One burning issue is how best to establish a regency government that will be robust enough to survive what will be the longest minority in English history. Who should govern? How should the necessary fiction of an active king be maintained for the long years of Henry VI's childhood? How hard should the English cling to the dream of the dual monarchy? What should be done with long-standing prisoners like the duke of Orléans and James I of Scotland?

The greatest question of all is what should be done about the war in

France. That matter has taken on unexpected piquancy in recent weeks, and not only because of Henry V's demise. On the very day that the parliament opens, a funeral is being held in Saint-Denis to honor another king. Just six weeks after Henry's death Charles VI also died, on October 21, 1422, having "wasted away in sorrow and loneliness."[6] From his rebel kingdom of Bourges, his son, the dauphin, is advancing his claim to be Charles VII. In the north, John, duke of Bedford, represents the interests of the rival king, the eleven-month-old Henry VI. Which of them has the true right? How should it be decided? Can the quarrel ever be resolved?

A new world is opening up, with challenges of an entirely different order to the old. There are many more battles to be fought, sieges to be endured, and diplomatic puzzles to be solved. Only one thing is certain. It will be many years before English and French can live cheerfully ignorant of the legacy of Henry V.

What sort of man was Henry? Why did God allow him to die so suddenly? Was it sheer bad luck, evidence of divine caprice, or punishment for his misdeeds, as his military ambition outran his original righteous cause? Was he a brilliant king struck down before his time, or a warmonger whose addiction to conquest eventually brought him the end he deserved? The writers who wrestled with that question at around the time of his death came to very different conclusions.

According to one Burgundian chronicler, Henry was warned that he was going too far with his war with France but would not listen. In this telling, Henry was approached by a hermit who explained to him that God had allowed him a large degree of success in life to make up for the terrible injury he had suffered at the battle of Shrewsbury—but that he had now overreached, and unless he ceased his torments of the French, God would put an end to his life.[7]

A Welsh chronicler, who lived long enough to remember the tumult of Richard II's and Henry IV's reigns, agreed. Writing in 1421, he expressed his bitter dismay about the impositions Henry was then laying on his people by continuing his war even after Normandy had fallen. "The lord king is now fleecing everyone with any money, rich or poor, throughout the realm, in readiness for his return to France in great force," the chronicler wrote. "I fear, alas, that both the great men and the money of the kingdom will be miserably wasted on this enterprise." Henry's financial demands seemed to be encouraging "dark—though private—mutterings and curses and . . . hatred of such extortions."

If the king did not take care, this writer believed, a familiar pattern of history would assert itself. Henry had been a magnificent conqueror, no doubt, but now he was going too far, and risked losing everything he had. Citing the examples of Julius Caesar, Alexander the Great, and the Persian rulers Xerxes I, Cyrus II, and Darius III, the chronicler prayed "that my supreme lord [i.e., Henry] may not in the end . . . incur the sword of the Lord's fury."[8]

Such reactions as these were understandable and—with hindsight—looked brilliantly prophetic. But they were not mainstream views. A more measured—and typical—response to Henry's death was one recorded by a French monk of Saint-Denis, a brilliant chronicler and far from an acolyte of the English king. In his view, Henry's claim to the French "crown of lilies" was poorly founded. Yet there was little to criticize in Henry's conduct and bearing.

"Throughout his reign, and particularly since his invasion of France, [Henry] showed much magnanimity, valor, prudence and wisdom: a great sense of justice, judging the mighty as well as the small," wrote this monk. "He was feared and respected by all his relatives and subjects, and even by those neighbors who were not his subjects. No prince of his time seemed more capable than him of subduing and conquering a country, by the wisdom of his government, by his prudence, and by the other qualities with which he was endowed."[9]

There were many other, similar encomia for Henry, particularly from churchmen. An English monk wrote that Henry "had a pious mind" and that his words were "few but well judged." He was "far-sighted in his planning and shrewd in judgment." Modest and generous, Henry "worked unceasingly, frequently went on pilgrimage and was a generous alms-giver. He was a devout Christian [and] a distinguished and fortunate leader in war, who in all his battles always came off the victor. His construction of new buildings and his foundation of monasteries were on a magnificent scale . . . in all matters he hunted down and fought against the enemies of the faith and the church."[10]

In the eyes of Henry's subjects, these were the things that mattered. To a Londoner, he was "that good and noble king, Harry the Vth after the conquest, flower of chivalry of Christian men." To a Lancastrian writer he was as brave as Hector, as manly as Achilles, as imperious as Augustus, as eloquent as Paris, and as wise as Solomon.[11]

This, maybe, was a level of flattery too far. But even to the Burgundian chronicler who recorded the story of the hermit who told Henry to lay down his arms or die, this was a great man. Henry was a "prince of justice both toward himself and others . . . sober in nature, true in speech, high and lofty in courage, [he] turned his face away from vile and base things." He indulged in "no fruitless labors."[12] He fled idleness.

In the six centuries that have passed since the shock of Henry's death prompted these outpourings of praise for his upstanding character, ideas about him have changed somewhat, but until recently, the consensus—in the English-speaking world—has been that he was a paragon of a certain type of late medieval kingship.

During the decades immediately following his death, Henry's legacy was defended jealously by those who had known him and fought alongside him. The English kingdom of France lasted more or less intact under the stewardship of his brother John, duke of Bedford, until 1435, for if there was any man alive who was the equal to Henry V in terms of ability, personal gravity, experience, and judgment, it was John. Under him, the English won a battle at Verneuil, in 1424, that was as magnificent a victory as Agincourt. Like Henry, Bedford was respected, even if he was not loved, by the French over whom he attempted to rule. Under his regency, the ultimate goal of the Treaty of Troyes was achieved, when Henry VI was crowned king of France in 1431, albeit in Paris rather than the traditional venue of Reims. For more than a decade John's regency suggested that God's interest in the English kingdom of France was general, and not particular to the late Henry V.

Yet by the time John died in 1435, it was also obvious that without another Henry V, it was hard to see how a long-term English presence in France could be maintained. By this time, Joan of Arc had appeared, made contact with the dauphin, and accompanied him to his own coronation, as Charles VII. Joan was caught and eventually burned by the English, but her short career coincided with a turning of the tide. The same year that John, duke of Bedford, died, the Burgundians and Armagnacs finally settled their quarrel, making peace in the Treaty of Arras. From this point onward, Charles VII began steadily to reverse the disastrous losses of his father's reign. By 1436 Charles had taken back Paris. During the 1440s he retook Normandy. By 1453 the English had lost more than Henry V ever won, for their grip on Guyenne was loosened and then broken for good at the battle of Castillon. After this, the only place on the French mainland controlled by England was Calais and the heavily fortified "pale" around it, which was finally recaptured during the reign of Mary Tudor, in 1558. Just as the chronicler Adam Usk had predicted, Henry's conquests went the way of Alexander the Great's and Augustus's: worn down by time, unholdable by any lesser man—which meant almost every man who came afterward.

Yet if Henry's achievements proved as transitory as every great conqueror's, his personal legacy endured in much better shape over the generations that followed him. At first it was curated and maintained through the efforts of his youngest brother, Humphrey, who never forgot—or let it be forgotten—that he was at Agincourt, and found it harder than most to stomach the erosion of what he and his brothers had won together. Humphrey commissioned a Latin biography of Henry, known as the *Vita Henrici Quinti*, from the Italian humanist Tito Livio in the 1430s. This heroic life, along with other memorials of Henry, including that known today as the Pseudo-Elmham (also dating to the 1430s) and the vivid account of the Agincourt campaign and siege of Rouen (known as the *Gesta Henrici Quinti*), which was made during Henry's lifetime by a royal chaplain, ensured that even as Henry's conquests fell back into French hands, and England itself was engulfed by the civil conflict known now as the Wars of the Roses, his legend burned bright in the English imagination.

By the early sixteenth century Henry's deeds were far enough away in time, but rendered colorfully enough in literature, that a young king Henry VIII (descended variously from Henry's Beaufort uncles, and his widow, Catherine de Valois) had Tito Livio's work translated into English, blended with other reminiscences of his ancestor, and used it as a virtual blueprint for his own ambitions to win military glory in France, which he invaded in 1513 with thirty thousand men, hoping to force a second Agincourt. It did not take Henry VIII long to realize that emulating his Lancastrian relative was beyond the reach of even his outsize ambition. All the same, the notion that just one century earlier England had been ruled by the best king it had ever had was well set.

As the sixteenth century went on, Henry's reputation continued to flourish. Tudor historians recognized in him an attractive combination of personal probity and bravery, and presented him as the embodiment—indeed, the forefather—of plucky English nationalism. To the mid-century historian Edward Hall, Henry was the flower of chivalry and the model all successful kings ought to follow if they wished to succeed. To the Elizabethan writer Richard Grafton, he was the "noblest king that ever reigned over the realm of England."[13] And at the very end of the century William Shakespeare gave Henry's life perfect dramatic form, as a rake, converted, just in the nick of time, into a nerveless military hero. Seen within the cycle of Shakespeare's other fifteenth-century "history plays," Henry's story serves as an admonition to those who followed him: the selfish nobles whose bloody factional squabbles bathed England in blood, until the arrival of the house of Tudor finally restored the realm to peace.

Only from the nineteenth century, with Europe wracked by warfare between English and French once more, did historians begin to look on Henry with a critical eye, wondering aloud and in print whether his pursuit of his personal claim in France was really worth the lives lost, the cities starved and blown to pieces, and the wealth squandered on a military project whose net gain was less than zero. Although orthodox opinion, most memorably expressed by the arch-Victorian bishop-historian William Stubbs, was still that Henry should be regarded as the noblest and purest man who ever governed England, there were dissenters. These were best represented by the popular historian J. R. Green, who accused Henry of wanton aggression and an ultimate failure to make good on his miraculous victory at Agincourt, and that great Victorian living out of time, Winston Churchill, who, after the Second World War had issued another reminder of the hideous reality of war in France, called Henry's fight in France "the greatest tragedy of our medieval history."

Broadly speaking, these have remained the two poles of historical opinion ever since. Henry was either what the Edwardian scholar C. L. Kingsford called a "typical medieval hero" or the exemplar of all that was most depressing about the Middle Ages: a time of barbarity dressed up as chivalry, during which the private ambitions of warlords were cloaked in the humbug of religion and used as the pretext to shed the blood of thousands, for the gain of a town here and a castle there, both of which might well be lost again the following year.

Thus it is possible that Henry can be judged as hero and monster on the basis of the same evidence. To the influential and generally levelheaded medievalist K. B. McFarlane, Henry V was "the greatest man that ever ruled England."[14] Yet in the view of a more recent historian, Henry was a "deeply flawed individual," a misogynist, a religious fundamentalist, a reckless spender of other people's money, and a second-rate military commander.[15] In this view, Henry was "one of the cruelest and most cold hearted kings that England has had," breathtakingly arrogant, autocratic, heedless of the needs of those who served in his armies. His golden reputation is based on nothing more than the inconvenient fact that people at the time seemed to like that sort of thing.[16]

There is, famously, no accounting for taste.

What, then, should we conclude of Henry today—if we are determined to pass judgment, rather than simply to understand the unusual but utterly compelling story of his life? The charge that Henry V was cold, tough, uninterested in fornicating with women, and a devout Christian is so obvious that it scarcely merits making. He was certainly unsparing with the lives of those he felt had offended the laws of God and war—not only at Agincourt but throughout his military career.

It should also go without saying that these can seem unlikely qualities to prioritize in a leader. By our standards, Henry *was* a cruel zealot, quick to judge and fight, frigid and stiff-necked, impatient, exacting, unforgiving, largely sexless, and mostly humorless. Seen from the perspective of an age that positively embraces vulnerability, Henry can be a hard character to like, or even to admire. Our values are not his. His are not ours. We do not need to pretend otherwise.

History, however, is not a congeniality contest. How we rate Henry for likability today is of little consequence. What matters is what he did in his own time, how he optimized for the standards of his own age, and what the consequences were of his relatively short life and reign.

This is a more straightforward assessment to make. In his day, the weight of opinion was that Henry was somewhere close to the paragon of kingship, measured both by his personal bearing and by his political and military achievements.

As a prince he navigated a long apprenticeship, largely successfully, and though he clashed with his father as the transition to rule approached, he stopped just short of allowing his personal frustrations to boil over into full-blown political crisis. He was unusually alert to the lessons that his youth and adolescence taught him: learning as much from the dazzling theatrical kingship of Richard II as he did from the dogged pragmatism of his father, and applying the best of both styles to his own rule when the time came.

As a result, his actions were endorsed time and again by a political community that was well practiced in making trouble for kings they felt were working against their common interest. The evidence of his times cannot be read without concluding that Henry presented to most of his contemporaries as a rare leader who had somehow secured the full approval of God: a man whom they could trust with their money, their faith, and their lives; a general who would hold his nerve, come what may, never weakened or moved by sentimentality, but utterly consumed by the act of leadership.

This, in the end, is as much as we can say, and as much as Henry could have done. I hope in this book, in which I have tried to move us as close as the surviving evidence allows to the immediacy of Henry's decisions—the pressures that weighed on him, the dangers he faced, and the rare moments of calm, quiet, and pleasure he enjoyed—I have presented a Henry who is a little more rounded and human than is often available to us outside the imaginative realms of theater and cinema. For all that he can be hard to find—for all that Henry actively tried to hide himself—there was a man behind the mask, who was complex and sometimes conflicted, despite the rare array of abilities and experience with which he was blessed.

It is sometimes suggested today that Henry V was lucky to have died when he did—before he got unlucky and lost, before the war turned in the dauphin's favor, before the strain of sustaining the dream of the dual kingdom exhausted French and English taxpayers alike. And it is certainly possible to argue that the greatest weakness of Henry's policies was the degree to which their success rested squarely on his own shoulders.

Yet to criticize him for being too successful, and to assume that he would have been helpless when the tide went out on his campaigns, is to underestimate Henry, and to ignore the frequency with which he defied what was considered politically and militarily possible by everyone but him. He believed he would win the war in France and go on to lead a successful crusade. We may snigger into our sleeves, but as we do so, we must remember that those who doubted Henry in his lifetime were usually proven wrong.

Henry's contemporaries saw in him a paragon of Christian, knightly virtue and the living embodiment of traditional kingship. They perceived—rightly—a ruler who made the systems of English government work as they were supposed to without resorting to novelty or swindling the system. They saw a defender of religious orthodoxy and a severe but consistent disciplinarian who seldom acted rashly or unpredictably and usually kept his word. They saw a master of war who learned from his mistakes and proved, until his final illness, freakishly hard to kill.

To know that the sixteen-year-old boy who lay close to death in Kenilworth Castle after the battle of Shrewsbury, awaiting the surgeon John Bradmore's knife, should have survived, let alone grown up to become such a man, would have shocked anyone who heard it.

Anyone, that is, except Henry V.

NOTES

INTRODUCTION

1. Winston Churchill, *History of the English-Speaking Peoples: Volume 1, The Birth of Britain* (London: Cassell and Company Ltd., 1956), 247.

1. THE BOY IN THE BLACK STRAW HAT

1. The dedication image in a Lancastrian family psalter shows Mary de Bohun kneeling between her namesakes Mary Magdalene and Mary the Virgin. She asks Christ, sitting in his mother's lap, to have mercy upon her. Bodleian MS. Auct. D. 4. 4 181v. For context see Jill C. Havens, "A Gift, a Mirror, a Memorial: The Psalter-Hours of Mary de Bohun," in *Medieval Women and Their Objects*, eds. Jenny Adams and Nancy Mason Bradbury (Ann Arbor: University of Michigan Press, 2017), 144–70.
2. *The Book of Margery Kempe*, trans. William Erdeswick Ignatius Butler-Bowdon. (London: Oxford University Press, 1954), 9, 63.
3. Not the second, as sometimes stated. See Anne Curry, *Henry V: From Playboy Prince to Warrior King* (London: Allen Lane, 2015), 3.
4. The treatise is entitled *Nativitas Nocturna*. For details, see Hilary Mary Carey, *Courting Disaster: Astrology at the English Court and University in the Later Middle Ages* (London: Macmillan, 1992), 129.
5. The name "young lord Henry" is that given to him in his family's accounts. See Curry, "The Making of a Prince: The Finances of the 'Young Lord Henry,' 1386–1400," in *Henry V: New Interpretations*, ed. Gwilym Dodd (Woodbridge, UK: York Medieval Press, University of York, 2013), 13.
6. Josiah Cox Russell, *British Medieval Population* (Albuquerque: University of New Mexico Press, 1948), 146. This figure is based on analysis of the 1377 poll tax returns.
7. The most recent history of the Peasants' Revolt of 1381 is Juliet Barker, *England, Arise: The People, the King and the Great Revolt of 1381* (London: Little, Brown Book Group, 2014).
8. Thomas Aquinas, *On Kingship to the King of Cyprus*, trans. Gerald B. Phelan (Toronto: Pontifical Institute of Mediaeval Studies, 1949), 6. For the field of conceptions of the composition of society and the medieval state (if such a thing existed), the best introduction is James Henderson Burns, *The Cambridge History of Medieval Political Thought: c. 350–c. 1450* (Cambridge: Cambridge University Press, 1988).
9. On Bolingbroke's childhood relationship with Richard II, see Chris Given-Wilson, *Henry IV* (New Haven; London: Yale University Press, 2016), 29–47.
10. George B. Stow, "Richard II in Thomas Walsingham's Chronicles," *Speculum* 59 (1984): 87–88.
11. Christopher Allmand, *Henry V*, new ed. (New Haven; London: Yale University Press, 1997), 8.

12. Nicholas Orme, *From Childhood to Chivalry: The Education of the English Kings and Aristocracy, 1066–1530* (London: Routledge, 2017), 3. This may be an underestimate—childhood mortality is rated closer to an astonishing 60 percent by G. Hühne-Osterloh and G. Grupe in "Causes of Infant Mortality in the Middle Ages Revealed by Chemical and Palaeopathological Analyses of Skeletal Remains," *Zeitschrift für Morphologie und Anthropologie* 77, no. 3 (1989): 247–58.
13. S. K. Cohn Jr., "Epidemiology of the Black Death and Successive Waves of Plague," *Medical History Supplement* 27 (2008): 74–100.
14. Rosemary Horrox, trans. and ed., *The Black Death* (Manchester; UK: Manchester University Press, 1994), 193–94.
15. Margaret Amassian, "A Verse Life of John of Bridlington," *Neuphilologische Mitteilungen* 71, no. 1 (1970): 136–45.
16. James Hamilton Wylie, *The History of England under Henry IV* (London: Longmans & Co, 1884–1898), vol. 3, 335–36.
17. Orme, *From Childhood to Chivalry*, 6; M. A. Jonker, "Estimation of Life Expectancy in the Middle Ages," *Journal of the Royal Statistical Society* 166 (2003): 105–17.
18. For his petticoats, or "demigown," Wylie, *Henry IV*, vol. 3, 325–26.
19. Wylie, *Henry IV*, vol. 3, 177.
20. Orme, *From Childhood to Chivalry*, 13.
21. Given-Wilson, *Henry IV*, 77–78.
22. *Versus Rhythmici*, in *Memorials of Henry the Fifth, King of England*, ed. Charles Augustus Cole (London: Longman, Brown, Green, Longmans, and Roberts, 1858), 64.
23. Wylie, *Henry IV*, vol. 3, 327.
24. Russell Hope Robbins, ed., *Historical Poems of the XIVth and XVth Centuries* (New York: Columbia University Press, 1959), 231.
25. Partially preserved in the British Library MS Royal 20 D III and IV. For the illustration Royal D IV f. 1r.
26. K. B. McFarlane, *Lancastrian Kings and Lollard Knights* (Oxford: Clarendon Press, 1972), 115.
27. Jeanne E. Krochalis, "The Books and Reading of Henry V and His Circle," *Chaucer Review* 23 (1988): 61.
28. Judging by the speed with which he orders her new tomb on becoming king. See chapter 18.

2. THE PRICE OF PEACE

1. Curry, "Making of a Prince," 13.
2. Louis François Bellaguet, ed., *Chronique du Religieux de Saint-Denys, Contenant le Règne de Charles VI., de 1380 à 1422* (Paris: Crapelet, 1839–1852) vol. 2, 446.
3. Bellaguet, *Chronique du Religieux de Saint-Denys*, vol. 2, 455.
4. *Chronica Maiora of Thomas Walsingham, 1376–1422*, ed. David Preest (Woodbridge, UK: Boydell, 2005), 296.
5. *Sir John Froissart's Chronicles of England, France, Spain and the Adjoining Countries* vol. 11, 338–40.
6. Sir John Clanvowe, quoted in Jonathan Sumption, *Divided Houses: The Hundred Years War III* (London: Faber, 2011), 776.
7. Jean de Montreuil, quoted in Kelly DeVries and Michael Livingston, eds., *Medieval Warfare: A Reader* (Toronto: University of Toronto Press, 2019), 31.
8. Jean de Montreuil, quoted in DeVries and Livingston, *Medieval Warfare*, 823–24.
9. English narrative of the meeting between Richard II and Charles VI preserved in Oxford, Oriel College MS 46 ff 104v-106. Most easily accessed in Jenny Stratford, *Richard II and the English Royal Treasure* (Woodbridge, UK: The Boydell Press, 2012), 387–91.
10. "Annales Ricardi Secundi et Henrici Quarti, Regum Angliae," in Henry T. Riley, ed., *Johannis de Trokelowe et Henrici de Blaneforde, monachorum S. Albani, necnon quorundam anonymo-rum chronica et annales, regnantibus Henrico Tertio, Edwardo Primo, Edwardo Secundo, Ricardo Secundo, et Henrico Quarto* (London: Longmans & Co, 1866), 189.
11. Bellaguet, *Chronique du Religieux de Saint- Denys*, 463.

3. "BEHOLD, I WILL OPEN YOUR GRAVES"

1. Curry, "Making of a Prince," 14.
2. *Knighton's Chronicle, 1337–1396*, ed. G. H. Martin (Oxford: Clarendon Press, 1995), 422–23.
3. *Knighton's Chronicle*, 422–23.
4. "Vita Ricardi Secundi," 137–38, in *Chronicles of the Revolution, 1397–1400: The Reign of Richard II*, ed. and trans. Christopher Given-Wilson (Manchester: Manchester University Press, 1993), 55.
5. "Vita Ricardi Secundi," 138, in Given-Wilson, *Chronicles of the Revolution*, 55.
6. Thomas Walsingham, "Annales Ricardi Secundi," 199–239, trans. in Given-Wilson, *Chronicles of the Revolution*, 73.
7. "Richard II: September 1397, Part 1," in *Parliament Rolls of Medieval England*, British History Online, british-history.ac.uk/no-series/parliament-rolls-medieval/september-1397-pt-1.
8. "Richard II: September 1397, Part 1," in *Parliament Rolls of Medieval England*.
9. For Bussy's political career, see John Smith Roskell, Linda Clark, and Carole Rawcliffe, eds., *The House of Commons, 1386–1421* (Sutton: Boydell & Brewer, 1992), vol. 2, 449–54.
10. Chris Given-Wilson, ed., *The Chronicle of Adam Usk 1377–1421* (Oxford: Clarendon Press, 1997), 28–29.
11. Given-Wilson, *Adam Usk*, 30–31.
12. "Vita Ricardi Secundi," in Given-Wilson, *Chronicles of the Revolution*, 60.
13. *Chronica Maiora*, 300–301.
14. "Annales Ricardi Secundi," in Riley, *Johannis de Trokelowe*, 218.
15. Given-Wilson, *Adam Usk*, 30–31.
16. "Vita Ricardi Secundi," in Given-Wilson, *Chronicles of the Revolution*, 61.
17. Walsingham, "Annales Ricardi Secundi," 74.

4. ROUGH JUSTICE

1. K. B. McFarlane, *The Nobility of Later Medieval England: The Ford Lectures for 1953 and Related Studies* (Oxford: Clarendon Press, 1973), 243.
2. The classic account of Richard's tyranny from 1397 is Caroline M. Barron, "The Tyranny of Richard II," *Bulletin of the Institute of Historical Research* 41, no. 103 (May 1968): 1–18.
3. Walsingham, "Annales Ricardi Secundi," 74.
4. The so-called Wilton Diptych is one of the treasures of the National Gallery in London. See Dillian Gordon, *The Wilton Diptych* (London: National Gallery Company, 2015).
5. Nigel Saul, in *Richard II* (London: Yale University Press, 1997), 459–65, plumps for narcissism, over earlier historical diagnoses of schizophrenia.
6. "Short Kirkstall Chronicle," in Given-Wilson, *Chronicles of the Revolution*, 96.
7. This translation via Charles Lethbridge Kingsford, ed., *The First English Life of King Henry V* (Oxford: Clarendon Press, 1911), 8. Cf. original source, Titus Livius de Frulovisiis, *Livii Foro-Juliensis Vita Henrici Quinti, Regis Angliæ*, ed. Thomas Hearne (Oxford: n.p., 1716), 3.
8. "Richard II: September 1397, Part 2," in *Parliament Rolls of Medieval England*.
9. "Richard II: September 1397, Part 2," in *Parliament Rolls of Medieval England*.
10. Given-Wilson, *Henry IV*, 62.
11. Given-Wilson, *Henry IV*, 72–74.
12. Given-Wilson, *Henry IV*, 113.
13. Benjamin Williams, *Chronicque de la Traïson et Mort de Richart Deux Roy Dengleterre* (London: English Historical Society, 1846), 152.
14. Williams, *Chronicque de la Traïson*, 156.
15. Williams, *Chronicque de la Traïson*, 157.
16. Williams, *Chronicque de la Traïson*, 158.
17. Froissart believed that the king had commuted Bolingbroke's sentence to six years even before he left England. *Froissart*, vol. 12, 55–56.
18. Given-Wilson, *Adam Usk*, 50–51.
19. Jenny Stratford, "John [John of Lancaster], duke of Bedford (1389–1435), regent of France and prince," *Oxford Dictionary of National Biography* 23 Sep. 2004; Accessed 21 May. 2024. https://

www.oxforddnb.com/view/10.1093/ref:odnb/9780198614128.001.0001/odnb-9780198614128-e-14844.

5. "FAIR COUSIN"

1. *Froissart*, vol. 12, 64, 83.
2. Orme, *From Childhood to Chivalry*, 166.
3. Charles Lethbridge Kingsford, *Henry V: The Typical Mediaeval Hero* (New York: G. P. Putnam's Sons, 1901).
4. McFarlane, *Lancastrian Kings and Lollard Knights*, 116.
5. Curry, "Making of a Prince," 18–19.
6. *The Orygynale Cronykil of Scotland by Andrew of Wyntoun*, vol. 3, ed. David Laing (Edinburgh: Edmonston & Douglas, 1879), 68.
7. Described in his will, when he left it to St. Paul's Cathedral. The will is printed in James Raine, *Testamenta Eboracensia; or, Wills Registered at York, Illustrative of the History, Manners, Language, Statistics, etc., of the Province of York, from the Year 1300 Downwards*, vol. 1 (London: Publications of the Surtees Society, 1836), 223–39.
8. *Froissart*, vol. 12, 87.
9. *The Orygynale Cronykil of Scotland by Andrew of Wyntoun*, 69.
10. Thomas Gascoigne, *Loci e Libro Veritatum. Passages Selected from Gascoigne's Theologica Dictionary, Illustrating the Condition of Church and State, 1403–1458*, ed. James Edwin Thorold Rogers (Oxford: Clarendon Press, 1881), 137.
11. Sometimes given, probably incorrectly, as February 4. See J. B. Post, "The Obsequies of John of Gaunt," *Guildhall Studies in London History* 5 (1981): 1–12.
12. Gascoigne, *Loci e Libro Veritatum*, 137.
13. Wylie, *Henry IV*, vol. 2, 436.
14. Post, "The Obsequies of John of Gaunt," 4.
15. *Froissart*, vol. 12, 90.
16. See Roskell et al., *House of Commons*, vol. 3, 713.
17. Curry, "Making of a Prince," 13.
18. This chronology is suggested and convincingly argued from the records by Curry, "Making of a Prince," 21.
19. Curry, "Making of a Prince," 90.
20. Saul, *Richard II*, 270–73. See also S. Egan, "Richard II and the Wider Gaelic World: A Reassessment," *Journal of British Studies* 57, no. 2 (2018): 221–52, and references therein.
21. Sir Harris Nicolas, ed., *Proceedings and Ordinances of the Privy Council of England*, vol. 1 (London: Record Commission, 1834), 56.
22. J. Webb, "Translation of a French Metrical History of the Deposition of King Richard the Second," *Archaeologia* 20 (1824): 22.
23. Webb, "Translation of a French Metrical History," 30.
24. Webb, "Translation of a French Metrical History," 29.
25. Webb, "Translation of a French Metrical History," 46.
26. Webb, "Translation of a French Metrical History," 50.
27. "Annales Ricardi Secundi," in Riley, *Johannis de Trokelowe*, 246–47.

6. "A MAN IS RULING"

1. Given-Wilson, *Adam Usk*, 56–57.
2. Given-Wilson, *Adam Usk*, 54–55.
3. Given-Wilson, *Adam Usk*, 54–55.
4. Given-Wilson, *Adam Usk*, 61.
5. Krochalis, "Books and Reading of Henry V," 51–52.
6. Webb, "Translation of a French Metrical History," 149–51.
7. Webb, "Translation of a French Metrical History," 181.
8. Williams, *Chronicque de la Traïson*," 181.

9. "The Record and Process of the renunciation of King Richard the Second since the conquest and of the acceptance of the same renunciation, together with the deposition of the same King Richard," in Given-Wilson, *Chronicles of the Revolution*, 169–89.
10. "The Manner of King Richard's Renunciation," in Given-Wilson, *Chronicles of the Revolution*, 163.
11. Given-Wilson, *Adam Usk*, 64–65.
12. "Manner of King Richard's Renunciation," in Given Wilson, *Chronicles of the Revolution*, 163.
13. "Record and Process," in Given-Wilson, *Chronicles of the Revolution*, 186.
14. "Record and Process," in Given-Wilson, *Chronicles of the Revolution*, 186.
15. On the "closed" imperial crown used for this coronation, and its probable design by Richard II, Given-Wilson, *Henry IV*, 152.
16. Given-Wilson, *Adam Usk*, 50–53. See also Michael J. Bennett, "Prophecy, Providence and the Revolution of 1399," in *Prophecy, Apocalypse and the Day of Doom*, ed. Nigel Morgan (Linconshire: Paul Watkins Publishing, 2004), 1–18.

7. PRINCE OF WALES

1. Given-Wilson, *Adam Usk*, 78–79n3.
2. Given-Wilson, *Adam Usk*, 78–79.
3. "Annales Ricardi Secundi," in Riley, *Johannis de Trokelowe*, 322.
4. Given-Wilson, *Adam Usk*, 88–89.
5. "Vita Ricardi Secundi," in Given-Wilson, *Chronicles of the Revolution*, 241.
6. Webb, "Translation of a French Metrical History," 221, suggests that the body displayed in London was that of Richard's manservant "Maudelain."
7. *Rymer's Foedera*, vol. 8, British History Online, 75–76.
8. *Versus Rhythmici*, in Cole, *Memorials of Henry the Fifth*, 65.
9. *Liber Metricus*, in Cole, *Memorials of Henry the Fifth*, 136–50.
10. For a detailed account of the campaign, see A. L. Brown, "The English Campaign in Scotland, 1400," in *British Government and Administration: Studies Presented to S.B. Chrimes*, eds. H. R. Loyn and H. Hearder, (Cardiff: University of Wales Press, 1974), 40–54.
11. Gruffudd Llwyd, "Owain's Exploits in Scotland," in *Owain Glwndŵr: A Casebook* eds. Michale Livingston and John K. Bollard (Liverpool: Liverpool University Press, 2013), 12–13.
12. For as good an attempt to construct a personal portrait of Glyndŵr as is possible, see Davies, *The Revolt of Owain Glyn Dŵr* (Oxford: Oxford University Press, 1995), 129–52.
13. Curry, *Henry V*, 13.
14. *Froissart*, vol. 9, 248.
15. Given-Wilson, *Adam Usk*, 170–71.
16. D. M. Nicol, "A Byzantine Emperor in England: Manuel II's Visit to London in 1400–1401," in *University of Birmingham Historical Journal* 12 (1970): 204–25.
17. "Henry IV: January 1401," in *Parliament Rolls of Medieval England*, British History Online, british-history.ac.uk/no-series/parliament-rolls-medieval/january-1401.
18. Keith Williams-Jones, "The Taking of Conwy Castle, 1401," in *Transactions of the Caernarvonshire Historical Society* 39 (1978): 7–43.
19. Given-Wilson, *Adam Usk*, 128–29.
20. M. Dominica Legge, ed. *Anglo-Norman Letters and Petitions from All Souls MS. 182* (Oxford: Anglo-Norman Text Society, 1941), 310–12.
21. Livingston and Bollard, *Owain Glyndŵr*, 54–55.

8. "GREAT PAIN AND DILIGENCE"

1. Francis Charles Hingeston, ed., *Royal and Historical Letters During the Reign of Henry the Fourth, King of England and of France, and Lord of Ireland* (London: Longman & Co, 1860), 71.
2. Wylie, *Henry IV*, vol. 1, 232.
3. Given-Wilson, *Adam Usk*, 146–47.
4. The messengers were caught and beheaded; their letters are preserved in Given-Wilson, *Adam Usk*, 148–53.

5. "Annales Ricardi Secundi," in Riley, *Johannis de Trokelowe*, 341.
6. Given-Wilson, *Adam Usk*, 160–61.
7. Given-Wilson, *Adam Usk*, 160–61.
8. Wylie, *Henry IV*, vol. 1, 310.
9. Allmand, *Henry V*, 24n30.
10. Livingston and Bollard, *Owain Glyndŵr*, 80–83.
11. For a discussion of the Percy family's grievances, and a clear examination of the lines of credit they extended to Henry IV's treasury, J. M. W. Bean, "Henry IV and the Percies," *History* 44 (1959): 212–27.
12. According to the Dieulacres Chronicle, in M. V. Clarke and V. H. Galbraith, "The Deposition of Richard II," *Bulletin of the John Rylands Library* 14 (1930): 177–78.
13. Frank Scott Haydon, ed., *Eulogium Historiarum sive Temporis*, vol. 3 (London: Longman & Co, 1863), 397.
14. Wylie, *Henry IV*, vol. 1, 358.
15. Wylie, *Henry IV*, vol. 1, 359.
16. "Annales Ricardi Secundi," in Riley, *Johannis de Trokelowe*, 365.
17. Dieulacres Chronicle, in M. V. Clarke and V. H. Galbraith, "The Deposition of Richard II," 179.
18. Friedrich W. D. Brie, ed., *The Brut, or, The Chronicles of England*, vol. 2 (London: Kegan Paul, Trench, Trübner & Co., 1908), 549.
19. Given-Wilson, *Henry IV*, 225.
20. Wylie, *Henry IV*, 362.
21. The Wigmore chronicler, quoted in Given-Wilson, *Henry IV*, 226.
22. On the likely removal of the arrow shaft from the arrow that hits Henry, I follow Michael Livingston, *Agincourt: Battle of the Scarred King* (London: Osprey Publishing, 2023), 28.

9. "HIS MIRACULOUS POWER"

1. Michael Livingston, "The Depth of Six Inches Prince Hal's Head-Wound at the Battle of Shrewsbury" in *Wounds and Wound Repair in Medieval Culture*, eds. Larissa Tracey and Kelly DeVries (Leiden: Brill, 2015), 215–30. For Bradmore's notes, DeVries and Livingston, *Medieval Warfare*, 284–85.
2. Livingston, *Agincourt*, 32.
3. Allmand, *Henry V*, 27.
4. On the shrine's appearance, John Jenkins, ed., *The Customary of the Shrine of St. Thomas Becket at Canterbury Cathedral* (Leeds: Arc Humanities Press, 2022), 12–14.
5. Geoffrey Chaucer, "General Prologue," *Canterbury Tales*, lines 17–18, in *The Riverside Chaucer*, eds. Larry D. Benson and F. N. Robinson, 3rd ed. (Oxford: Oxford University Press, 2008), 23.
6. *Ninth Report of Royal Commission of Manuscripts* (London: Eyre and Spottiswoode for HMSO 1883), 138.
7. J. C. Dickinson, *The Shrine of Our Lady of Walsingham* (Cambridge: Cambridge University Press, 1956), 29.
8. "Henry IV: January 1404," in *Parliament Rolls of Medieval England*, British History Online, british-history.ac.uk/no-series/parliament-rolls-medieval/january-1404.
9. R. Griffiths, "Prince Henry and Wales, 1400–1408," in *Profit, Piety and the Professions in Later Medieval England*, ed. Michael A. Hicks (Gloucester: Sutton, 1990), 55–56.
10. Translated in Frederick Solly-Flood, "Prince Henry of Monmouth: His Letters and Despatches during the War in Wales, 1402–1405," *Transactions of the Royal Historical Society* 4 (1889): 133.
11. Griffiths, "Prince Henry and Wales," 58.
12. "Henry IV: October 1404," in *Parliament Rolls of Medieval England*, British History Online, british-history.ac.uk/no-series/parliament-rolls-medieval/october-1404.
13. Solly-Flood, "Prince Henry of Monmouth," 136.
14. Solly-Flood, "Prince Henry of Monmouth," 137.
15. Solly-Flood, "Prince Henry of Monmouth," 133–36.

10. CRIMES AND PUNISHMENTS

1. Given-Wilson, *Henry IV*, 267–69.
2. Haydon, *Eulogium* 408.
3. Gascoigne, *Loci e Libro Veritatum*, 228.
4. The standard discussion of Henry IV's illness is Peter McNiven, "The Problem of Henry IV's Health, 1405–1413," *English Historical Review* 100, no. 397 (1985): 747–72.
5. Gascoigne, *Loci e Libro Veritatum*, 228.
6. Nicolas, *Proceedings and Ordinances*, vol. 1, 275.
7. Wylie, *Henry IV*, vol. 4, 153.
8. This interpretation of the 1406 parliament is best laid out by Douglas Biggs, "The Politics of Health: Henry IV and the Long Parliament of 1406," in *Henry IV: The Establishment of the Regime, 1399–1406* eds. Gwilym Dodd and Douglas Biggs (Woodbridge, UK: York Medieval Press in association with Boydell Press, 2003), 185–202.
9. "Henry IV: March 1406, Part 1," in *Parliament Rolls of Medieval England*, British History Online, british-history.ac.uk/no-series/parliament -rolls-medieval/march-1406-pt-1.
10. Biggs, "The Politics of Health," 196.
11. "Henry IV: March 1406, Part 1," in *Parliament Rolls of Medieval England.*
12. "Henry IV: October 1399, Part 1," in *Parliament Rolls of Medieval England*, British History Online, https://www.british-history.ac.uk/no-series/parliament-rolls-medieval/october-1399-pt-1.
13. "Henry IV: March 1406, Part 1," in *Parliament Rolls of Medieval England.*

11. "VIRTUOUS PRINCE"

1. Given-Wilson, *Henry IV*, 293.
2. Douglas Biggs, "The Politics of Health," 198–99.
3. Wylie, *Henry IV*, vol. 2, 442–43.
4. Wylie, *Henry IV*, vol. 2, 444–45.
5. The book of hours is held by Det Kongelige Bibliotek in Copenhagen, MS Thott 547. It can be viewed online at www5.kb.dk/permalink/2006/manus/76. See also Krochalis, "Books and Reading of Henry V," 54.
6. Roskell et. al, *House of Commons*, vol. 3, 713.
7. Griffiths, "Prince Henry and Wales," 56–57.
8. "Henry IV: March 1406, Part 1," in *Parliament Rolls of Medieval England.*
9. "Henry IV: March 1406, Part 1," in *Parliament Rolls of Medieval England.*
10. Davies, *Revolt of Owain Glyn Dŵr*, 124.
11. For the relatively paltry bill for repairs after the siege, see R. A. Brown, H. M. Colvin, and A. J. Taylor, eds., *The History of the King's Works: The Middle Ages*, vol. 1 (London: Ministry of Public Building and Works, 1963), 308.
12. *Chronica Maiora*, 358.
13. "Henry IV: October 1407," in *Parliament Rolls of Medieval England*, British History Online, british -history.ac.uk/no-series/parliament-rolls-medieval/october-1407.
14. "Henry IV: October 1407," in *Parliament Rolls of Medieval England.*
15. *Chronica Maiora*, 358; Allmand, *Henry V*, 32n78.
16. *Chronica Maiora*, 361.
17. "Annales Owain Glyndwr," in Livingston and Bollard, *Owain Glyndŵr*, 174–75.
18. See Livingston and Bollard, *Owain Glyndŵr*, 218–19.
19. Given-Wilson, *Adam Usk*, 160–61.

12. COUPS AND COUNCILS

1. For the background to and narrative of Louis d'Orléans's murder, see Jonathan Sumption, *Cursed Kings: The Hundred Years War IV* (London: Faber, 2015), 234–45.

2. Wylie, *Henry IV*, vol. 3, 239.
3. Henry's will is printed in John Nichols and Richard Gough, eds., *A Collection of All the Wills Now Known to Be Extant of the Kings and Queens of England* (London: John Nichols, 1780), 203–5.
4. Wylie, *Henry IV*, vol. 3, 245.
5. Given-Wilson, *Henry IV*, 464n1.
6. Livingston and Bollard, *Owain Glyndŵr*, 134–35.
7. These were some of the dishes served at the Smithfield (London) jousts of July 1409. For the full menu, see Mrs. Alexander Napier, ed., *A Noble Boke Off Cookry ffor a Pynce Houssolde or Eny Other Estately Houssolde* (London: Elliot Stock, 1882), 5–6.
8. Given-Wilson, *Henry IV*, 466n5.
9. *Calendar of the Patent Rolls Preserved in the Public Record Office—Henry IV, Vol. 4, 1408–1413*. (London: Anthony Brothers Limited, 1909), 113.
10. J. L. Kirby, "Councils and Councilors of Henry IV, 1399–1413," *Transactions of the Royal Historical Society* 14 (1964): 62–65.
11. *La Chronique d'Enguerran de Monstrelet Avec Pièces Justificatives, 1400–1444*, vol. 1, ed. L. Douët-d'Arcq (Paris: Vueve J. Renouard, 1857), 126.

13. HOLY FIRE

1. The standard text on the Badby case is Peter McNiven, *Heresy and Politics in the Reign of Henry IV: The Burning of John Badby* (Woodbridge, UK: Boydell, 1987).
2. *Chronica Maiora*, 372.
3. "Henry IV: January 1401," in *Parliament Rolls of Medieval England*.
4. *Chronica Maiora*, 375.
5. "Henry IV: January 1410," in *Parliament Rolls of Medieval England*, British History Online, british-history.ac.uk/no-series/parliament-rolls-medieval/january-1410.
6. McNiven, *Heresy and Politics in the Reign of Henry IV*, 216.
7. "Gregory's Chronicle: 1403–1419," in *The Historical Collections of a Citizen of London in the Fifteenth Century*, ed. James Gairdner (London: Camden Society, 1876), 103–28, british-history.ac.uk/camden-record-soc/vol17/pp103-128.
8. Gairdner, "Gregory's Chronicle."
9. *Chronica Maiora*, 376.
10. *Chronica Maiora*, 376.
11. "Henry IV: January 1410," in *Parliament Rolls of Medieval England*.
12. Nicolas, *Proceedings and Ordinances of the Privy Council*, vol. 1, 351; Curry, *Henry V*, 24.
13. Nicolas, *Proceedings and Ordinances of the Privy Council*, vol. 1, 348.
14. Given-Wilson, *Henry IV*, 473.
15. J. L. Bolton, *The Medieval English Economy, 1150–1500* (London: Dent, 1980), 297–98.
16. See particularly Helen Castor, *The King, the Crown, and the Duchy of Lancaster: Public Authority and Private Power 1399–1461*. (Oxford: Oxford University Press, 2000), 212–24.

14. BALLADS AND BRAWLS

1. Krochalis, "Books and Reading of Henry V," 50–77.
2. John Stow, "Vintrie warde," in *A Survey of London. Reprinted from the Text of 1603*. ed. Kingsford (Oxford: Clarendon Press, 1908), 238–50, British History Online, british-history.ac.uk/no-series/survey-of-london-stow/1603/pp238-250.
3. Stow, "Vintrie warde."
4. Walter W. Skeat, *Chaucerian and Other Pieces* (Oxford: Clarendon Press, 1897), 237–44.
5. Walter W. Skeat, *The Complete Works of Geoffrey Chaucer*, vol. 7 (Oxford: Oxford University Press), 237–44.
6. Gairdner, "Gregory's Chronicle."
7. John Stow, "Candlewicke streete warde," in *A Survey of London*, 216–23, British History Online, british-history.ac.uk/no-series/survey-of-london-stow/1603/pp216-223.
8. Chaucer, *Troilus and Criseyde*, book 1, line 34, in Benson and Robinson, *The Riverside Chaucer*, 473.

9. Chaucer, *Troilus and Criseyde*, book 5, lines 1745, 1749–50, in Benson and Robinson, *The Riverside Chaucer*, 573.
10. Cf. Lydgate's prologue to the Troy Book: *Lydgate's Troy Book: A.D. 1412–20, Part 1*, ed. Henry Bergen (London: Early English Text Society, 1906), 3.
11. A rather dated modern edition exists: Edward, Second Duke of York, *The Master of Game*, eds. William A. Baillie-Grohman and F. Baillie-Grohman (London: Chatto & Windus, 1909).
12. Baillie-Grohman and Baillie-Grohman, *Master of Game*, 4, 11.
13. Krochalis, "Books and Reading of Henry V," 50–62.
14. Thomas Hoccleve, *The Regiment of Princes*, ed. Charles Blyth (Kalamazoo: Medieval Institute, 1999), 103.
15. Hoccleve, *The Regiment of Princes*, 123.
16. Hoccleve, *The Regiment of Princes*, 41.
17. Chaucer, *Troilus and Criseyde*, book 3, line 615, in Benson and Robinson, *The Riverside Chaucer*, 522.

15. "THE STORM OF DESCENDING"

1. Sumption, *Cursed Kings*, 284.
2. The standard account of this crisis is Peter McNiven, "Prince Henry and the English Political Crisis of 1412," *History* 65, no. 213 (1980): 1–16.
3. Curry, *Henry V*, 26.
4. Wylie, *Henry IV*, vol. 4, 60.
5. For ointment, Wylie, *Henry IV*, vol. 4, 62.
6. John Silvester Davies, ed., *An English Chronicle of the Reigns of Richard II, Henry IV, Henry V and Henry VI, Written Before 1470* (London: Camden Society, 1856), 36.
7. Chris Given-Wilson, ed., *Continuatio Eulogii: The Continuation of the Eulogium Historiarum, 1364–1413* (Oxford: Clarendon Press, 2019), 158–59. The chronicler assigns this event to 1413, but it seems almost certainly to belong to the autumn of 1411.
8. Johannes Allen, ed., Giles, *Incerti Scriptoris Chronicon Angliae* (London: D. Nutt, 1848), 63.
9. "Henry IV: November 1411," in *Parliament Rolls of Medieval England*, British History Online, https://www.british-history.ac.uk/no-series/parliament-rolls-medieval/november-1411.
10. "Henry IV: November 1411," in *Parliament Rolls of Medieval England*.
11. Sumption, *Cursed Kings*, 310.
12. *Chronica Maiora*, 387.
13. Wylie, *Henry IV*, vol. 4, 72–73.

16. "SONS OF INIQUITY"

1. R. L. J. Shaw (May 21, 2009), "Holland [married name Beaufort], Margaret, duchess of Clarence (b. in or before 1388, d. 1439), wealthy widow and monastic patron," *Oxford Dictionary of National Biography*. 4 Oct. 2008; Accessed 24 May. 2024. https://www.oxforddnb.com/view/10.1093/ref:odnb/9780198614128.001.0001/odnb-9780198614128-e-98133.
2. Hoccleve, *The Regiment of Princes*, 103.
3. The letter is printed in B. A. Pocquet du Haut-Jussé, "La Renaissance Littéraire Autour de Henri V, Roi d'Angleterre (Deux Lettres Inédites, 1412)," *Revue Historique* 224, no. 2 (1960): 335–36.
4. This story is later recounted by Beaufort during the parliament of 1426. "Henry VI: February 1426," in *Parliament Rolls of Medieval England*, British History Online, https://www.british-history.ac.uk/no-series/parliament-rolls-medieval/february-1426.
5. The letter is preserved by Thomas Walsingham, who places it in his chronicle directly after a passage explaining that Henry IV had put the French invasion in the hands of Thomas. *Chronica Maiora*, 386.
6. A convincing parse of Henry's claims in his letter may be found in McNiven, "Prince Henry and the English Political Crisis of 1412."
7. *Chronica Maiora*, 387.
8. Kingsford, *First English Life*, 11–12.
9. Kingsford, *First English Life*, 11–12.
10. Given-Wilson, *Henry IV*, 513.

11. John Capgrave, *The Book of the Illustrious Henries*, trans. Francis Charles Hingman (London: Longmans & Co., 1858), 123–24.
12. Kingsford, *First English Life*, 14.
13. Jean de Wavrin, *A Collection of the Chronicles and Ancient Histories of Great Britain, Now Called England, from AD 1399 to AD 1422*, vol. 2., trans. and eds. William Hardy and Edward L. C. P. Hardy (London: Longmans & Co, 1887), 165–67.

17. "A DIFFERENT MAN"

1. Gairdner, "Gregory's Chronicle," 107. The claim that snow fell in London on Henry's coronation day: derives from Thomas of Walsingham and Adam Usk. It may be taken from both that snow fell heavily across much of England, and that this was connected with the event of the coronation. Neither Walsingham nor Usk, however, was in London.
2. *Chronica Maiora*, 389.
3. Given-Wilson, *Adam Usk*, 242–43.
4. Song of Songs 2:11–12. Quoted in, *Chronica Maiora*, 389.
5. Roskell et. al, *House of Commons*, vol. 3, 713.
6. Wylie, *Henry IV*, vol. 4, 111–14.
7. See Leopold George Wickham-Legg, ed., *English Coronation Records* (London: Archibald Constable, 1901), 172–90.
8. Allmand, *Henry V*, 65, makes a convincing case for the use of this oil.
9. *Versus Rhythmici*, in Cole, *Memorials of Henry the Fifth*, 58. For other details, Kingsford, *First English Life*, 16–17.
10. James Hamilton Wylie and James Templeton Waugh, *The Reign of Henry V* (Cambridge: Cambridge University Press, 1914–1929), vol. 1, 7.
11. *Chronica Maiora*, 289.
12. John S. Roskell and Frank Taylor, trans. and eds. *Gesta Henrici Quinti The Deeds of Henry the Fifth* (Oxford: Clarendon Press, 1975), 155.
13. Kingsford, *First English Life*, 17.
14. Brie, *The Brut*, vol. 2, 594–95.
15. Thomae de Elmham, *Vita et Gesta Henrici Quinti Angulorum Regis*, ed. Thomas Hearne (Oxford: Oxonii, 1727), 14.
16. Kingsford, *First English Life*, 17.
17. Kingsford, *First English Life*, 17.
18. Kingsford, *Henry V*, 87–91.
19. Kingsford, *First English Life*, 18–19.
20. Brie, *The Brut*, vol. 2, 594–95.
21. Curry, *Henry V*, 36.
22. Sumption, *Cursed Kings*, 366.
23. Malcolm Vale, *Henry V The Conscience of a King* (New Haven; London: Yale University Press, 2016), 219–20.

18. FALSE FRIENDS

1. Brown, Colvin, and Taylor, *History of the King's Works*, vol. 2, 970–77.
2. Wylie and Waugh, *Henry V*, vol. 1, 209.
3. See especially Gwilym Dodd, "Henry V's Establishment: Service, Loyalty and Reward in 1413," in Dodd, *Henry V: New Interpretations*, 35–61, and Allmand, *Henry V*, 349–55.
4. Ecclesiastes 37:16.
5. See G. L. Harriss, *Henry V: The Practice of Kingship* (Oxford: Oxford University Press, 1985), 144.
6. "Henry V: May 1413," in *Parliament Rolls of Medieval England*, British History Online, https://www.british-history.ac.uk/no-series/parliament-rolls-medieval/may-1413.
7. Robbins, *Historical Poems*, 45–46.
8. *Chronica Maiora*, 390.

9. Wylie and Waugh, *Henry V*, vol. 1, 244.
10. Wylie and Waugh, *Henry V*, 246.
11. *Chronica Maiora*, 390.
12. *Chronica Maiora*, 392.
13. *Chronica Maiora*, 393.
14. Roskell and Taylor, *Gesta Henrici Quinti*, 6–7.
15. Gairdner, "Gregory's Chronicle," 107.
16. Robbins, *Historical Poems*, 107–8.
17. Brown, Colvin, and Taylor, *History of the King's Works*, vol. 2, 1000–1001.
18. Brown, Colvin, and Taylor, *History of the King's Works*, vol. 2, 1000–1001.
19. Wylie, Henry the Fifth, 262.
20. See M. Jurkowski, "Henry V's Suppression of the Oldcastle Revolt," in Dodd, *Henry V: New Interpretations*, 109.
21. *Chronica Maiora*, 394.
22. Roskell and Taylor, *Gesta Henrici Quinti*, 9.

19. THE ROAD TO WAR

1. Kingsford, *First English Life*, 23.
2. Jurkowski, "Henry V's Suppression," 114–17.
3. Capgrave, *Book of the Illustrious Henries*, 128.
4. Roskell and Taylor, *Gesta Henrici Quinti*, 12–13.
5. Roskell and Taylor, *Gesta Henrici Quinti*, 15.
6. For his residence in the castle, Wylie and Waugh, *Henry V*, vol. 1, 322.
7. Given-Wilson, *Adam Usk*, 248–49.
8. "Henry V: April 1414," in *Parliament Rolls of Medieval England*, British History Online, https://www.british-history.ac.uk/no-series/parliament-rolls-medieval/april-1414.
9. The classic consideration of Henry's policy regarding law and order is E. Powell, "The Restoration of Law and Order," in Harriss, *Henry V*, 53–74.
10. Taylor, "The Chronicle of John Strecche," 147.
11. *Chronica Maiora*, 397.
12. Sumption, *Cursed Kings*, 385–86.
13. Brie, *The Brut*, vol. 2, 595–96.
14. "Henry V: November 1414," in *Parliament Rolls of Medieval England*, British History Online, https://www.british-history.ac.uk/no-series/parliament-rolls-medieval/november-1414.

20. "FICKLE AND CAPRICIOUS FORTUNE"

1. E. Jamieson and R. Lane, "Monuments, Mobility and Medieval Perceptions of Designed Landscapes: The Pleasance, Kenilworth," *Medieval Archaeology* 59, no. 1 (2015): 255–71.
2. Brown, Colvin, and Taylor, *History of the King's Works*, vol. 2, 995–96.
3. *Liber Metricus*, in Cole, *Memorials of Henry the Fifth*, 100–101.
4. *Liber Metricus*, in Cole, *Memorials of Henry the Fifth*, 101.
5. John Strecche, *The Deeds of King Henry V*, ed. Geoffrey M. Hilton (Kenilworth: G M Hilton, 2014), 5.
6. Sumption, *Cursed Kings*, 410–12.
7. Harriss, *Henry V*, 163.
8. Sumption, *Cursed Kings*, 419.
9. Harriss, *Henry V*, 164.
10. Harriss, *Henry V*, 168–70.
11. Michael McCarthy, *Citizen of London: Richard Whittington, the Boy Who Would Be Mayor* (London: C Hurst & Co, 2022), 312.

12. Jenny Stratford, "'Par le special commandement du roy': Jewels and Plate Pledged for the Agincourt Expedition," in Dodd, *Henry V: New Interpretations*, 163.
13. Stratford, "'Par le special commandement du roy,'" 164.
14. For the naval aspect of preparations for Agincourt, see Craig Lambert, "Henry V and the Crossing to France: Reconstructing Naval Operations for the Agincourt Campaign, 1415," *Journal of Medieval History* 43 (2017): 24–39.
15. Lambert, "Henry V and the Crossing to France."
16. Brie, *The Brut*, vol. 2, 375.
17. The standard account of the Southampton Plot is T. B. Pugh, *Henry V and the Southampton Plot of 1415* (Southampton: Southampton University Press, 1988).
18. Given-Wilson, *Adam Usk*, 262–63.
19. *Chronica Maiora*, 407.
20. *Historia Henrici Quinti*, in Cole, *Memorials of Henry the Fifth*, 40–41.
21. *Chronica Maiora*, 407.
22. Vale, *Henry V*, 234.
23. Roskell and Taylor, *Gesta Henrici Quinti*. See also Wylie and Waugh, *Henry V*, vol. 2, 6.

21. "FIRES OF HELL"

1. Roskell and Taylor, *Gesta Henrici Quinti*, 22–23.
2. Roskell and Taylor, *Gesta Henrici Quinti*, 22–23.
3. Wylie and Waugh, *Henry V*, vol. 2, 15.
4. Roskell and Taylor, *Gesta Henrici Quinti*, 24–25.
5. Kingsford, *First English Life*, 33.
6. *La Chronique d'Enguerran de Monstrelet*, vol. 2, 79.
7. Roskell and Taylor, *Gesta Henrici Quinti*, 34–35.
8. Roskell and Taylor, *Gesta Henrici Quinti*, 36–37. See also Sumption, *Cursed Kings*, 435–36.
9. Deuteronomy 20:10–15.
10. Wylie and Waugh, *Henry V*, vol. 2, 30.
11. Kingsford, *First English Life*, 36.
12. Kingsford, *First English Life*, 37.
13. Roskell and Taylor, *Gesta Henrici Quinti*, 40–41.
14. Roskell and Taylor, *Gesta Henrici Quinti*, 39.
15. Wylie and Waugh, *Henry V*, vol. 2, 36.
16. Bellaguet, *Chronique du Religieux de Saint-Denys*, vol. 5, 536–37.
17. Roskell and Taylor, *Gesta Henrici Quinti*, 36–37.
18. Kingsford, *First English Life*, 38.
19. Charles Lethbridge Kingsford, *Chronicles of London* (Oxford: Clarendon Press, 1905), 117.
20. Kingsford, *Chronicles of London*, 117.
21. Text of correspondence between the camp at Harfleur and the city of Bordeaux is printed in Anne Curry, *The Battle of Agincourt: Sources and Interpretations* (Woodbridge, UK: Boydell, 200), xx. Cf. Wylie and Waugh, *Henry V*, vol. 2, 42.
22. Kingsford, *Chronicles of London*, 118.
23. Roskell and Taylor, *Gesta Henrici Quinti*, 52–53.
24. "Rymer's Foedera with Syllabus: September 1415," in *Rymer's Foedera*, vol. 9, (London: 1739–1745), 310–13, British History Online, british-history.ac.uk/https://www.british-history.ac.uk/rymer-foedera/vol9/pp310-313.
25. According to Roskell and Taylor, *Gesta Henrici Quinti*, 58–59.
26. Roskell and Taylor, *Gesta Henrici Quinti*, 44–45.

22. "HIS LITTLE BLESSED MANY"

1. The exact numbers are a matter of live historical dispute. Livingston, *Agincourt*, 141, and Sumption, *Cursed Kings*, 441, reckon on around 6,000. Anne Curry, *Agincourt* (Oxford: Oxford University Press,

2015), 25, reckons on a "reasonable maximum" of 8,680 men. For a full tabulated list of contemporary estimations of the army's size, see Curry, *Battle of Agincourt*, 12.

2. Roskell and Taylor, *Gesta Henrici Quinti*, 60–61.
3. Roskell and Taylor, *Gesta Henrici Quinti*, 60–61.
4. Curry, *Battle of Agincourt*, 441.
5. Wylie and Waugh, *Henry V*, vol. 2, 89–90.
6. Roskell and Taylor, *Gesta Henrici Quinti*, 62–63.
7. Kingsford, *First English Life*, 44.
8. Roskell and Taylor, *Gesta Henrici Quinti*, 70–71.
9. Roskell and Taylor, *Gesta Henrici Quinti*, 74–75.
10. See Livingston, *Agincourt*, 155–58, for a convincing attempt to reconcile the conflicting English and French evidence about the conversation with the heralds.
11. Roskell and Taylor, *Gesta Henrici Quinti*, 78–79.
12. Roskell and Taylor, *Gesta Henrici Quinti*, 76–77.
13. Gairdner, "Gregory's Chronicle," 111.
14. Roskell and Taylor, *Gesta Henrici Quinti*, 76–77.
15. Gairdner, "Gregory's Chronicle," 111.
16. Roskell and Taylor, *Gesta Henrici Quinti*, 78–79.
17. Roskell and Taylor, *Gesta Henrici Quinti*, 80–81.
18. Gairdner "Gregory's Chronicle," 111.
19. *Chronica Maiora*, 410.
20. "The Religioux (Monk) of Saint-Denis, *Histoir de Charles VI* (*c*. 1455–22, Latin)", in Curry, *Battle of Agincourt*, 105.
21. Brie, *The Brut*, vol. 2, 378.
22. Allmand, *Henry V*, 91n17.
23. "Pseudo Elmham, *Vita et Gesta Henrici Quinti* (*c*. 1446–49, Latin)," in Curry, *Battle of Agincourt*, 105.
24. Livingston, *Agincourt*, makes a compelling case for only a partial forward move of Henry's army, with the archers on the wings remaining in place.
25. Curry, *Battle of Agincourt*, 158.
26. Curry, *Battle of Agincourt*, 157.
27. *Chronica Maiora*, 411.
28. Roskell and Taylor, *Gesta Henrici Quinti*, 88–89.
29. Curry, *Battle of Agincourt*, 157.
30. Robbins, *Historical Poems*, 76.
31. Allmand, *Henry V*, 94.
32. Arthur de Richemont in Curry, *Battle of Agincourt*, 182.
33. Curry, *Battle of Agincourt*, 164.
34. *Poetry of Charles d'Orléans and His Circle: A Critical Edition of BnF MS. fr. 25458, Charles d'Orléans's Personal Manuscript*, eds. John Fox and Mary-Jo Arn (Tempe: Arizona Center for Medieval and Renaissance Studies, 2010), xvi.
35. Curry, *The Battle of Agincourt*, 166.

23. TRIUMPHS

1. Gairdner, "Gregory's Chronicle," 112.
2. Given-Wilson, *Adam Usk*, 260–61.
3. Given-Wilson, *Adam Usk*, 260–61.
4. Given-Wilson, *Adam Usk*, 260–61.
5. Roskell and Taylor, *Gesta Henrici Quinti*, 102–3.
6. Roskell and Taylor, *Gesta Henrici Quinti*, 104–11.
7. Frulovisiis, *Livii Foro-Juliensis*, 22.
8. Robbins, *Historical Poems*, 90–91.
9. Roskell and Taylor, *Gesta Henrici Quinti*, 112–13.
10. "Henry V: November 1415," in Given-Wilson, *Parliament Rolls of Medieval England*, British History Online, british-history.ac.uk/no-series/parliament-rolls-medieval/november-1415.

11. Judges 15:11.
12. Curry, *The Battle of Agincourt*, 273.
13. "Rymer's Foedera with Syllabus: October–December 1415," in *Rymer's Foedera*, vol. 9, 327, British History Online, https://www.british-history.ac.uk/rymer-foedera/vol9/pp314-327.
14. Given-Wilson, *Adam Usk*, 262–63.
15. For this legend and the history of the shrine at Holywell, see Rick Turner, "The Architecture, Patronage and Date of St. Winefride's Well, Holywell," *Archaeologia Cambrensis* 168 (2019): 245–75.
16. Turner, "Architecture, Patronage and Date," 250–51.
17. Bellaguet, *Chronique du Religieux de Saint-Denys*, vol. 5, 586–89.
18. Nicholas Harris Nicolas, *Proceedings and Ordinances of the Privy Council of England*, vol. 2, (London: Commissioners of the Public Records of the UK, 1834) 196–97.
19. Sumption, *Cursed Kings*, 476–77.
20. Anne Curry and Susan Jenkins, eds., *The Funeral Achievements of Henry V at Westminster Abbey: The Arms and Armour of Death* (Woodbridge, UK: Boydell Press, 2020), 8.
21. Kingsford, *First English Life*, 69.
22. Susan Rose, ed., *The Navy of the Lancastrian Kings: Accounts and Inventories of William Soper, Keeper of the King's Ships, 1422-1427* (Abingdon: Rutledge, 2019), 49.
23. Roskell and Taylor, *Gesta Henrici Quinti*, 144–45.
24. Roskell and Taylor, *Gesta Henrici Quinti*, 146–47.
25. Roskell and Taylor, *Gesta Henrici Quinti*, 148–49.
26. Roskell and Taylor, *Gesta Henrici Quinti*, 150–51.

24. "FEARED BY EVERYBODY"

1. For the gift of the heart, Wylie and Waugh, *Henry V*, vol. 3, 14. For a golden statue of St. George, also donated to the chapel at Windsor, *Chronica Maiora*, 415.
2. Kingsford, *First English Life*, 77.
3. For details of the *Jesus*'s construction, see Rose, *The Navy of the Lancastrian Kings*, 214–16.
4. Wylie and Waugh, *Henry V*, vol. 3, 45.
5. "Henry V: October 1416," in *Parliament Rolls of Medieval England*, British History Online, british-history.ac.uk/no-series/parliament-rolls-medieval/october-1416.
6. Vale, *Henry V*, 62–87.
7. J. L. Kirby, ed., *Calendar of Signet Letters of Henry IV and Henry V (1399–1422)*, (London: HMSO, 1978), 164–65. Cf. Curry, *Henry V*, 80.
8. Kingsford, *First English Life*, 81.
9. Henry Thomas Riley, trans. and ed., *Memorials of London and London Life in the XIIIth, XIVth, and XVth Centuries* (London: Longmans, Green, and Co., 1868), 664–60.
10. See W. Mark Ormrod, "Henry V and the English Taxpayer," in Dodd, *Henry V: New Interpretations*, 187–216.
11. Curry, *Henry V*, 79.
12. Ormrod, "Henry V and the English Taxpayer," 195.
13. Ormrod, "Henry V and the English Taxpayer," 417.
14. Calendar of Patent Rolls, 1416–1422, Henry V, vol. 2, 84.
15. *Chronica Maiora*, 418.
16. Sumption, *Cursed Kings*, 530.
17. "Rymer's Foedera with Syllabus: August 1417," in *Rymer's Foedera*, vol. 9, 479–87, British History Online, british-history.ac.uk/rymer-foedera/vol9/pp479-487.
18. *Chronica Maiora*, 424–25.
19. Sumption, *Cursed Kings*, 534, and cf. Juliet Barker, *Conquest: The English Kingdom of France, 1417–1450* (Cambridge: Harvard University Press, 2013), 12–13.
20. Sumption, *Cursed Kings*, 536.
21. Riley, *Memorials of London*, 664–60.
22. *Historia Henrici Quinti*, in Cole, *Memorials of Henry the Fifth*, 51.
23. *Chronica Maiora*, 427.

24. Kingsford, *First English Life*, 92.
25. *Chronica Maiora*, 428–29.

25. "WHO IS THE GREAT LORD?"

1. For an account of Bedford's extraordinary collection of fine things, see Jenny Stratford, *The Bedford Inventories: The Worldly Goods of John, Duke of Bedford, Regent of France (1389–1435)* (London: Society of Antiquaries of London, 1993).
2. *Chronica Maiora*, 426.
3. "Henry V: November 1417," in *Parliament Rolls of Medieval England*, British History Online, british-history.ac.uk/no-series/parliament-rolls-medieval/november-1417.
4. *Chronica Maiora*, 427.
5. John A. F. Thomson, "Oldcastle, John, Baron Cobham (d. 1417), soldier, heretic, and rebel." *Oxford Dictionary of National Biography*. 23 Sep. 2004; Accessed 24 May. 2024. https://www.oxforddnb.com/view/10.1093/ref:odnb/9780198614128.001.0001/odnb-9780198614128-e-20674.
6. Wylie and Waugh, *Henry V*, vol. 3, 92.
7. Capgrave, *Book of the Illustrious Henries*, 141.
8. "Henry V: November 1417," in *Parliament Rolls of Medieval England*.
9. *Chronica Maiora*, 428.
10. Given-Wilson, *Adam Usk*, 267.
11. *Chronica Maiora*, 428.
12. *Chronica Maiora*, 429.
13. Jules Delpit, *Collection Générale des Documents Français que se Trouvent en Angleterre*, vol. 1 (Paris: Dondey-Dupré, 1847), 222.
14. Wylie and Waugh, *Henry V*, vol. 3, 131.
15. Delpit, *Collection Générale des Documents Français*, vol. 1, 223.
16. Sumption, *Cursed Kings*, 583–86.
17. John Page, "The Siege of Rouen," in Gairdner, *Historical Collections of a Citizen of London*, 1. See also an alternative version recorded in J. J. Conybeare, "IX. Poem, entitled the 'Siege of Rouen:' written in the Reign of Henry the Fifth. Communicated in a Letter from the Rev. J. J. Conybeare, late Professor of Poetry in the University of Oxford, to Henry Ellis, Esq. F.R.S. Secretary," *Archaeologia* 21 (1827): 43–78.
18. Delpit, *Collection Générale des Documents Français*, vol. 1, 222.
19. Page, "The Siege of Rouen," 1.
20. Sumption, *Cursed Kings*, 594.
21. Kirby, *Calendar of Signet Letters*, 173.
22. Page, "The Siege of Rouen," 30.
23. Conybeare, "IX. Poem, entitled 'The Siege of Rouen,'" 76.
24. Page, "The Siege of Rouen," 42.
25. Page, "The Siege of Rouen," 34, 43.

26. "THIS UNLUSTY SOLDIER'S LIFE"

1. For Isabeau of Bavaria's description, see Rachel Gibbons, "Isabeau of Bavaria, Queen of France (1385–1422): The Creation of an Historical Villainess: The Alexander Prize Essay," *Transactions of the Royal Historical Society* 6 (1996): 51–73.
2. See *Rymer's Foedera*, vol. 9, 751.
3. Wylie and Waugh, *Henry V*, vol. 3, 163.
4. *Rymer's Foedera*, vol. 9, 779.
5. Sumption, *Cursed Kings*, 626.
6. Henry Ellis, ed., *Original Letters, Illustrative of English History*, Second Series, vol. 1 (London: Harding and Lepard, 1827), 78.
7. *La Chronique d'Enguerran de Monstrelet*, vol. 3, 321.

8. Wylie and Waugh, *Henry V*, vol. 3, 168.
9. This translation, Maurice Keen, "Diplomacy," in Harriss, *Henry V*, 189.
10. Delpit, *Collection Générale des Documents Français*, vol. 1, 227.
11. Delpit, *Collection Générale des Documents Français*, vol. 1, 227.
12. Delpit, *Collection Générale des Documents Français*, vol. 1, 227.
13. There are numerous contradictory accounts concerning the choreography of the violence; compare Sumption, *Cursed Kings*, 653, and Wylie and Waugh, *Henry V*, vol. 3, 185–86.

27. "THINGS ARE DIFFERENT NOW"

1. *Rymer's Foedera*, vol. 9, 801.
2. For a modern edition of Charles of Orléans's poetry, *Poetry of Charles d'Orléans*.
3. Sumption, *Cursed Kings*, 658.
4. Curry, *Henry V*, 94.
5. Vale, *Henry V*, drawing on Parliament Rolls (1423).
6. Bellaguet, *Chronique du Religieux de Saint-Denys*, vol. 6, 379.
7. Bellaguet, *Chronique du Religieux de Saint-Denys*, vol. 6, 379.
8. Alexandre Tuetey, *Journal d'un Bourgeois de Paris*, 129–31.
9. Tuetey, *Journal d'un Bourgeois de Paris*, 135.
10. *Rymer's Foedera*, vol. 9, 825.
11. Sumption, *Cursed Kings*, 679.
12. "Henry V: October 1419," in *Parliament Rolls of Medieval England*, British History Online, british-history.ac.uk/no-series/parliament-rolls-medieval/october-1419.
13. See A. R. Myers, "The Captivity of a Royal Witch: The Household Accounts of Queen Joan of Navarre, 1419–21," *Bulletin of the John Rylands Library* 24 (1940): 263–84.
14. Allmand, *Henry V*, 143.
15. For the gold-crowned helm, Tuetey, *Journal d'un Bourgeois de Paris*, 139.
16. *Oeuvres de Georges Chastellain*, vol. 1, edited by JMBC Lettenhove (Brussels: Heussners, 1863), 131.
17. *Oeuvres de Georges Chastellain*, vol. 1, 133.
18. Wylie and Waugh, *Henry V*, vol. 3, 202.
19. *Oeuvres de Georges Chastellain*, vol. 1, 131–32.
20. *Rymer's Foedera*, vol. 9, 895, 907.
21. *Rymer's Foedera*, vol. 9, 906.
22. *Rymer's Foedera*, vol. 9, 910.
23. Sumption, *Cursed Kings*, 701.
24. Tuetey, *Journal d'un Bourgeois de Paris*, 140.

28. "A LONG BATTLE"

1. *Chronica Maiora*, 438.
2. Wylie and Waugh, *Henry V*, vol. 3, 208.
3. *La Chronique d'Enguerran de Monstrelet*, vol. 3, 404.
4. *Oeuvres de Georges Chastellain*, vol. 1, 156.
5. Strecche, *The Deeds of King Henry V*, 51.
6. Kingsford, *First English Life*, 168–69. See also *Oeuvres de Georges Chastellain*, vol. 1, 157.
7. Frederick Devon, ed., *Issues of the Exchequer* (London: John Murray, 1837), 362.
8. Krochalis, "Books and Reading of Henry V," 66; Allmand, *Henry V*, 153.
9. *Oeuvres de Georges Chastellain*, vol. 1, 177.
10. *Oeuvres de Georges Chastellain*, vol. 1, 185.
11. Curry, *Henry V*, 98.
12. Tuetey, *Journal d'un Bourgeois de Paris*, 146.
13. *La Chronique d'Enguerran de Monstrelet*, vol. 4, 17.
14. *Rymer's Foedera*, vol. 10, 33, British History Online, https://www.british-history.ac.uk/rymer-foedera/vol10.
15. *Rymer's Foedera*, vol. 10, 33.

16. "Henry V: December 1420," in *Parliament Rolls of Medieval England*, British History Online, https://www.british-history.ac.uk/no-series/parliament-rolls-medieval/december-1420.
17. *Chronica Maiora*, 439.
18. Devon, *Issues of the Exchequer*, 364.

29. "À CLARENCE!"

1. *La Chronique d'Enguerran de Monstrelet*, vol. 4, 24.
2. *Oeuvres de Georges Chastellain*, vol. 1, 206.
3. Brie, *The Brut*, vol. 2, 425.
4. *Chronica Maiora*, 439.
5. Allmand, *Henry V*, 156.
6. Brie, *The Brut*, vol. 2, 426.
7. *Chronica Maiora*, 439.
8. Brie, *The Brut*, vol. 2, 426.
9. Brie, *The Brut*, vol. 2, 426.
10. Gairdner, "Gregory's Chronicle," 141.
11. For Henry's itinerary and a detailed commentary on this progress, J. Doig, "Propaganda and Truth: Henry V's Royal Progress in 1421," *Nottingham Medieval Studies* 40 (1996): 167–202.
12. Henry's letter is printed in Richard Ager Newhall, *The English Conquest of Normandy, 1416–1424: A Study in Fifteenth Century Warfare* (New York: Russell & Russell, 1971), 266.
13. Newhall, *English Conquest of Normandy*, 264.
14. Nicolas, *Proceedings and Ordinances*, vol. 2, 362.
15. Elmham, *Vita et Gesta Henrici Quinti*, 300.
16. Doig, "Propaganda and Truth," 172.
17. *La Chronique d'Enguerran de Monstrelet*, vol. 4, 25.
18. Gairdner, "Gregory's Chronicle," 142.
19. Doig, "Propaganda and Truth," 172.
20. Strecche, *The Deeds of King Henry V*, 54.
21. *Chronica Maiora*, 441.
22. Brie, *The Brut*, vol. 2, 428.
23. Wylie and Waugh, *Henry V*, vol. 3, 310.
24. "Henry V: May 1421," in *Parliament Rolls of Medieval England*, British History Online, https://www.british-history.ac.uk/no-series/parliament-rolls-medieval/may-1421.
25. For a detailed discussion of this episode, G. L. Harriss, *Cardinal Beaufort: A Study of Lancastrian Ascendancy and Decay* (Oxford: Clarendon Press, 1988), 91–114.
26. Vale, *Henry V*, 228, which seems to misdate this to 1420, when the king was not in England.

30. TO JERUSALEM

1. *Rymer's Foedera*, vol. 10, 131.
2. Tuetey, *Journal d'un Bourgeois de Paris*, 150–54.
3. Krochalis, "Books and Reading of Henry V," 65.
4. Krochalis, "Books and Reading of Henry V," 65.
5. Vale, *Henry V*, 219; Devon, *Issues of the Exchequer*, 367.
6. Delpit, *Collection Générale des Documents Français*, vol. 1, 231.
7. G. du Fresne de Beaucourt, *Histoire de Charles VII*, vol. 1 (Paris: Librairie de la Société Bibliographique, 1881), 461.
8. Bellaguet, *Chronique du Religieux de Saint-Denys*, vol. 6, 464–65.
9. Delpit, *Collection Générale des Documents Français*, vol. 1, 231.
10. Tuetey, *Journal d'un Bourgeois de Paris*, 172.
11. Brie, *The Brut*, vol. 2, 428.
12. Allmand, *Henry V*, 168.
13. Buchon, *ed. Choix de Chroniques et Mémoires sur l'Histoire de France* Paris: Mairet et Fournier, 1841), 566.

14. Kirby, *Calendar of Signet Letters*, 186.
15. "Henry V: December 1421," in *Parliament Rolls of Medieval England*, British History Online, https://www.british-history.ac.uk/no-series/parliament-rolls-medieval/december-1421.
16. Newhall, *The English Conquest of Normandy*, 264.
17. *Rymer's Foedera*, vol. 10, 161.
18. Vale, *Henry V*, 219.
19. Printed in J. Webb, "A Survey of Egypt and Syria, undertaken in the year 1422, by Sir Gilbert de Lannoy," *Archaeologia* 21 (1827): 281–444.
20. Denis de Sainte-Marthe, ed. *Gallia Christiana*, vol. 8 (Paris: Lutetiae Parisiorum, Coignard, 1744), 389.
21. Brie, *The Brut*, vol. 2, 428.
22. Brie, *The Brut*, vol. 2, 428.
23. Sumption, *Cursed Kings*, 755.
24. Krochalis, "Books and Reading of Henry V," 68. See also McFarlane, *Lancastrian Kings and Lollard Knights*, 233.
25. Tuetey, *Journal d'un Bourgeois de Paris*, 174.
26. *La Chronique d'Enguerran de Monstrelet*, vol. 4, 99.
27. Tuetey, *Journal d'un bourgeois de Paris*, 174; Bellaguet, *Chronique du Religieux de Saint-Denys*, vol. 6, 461.
28. *Chronica Maiora*, 445.
29. Sumption, *Cursed Kings*, 763.
30. Patrick Strong and Felicity Strong, "The Last Will and Codicils of Henry V," *English Historical Review* 96, no. 378 (1981): 79–102.
31. *La Chronique d'Enguerran de Monstrelet*, vol. 4, 110.
32. *La Chronique d'Enguerran de Monstrelet*, vol. 4, 111.
33. *La Chronique d'Enguerran de Monstrelet*, vol. 4, 112.
34. *Chronica Maiora*, 445.

EPILOGUE

1. Bellaguet, *Chronique du Religieux de Saint-Denys*, vol. 6. 482–83; Brie, *The Brut*, vol. 2, 493; Allmand, *Henry V*, 174.
2. "Henry VI: October 1423," in *Parliament Rolls of Medieval England*, British History Online, https://www.british-history.ac.uk/no-series/parliament-rolls-medieval/october-1423.
3. *Rymer's Foedera*, vol. 10, 255.
4. *Chronica Maiora*, 447.
5. *Chronica Maiora*, 447.
6. *Chronica Maiora*, 446.
7. Wylie and Waugh, *Henry V*, vol. 3, 418–19.
8. Given-Wilson, *Adam Usk*, 270–71.
9. Bellaguet, *Chronique du Religieux de Saint-Denys*, vol. 6, 480–81.
10. *Chronica Maiora*, 445–46.
11. Strecche, *The Deeds of King Henry V* 57.
12. *Oeuvres de Georges Chastellain*, vol. 1, 553–54.
13. Keith Dockray, *Warrior King: The Life of Henry V* (Stroud: Tempus, 2007), 49.
14. McFarlane, *Lancastrian Kings and Lollard Knights*, 133.
15. Ian Mortimer, *1415: Henry V's Year of Glory* (London: Vintage Books, 2009).
16. Ian Mortimer, "Henry V: The Cruel King," *BBC History Magazine* (October 2009).

BIBLIOGRAPHY

ONLINE

The Parliament Rolls of Medieval England, accessed via British History Online, https://www.british-history.ac.uk.

Rymer's Foedera, volumes 8–10, accessed via British History Online, https://www.british-history.ac.uk/series/rymers-foedera.

PRIMARY

Andrew of Wyntoun. *The Orygynale Cronykil of Scotland by Andrew of Wyntoun*, vol. III. Edited by David Laing. Edinburgh: Edmonston & Douglas, 1879.

Aquinas, Thomas. *On the Governance of Rulers*. Translated by Gerald B. Phelan. Toronto: St. Michael's College Philosophical Texts, 1935.

Bellaguet, Louis François, ed. *Chronique du Religieux de Saint-Denys, Contenant le Règne de Charles VI., de 1380 à 1422* (6 vols). Paris: Crapelet, 1839–1852.

Brie, Friedrich W. D., ed. *The Brut, or, The Chronicles of England*, vol. 2. London: Kegan Paul, Trench, Trübner & Co., 1908.

Calendar of the Patent Rolls Preserved in the Public Record Office—Henry IV, Vol. 4, 1408–1413. London: Anthony Brothers Limited, 1909.

Capgrave, John. *The Book of the Illustrious Henries*. Translated by Francis Charles Hingeston. London: Longmans & Co, 1858.

Chastellain, Georges. *Oeuvres de Georges Chastellain*, vol. 1. Edited by JMBC Lettenhove. Brussels: Heussners, 1863.

Chaucer, Geoffrey. *The Riverside Chaucer*, 3rd edition. Edited by Larry D. Benson and F. N. Robinson. Oxford: Oxford University Press, 2008.

Cole, Charles Augustus, ed. *Memorials of Henry the Fifth, King of England*. London: Longmans & Co, 1858.

Curry, Anne. *The Battle of Agincourt: Sources and Interpretations*. Woodbridge, UK: Boydell, 2000.

Davies, John Silvester, ed. *An English Chronicle of the Reigns of Richard II, Henry IV, Henry V and Henry VI, Written Before 1470*. London: Camden Society, 1856.

Delpit, Jules. *Collection Générale des Documents Français que se Trouvent en Angleterre*, vol. 1. Paris: Dondey-Dupré, 1847.

Devon, Frederick, ed. *Issues of the Exchequer*. London: John Murray, 1837.

d'Orléans, Charles. *Poetry of Charles D'Orléans and His Circle: A Critical Edition of BnF MS. Fr. 25458, Charles D'Orléans's Personal Manuscript*. Edited by John Fox and Mary- Jo Arn. Tempe: Arizona Center for Medieval and Renaissance Studies, 2010.

Edward, Second Duke of York. *The Master of Game*. Edited by William A. Baillie-Grohman and F. N. Baillie-Grohman. London: Chatto & Windus, 1909.

Ellis, Henry, ed. *Original Letters, Illustrative of English History*, Second Series, vol. 1. London: Harding and Lepard, 1827.

Froissart, Jean. *Sir John Froissart's Chronicles of England, France, Spain and the Adjoining Countries*, volumes I–XIII (second edition). Edited by Thomas Johnes. London: Longmans & Co, 1806.

Frulovisiis, Titus Livius de. T. *Livii Foro-Juliensis Vita Henrici Quinti, Regis Angliæ*. Edited by Thomas Hearne. Oxford: n.p., 1716.

Gairdner, James, ed. *The Historical Collections of a Citizen of London in the Fifteenth Century*. London: Camden Society, 1876.

Gascoigne, Thomas. *Loci e Libro Veritatum. Passages Selected from Gascoigne's Theologica Dictionary, Illustrating the Condition of Church and State, 1403–1458*. Edited by James Edwin Thorold Rogers. Oxford: Clarendon Press, 1881.

Giles, Johannes Allen, ed. *IIncerti Scriptoris Chronicon Angliae*. London: D. Nutt, 1848.

Given-Wilson, Christopher, trans. and ed. *Chronicles of the Revolution, 1397–1400: The Reign of Richard II*. Manchester: Manchester University Press, 1993.

Given-Wilson, Christ, ed. *The Chronicle of Adam Usk, 1377–1421*. Oxford: Clarendon Press, 1997.

Given-Wilson, Christ, ed. *Continuatio Eulogii: The Continuation of the Eulogium Historiarum, 1364–1413*. Oxford: Clarendon Press, 2019.

Haydon, Frank Scott, ed. *Eulogium Historiarum sive Temporis*, vol. 3. London: Longman & Co, 1863.

Hingeston, Francis Charles, ed. *Royal and Historical Letters During the Reign of Henry the Fourth, King of England and of France, and Lord of Ireland*. London: Longman & Co, 1860.

Jenkins, John, ed. *The Customary of the Shrine of St. Thomas Becket at Canterbury Cathedral*. Leeds: Arc Humanities Press, 2022.

Juvenal des Ursins, Jean. Choix de Chroniques et Mémoires sur l'Histoire de France. Edited by J. A. C. Buchon. Paris: Mairet et Fournier, 1841.

Kempe, Margery. *The Book of Margery Kempe*. Translated by William Erdeswick Ignatius Butler-Bowdon. London: Oxford University Press, 1954.

Kingston, Charles Lethbridge, ed. *Chronicles of London*. Oxford: Clarendon Press, 1905.

Kingsford, Charles Lethbridge, ed. *The First English Life of Henry V*. Oxford: Clarendon Press, 1911.

Kirby, J. L., ed. *Calendar of Signet Letters of Henry IV and Henry V (1399–1422)*. London: HMSO, 1978.

Knighton, Henry. *Knighton's Chronicle, 1337–1396*. Edited by G. H. Martin. Oxford: Clarendon Press, 1995.

Legge, M. Dominica, ed. *Anglo-Norman Letters and Petitions from All Souls MS. 182*. Oxford: Anglo-Norman Text Society, 1941.

Lydgate, John. *Lydgate's Troy Book AD 1412–20, Part 1*. Edited by Henry Bergen. London: Early English Text Society, 1906.

Monstrelet, Enguerrand de. *La Chronique d'Enguerran de Monstrelet, Avec Pièces Justificatives, 1400–1444* (4 vols). Edited by L. Douët d'Arcq. Paris: Veuve J. Renouard, 1857.

Napier, Alexander, Mrs., ed. *A Noble Boke off Cookry ffor a Pynce Houssolde or Eny Other Estately Houssolde*. London: Elliot Stock, 1882.

Nicolas, Sir Harris, ed. *Proceedings and Ordinances of the Privy Council of England*, vols. 1, 2. London: Record Commission, 1834.

Nichols, John, and Richard Gough, eds. *A Collection of All the Wills Now Known to Be Extant of the Kings and Queens of England*. London: John Nichols, 1780.

Raine, James, ed. *Testamenta Eboracensia; or, Wills Registered at York, Illustrative of the History, Manners, Language, Statistics, etc., of the Province of York, from the Year 1300 Downwards*, vol. 1. London: Publications of the Surtees Society, 1836.

Riley, Henry T., ed. *Johannis de Trokelowe et Henrici de Blaneforde, monachorum S. Albani, necnon quorundam anonymo-rum chronica et annales, regnantibus Henrico Tertio, Edwardo Primo, Edwardo Secundo, Ricardo Secundo, et Henrico Quarto*. London: Longmans & Co, 1866.

Robbins, Rossell Hope, ed. *Historical Poems of the XIVth and XVth Centuries*. New York: Columbia University Press, 1959.

Roskell, John S., and Frank Taylor, trans. and eds. *Gesta Henrici Quinti: The Deeds of Henry the Fifth*. Oxford: Clarendon Press, 1975.

Roskell, John Smith, Linda Clark, and Carole Rawcliffe, eds. *The House of Commons, 1386–1421* (4 vols). Sutton: Boydell & Brewer, 1992.

Sainte-Marthe, Denis de, ed. *Gallia Christiana*, vol. 8. Paris: Lutetiae Parisiorum, Coignard, 1744.

Stow, John. *A Survey of London. Reprinted from the Text of 1603*. Edited by Charles Lethbridge Kingsford. Oxford: Clarendon Press, 1908.

Stratford, Jenny. *The Bedford Inventories: The Worldly Goods of John, Duke of Bedford, Regent of France (1389–1435)*. London: Society of Antiquaries of London, 1993.

Strecche, John. *The Deeds of King Henry V*. Edited by Geoffrey M. Hilton. Kenilworth: G M Hilton, 2014.

Tuetey, Alexandre, ed. *Journal d'un Bourgeois de Paris, 1405–1449*. Paris: Nogent_le_Rotrou, 1881.

Wavrin, Jehan de, *A Collection of the Chronicles and Ancient Histories of Great Britain, Now Called England, from AD 1399 to AD 1422*, vol. 2. Edited and translated by William Hardy and Edward L. C. P. Hardy. London: Longmans & Co, 1887.

Walsingham, Thomas. *The Chronica maiora of Thomas Walsingham, 1376–1422*. Edited by David Preest. Woodbridge, UK: Boydell, 2005.

Wickham-Legg, Leopold George, ed. *English Coronation Records*. London: Archibald Constable, 1901.

Williams, Benjamin, ed. *Chronique de la Traïson et Mort de Richart Deux Roy Dengleterre*. London: English Historical Society, 1846.

SECONDARY

Adams, Jenny and Nancy Mason Bradbury, eds. *Medieval Women and Their Objects*. Ann Arbor: University of Michigan Press, 2017.

Allmand, Christopher. *Henry V*. New Haven; London: Yale University Press, 1997 (new ed).

Barker, Juliet. *England, Arise: The People, the King and the Great Revolt of 1381*. London: Little, Brown Book Group, 2014.

Beaucourt, G. du Fresne de. *Histoire de Charles VII*. Paris: Librairie de la Société Bibliographique, 1881.

Bolton, J. L. *The Medieval English Economy, 1150–1500*. London: Dent, 1980.

Brown, R. A., H. M. Colvin, and A. J. Taylor, eds. *The History of the King's Works: The Middle Ages* (2 vols). London: Ministry of Public Building and Works, 1963.

Burns, James Henderson. *The Cambridge History of Medieval Political Thought c.350–c.1450*. Cambridge: Cambridge University Press, 1988.

Carey, Hilary Mary. *Courting Disaster: Astrology at the English Court and University in the Later Middle Ages*. London: Macmillan, 1992.

Castor, Helen. *The King, the Crown and the Duchy of Lancaster: Public Authority and Private Power 1399–1461*. Oxford: Oxford University Press, 2000.

Curry, Anne. *Agincourt*. Oxford: Oxford University Press, 2015.

Curry, Anne. *Henry V: From Playboy Prince to Warrior King*. London: Allen Lane, 2015.

Davies, R. R. *Owain Glyn Dwr: Prince of Wales*. Talybont: Y Lolfa, 2009.

Davies, R. R. *The Revolt of Owain Glyn Dwr*. Oxford: Oxford University Press, 1995.

DeVries, Kelly, and Michael Livingston, eds. *Medieval Warfare: A Reader* (Readings in Medieval Civilizations and Cultures). Toronto: University of Toronto Press, 2019.

Dickinson, J. C. *The Shrine of Our Lady of Walsingham*. Cambridge: Cambridge University Press, 1956.

Dockray, Keith. *Warrior King: The Life of Henry V*. Stroud: Tempus, 2007.

Dodd, Gwilym, and Douglas Biggs, eds. *Henry IV: The Establishment of the Regime, 1399–1406*. Woodbridge, UK: York Medieval Press in association with Boydell Press, 2003.

Dodd, Gwilym, ed. *Henry V: New Interpretations*. Woodbridge, UK: York Medieval Press, University of York, 2013.

Given-Wilson, Chris. *Henry IV*. New Haven; London: Yale University Press, 2016.

Gordon, Dillian. *The Wilton Diptych*. London: National Gallery Company, 2015.

Harriss, G. L. *Cardinal Beaufort: A Study of Lancastrian Ascendancy and Decay*. Oxford: Clarendon Press, 1988.

Harriss, G. L. *Henry V: The Practice of Kingship*. Oxford: Oxford University Press, 1985.

Hicks, Michael A., ed. *Profit, Piety and the Professions in Later Medieval England*. Gloucester: Sutton, 1990.

Horrox, Rosemary, trans. and ed. *The Black Death*. Manchester; UK: Manchester University Press, 1994.

Livingston, Michael, and John K. Bollard, eds. *Owain Glwndŵr: A Casebook*. Liverpool: Liverpool University Press, 2013.

Livingston, Michael. *Agincourt: Battle of the Scarred King*. London: Osprey Publishing, 2023.

Loyn, H. R., and H. Hearder, eds. *British Government and Administration: Studies Presented to S.B. Chrimes*. Cardiff: University of Wales Press, 1974.

McCarthy, Michael. *Citizen of London: Richard Whittington, the Boy Who Would Be Mayor*. London: C Hurst & Co, 2022.

McFarlane, K. B. *Lancastrian Kings and Lollard Knights*. Oxford: Clarendon Press, 1972.

McFarlane, K. B. *The Nobility of Later Medieval England: The Ford Lectures for 1953 and Related Studies*. Oxford: Clarendon Press, 1973.

McNiven, Peter. *Heresy and Politics in the Reign of Henry IV: The Burning of John Badby*. Woodbridge, UK: Boydell, 1987.

Morgan, Nigel J., ed. *Prophecy, Apocalypse and the Day of Doom: Proceedings of the 2000 Harlaxton Symposium*. Donington: Shaun Tyas, 2004.

Mortimer, Ian. *1415: Henry V's Year of Glory*. London: Vintage Books, 2009.

Newhall, Richard Ager. *The English Conquest of Normandy, 1416–1424: A Study in Fifteenth Century Warfare*. New York: Russell & Russell, 1971.

Orme, Nicholas. *From Childhood to Chivalry: The Education of the English Kings and Aristocracy, 1066–1530*. London: Routledge, 2017.

Pugh, T. B. *Henry V and the Southampton Plot of 1415*. Southampton: Southampton University Press, 1988.

Rose, Susan, ed. *The Navy of the Lancastrian Kings Accounts and Inventories of William Soper, Keeper of the King's Ships, 1422–1427*. Abingdon: Routledge, 2019.

Russell, Josiah Cox. *British Medieval Population*. Albuquerque: University of New Mexico Press, 1948.

Saul, Nigel. *Richard II*. London: Yale University Press, 1997.

Skeat, Walter W. *Chaucerian and Other Pieces*. Oxford: Clarendon Press, 1897.

Stratford, Jenny. *Richard II and the English Royal Treasure*. Woodbridge, UK: The Boydell Press, 2012.

Sumption, Jonathan. *Cursed Kings: The Hundred Years War IV*. London: Faber, 2015.

Sumption, Jonathan. *Divided Houses: The Hundred Years War III*. London: Faber, 2011.

Vale, Malcolm. *Henry V: The Conscience of a King*. New Haven; London: Yale University Press, 2016.

Wylie, James Hamilton and James Templeton Waugh. *The Reign of Henry V* (3 vols). Cambridge: Cambridge University Press, 1914–1929.

Wylie, James Hamilton. *The History of England under Henry IV* (4 vols). London: Longmans & Co, 1884–1898.

ARTICLES

Amassian, Margaret. "A Verse Life of John of Bridlington." *Neuphilologische Mitteilungen* 71, no. 1 (1970): 136–45.

Barron, Caroline M. "The Tyranny of Richard II." *Bulletin of the Institute of Historical Research* 41, no. 103 (May 1968): 1–18.

Bean J. M. W. "Henry IV and the Percies." *History* 44 (1959): 212–27.

Cohn S. K. Jr. "Epidemiology of the Black Death and Successive Waves of Plague." *Medical History Supplement* 27, (2008): 74–100.

Conybeare, JJ. "Poem, Entitled the 'Siege of Rouen': Written in the Reign of Henry the Fifth. Communicated in a Letter from the Rev. J. J. Conybeare, Late Professor of Poetry in the University of Oxford, to Henry Ellis, Esq. F.R.S. Secretary." *Archaeologia* 21 (1827): 43–78.

Clarke M. V., and V. H. Galbraith. "The Deposition of Richard II." *Bulletin of the John Rylands Library* 14 (1930): 125–181.

Doig, J. "Propaganda and Truth: Henry V's Royal Progress in 1421." *Nottingham Medieval Studies* 40 (1996): 167–202.

du Haut-Jussé, B. A. Pocquet. "La Renaissance Littéraire Autour de Henri V, Roi d'Angleterre (Deux Lettres Inédites, 1412)." *Revue Historique* 224, no. 2 (1960): 335–6.

Egan, S. "Richard II and the Wider Gaelic World: A Reassessment." *Journal of British Studies* 57, no. 2 (2018): 221–52.

Flood, Frederick Solly. "Prince Henry of Monmouth: His Letters and Despatches during the War in Wales, 1402–1405." *Transactions of the Royal Historical Society* 4 (1889): 125–41.

Gibbons, Rachel. "Isabeau of Bavaria, Queen of France (1385–1422): The Creation of an Historical Villainess: The Alexander Prize Essay." *Transactions of the Royal Historical Society* 6 (1996): 51–73.

Hühne-Osterloh, G., and G. Grupe. "Causes of Infant Mortality in the Middle Ages Revealed by Chemical and Palaeopathological Analyses of Skeletal Remains." *Zeitschrift für Morphologie und Anthropologie* 77, no. 3 (1989): 247–58.

Jamieson, E., and Lane, R. "Monuments, Mobility, and Medieval Perceptions of Designed Landscapes: The Pleasance, Kenilworth." *Medieval Archaeology* 59, no. 1 (2015): 255–71.

Jonker, M. A. "Estimation of Life Expectancy in the Middle Ages." *Journal of the Royal Statistical Society* 166 (2003): 105–17.

Kirby, J. L. "Councils and Councillors of Henry IV, 1399–1413." *Transactions of the Royal Historical Society* 14 (1964): 35–65.

Krochalis, Jeanne E. "The Books and Reading of Henry V and His Circle." *The Chaucer Review* 23 (1988): 50–77.

Lambert, Craig. "Henry V and the Crossing to France: Reconstructing Naval Operations for the Agincourt Campaign, 1415." *Journal of Medieval History* 43 (2017): 24–39.

McNiven, Peter. "Prince Henry and the English Political Crisis of 1412." *History* 65, no. 213 (1980): 1–16.

McNiven, Peter. "The Problem of Henry IV's Health, 1405–1413." *The English Historical Review* 100, no. 397 (1985): 747–72.

Nicol, D. M. "A Byzantine Emperor in England: Manuel II's Visit to London in 1400–1401." *University of Birmingham Historical Journal* 12 (1970): 204–25.

Post, J. B. "The Obsequies of John of Gaunt." *Guildhall Studies in London History* 5 (1981): 1–12.

Stow, George B. "Richard II in Thomas Walsingham's Chronicles." *Speculum* 59 (1984): 68–102.

Strong, Patrick, and Felicity Strong. "The Last Will and Codicils of Henry V." *The English Historical Review* 96, no. 378 (1981): 79–102.

Turner, Rick. "The Architecture, Patronage and Date of St Winefride's Well, Holywell." *Archaeologia Cambrensis* 168 (2019): 245–75.

Webb, J. "A Survey of Egypt and Syria, Undertaken in the Year 1422, by Sir Gilbert de Lannoy." *Archaeologia* 21 (1827): 281–444.

Webb, J. "Translation of a French Metrical History of the Deposition of King Richard the Second." *Archaeologia* 20 (1824): 1–423.

Williams-Jones, Keith. "The Taking of Conwy Castle, 1401." *Transactions of the Caernarvonshire Historical Society* 39 (1978): 7–43.

ILLUSTRATION CREDITS

Insert 1

page

1 The Bodleian Libraries, University of Oxford, [Bodleian Library MS. Auct. D. 4. 4], [folio. 181v]

2 *(Top)* OgreBot / Wikimedia Commons; *(Bottom)* Ashley Cooper pics / Alamy Stock Photo

3 from the archive of the British Library (MS Royal 17 B XLIII, f 132v).

4 *(Top)* jvoisey / Getty Images; *(Bottom)* David Taylor Photography / Alamy Stock Photo

5 *(Top)* from the archive of the British Library (Harley 1319, f.5); *(Bottom)* © Amgueddfa Cymru—Museum Wales

6 *(Top)* Pictorial Press Ltd / Alamy Stock Photo; *(Bottom)* from the archive of the British Library (Harley 4866, f.88)

7 *(Top)* from the archive of the British Library / jenikirbyhistory; *(Bottom)* Royal Collection Trust / © His Majesty King Charles III 2024

8 *(Top)* World History Archive / Alamy Stock Photo; *(Bottom)* Bibliothèque nationale de France

Insert 2

1 (*Top*) Nicholas E. Jones / Shutterstock; (*Bottom*) Département des Manuscrits / Wikimedia Commons

2 *Painted Chamber* 1799 Interior view looking east with Trojan War tapestries shown. Watercolor by Mr. William Capon UK Parliament; WOA 1648. heritagecollections. parliament.uk

3 (*Top*) The Picture Art Collection / Alamy Stock Photo; (*Bottom*) Bibliothèque nationale de France

4 (*Top*) E101/69/7/509 / The National Archives; (*Left*) Copyright: Dean and Chapter of Westminster; (*Right*) RMN-Grand Palais / Jacques Quecq d'Henripret / RMN- / Dist. Foto SCALA, Florence

5 Selbymay / Wikimedia Commons

6 From the archive of the British Library / (MS 18850, f. 256v)

7 (*top*) E 30/411 / The National Archives; (*Bottom*) AF Fotografie / Alamy Stock Photo

8 (*Top*) Pictorial Press Ltd / Alamy Stock Photo; (*Bottom*) Angelo Hornak / Alamy Stock Photo

INDEX